Germany's Vision of Empire in Venezuela 1871-1914

GERMANY'S VISION OF EMPIRE IN VENEZUELA 1871-1914

Holger H. Herwig

Princeton University Press
Princeton, New Jersey

Copyright © 1986 by Princeton University Press
Published by Princeton University Press,
41 William Street, Princeton, New Jersey 08540
In the United Kingdom: Princeton University Press,
Guildford, Surrey

All Rights Reserved
Library of Congress Cataloging in Publication Data will be
found on the last printed page of this book

ISBN 0-691-05483-5

Publication of this book has been aided by a grant from
The Andrew W. Mellon Foundation

This book has been composed in Linotron Bodoni
Clothbound editions of Princeton University Press books
are printed on acid-free paper, and binding materials are
chosen for strength and durability

Printed in the United States of America by
Princeton University Press, Princeton, New Jersey

CONTENTS

TABLES

ACKNOWLEDGMENTS

I first came across the naval record of the German blockade of Venezuela in 1902-1903 more than a decade ago at the Bundesar-chiv-Militärarchiv, Freiburg, in the Federal Republic of Germany. Subsequent research at the Bundesarchiv, Koblenz, as well as at the Auswärtiges Amt, Bonn, broadened the study to embrace its political and diplomatic ramifications. A grant from the International Research and Exchanges Board in New York permitted me to explore German economic records at the Zentrales Staatsarchiv, Potsdam and Merseburg, as well as at the Staatsarchiv, Dresden, in the German Democratic Republic. Further assistance from the Research Council of Vanderbilt University and the American Council of Learned Societies widened the investigation to include the holdings of the Bayerisches Hauptstaatsarchiv and the Institut für Zeitgeschichte at Munich, the Staatsarchiv at Bremen, the Staatsarchiv and the Handelskammer at Hamburg, the Evangelisches Zentralarchiv at West Berlin, and the Historisches Archiv of Friedrich Krupp at Essen-Bredeney, all in the Federal Republic of Germany. Finally, the American Philosophical Society and the National Endowment for the Humanities permitted me to visit the Public Record Office, then still in London, and the N. M. Rothschild Archives, City of London; the latter was especially useful because the files of the two banks most intimately involved with Venezuela—Disconto and Norddeutsche—were destroyed during the Second World War while being stored with the Deutsche Bank at Frankfurt. The staffs of all these depositories were most generous in their assistance and counsel.

I owe by far the greatest debt to the Alexander von Humboldt-Stiftung in general and to Drs. Heinrich Pfeiffer and Thomas Berberich in particular. This book is dedicated to the Stiftung for its untiring and generous support of my research activities over the past fifteen years; without Humboldt at Bonn-Bad Godesberg, I, like so many of my North American colleagues, could never have experienced such munificent opportunities to undertake archival research in the Federal Republic. Hence, it is perhaps fitting that this book should concern itself with Germany and Venezuela, for Alexander von Humboldt began his magnificent voyages of discovery in the Americas on July 16, 1799, at Cumaná, "this most heavenly and abundant land."

Finally, I am once more indebted to my wife, Lorraine, not only for critically reading the manuscript but, above all, keeping it before me at times when other projects threatened to deter its completion. Obviously, whatever failings come to light are due to my own ignorance.

Holger H. Herwig
Newport, Fall 1985

Germany's Vision of Empire in Venezuela 1871-1914

INTRODUCTION

This book deals with German "imperialist" policies in South America in general and Venezuela in particular between 1871 and 1914. It studies German leaders and their thoughts, the German government and its diplomacy, German entrepreneurs and their commercial policies, the German navy and its overseas aspirations, the German Evangelical Church and its missions abroad, and the various German domestic pressure groups and their vociferous advocacy of the *Deutschtum* (German nationals) overseas. Specifically, it attempts to analyze the role of German trade, overseas financial investments, armaments sales, military missions, coaling stations, naval bases, and emigration patterns in South America with an eye especially toward the motivation behind the Reich's participation in an Anglo-German-Italian blockade of Venezuela in 1902-1903.[1]

The book is not intended as a general history of German-Venezuelan relations. Indeed, Venezuela simply serves as the "laboratory" in which to examine the greater German drive toward the Caribbean basin—and its resulting clash with the self-appointed hemispheric guardian, the United States. Nor is the book offered as a theoretical treatise (much less anthology) on classical nineteenth-century European imperialism. Yet, as a case study, it addresses, on the basis of extensive multinational archival research, several of the more prominent theories of imperialism that have been put forth ever since John Hobson's seminal *Imperialism: A Study* appeared in 1902—always with the caution expressed by Joseph Schumpeter more than sixty years ago that historical examples do not necessarily

---

[1] See Holger H. Herwig, *Alemania y el bloqueo internacional de Venezuela 1902/03* (Caracas, 1977), in both English and Spanish. This work, which stressed primarily the naval activity of the blockade, led to the present expanded analysis.

"prove" one theory or another, but merely offer a basis for future discussion.[2]

German policies with regard to Venezuela around the turn of the century must appear simple and direct to the reader. Men such as Emperor Wilhelm II, Chancellor Bernhard von Bülow, Foreign Secretary Oswald von Richthofen, and Admiral Alfred von Tirpitz were guided by vague, albeit persistent, notions of economic determinism. They talked about markets, weapons sales, training missions, targets for emigration, cultural missions, and the like. Strategic and economic motives, laced with a liberal dose of social Darwinism, were uppermost in their minds. They paid scant attention to Venezuelan affairs—either foreign or domestic—and by and large viewed the Venezuelan economy as being much too primitive before 1900 to permit any sophisticated reactions to German moves, both economic and diplomatic. Indeed, Berlin's relations with Caracas never matured to the state where one could speak of a "client state relationship." Finally, current notions concerning "informal" empire or "client state dependency" did not exist in the vocabulary of German leaders before 1914. As a result, this book will concentrate upon the nature of German "imperialist" expansion south of the Río Grande as it was understood and practiced in Berlin around 1900.

For the sake of simplicity, the numerous "imperialism" schools have been divided into two major categories, the economic and the noneconomic. Both are mainly Eurocentric insofar as they deal almost exclusively with Europe's needs and desires. While the economic school generally stresses Europe's need to export capital or goods and services abroad, the noneconomic school favors the rivalries among nations, "priorities and perceptions within governments," and the "notions and commitments of social classes." Finally, a recent rebuttal to these two major schools stressing developments overseas will also be covered.[3] Above all, it should be remembered that the following brief comments upon several "imperialism" schools are offered primarily in order to provide the theo-

[2] Joseph Schumpeter, *Zur Soziologie des Imperialismus* (Tübingen, 1919), 90ff.

[3] See D. K. Fieldhouse, *Economics and Empire, 1830-1914* (London, 1973), 3-87; and R. V. Kubicek, *Economic Imperialism in Theory and Practice* (Durham, N.C., 1979), 5-6.

retical framework within which the German policies toward Venezuela before 1914 will be evaluated; they are in no way intended to be complete. Their applicability to the case study at hand will be dealt with in the Conclusion.

Certainly the classical model of imperialism is the economic, or Marxist, interpretation. Its monocausal simplicity has a certain seductive attraction on first reading. While Rosa Luxemburg stressed the role of the market, Hobson as well as Rudolf Hilferding and V. I. Lenin concentrated on the export of capital.[4] Especially the English radical Hobson saw the essence of a modern foreign policy as "primarily a struggle for profitable markets of investment." Hobson noted the pressure to find "foreign markets for goods and investments" owing to a financial glut on the domestic market as the "taproot" of imperialism. This "pressure" resulted from the periodic depressions in the free-market economic cycle, and led Hobson to propose his famous "over-saving" theory: the competitive labor market, which prevented a proper redistribution of profits, increased at such a rapid rate that capitalists constantly had to search out new markets for their goods and new opportunities to export their profit (or finance) capital. "It is not industrial progress that demands the opening up of new markets and areas of investment, but mal-distribution of consuming power which prevents the absorption of commodities and capital within the country." This imbalance between savings and consumption arising from the unequal distribution of the national income was but a practical response to a certain maladjustment within capitalism, one that could easily be corrected by raising labor's share of the profits. Yet in the meantime, "It is not too much to say that the modern foreign policy of Great Britain has been primarily a struggle for profitable markets for investment. . . . What was true of Great Britain was true likewise of France, Germany, and the United States."[5]

---

[4] John A. Hobson, *Imperialism: A Study* (London, 1902); Rosa Luxemburg, *Die Akkumulation des Kapitals* (Berlin, 1913); Rudolf Hilferding, *Das Finanzkapital* (Vienna, 1910); and V. I. Lenin, *Der Imperialismus als jüngste Etappe des Kapitalismus* (Hamburg, 1921), as well as "Der Imperialismus als höchstes Stadium des Kapitalismus," in *Werke*, XXII (East Berlin, 1960).

[5] Hobson, *Imperialism*, 48, 53-54, 70, 75. See also Holger H. Herwig, "German

Erich Preiser, a West German scholar, has taken what he terms Hobson's "primitive over-saving theory" one step further, describing the export of capital as a "sustentative" measure, or as a "safety valve," designed to ward off lasting stagnation on the domestic market. In other words, given the instability of the capitalist free-market economy, the export of capital arises less out of pure profit motives—although these are always present—than out of a crisis situation that demands action in order to overcome a depression affecting entrepreneurs, workers, and government alike. This development, Preiser argues, alone explains why capitalism is able to overcome its periodic depressions at a time when there is insufficient confidence in, or means to stimulate, the domestic economy. He further posits that overseas investments have always increased when those at home fell off; total investments at home and abroad have rarely shown great overall fluctuations in quantity. In almost pre-Keynesian terms, Preiser claims that entrepreneurs exported their capital around the turn of the century as a "safety valve" as they sought to ameliorate the depressions of the economic cycle, to stabilize the gross national product as well as employment, and generally to offer a genuine alternative to stagnation of the entire economy during "low" periods in the business cycle.[6]

To be sure, there were two major long-term cycles for the period under discussion: the "great depression" of 1874 to 1894 and the economic boom from 1895 to 1914. While the former period recorded fifteen years of depression and only six of boom, the latter showed fifteen years of boom and a mere four of depression.[7] For our immediate purposes, the export of German capital after 1888 for the

Imperialism and South America before the First World War: The Venezuelan Case 1902/03," in Alexander Fischer, Günter Moltmann, and Klaus Schwabe, eds., *Russland-Deutschland-Amerika: Festschrift für Fritz T. Epstein zum 80. Geburtstag* (Wiesbaden, 1978), 117-30.

[6] Erich Preiser, "Die Imperialismusdebatte. Rückschau und Bilanz," in *Wirtschaft, Geschichte und Wirtschaftsgeschichte: Festschrift zum 65. Geburtstag von Friedrich Lütge* (Stuttgart, 1966), 368-69.

[7] See Peter Hampe, *Die "ökonomische Imperialismustheorie": Kritische Untersuchungen* (Munich, 1976), 307-08.

construction of the Great Venezuelan Railroad (Grosse Venezuela-Eisenbahngesellschaft) by the Disconto Gesellschaft (hereafter Disconto Bank) in Berlin should offer some insights into Preiser's economic theories. In other words, was the overseas railroad investment undertaken with the specific purpose of stimulating German heavy industry during a depression? Unfortunately, the destruction of the pertinent banking records for the Great Venezuelan Railroad during the Second World War does not allow an analysis of Hobson's often overlooked remark concerning the "great capitalist proletariat," that is, small and middling investors who were largely at the mercy of the financial system.[8]

Another "economic" category of imperialism studies revolves around the so-called "export-monopoly" thesis most closely associated with Hilferding; Schumpeter later adopted it and Lenin assumed its main tenets. Hallmarks of this interpretation are the formation of cartels and trusts, and the close cooperation between banks and industry—popularly termed "finance capital" (*Finanzkapital*). The emphasis here is on production. The cartels strive for "monopoly profits" and use high tariff walls against foreign competitors in order to conquer the domestic market. Thereafter, they deploy cheaper export prices and "dumping" tactics in order to penetrate overseas markets. This practice, in turn, leads at home to social unrest, abroad to severe competition among states. And as other nations create their own high tariff barriers, markets disappear and production as well as profits fall. Entrepreneurs at this stage seek to circumvent foreign tariff walls by exporting capital rather than goods. "Finance capital," the accumulated surplus profits of banks and industry, forces expansion upon capitalists into less industrialized lands where the profit-loss scheme has not yet taken hold. Hilferding termed this overseas expansion in order to maintain high production at home the final phase of the capitalist economy, its "highest stage," in short: imperialism. Nevertheless, Hilferding admitted that the economic collapse of the capitalist order was not

---

[8] See Kubicek, *Economic Imperialism*, 200-01.

unavoidable; politics rather than economics could lead to war and thereby bring about the collapse of capitalism.[9]

At first glance the requisite preconditions seem evident. The number of price-fixing agreements among producers of uniform commodities, that is, *Kartells*, increased from a mere 14 in 1877 to 90 in 1885 and a staggering 385 twenty years later. German banks vastly increased their available capital from 1,291 million Mark in 1890 to 2,291 million Mark by 1900; Disconto, which financed the railroad in Venezuela, alone upped its holdings from 30 million Mark in 1856 to 130 million Mark by 1900. Moreover, the close tie of banks to industry was also highly visible: the Deutsche Bank was intimately linked to Friedrich Krupp as well as to Siemens–Halske, the Dresdner Bank to August Thyssen, the Disconto Bank to Emil Kirdorf's Gelsenkirchener Bergwerks A. G., and the Berliner Handelsgesellschaft to German General Electric (AEG). Finally, many prominent members of German ruling houses, such as King Wilhelm II of Württemberg, King Friedrich August III of Saxony, Crown Prince Wilhelm of Prussia, and Prinzregent Luitpold of Bavaria, to name but a few, were involved in the export of capital.[10]

By and large, the "export-monopoly" thesis, in the words of Preiser, is dominated more by "an amusing tone of sneering superiority" than by "accuracy."[11] Indeed, for this thesis to hold, it would be necessary to produce hard evidence that "monopolist capitalists" forced the state into an expansionist and aggressive foreign policy. Profits, investments, and the export of capital are part and parcel of the capitalist order: their mere existence or repeated recitation does not "prove" the existence of "imperialism." In the present case, the role of the Great Venezuelan Railroad as well as that of other German

[9] Hilferding, *Finanzkapital*, 458, 460, 512. These citations are from a reprint (Berlin, 1947).

[10] See Jürgen Kuczynski, *Studien zur Geschichte des deutschen Imperialismus* (East Berlin, 1952), I, 86-90, 144, and II, 130; A. S. Jerussalimski, *Die Aussenpolitik und die Diplomatie des deutschen Imperialismus Ende des 19. Jahrhunderts* (East Berlin, 1954), 53-56; and Klaus Kannapin, "Die deutsch-argentinischen Beiziehungen von 1871 bis 1914 unter besonderer Berücksichtigung der Handels- und Wirtschaftsbeziehungen und der Auswanderungspolitik" (diss., East Berlin, 1968), 35.

[11] Preiser, "Die Imperialismusdebatte," 365 n. 19.

undertakings in Venezuela, such as the Aktiengesellschaft für Be-
ton- und Monierbau, the Deutsch-Venezolanische Schwefelgruben
A.-G., and Karl Henkel's Caracas Slaughterhouse before and during
the blockade of 1902-1903 will serve as a case study. Put in other
words, were profit-seeking and capital-export the deciding factors in
the international action against President Cipriano Castro, and did
"big business" coerce the government in Berlin to take action
against Venezuela?

A recent French scholar, Raymond Poidevin, has suggested that
the international economic community in general, and its branches
in France and Germany in particular, tended largely toward cooperation rather than confrontation before 1914.[12] Again, this observation will be tested in light of the role that British and German
financiers played during the critical Anglo-German alliance negotiations between 1899 and 1902 that provided the background for the
international blockade of Venezuela.

A final "economic" category of imperialism scholars has suggested that this phenomenon was born out of a need of industrial
states to secure their supplies of raw materials and, in turn, to create
a market for their finished products. Rudolf Kjellén, Paul Mombert,
Arthur Salz, and the Social Democrat Gerhard Hildebrand—inves-
tigators looking back at Wilhelmian *Weltpolitik* (global politics) during the Weimar Republic—enthusiastically touted this "neo-mercantilist" or "industrial-state" theory, arguing that industrialized
European nations had been forced to exploit African, Asian, or
South American lands once their *Autarkie* aspirations concerning
food stuffs and raw materials were no longer secure at home. In
pseudo-Darwinistic terms, these writers to varying degrees una-
bashedly trumpeted the theme of the "white man's burden." They
upheld past directed emigration to, private investment in, and armaments sales to the underdeveloped nations earmarked for economic and, if need be, political and/or military domination.[13] And

[12] Raymond Poidevin, *Les Relations économiques et financières entre la France et l'Allemagne de 1898 à 1914* (Paris, 1969).
[13] Rudolf Kjellén, *Der Staat als Lebensform* (Leipzig, 1917); Paul Mombert, "Be-völkerungsproblem und Bevölkerungstheorie im Lichte des Weltkrieges," in *Die Wirtschaftswissenschaft nach dem Kriege: Festgabe für Lujo Brentano* (Munich/Leip-

while Venezuela could hardly be seen as a great future market for German industrial goods, or even as a source of raw materials other than beef, hides, coffee, and grains—oil had not been fully appreciated by 1900—this school will nevertheless be addressed in the broader light of German emigration to the regions south of the Río Grande and the various schemes put forth to uphold the *Deutschtum* there, primarily through German schools and churches.

Still Eurocentric, although no longer "economic," is the "sociological" category of imperialism. Pioneered in 1918-1919 by the Austro-American economist Joseph Schumpeter, the "Sociology of Imperialism" eschews the short nineteenth-century interpretation of that phenomenon and instead offers a longer historical analysis of pre-capitalist empire building. Schumpeter spied the roots of "imperialism," not in capital or in its export but rather in the social structure of nations. Specifically, he argued that in every European state there existed remnants of social classes that had lost their historical function, that is, a warrior class in a society no longer constantly threatened by war. This obsolete class, Schumpeter argued, maintained its values, mentality, and even membership intact, and over the course of time transferred them to overseas expansion and conquest. Memories of past battles, the soldierly tradition, the pomp and glory of battle—all hereditary vestiges of a past or passing age—encouraged this "atavism."[14]

Partly in this vein, A. S. Kanya-Forstner has recently suggested that the military, rather than the government, "determined the pace, the extent and the nature" at least of French "imperialism" in the Western Sudan. Especially the inadequate state of communications at the time rendered it difficult for governments in Europe to do other than to rely upon the military on the scene, who thereby "became the

---

zig, 1925), II, 379ff.; Arthur Salz, "Der Imperialismus der Vereinigten Staaten," in *Archiv für Sozialwissenschaft und Sozialpolitik*, 50 (1923), 565ff.; and Gerhard Hildebrand, *Die Erschütterung der Industrieherrschaft und des Industriesozialismus* (Jena, 1910). The latter work inspired Hans Grimm to write his two-volume classic: *Volk ohne Raum* (Munich, 1926).

[14] Joseph Schumpeter, "The Sociology of Imperialism," in *Social Classes and Imperialism* (Cleveland, 1968), 1-98.

experts on whose advice the Government was forced to rely." And
when back home in Europe, these officers formed an effective pressure group to exert direct influence upon the formulation of "imperialist" policies.[15]

In the case of German policies vis-à-vis Venezuela, that "atavism" was evident primarily in the form of overseas ship commanders who constantly plied the waters of the Caribbean basin and who
regularly reported to both Emperor and government upon the
chances for German expansion in the region. Moreover, many of
those officers in retirement became active members of domestic lobbies such as the Pan-German League, Colonial League, and Navy
League in order to pressure the government into a more active—indeed aggressive—overseas policy. It remains to be seen how effective their actions were with regard to South America.

Secondly, there are the very recent non-Eurocentric explanations
of imperialism that stress political developments in the "victim" nations overseas. Ronald Robinson especially has suggested that
"imperialism was as much a function of its victims' collaboration or
non-collaboration—of their indigenous politics, as it was of European expansion." In other words, imperialism was a two-way street.
"The expansive forces generated in industrial Europe had to com-
bine with elements within the agrarian societies of the outer world to
make empire at all practicable."[16] Of course, a detailed examination
of Venezuelan internal politics goes far beyond the scope of this
book, and hence only brief reference will be made to Caracan affairs
insofar as they had a direct bearing upon German actions in the
country. It is worth noting that Robinson's use of the term "outer
world" suggests that crises on the periphery of metropolitan Europe
often impelled Europe to act—regardless of the "internal stresses"
engendered by "imperialism."

Most prolifically, D. K. Fieldhouse has put forth certain variants

[15] A. S. Kanya-Forstner, *The Conquest of the Western Sudan: A Study of French Military Imperialism* (Cambridge, 1969), 266-68.

[16] Ronald Robinson, "Non-European Foundations of European Imperialism: Sketch for a Theory of Collaboration," in E.R.J. Owen and R. B. Sutcliffe, eds., *Studies in the Theory of Imperialism* (London, 1972), 118.

upon the "peripheral" explanation. In stressing the "diplomatic" nature of imperialism, Fieldhouse has suggested that with Europe increasingly deadlocked between two hard alliance blocks (Triple Alliance and Triple Entente), statesmen began to look beyond the Continent's periphery for diplomatic advantage. Overseas possessions thus became pawns in the European power struggle. "Imperialism may best be seen as the extension into the periphery of the political struggle in Europe. At the center the balance was so nicely adjusted that no positive action, no major change in the status of territory of either side was possible." Hence, the symbolic value of bases and markets—what I would term *prestige*—came into play. Put in other words, the "periphery" of, say, South America could permit an outlet for competition or even confrontation—"atavism"?—without endangering the fragile security of the metropolitan center.[17]

With regard to Venezuela, Robinson's thesis will be tested against the role played during the 1890s and 1900s not only by the various Venezuelan presidents in power, but also by the German merchant houses that controlled much of that nation's domestic as well as overseas commerce. The very delicate Anglo-German alliance negotiations around the turn of the century will need to be assessed in terms of how aware planners in Berlin and London were that their European confrontation might be "defused" by agreement and cooperation on the Continent's "periphery." And with an eye directed toward Fieldhouse, the international blockade undertaken by three otherwise competing European powers ought certainly to lend itself to analysis.

Finally, given what we know today about the impulsive nature of Wilhelmian Germany, it might be highly profitable to glance at various "irrational" motivations that undoubtedly gave impetus to the peculiar nature of German imperialism by the 1890s. Among these, I would certainly include public opinion, maritime grand strategy, national honor, diplomatic gamesmanship, prestige, and even national

[17] D. K. Fieldhouse, " 'Imperialism': An Historiographical Revision," *Economic History Review*, 14 (December 1961), 205-06. See also Benjamin J. Cohen, *The Question of Imperialism: The Political Economy of Dominance and Dependence* (New York, 1973), 78-79.

idiosyncracies.[18] Nor should the human factor be overlooked when dealing with people such as Wilhelm II, Bernhard von Bülow, and Alfred von Tirpitz—each a unique personality and in his own way a contributor to the course of Germany's overseas policy.

Turning from this brief general framework of analysis to the specific case of German aspirations and policies in South America, we should note that much of the work was pioneered nearly two decades ago by an East German group headed by Friedrich Katz (Mexico) and a host of students including Jürgen Hell (South Brazil), Manfred Scharbius (Cuba), Ingrid Uhlich (Peru), and Klaus Kannapin (Argentina).[19] Katz summarized many of their findings, suggesting four "peaceful" avenues for German expansion: a concentrated trade offensive in all lands, which by 1914 had secured the Reich second place in world trade; financial investment in neighboring nations designed to provide a source of raw materials; agreements with Great Britain and the United States to divide the colonial possessions of "dying" empires such as Spain and Portugal; and political as well as economic offensives in independent states such as China, Turkey, the Balkans, and South America.[20]

Classical imperialism, of course, revolves around preferential trade agreements, directed emigration, and aggressive armaments sales as well as military training missions to the states to be exploited. Katz as well as Fritz T. Epstein and Jürgen Schaefer[21] have

[18] See, for example, Winfried Baumgart, *Deutschland im Zeitalter des Imperialismus (1890-1914)* (Frankfurt, 1972).

[19] Friedrich Katz, *Deutschland, Diaz und die Mexikanische Revolution* (East Berlin, 1964); Jürgen Hell, "Die Politik des deutschen Reiches zur Umwandlung Südbrasiliens in ein überseeisches Neudeutschland (1890-1914)" (diss., East Berlin, 1966); Manfred Scharbius, "Die ökonomischen Rivalitäten der imperialistischen Hauptmächte und Kuba und ihre Auswirkungen auf die wirtschaftliche Entwicklung der Insel (Vom Ausgang der spanischen Kolonialherrschaft bis 1914)" (diss., East Berlin, 1970); Ingrid Uhlich, "Die Politik des deutschen Kaiserreichs und der Grossmächte in Peru von 1871 bis zum Beginn des 1. Weltkrieges" (diss., East Berlin, 1971); and Kannapin, "Die deutsch-argentinischen Beziehungen" (n. 10).

[20] Katz, *Deutschland, Diaz und die Mexikanische Revolution*, 88. Katz has included much of this information in his *The Secret War in Mexico: Europe, the United States and the Mexican Revolution* (Chicago, 1981).

[21] Fritz T. Epstein, "European Military Influences in South America" (ms., Library of Congress, 1941); and Jürgen Schaefer, *Deutsche Militärhilfe an Südamerika: Mi-*

suggested that by 1914 the armies of Argentina, Chile, and Bolivia "stood fully under German influence," while those of Paraguay, Uruguay, Ecuador, Colombia, and Venezuela were gravitating toward the German camp. What I have termed "the military advisors game" touches upon Robinson's thesis of "outer world collaboration" as the South American states played a major role in bringing German missions and weapons to that continent. As for Reich emigration, Katz points out that this tended to devolve upon the southern states of Argentina, Brazil, Chile, and Uruguay, largely because of the uninviting tropical climate and partly because of the strong "feudal system" that dominated the northern states. As a result, emigration to the latter consisted mainly of merchants, plantation owners, and skilled technicians, "whose number never surpassed several thousand and who belonged to the ruling classes." According to Katz, these German nationals "rarely assimilated" with the indigenous populace "and most often displayed great disdain for their new homeland."[22] This hypothesis will be tested for the German nationals in Venezuela on the basis of reports received at home from ship commanders and diplomatic envoys as well as pastors who visited that land frequently and who left quite detailed accounts of their impressions.

Preferential trade agreements were the most visible "evidence" of German "imperialism" in South America. In neo-mercantilist fashion, it was expected that Germany would sell expensive finished products to the nations of South America in return for cheap raw materials, that all trade would be carried in German bottoms both ways, that the trade would be centered in the hands of German export and import houses, and that overseas branches or subsidiaries of the major German banks would finance South American states so that they could purchase German goods and services.[23] To be sure, Reich trade with South America rose from 0.95 percent of overall German trade in 1881 to 7.6 percent by 1913—which accorded it third place behind the United States (28 percent) and Great Britain (22 per-

litär- und Rüstungsinteressen in Argentinien, Bolivien und Chile vor 1914 (Düsseldorf, 1974). Also most recently, Frederick M. Nunn, Yesterday's Soldiers: European Military Professionalism in South America, 1890-1940 (Lincoln/London, 1983).

[22] Katz, Deutschland, Diaz und die Mexikanische Revolution, 89.

[23] Ibid., 90.

cent). South American states, for their part, in 1913 imported 16.45 percent of their goods from, and exported 12.2 percent to Germany. The latter's investments in South America, according to Katz, stood at 600 million dollars, or 10.5 percent of all foreign holdings, by 1913; this figure pales considerably when compared to British investments of 5 billion dollars, United States credits of 1.3 billion dollars, and French holdings of 1.2 billion dollars.[24] It remains to be seen whether German merchants and bankers were able to assert their presence in Venezuela and to push aside their British counterparts. In other words, could Hamburg, Bremen, and Berlin squeeze the City of London out of its central role in financing and insuring overseas trade?

By and large, Katz suggests that it was the "discovery" of South America in the 1890s by the various German expansionist pressure groups (Pan-German, Colonial, and Navy Leagues) that helped to shape the nature as well as pace of Berlin's "imperialism" south of the Río Grande through an outpouring of books, articles, brochures, and public lectures, all stressing the future "mission of Deutschtum in Latin America." Specifically, these domestic lobbies attempted to influence official governmental policy toward South America in several directions: non-recognition of the Monroe Doctrine, acquisition of coaling stations and naval bases, direction of emigration to specially selected points, and affiliation of South Brazil (New Germany) with the homeland. Katz concludes that Berlin's ultimate objective was to partition South America into three spheres of interest: Mexico and Central America to the United States; northern South America to Britain; and the southern states of Argentina, South Brazil, South Chile, and Uruguay to Germany.[25]

Specifically with regard to Venezuela, Katz claims that Germany sought to "penetrate Venezuela politically and economically in order to obtain a naval base" off its coast. In pursuing this course of action in the period between 1898 and 1904, Wilhelm II hoped to forge a sort of European "union" directed against the United States: in 1898, in order to save the Spanish possessions in the Western Hem-

[24] Ibid., 90-91.
[25] Ibid., 92.

isphere from United States control; and in 1904, in order to "internationalize" the Panama Canal.[26] Only during the international blockade of Venezuela in 1902-1903 did the Emperor ever approach realization of this dream. In the end, Germany's policy in South America failed owing to "pressure" from the United States and to "the primacy of the Anglo-German antagonism."[27] To a certain degree, then, this book will deal with American actions in the Caribbean base—to the extent that they interacted with German moves there.

To sum up, this book investigates German policy in South America in general and in Venezuela in particular in order to test several of Katz's hypotheses. Specifically, it will look at German emigration to, investments in, and trade with South America up to the start of the Great War. German attitudes—both official and popular—toward the Monroe Doctrine and the Panama Canal and attempts undertaken to acquire naval bases and coaling stations in the Caribbean basin will play a major role in this study. The Anglo-German-Italian blockade of 1902-1903 will be examined primarily with an eye toward its effects upon Anglo-German and German-American relations. Reich armaments sales and military training missions to several South American states will help to clarify the place of advisors and their wares in the overall pattern of "imperialism." And the role of the *Deutschtum* overseas will be taken up through a closer examination of the Reich's support of German nationals as well as their schools and churches in Venezuela. Above all, German hopes and aspirations will be measured against their realization. In the process, I hope that this case study will, as Schumpeter suggested many years ago, offer a basis for future discussion concerning German "imperialism" in South America in the late nineteenth and early twentieth centuries.

[26] Ibid., 93-94. Much of this is taken from Alfred Vagts, *Deutschland und die Vereinigten Staaten in der Weltpolitik* (New York, 1935), II, 1278, 1490ff. Vagts' *magnum opus* still remains the seminal work on Imperial Germany's policy toward the Americas.

[27] Katz, *Deutschland, Diaz und die Mexikanische Revolution*, 93-94.

CHAPTER I

FROM COFFEE TO RAILROADS: GERMAN MERCHANTS AND INVESTMENTS

Germany's economic relations with Venezuela basically can be divided into a pre-industrial and an industrial period. Indeed, it would be more accurate before the 1880s to speak of Hamburg's trade with "Little Venice" in terms of coffee, cacao, tobacco, and cotton imports; according to one estimate, Hanseatic merchants in 1845 accounted for sixty-seven of the ninety-eight German firms engaged in commerce in South America. Exports of iron wares, machine tools, chemicals, and weapons take on meaningful proportions only well after German unification in 1871. Thus it is to the early Hanseatic coffee trader that one must look in order to garner some understanding of what a later generation would celebrate as the *Deutschtum* overseas. To be sure, there had been a brief period in the sixteenth century when the brothers Bartholomäus and Anton Welser of Augsburg had tried to attract colonists to and establish trade with Coro and its hinterland under a charter granted by Emperor Charles V. Yet, despite highly advantageous terms—tax exemption for all settlers, relaxation of the Spanish twenty-percent tax on mining precious metals, and a net return of five percent on all incomes—the venture had not succeeded within two decades.[1] Thereafter, individual enterprising *Hansa* merchants plied the South American trade either through Cadiz or through Amsterdam in the Spanish Netherlands. And while some Hamburg skippers as early as

[1] Heinrich Schnee, ed., *Deutsches Kolonial-Lexikon* (Leipzig, 1920), III, 700-01; Wilhelm Sievers, *Zweite Reise in Venezuela in den Jahren 1892/93* (Hamburg, 1896), 60; Percy Ernst Schramm, *Deutschland und Übersee: Der Deutsche Handel mit den anderen Kontinenten, insbesondere Afrika, von Karl V. bis zu Bismarck* (Braunschweig/Berlin/Hamburg/Kiel, 1950), 21, 55.

1801 had sailed directly to La Guayra and Puerto Cabello, the number of such passages never exceeded ten per annum by the 1820s.[2]

Caracas cotton reached Hamburg markets in the 1780s, but the greatest single boon to Hamburg-Venezuela trade was to be coffee. Wilhelm Sievers, who travelled extensively in Venezuela around 1900, claims that the bean was first brought to the West Indies from Africa and Arabia in 1717, and that it was taken to Venezuela perhaps as early as 1730 and certainly by 1740. Coffee plantations flourished in the state of Táchira and around Caracas by the mid-1780s, expanding thereafter into the Aragua valleys near La Victoria and to Trujillo. The first regular exports of coffee to Hamburg were noted between 1786 and 1790. By the mid-1830s, Hanseatic merchants sent mainly coffee, cacao, tobacco, and cotton home in the value of about 1.3 million Mark, while exporting to Venezuela mostly linens, iron wares, glass, brandy, butter, and beer estimated at about 500,000 Mark.[3]

Unfortunately, this trade was severely crippled when Britain, France, the Netherlands, and the United States concluded favorable trade agreements with Venezuela by the mid-1830s. In fact, traders whose countries had not concluded formal treaties with Caracas were forced to pay special surcharges of as much as fifty percent upon all imports. In addition, they had to ship their goods in bottoms belonging to those nations which had established formal trade agreements—at an additional charge of two to three percent. In the process, their own shipping lines suffered accordingly.[4] Unsurprisingly, Hamburg rushed to conclude a trade treaty with Venezuela in May 1837, and commerce quickly blossomed to around 5 million Mark per year, or an increase of 130 percent over the earlier period. The

[2] Ernst von Halle, ed., *Amerika: Seine Bedeutung für die Weltwirtschaft und seine wirtschaftlichen Beziehungen zu Deutschland insbesondere zu Hamburg* (Hamburg, 1905), 549-50.

[3] Wilhelm Sievers, *Venezuela und die deutschen Interessen* (Halle, 1903), 45ff.; Sievers, *Venezuela* (Hamburg, 1921), 17; Sievers, *Südamerika und die deutschen Interessen* (Stuttgart, 1903), 28. The Bolívar stood equal to the French franc, at U.S. 0.20, and at German goldmark 0.80; the British pound sterling was worth between 25 and 27 Bolívars.

[4] Halle, ed., *Amerika*, 550.

nature of the trade also changed: Venezuela now sent mainly cacao, coffee, dividivi, and cow hides to Hamburg in return for machine-made textiles and silk products as well as cement, drugs, and steel. It is estimated that about a dozen German firms dominated the Hamburg trade at La Guayra and Puerto Cabello.

The issue of a formal trade treaty continued to trouble German-Venezuelan relations. Prussia and the German Customs Union (*Zollverein*) had concluded trade accords with Argentina (1857), Paraguay (1859), Chile (1862), and Peru (1863), but a formal agreement with Venezuela drafted in April 1858 was never ratified by either side.[5] Nor was a similar pact negotiated between Hamburg and Caracas in March 1860 formally adopted, mainly because Venezuela insisted upon a clause stating that in case of damages arising from domestic unrest—as had been the case in 1847—foreign merchants were to submit their claims only to Venezuelan courts under local law. The newly formed German Empire in 1871 likewise refused to ratify a trade accord with Venezuela; the two countries in 1883 agreed only to honor each other's patent rights.[6] In the following years, Berlin concluded formal trade pacts with Brazil and Mexico (1882), the Dominican Republic (1885), Ecuador, Guatemala, Honduras, and Paraguay (1887), El Salvador (1888), and Uruguay (1892). Chancellor Leo von Caprivi in 1891 stated that these trade pacts had been negotiated "mainly as a counterweight to American aspirations" in South America.[7] But a trade treaty with Colombia in July 1892, especially, wherein Berlin agreed that Bogotá could not

[5] Zentrales Staatsarchiv (ZStA) Merseburg, Königliches Geheimes Civil-Cabinet Nr 13361, Die Südamerikanischen Staaten . . . 1873-1918, pp. 6, 10, 19, 21, 25.

[6] Zentrales Staatsarchiv (ZStA) Potsdam, Auswärtiges Amt, Abt. II, Marken- resp. Musterschutz in Venezuela Nr 12561, pp. 106-26; *Reichs-Gesetzblatt*, Nr 27 (December 1883), p. 339. See also Halle, ed., *Amerika*, 552-53; Ernst Baasch, *Beiträge zur Geschichte der Handelsbeziehungen zwischen Hamburg und Amerika* (Hamburg, 1892), 159ff., 165ff.

[7] ZStA-Potsdam, Reichs Justizamt, Sammlung der Handels- und Schiffahrtsverträge Deutschlands mit dem Auslande Nr 3346, pp. 2-22. Foreign Office tabulation of Mar. 11, 1897. Agreements had also been reached with Costa Rica in 1875 and Mexico in 1869. Caprivi is cited in Ingrid Uhlich, "Die Politik des deutschen Kaiserreichs und der Grossmächte in Peru von 1871 bis zum Beginn des 1. Weltkrieges" (diss., East Berlin, 1971), 161.

be held accountable for damages arising from domestic violence, was firmly rejected by the leading 200 firms in Hamburg, which argued that it would only "encourage" South American states to "seize German property with impunity."[8] The issue of state liability for revolutionary violence, of course, would bring irritation and confusion right down to the international blockade of Venezuela in 1902-1903, with the result that Berlin did not pen a formal trade treaty with Caracas until the summer of 1909.[9]

The lack of a formal *Handelsvertrag* notwithstanding, German-Venezuelan trade grew rapidly, increasing fully 143 percent in the first five years of the 1890s. Indeed, if we look at the longer range from 1837 until 1890, Hamburg's imports from Venezuela increased 1,100 percent, and its exports 1,500 percent. And in the final five years before the Great War, the Reich's trade with Venezuela stood at 26 million Mark, placing it on the same level as that with Colombia, Peru, Cuba, and several of the smaller Central American states.[10]

---

[8] ZStA-Potsdam, Auswärtiges Amt, Abt. IIu, Handelsvertragsverhandlungen Deutschlands mit Venezuela Nr 12573, pp. 78-80. Hamburg to Foreign Office (Berlin), April 1893.

[9] ZStA-Potsdam, Reichs Justizamt, Freundschafts- Handels- und Schiffahrtsvertrag mit Venezuela Nr 3478, pp. 8-17. The agreement passed third reading in the Reichstag on July 13, 1909, and was officially published in the *Reichs-Gesetzblatt* on Sept. 1. By the turn of the century, Germany had concluded "most-favored-nation" agreements with Argentina, Colombia, Ecuador, Guatemala, Honduras, Mexico, Nicaragua, Paraguay, El Salvador, Uruguay; none existed with Chile, Brazil, Bolivia, Costa Rica, the Dominican Republic, Haiti, Peru, and Venezuela. Uhlich, "Politik des deutschen Kaiserreichs," 167.

[10] Politisches Archiv, Auswärtiges Amt (AA) Bonn, Preussen 1 Nr 3 Nr 3, S.K.H. Prinz Heinrich von Preussen, vol. 14. Report from the Embassy at Montevideo to Chancellor von Bethmann Hollweg, Apr. 14, 1914, for the planned visit of the Emperor's brother to South America, gives the following summary of trade between 1909 and 1913:

Average per annum, total imports and exports, in millions Mark:

Argentina	656.2	Central America	49.7
Brazil	430.5	Cuba	37.2
Chile	256.7	Colombia	25.3
Uruguay	70.1	Peru	29.8
Mexico	72.0	Venezuela	25.8

In order to handle this increasing volume, German merchant lines began to offer direct sailings between Hamburg and Venezuela, thus bypassing the customary stops at Southampton and Liverpool en route. As early as 1855, packets sailed directly to La Guayra and Puerto Cabello; non-stop sailings to Maracaibo began in 1860. The greatest impetus to trade with Venezuela came after 1871, when both the Hamburg-America Line and the North German Lloyd inaugurated regular service with Venezuela via the West Indies. And while this direct connection proved highly irregular owing to Venezuela's repeated domestic troubles and the notoriously volatile nature of the coffee market—where fluctuations of nearly 300 percent (from 85 to 30 Bolívars per *quintal*) in a short span were not at all uncommon—the Hamburg-America Line profited from the trade with the West Indies and Venezuela. By the turn of the century, it not only carried fully one-half of Venezuela's coffee exports, but purchased two shipping lines, de Freitas and Kosmos, for that trade.[11] Moreover, South American shipping was conducted without the benefit of state subsidies.[12]

See also the figures in *Deutsche Übersee Bank 1886-1936* (Berlin, n.d.), 104-07, for the years 1889-1913; and Richard van der Borght, *Das Wirtschaftsleben Südamerikas insbesondere in seinen Beziehungen zu Deutschland* (Cöthen, 1919), 184ff. All these statistics basically come from *Statistik des Deutschen Reichs, Auswärtiger Handel des deutschen Zollgebietes im Jahre 1903* (Berlin, 1904), vol. 158, pp. 138-60.

[11] For the development of Hamburg's sea trade with Venezuela, see Baasch, *Handelsbeziehungen zwischen Hamburg und Amerika*, 220ff.; Kurt Himer, *Die Hamburg-Amerika Linie: Im Sechsten Jahrzehnt ihrer Entwicklung 1897-1907* (Hamburg, 1907), 53, 123; Frank Bernard Herschel, *Entwicklung und Bedeutung der Hamburg-Amerika Linie* (Berlin, 1912), 24, 66, 81, 102, 116; Walter Kresse, *Die Fahrtgebiete der Hamburger Handelsflotte 1824-1888* (Hamburg, 1972), 230-31, 351; and Otto Mathies, *Hamburgs Reederei 1814-1914* (Hamburg, 1924), 16-17, 81, 98-99, 169. Much of the Hamburg trade can be gleaned from the annual consular reports from La Guayra: ZStA-Potsdam, Auswärtiges Amt, Abt. Ic, Kais. Konsulat La Guayra Nr 52796.

[12] ZStA-Potsdam, Auswärtiges Amt, Abt. II, Handels- und Schiffahrtsverhältnisse mit Venezuela, vol. 20, p. 73, Foreign Office memorandum of Mar. 11, 1899, concludes: "There exist no German steamship lines to South America which are subsidized." A request from the German minister at Caracas in March 1905 to extend subsidies to the Hamburg-America Line was rejected in Berlin. Ibid., vol. 26, p. 56, Pelldram to Chancellor von Bülow, Mar. 27, 1905. In fact, German lines were sub-

Before additional statistics are presented concerning either the value or the volume of German-Venezuelan trade, a word of caution is in order. Statistics are notoriously inaccurate and can at best be taken as relative indicators of overall trade. In the first place, German commerce figures as late as 1888 contain only the activities of states associated with the *Zollverein*, to which the vital Hanseatic cities did not belong. Hamburg was listed as a "foreign country," and hence no records were kept of the final destination of goods passing through its duty-free port either overseas or to Europe. And when the "free-port" regions were incorporated into the German Empire in 1906, Hamburg was again conspicuous by its absence. Finally, a host of other technicalities combined to render trade statistics suspect: volumes rather than values were usually listed; goods were classified according to tariff rates rather than to actual description; no records were kept either as to place of production or final destination; goods crossing more than one border, including Hamburg's duty-free port, were excluded from all tabulations; and the very area of the *Zollverein* was not static but rather in flux.[13]

By the turn of the century, most observers in Venezuela agreed that the German merchant colony was dominant, controlling nearly one-third of all commerce and two-thirds of the trade in manufactured goods. It therefore becomes necessary to take a closer look at this group. There were thirty-eight German houses operating in Venezuela by the end of the nineteenth century. Of these, eight had established bases at Caracas, six each at Maracaibo and Valencia, five each at Puerto Cabello and Ciudad Bolívar, four at La Guayra, three at Barcelona, two at La Victoria, and one at Carúpano. From Caracas, they had cast a web over much of the land, monopolizing the import and export trade, mortgaging harvests, and lending money at

---

sidized only to the extent of 1.85 Mark per registered ton, compared to 28 Mark for France, 24.70 Mark for Japan, 12.10 Mark for Italy, and 1.95 Mark for Britain. See ZStA-Potsdam, Auswärtiges Amt, Abt. IIs, Schiffahrtsgesellschaften, Hamburg-Amerika Linie Nr 17661, pp. 98-101. Hanseatic Ambassador Götzen to Chancellor von Bethmann Hollweg, Jan. 15, 1910.

[13] See Paul M. Kennedy, *The Rise of the Anglo-German Antagonism 1860-1914* (London, 1980), 471-72.

twenty-percent interest rates.[14] Their estimated real property holdings of 20 million Mark were mainly in coffee plantations, with F. H.
Ruete of Hamburg leading the list with seven coffee *haciendas* under
cultivation. By far the largest house was that of H. G. & L. F. Blohm
of Hamburg, with branches located at Caracas, Ciudad Bolívar, Barquisimeto, La Guayra, Puerto Cabello, Valencia, and Maracaibo.
Breuer, Möller & Co. as well as Van Dissel, Rhode & Co. came next,
with trade centered on Maracaibo and San Cristóbal.[15] Unfortunately, very little is known of the Blohms' commercial empire; they
left neither diaries nor letters and no family archive has survived. By
and large, the family network operated in great secrecy and apparently concluded many of their transactions by word of mouth or
handshake.

A glance at the German merchant colony at Maracaibo will provide some insight into the activities of the Hanseatic traders. Maracaibo's foreign trade was largely in the hands of five major German
houses: Blohm, Breuer, Van Dissel, H. Bornhorst, and Schon-Will-
son; lesser *Hansa* firms included Beckmann & Co., E. Herrnbrück,
Christern & Co., and Ad. Kehrkahn. Their direct holdings—not
counting business credits—were estimated at 12 to 15 million Mark.
The Germans dominated the local *club de commercio*, maintained a
"German Rowing Club," organized a chapter of the German Navy
League, and alleviated the torrid climate through the 300,000-bottle
annual production of the Cervecería de Maracaibo, built with Ger-

[14] Wilhelm Wintzer, *Der Kampf um das Deutschtum: Die Deutschen im tropischen Amerika* (Munich, 1900), 49; William S. Sullivan, "The Rise of Despotism in Venezuela: Cipriano Castro, 1899-1908" (diss., University of New Mexico, 1974), 27. The
credits extended against projected harvests, of course, often led to loss of land by the
Venezuelans. In 1901, for example, coffee planters lost about 4,000 hectares valued
at 3 million Mark to German merchants at San Cristóbal in this manner. ZStA-Potsdam, Auswärtiges Amt, Abt. II, Jahresberichte San Cristobal Nr 54119, pp. 2-5.
Consul Gerstaecker to Chancellor von Bülow, Feb. 8, 1901.

[15] A "black list" of the allegedly sixty to eighty German houses in Venezuela was
published by the United States in December 1917. See *Beilage zu Nr 5718 der
"Nachrichten für Handel, Industrie und Landwirtschaft,"* published by the Reich-
swirtschaftsamt in Berlin. See also *Der Wirtschaftskrieg* (Jena, 1918), IV, 154; and V
(Jena, 1919), 449.

man machinery and run by a German brewmaster.[16] And while opinions as to the quality of the Maracaibo Pilsner differed greatly, the merchants nevertheless agreed that it had been a boon to German industry as all hops, malt, bottles, boilers, instruments, ice plant, and the like had come from Hamburg.[17] Consul Eduard von Jess of the *casa* Breuer, Möller & Co. merely lamented that the searches for artesian wells had only brought in unwanted "petroleum springs."[18]

The United States Consul at Maracaibo, Eugene H. Plumacher, left a detailed description of the business activities of the Maracaibo Germans. He noted that they "practically monopolized" the coffee trade not only at Maracaibo, but also of the entire Táchira region at San Cristóbal, Tovar, Mérida, and Valera as well as San José de Cúcuta in Santander, Colombia (despite a special twenty-percent tax on all coffee brought out from Colombia through Maracaibo). "They are thoroughly acquainted with all the wants of the people in the interior, and are in fact personally known to most of the leading men." Above all, the Germans "know what the market needs and supply it. . . . These Germans not only speak Spanish fluently, but also speak French and English." Rating the German business system "far superior to all others," Plumacher detailed that effectiveness:

> Some of these firms had a dozen or more young Germans in their service engaged for a term of years, who rise from position to position until they become partners, and finally Chiefs, the Seniors retiring as rich men and fixing their residence chiefly at Hamburg where they attend to the export of merchandise for the Maracaibo houses and receive and dispose of the produce shipped from here.

[16] ZStA-Potsdam, Auswärtiges Amt, Abt. II, Handels- und Schiffahrtsverhältnisse mit Venezuela, vol. 16, pp. 127-29. Minister von Rotenhahn to Chancellor von Bülow, July 8, 1905.

[17] See the Consular reports of July 1895, April 1896, June 1897, and September 1905 in ZStA-Potsdam, Auswärtiges Amt, Abt. II, Jahresberichte des Kaiserl. Konsulats in Maracaibo 1887-1906 Nr 54112, pp. 83-97, 98-109, 113-22, and Nr 54113, pp. 74-91.

[18] Ibid., Nr 54112, pp. 126-40. Jess' report of March 1898.

The Chiefs housed and fed their staffs, clothed them and provided medical care, while maintaining "strict control and discipline." Even a rigid dress code furthered the appearance of the Germans in the eyes of the natives: dinner was taken only in black tie. The "recruits" from Hamburg were often a sorry lot "with their heavy, clumsy boots, ill fitting German clothes, and coarse linen, and with a general air of rusticity." In short order, however, they were observed on the streets of Maracaibo "in white duck costumes of elegant cut and fit, fine straw hats, neat polished boots and with shirts and collars of the latest mode." Above all, they impressed the Venezuelans with their social cohesiveness. "They had their club, their glee club, their boat club with all the members elegantly dressed."[19] Moreover, the German merchants had pooled their financial resources in order to purchase and operate a small fleet of ships that dominated the traffic not only on Lake Maracaibo, but also on the vital Zulia-Catatumbo River system that brought Colombian coffee to Maracaibo.[20] Finally, the American consul observed much the same pattern of German trade practices at San Cristóbal, where four German houses dominated with 12 million Mark capital, and at La Guayra and Puerto Cabello, where the Germans worked with capital of 10 to 12 million Mark and property holdings of about 1 million Mark in each.[21]

This German business system reached into the interior of the land, where it recruited the most energetic young Venezuelans to act

[19] ZStA-Potsdam, Auswärtiges Amt, Abt. II, Handel . . . mit Venezuela, vol. 25, p. 53, Plumacher's report dated June 28, 1904, and somehow received by Berlin from Washington. Plumacher's detailed treatment of the Germans at Maracaibo is in Tennessee State Archives, Manuscript Division, Nashville, "Eugene H. Plumacher Memoirs 1877-1890," Accession Number 442, Chapter VIII, 167-70.

[20] ZStA-Potsdam, Auswärtiges Amt, Abt. IIu, Handel- und Schiffahrtsverhältnisse mit Venezuela Nr 4718, pp. 18-20. Prollius to Chancellor von Bethmann Hollweg, Mar. 12, 1913.

[21] See ZStA-Potsdam, Auswärtiges Amt, Abt. II, Jahresberichte San Cristobal Nr 54119, pp. 2-5, Gerstaecker to Chancellor von Bülow, Feb. 8, 1901; and AA-Bonn, Venezuela 1, Allgemeine Angelegenheiten Venezuelas, vol. 14, Commander Jacobsen (*Geier*) to Commanding Admiral, Berlin, Mar. 6, 1898, on La Guayra and Puerto Cabello.

either as intermediaries or as direct buyers. Especially from Maracaibo, the Germans expanded their businesses into Venezuela's Andean states and into northeastern Colombia, sending apprentice clerks to these regions to learn the language and local trade practices; Cipriano Castro was but one such journeyman recruited by Breuer, Möller & Co. in Táchira State. And the system proved highly effective. Consul Plumacher in 1893 noted that the "Hamburg market has gobbled up" all the Maracaibo coffee trade. "In all the other ports it is the same." The following year, he again lamented that "All our business is in the hands of the Germans," advising Washington "simply [to] recall our consuls."[22] And, while the pessimism of these reports may have been exaggerated, Plumacher, as a native of Stein am Rhein in Switzerland, was nevertheless in a position to learn intimately the workings of the Hamburg merchants at Maracaibo.

Indeed, the British at about the same time discovered the validity of Plumacher's observations. Both the government and the Board of Trade joined in the so-called "Made in Germany" alarm in 1896, and began to gather information from around the world regarding the efficacy of the German business system. From consuls in Venezuela came the news that the Germans had attained their dominant position there "by steady perseverance." Above all, the Hamburg merchants "assimilate themselves to the natives of their adopted home, acquire the language quickly and thoroughly, and in that way gain the sympathies of the people with whom they have intercourse."[23] The final report on the "Made in Germany" alarm gave further evidence of the German manner of using local weights, measures, and currency; publishing their trade catalogs in Spanish and Portuguese; paying great attention to the needs of local markets; taking care over even small orders and packaging and invoicing; being willing to work for smaller profits; and using commercial travellers schooled in

---

[22] Tennessee State Archives, Manuscript Division, "Plumacher Papers, Correspondence, 1886-1898," Accession Number 70-76, folder 12. Letters to Morton B. Howell, Nashville, Mar. 10 and Nov. 30, 1893, Jan. 23 and Mar. 24, 1894. Also Sullivan, "Rise of Despotism in Venezuela," 69.

[23] ZStA-Potsdam, Auswärtiges Amt, Abt. II, Handel . . . mit Venezuela, vol. 19, p. 102. British Foreign Office Consular Report on Trade and Finances, 1896.

the language and customs of the country they worked.[24] Not specifically stated was the fact that German home industry also used "dumping" tactics and set lower prices for overseas in order to capture foreign markets from established American, British, Dutch, French, and Italian entrepreneurs.

Banking and insurance, however, remained mainly with London. Eighty percent of Hamburg's imports in 1913, valued at 4,716 million Mark, was financed by London's Merchant Bankers, and while the German Mark by 1900 was an established alternative to the universally accepted British pound sterling, it never quite equalled the latter in influence or prestige. Both the Hamburg-America Line and the North German Lloyd insured their vessels as well as cargos with Lloyds of London. German banks by and large continued to rely upon the London Discount Market to handle their overseas accounts, which netted the British financial institutions as much as 12 million Mark in charges from the ABC states in 1913 alone.[25] The German merchants overseas, for their part, did not restrict themselves to German banking concerns, but financed much of their trade, especially through the French *haute banques* such as Vernes & Cie., de Neuflize & Cie., Heine & Cie., Louis Dreyfus & Cie., Gans & Cie., and Marcuard, Meyer-Boreil & Cie.[26] The largest German house in Venezuela, Blohm, as well as its major competitor, Van Dissel, for instance, relied heavily upon de Neuflize & Cie. for their transactions.[27] Nor should it be overlooked that N. M. Rothschild in London handled much of the foreign investments of S. Bleichröder to about 1890, and thereafter of Adolph von Hansemann's Diskonto-Gesell-

[24] See Ian L. D. Forbes, "German Commercial Relations with South America, 1890-1914" (diss., University of Adelaide, 1975), 207. E. E. Williams' powerful book, *Made in Germany*, appeared at the height of the alarm in 1896. The *New Review* and *Saturday Review*, especially, warned the British public of the German economic danger.

[25] See W.T.C. King, *History of the London Discount Market* (London, 1936), 280; Forbes, "German Commercial Relations," 223, sets the amount received by British bankers for Argentina, Brazil, and Chile.

[26] Alfred Schuett, *Die Finanzierung des Hamburger Aussenhandels* (Marburg, 1925), 78, 138, 172.

[27] Raymond Poidevin, *Les Relations économiques et financières entre la France et l'Allemagne de 1898 à 1914* (Paris, 1969), 13, 156, 660.

schaft in Berlin. Commerce and banking, before the Great War, was very much a highly integrated, international cooperative undertaking and not a chauvinistic, national-monopolistic venture.

On the other hand, the existence of *some* narrow nationalistic impulses does permit a description of the extent of German holdings in South America in general and Venezuela in particular. In November 1897, the newly appointed State Secretary of the Navy Office, Alfred von Tirpitz, asked the Foreign Office to query all overseas missions concerning the extent as well as nature of German commercial interests abroad so that he could compile the data in order to convince the Reichstag of the need for a sizeable fleet.[28] Adolf von Prollius, then a junior staffer at the Caracas mission, replied at once: German merchants ranked first in Venezuela, with working capital estimated at between 50 and 60 million Mark, and land holdings at between 10 and 12 million Mark. Prollius suggested that the return on the coffee trade stood at ten to twenty percent per annum. Industrial investments in the form of breweries and coffee-processing machines were listed at 3 to 5 million Mark, with annual returns also in the ten to twenty percent range. Finally, the diplomat took note of the 60 million Mark investment in the Great Venezuelan Railroad—which will be taken up later in the chapter—and the 2 million Mark Caracas Slaughterhouse being built by Berlin's Beton- und Monierbau.[29]

Concurrently, the Hamburg Senate informed Berlin of two land holdings: Mariara, an 8,100-hectare coffee plantation recently purchased for 816,000 Bolívars by a Hamburg syndicate headed by F. H. Ruete, and the Venezuela Plantation Society, largely owned by the Railroad (Disconto). In addition, the German-Venezuelan Sulphur Company operated a pit near Carúpano with 1.5 million Bolívars capital; the firm hoped to displace Sicilian sulphur from the North American market. Finally, the Senate reported that it had learned "confidentially" that a very large merchant house—most

[28] ZStA-Potsdam, Auswärtiges Amt, Abt. IIu, Bedeutung der deutschen Seeinteressen im Auslande Nr 8598, pp. 2-3. Tirpitz to Foreign Office, Nov. 3, 1897.

[29] ZStA-Potsdam, Auswärtiges Amt, Abt. II, Handel . . . mit Venezuela, Prollius to Foreign Office, Dec. 15, 1897.

likely, Blohm—operated with 12 million Mark credits extended in Venezuela.[30]

Tirpitz's Navy Office in Berlin duly published the findings for all of South America (see Table I). The total German investment in the Caribbean basin, including Colombia and Venezuela, was placed at between 1,000 and 1,250 million Mark, that for the rest of South America at between 1,500 and 1,700 million Mark. The Navy Office

TABLE I
GERMAN TRADE WITH SOUTH AMERICA
(in millions of Mark)

| Country | Commerce and Banking | | | Land and | |
	Capital	Credits	Industry	Plantations	Total
Colombia	20	60	12	2-3	100
Venezuela	50-60	50-60	67	10-12	ca. 200
Chile	114	80-90	20-30	45	270-300
Argentina	200	160 + ?	6-7	200 + ?	570-600
Brazil	180	50-60	40 + ?	30	ca. 350
Uruguay/ Paraguay	42	50	1-2	13	ca. 110
Peru	25	50	}5.5	6 + ? } ca. 25	}100-120
Ecuador	3	6		7 + ?	
Mexico	70	20 + ?	28	28	over 200
Guatemala/ Nicaragua/ Costa Rica	35	60-70	45-50	100	240

[30] Staatsarchiv (SA) Hamburg, Senatskommission für die Reichs- und auswärtigen Angelegenheiten I, S I k 19.1, Nebenakten zu Convolutum I. Report by the Hamburg Board of Trade, Nov. 18, 1897; and ibid., C I d 172, Wirtschaftliche Verhältnisse in Venezuela, Auskunft über dortige Firmen, report from Schmidt-Leda (Caracas), May 5, 1899. It is interesting to note that the Board of Trade entrusted this information gathering not to the largest Hamburg merchant house in Venezuela, H. G. & L. F. Blohm, but rather to the Norddeutsche Bank of Max von Schinckel, which had virtually no experience in Venezuela other than its share of financing the Great Venezuelan Railroad alongside Disconto. Ekkehard Böhm, Überseehandel und Flottenbau: Hanseatische Kaufmannschaft und deutsche Seerüstung 1879-1902 (Düsseldorf, 1972), 104.

noted that German merchants in Venezuela had extended credits of "at least 50 to 60 million Mark" throughout that land, where the Reich maintained a mission and five consulates. It depicted Venezuela in glowing terms as the "premiere overseas territory, where German colonizers more than 400 years ago had attempted to establish a firm base."[31] The German Minister at Caracas, Dr. Schmidt-Leda, in January 1901 reduced these optimistic estimates somewhat, listing total German holdings at between 150 and 160 million Mark, and lowering the estimate of extended credits by fully one-half to 20 million Mark.[32]

While these reports sufficed to help pass the Navy Bills of 1898 and 1900, Tirpitz nevertheless was not convinced of their thoroughness, and in January 1904 the admiral requested a confidential reappraisal "in the greatest possible detail."[33] Alfred Pelldram, the new German minister at Caracas, replied in two lengthy reports of March and August. He raised total German investments to 65 to 70 million Mark, noting not only an increase of about 9 million Mark in the Maracaibo coffee trade, but caustically reporting that the *casa* Blohm seemed to have profited greatly from the recent political turmoil. German insurance firms in Caracas held policies valued at 6 million Mark; land holdings were estimated at 12 million Mark, although President Cipriano Castro had recently purchased one German-owned coffee plantation for 1 million Mark; but the return on investment now hovered just around ten percent. The small German merchant fleet that plied Lake Maracaibo and its tributaries was valued

---

[31] Navy Office Memorandum, "Die deutschen Kapitalanlagen in überseeischen Ländern," April 1900, in ZStA-Potsdam, Auswärtiges Amt, Abt. IIu, Bedeutung der deutschen Seeinteressen im Auslande Nr 8601, p. 109. See also the earlier, less detailed memorandum, "Die Seeinteressen des Deutschen Reichs," Nov. 30, 1897, in Sächsisches Hauptstaatsarchiv Dresden, Gesandschaft Berlin Nr 1748, Flottengesetz 1898. This latter document was compiled by Ernst von Halle of Berlin; Germany's most noted economist, Gustav Schmoller, had recommended Halle to Tirpitz. See Böhm, *Überseehandel und Flottenbau*, 103.

[32] ZStA-Potsdam, Auswärtiges Amt, Abt. II, Handel . . . mit Venezuela, Schmidt-Leda to Chancellor von Bülow, Jan. 24, 1901. See also the *Leipziger Neueste Nachrichten*, Dec. 20, 1901, and the *Vorwärts*, Jan. 5, 1902.

[33] ZStA-Potsdam, Auswärtiges Amt, Abt. IIu, Bedeutung der deutschen Seeinteressen im Auslande Nr 8604, pp. 87-88. Tirpitz to Foreign Office, Jan. 10, 1904.

at 800,000 Mark, holdings in breweries stood at 1.5 million Mark, and a German hat factory at Caracas was estimated at 150,000 Mark. Smaller holdings such as medicine factories, a candle factory, four soap factories, two coconut oil factories, and a marble quarry were listed without indication of value. On the negative side, both the German sulphur operation at Carúpano and an asphalt plant on the Lower Orinoco had been liquidated.[34] Although Count von Oriola of the *Gazelle* cautioned against further German capital investment in this revolution-torn land, the Navy Office in Berlin optimistically continued to claim total German investments of 200 million Mark in Venezuela.[35] And as late as March 1913, Minister von Prollius listed twelve German merchant houses flourishing at Caracas, seven at Valencia, four at Barquisimeto, seven at Puerto Cabello, nine at Maracaibo, four at San Cristóbal, five at Ciudad Bolívar, and one at El Callao.[36] A German publication, *Die Post*, the following year claimed that Germans still held 180 million Mark in investments: 60 million Mark in the "Gran Ferrocarril de Venezuela," 40 million Mark by the *casa* Blohm, 50 to 60 million Mark by the other roughly forty merchant houses, and 20 million Mark in plantations and small industries.[37]

One interesting observation on the German merchants in Venezuela is that they somehow managed to survive the numerous domestic revolts of the nineteenth century without having to call on Berlin for armed assistance. As early as 1879-1880, for example, the German merchants at Ciudad Bolívar simply paid off General Venancio Pulgar, thereby sparing the colony from the customary

[34] ZStA-Potsdam, Auswärtiges Amt, Abt. II, Handel . . . mit Venezuela, Pelldram to Bülow, Mar. 1 and Aug. 5, 1904. See also Clyde E. Hewitt, "Venezuela and the Great Powers, 1902-1909: A Study in International Investment and Diplomacy" (diss., University of Chicago, 1948), 190.

[35] AA-Bonn, Venezuela 1, vol. 20. Count von Oriola to Admiralty Staff, Mar. 20, 1902; Navy Office memorandum, "Die Entwicklung der deutschen Seeinteressen im letzten Jahrzehnt," Nov. 30, 1905, in ZStA-Merseburg, Reichskanzlei Nr 950, Flottengesetz, pp. 189-338.

[36] ZStA-Potsdam, Auswärtiges Amt, Abt. IIu, Bedeutung der deutschen Seeinteressen im Auslande. Prollius to Chancellor von Bethmann Hollweg, Mar. 13, 1913.

[37] *Die Post*, Jan. 6, 1914.

damages.[38] Again, in 1892 they were spared from pillage by timely financial support for General Joaquín Crespo. The house of Blohm had ingratiated itself with Crespo by not putting in claims for constriction of trade and by refusing to approach Minister Friedrich Count von Kleist-Tychow for help—an action that drew the ire not only of Kleist but also of Wilhelm II.[39] Of course, Blohm's opposition to the German blockade of 1902-1903 and its subsequent underwriting of the mediation efforts by the American minister at Caracas, Herbert W. Bowen, strained its relations with the Reich: Minister Giesbert von Pilgrim-Baltazzi sarcastically noted these actions by "the patriotic house Blohm and Cie.," while the Disconto Bank bluntly suggested that Blohm was undermining the entire German effort in Venezuela and opening that country up to North American interests.[40] Pilgrim-Baltazzi's successor, Alfred Pelldram, in 1903 bitterly complained that Blohm was obtaining special concessions from Castro as a favor for having opposed the blockade.[41] Not even Castro's deposition by President Juan Vicente Gómez altered Blohm's favorable position as the Hamburg house in 1909 successfully blocked the proposed lifting of the special thirty-percent Antilles tariff, which would have benefited British and Dutch traders. Indeed, the German envoy at Caracas in 1910 formally charged Blohm with conniving in Gómez's schemes to extort state funds![42]

[38] ZStA-Potsdam, Auswärtiges Amt, Abt. II, Handel . . . mit Venezuela, vol. 10, pp. 101-104, Stammann to Foreign Office, Feb. 20, 1880; and vol. 11, p. 38, Stammann to Foreign Office, Mar. 23, 1880.

[39] AA-Bonn, Venezuela 1, vol. 10, Kleist to Chancellor von Caprivi, Nov. 27, 1892, and Feb. 1, 1893; and Foreign Office to Kleist, Dec. 20, 1892. The incident was widely reported in the Hamburg press. See, for example, *Hamburger Nachrichten*, May 2, 1893.

[40] AA-Bonn, Venezuela 1, vol. 24, Pilgrim-Baltazzi to Mühlberg (Foreign Office), Feb. 10, 1903; ibid., vol. 25, Disconto to Foreign Office, July 8, 1903.

[41] See Pelldram's complaints to Chancellor von Bülow, Aug. 27 and Oct. 27, 1903, in ZStA-Potsdam, Auswärtiges Amt, Abt. II, Handel . . . mit Venezuela, vol. 23, pp. 126-27, 165. Pelldram repeated the charge on Dec. 13, 1903.

[42] See the Foreign Office's memorandum on Blohm, Jan. 16, 1909, in ZStA-Potsdam, Auswärtiges Amt, Abt. IIu, Handels- und Schiffahrtsverhältnisse mit Venezuela Nr 4715, pp. 78-79; and AA-Bonn, Venezuela 1, vol. 37, Rhomberg to Bethmann Hollweg, Jan. 4, 1910. Blohm was even accused of profiting from the internment of merchant ships in September 1914! See Bundesarchiv-Koblenz, R85/

This petty bickering obscured the fact that Castro rather than Blohm was responsible for the economic *malaise* that crippled Venezuela after the blockade. Castro and his family had by 1905 firmly established monopolies in the production and sale of salt, flour, cigarettes, cigarette paper, matches, tobacco, brandy, pearls, guns, dynamite, and cattle export.[43] Dr. Alfred Scharffenorth, former owner of the German asphalt plant on the Lower Orinoco, later confirmed that Castro's monopolies "have done nothing but ruin [once] blooming industries, damage countless commercial enterprises, and suck the blood out of both land and people." According to Scharffenorth, Gómez merely continued this system.[44] In other words, Blohm simply was able to swim with the current and to adjust to changing conditions, while many German industrial undertakings, on the other hand, had suffered greatly as a result of their support of the blockade.

The one notable exception to that was the Great Venezuelan Railroad. With a capitalization of 60 million Mark, it was Germany's largest railroad enterprise overseas. And whereas the more famous Berlin-to-Baghdad Railroad was built with forty percent French capital, the Venezuelan project was fully funded in Germany. For once, not even Lord Nathaniel Rothschild of London was offered shares in the undertaking.[45]

For much of the nineteenth century, railroad building in South America rested with the Americans and the British; German investments generally shied away from this speculative area—with the one notable exception of the Companhia Estrada de Ferro do Oeste de

6871, Haltung der Neutralen im europäischen Kriege 1914-1921. Prollius to Bethmann Hollweg, Sept. 15 and 24, 1914, and Feb. 18, 1915.

[43] For a partial listing of Castro's monopolies, see ZStA-Potsdam, Auswärtiges Amt, Abt. II, Handel . . . mit Venezuela, vol. 26, pp. 149-52. Minister von Rotenhahn to Bülow, July 27, 1905.

[44] ZStA-Potsdam, Auswärtiges Amt, Abt. IIu, Handels-und Schiffahrtsverhältnisse mit Venezuela Nr 4715, pp. 154-62. Rhomberg to Bethmann Hollweg, Aug. 11, 1909. Scharffenorth termed the present reaction against Castro's monopolies as "nothing more than a miserable comedy." "Basically, nothing has changed."

[45] N. M. Rothschild Archives London (RAL), XI/72/11A: 18960722. Disconto to Rothschild, July 22, 1896.

Minas in West Brazil.[46] But as Germany entered the industrial revolution by the 1880s, both its envoy at Caracas and its ship commanders visiting Venezuela began to recommend investment in railroad building in Venezuela, where only a small spur from Caracas to La Guayra existed.[47] Ernst von Hasse's South American Colonial Society at Leipzig as early as 1883 advised Berlin to follow the example of the United States by building railroads in order to control markets. "We *Germans* are lacking neither a steel industry, nor human resources, nor technical expertise, nor capital. . . . To date, we Germans have *lacked* only enterprise, or boldness."[48] And the Union of German Iron and Steel Industrialists three years later expressed a similar hope that German concerns undertake railroad construction in Venezuela, which promised "large orders" in the near future.[49]

The major reason for this sudden interest in overseas railroad construction—quite apart from the obvious fact that the industrial revolution had just provided the requisite plants, technology, and skilled labor—was that the deep and persistent "great depression" of 1873 to 1894 had sharply curtailed domestic markets and hence prompted entrepreneurs to look abroad for investment opportunities and new markets. Indeed, by the late 1870s, nearly one-half of the Reich's 435 blast furnaces stood idle, while the actual market value of its twenty largest iron and steel works had slumped to 21 million Mark as opposed to a nominal book value of 178 million Mark. As late as 1892, the *Frankfurter Zeitung* reported a further decrease in the value of banking and industrial portfolios of twenty-five percent,

---

[46] See RAL, XI/72/11B. Disconto "Prememoria" for Rothschild, December 1898, on the Oeste de Minas loan of 1889 in the amount of 22.45 million Mark.

[47] See ZStA-Potsdam, Auswärtiges Amt, Abt. IIE, Eisenbahnen in Central- und Südamerika Nr 15322, p. 88. Minister von Peyer to Bismarck, Mar. 20, 1882; and ibid., Abt. II, Handel . . . mit Venezuela, vol. 13, p. 124, Lieutenant Commander von Seckendorff (*Olga*) to Foreign Office, Nov. 26, 1883. For an excellent survey of the whole spectrum of Venezuelan railroading, see Eduardo Arcila Farías, *Historia de la Ingeniería en Venezuela* (Caracas, 1961), II, 167-278.

[48] ZStA-Potsdam, Deutsche Kolonial-Gesellschaft Nr 262, Südamerikanische Colonisations-Gesellschaft zu Leipzig, pp. 10-11. Undated memorandum of 1883.

[49] ZStA-Potsdam, Auswärtiges Amt, Abt. IIE, Eisenbahnen . . . Nr 15324, pp. 216-17. Report of May 2, 1887.

from 4,479 to 3,365 million Mark.[50] Above all, Europe and America reacted to economic depression by erecting a system of high tariff walls against each other: Russia abandoned economic liberalism in 1877, Germany in 1879, Italy in 1886-1887, the United States in 1890, and France in 1892. Moreover, Britain at the same time was stirring the movement toward imperial preference, which was seen in many quarters simply as a precursor to an imperial tariff. The United States, for its part, sought to overcome the domestic depression not only through the McKinley Tariff but also through the development of a Pan-American movement designed to secure the South American market. Given these circumstances, German entrepreneurs saw enhanced overseas trade as the only available means of regaining and maintaining economic prosperity and of stabilizing the domestic economy.[51] In other words, Germany resorted to what one might term "depression imperialism" by the 1880s.

The two bankers who would eventually build the Venezuelan railroad, Adolph von Hansemann of Disconto and Max von Schinckel of the Norddeutsche Bank, were keenly aware of the connection between their great overseas project and the slumping German economy.[52] Fully financed by German banks, fully supplied with materials by German industry, and fully built by German engineers, the Venezuelan rail link would soon be touted as a model of German entrepreneurship and *Kultur*, as a shining example of German *Weltpolitik*. Therein, rather than in its function within the Venezuelan economy, lies its great importance.

On July 8, 1887, Friedrich Krupp of Essen signed a contract with the government of President Antonio Guzmán Blanco, Venezuela's

---

[50] Kennedy, *Rise of the Anglo-German Antagonism*, 49; Hermann Münch, *Adolph von Hansemann* (Munich/Berlin, 1932), 268. See also the pessimistic reports on domestic investment opportunities and the need for overseas capital export by Disconto's Hansemann to Lord Rothschild, Jan. 1 and July 20, 1887, in RAL XI/72/7B.

[51] See Forbes, "German Commercial Relations," 25ff.

[52] See Peter Hampe, *Die "ökonomische Imperialismustheorie": Kritische Untersuchungen* (Munich, 1976), 307, 316, 364; Max von Schinckel, *Lebenserinnerungen* (Hamburg, 1929), 234; *Die Disconto-Gesellschaft 1851 bis 1901: Denkschrift zum 50 Jährigen Jubiläum* (Berlin, 1901), 129: *Jahres-Bericht der Norddeutschen Bank in Hamburg* (1888), passim.

greatest "builder-statesman,"[53] to build a small-spur, single-track line from Caracas to San Carlos via Cagua and Valencia. The 290-kilometer-long line was estimated to cost 256,000 Mark per kilometer, with the cost to be recouped by a seven-percent Venezuelan guarantee per kilometer built; the initial spur to Cagua was to be finished within three years. The terms of the contract were highly lucrative: Krupp would be freed from all existing import tariffs as well as future taxes; the company would receive a ninety-nine-year lease on the line as well as 500-meter-wide strips of land on both sides of the track; and, finally, Krupp would be given free use of forests for railroad ties.[54] The contract was negotiated by Krupp's engineer, L. A. Müller, through a German-Venezuelan middleman, Juan Rodolfo Leseur of Leseur, Römer & Cie.; the single document in the Krupp Archives that attests to the agreement listed a "broker's fee" of 35,000 pounds sterling to be divided among Leseur, Guzmán Blanco, J. Cecilio Castro, and unnamed "third persons."[55] Little else is known of Krupp's role in the project. According to Max von Schinckel, the Disconto Bank in Berlin and the Norddeutsche Bank in Hamburg entered into the contract late in 1887 through the good offices of F. H. Ruete, a wealthy Hamburg coffee plantation owner in Venezuela. Schinckel and Ruete met Guzmán Blanco ("and a gallery of beautiful women") at Carlsbad Spa that year and signed the deal to finance the railroad.[56] On November 20, 1888, Disconto and

[53] According to John J. Johnson, ed., *The Role of the Military in Underdeveloped Countries* (Princeton, 1962), 111. From 1884 to 1888, Guzmán Blanco had appointed himself "Enviado Extraordinario y Ministro Plenipotenciario" to Berlin, London, Madrid, and Paris. ZStA-Potsdam, Auswärtiges Amt, Abt. II, Mission der Republik Venezuela Nr 50944/1, pp. 88-90. Minister von Peyer to Chancellor von Bismarck, May 26, 1884.

[54] See the "Grosse Venezuela Eisenbahngesellschaft. Concessions-Urkunde," July 8, 1887, in ZStA-Potsdam, Auswärtiges Amt, Abt. II, Handel . . . mit Venezuela, vol. 16, p. 77. Also, ibid., Abt. IIE, Eisenbahnen . . . Nr 15325, pp. 81-82. Consul Heinrich (Caracas) to Bismarck, July 19, 1887.

[55] Historisches Archiv, Friedr. Krupp, Essen-Bredeney, FAH IV C 16, Briefwechsel Aufsichtsrat-Direktorium. Gustav Hartmann to Krupp, Sept. 19, 1903, seeking payment of the funds.

[56] Schinckel, *Lebenserinnerungen*, 234. The Venezuelan statesman apparently accepted the contract by declaring: "In this decision to extend to my country German technology and German entrepreneurship, I see a sunrise that will come up over all

the Norddeutsche Bank formed the "Grosse Venezuela-Eisenbahn-gesellschaft" in Hamburg with a capitalization of 10 million Mark—the latter figure was suggested by Gustav Goddefroy of Samoan fame.

Disconto at once turned to the Prussian Ministry of Public Works with a request for two railroad engineers to survey the projected Venezuelan line. The Ministry at first expressed fears that Venezuela was not suited "for great projects," but eventually relented because the project was "advantageous for German [industrial] interests," which only recently had begun to cooperate with banking concerns "in overseas areas." However, the Ministry noted that it was willing to endorse the request for the engineers only because the undertaking "was not connected with any responsibilities" on the part of the Berlin government.[57] The engineering specialists, Jungbecker and Plock, were placed on "permanent vacation" and allowed to travel to Venezuela.

Krupp, for its part, deemed the future prospects of the railroad to be "very good," even though two British lines at either terminal, one from Caracas to La Guayra and the other from Valencia to Puerto Cabello, could control traffic on the German spur. Above all, Krupp saw the line as the proverbial foot in the door, as opening up new vistas for "the future of German undertakings" in Venezuela. Without a worldwide economic empire and with national markets everywhere closed behind restrictive tariff barriers, Germany had no choice but to find and establish its own monopolized markets. The Essen industrial giant bluntly reminded Berlin "that it was becoming ever more difficult for German industry to expand its markets and [thereby] to offer profitable and lasting employment to its workers purely through exports."[58] Krupp's comments certainly lend credence to Erich Preiser's "safety-valve" thesis that Germany exported capital primarily in order to overcome domestic cyclical financial depressions—and to secure new markets. Apparently, the Ministry

---

of Venezuela." The Carlsbad negotiations were later confirmed in a Foreign Office memorandum of Aug. 3, 1888, in AA-Bonn, Venezuela 1, vol. 6.

[57] ZStA-Potsdam, Auswärtiges Amt, Abt. II, Handel . . . mit Venezuela, vol. 15, pp. 99-102. Ministry of Public Works to Foreign Office, Nov. 29, 1887, and Foreign Office to Ministry of Public Works, Dec. 1, 1887.

[58] Ibid., vol. 16, pp. 10-12, 16-18. Krupp to Foreign Office, Sept. 3 and 12, 1888.

of Public Works agreed, and in 1889 assured the railroad that two Royal Prussian master builders, Carl Plock and Hermann Müller, could remain in Venezuela "with a view toward the growing value of the Venezuelan railroad construction for German industry."[59]

The Prussian engineers completed their survey in the spring of 1888, and submitted an "extraordinarily optimistic" report. The first leg of the project, the 102-kilometer line from Caracas to Cagua, would require a capital of 24 million Mark. All materials would be imported from Germany, and only German engineers would be used, as Venezuela lacked capable technical personnel.[60] Engineer Jungbecker felt that Venezuelans "lacked the individual drive to work," being prone mainly "to drink and to satisfy their major lust."[61] And while Schinckel of the Norddeutsche Bank later claimed that he harbored doubts about these highly optimistic prognoses, he nevertheless joined Disconto in the project after an outside consultant from the Magdeburg-Halberstädter Bahn termed the undertaking mere "child's play." Alfred Lent, the noted Berlin architect who had designed the famous Zirkus Busch and the Lehrter Bahnhof, also attested to the feasibility of the Venezuelan railroad.[62]

On the other hand, the German consul at Puerto Cabello, Richard Beselin, was not as optimistic. As early as February 1888, he warned that the German railroad would be economically viable only if it purchased the Caracas-La Guayra line; otherwise, it would constitute but a "tributary" link for the British railroad. Moreover, the consul cautioned that while the project would be "good business for the large capitalists," small investors should be "warned against placing their investments" in Venezuela.[63] The German minister at Caracas, Otto von Peyer, three years later likewise stressed that the

[59] Ibid., vol. 16, pp. 31-32. Ministry of Public Works to Bismarck, June 25, 1889.

[60] Ibid., vol. 15, pp. 113-15. Peyer to Bismarck, May 6, 1888. See also Münch, *Adolph von Hansemann*, 272.

[61] ZStA-Potsdam, Auswärtiges Amt, Abt. II, Handel . . . mit Venezuela, vol. 15, pp. 122-28. Jungbecker's report of July 2, 1888.

[62] Schinckel, *Lebenserinnerungen*, 234. See also Elsabea Rohrmann, *Max von Schinckel: Hanseatischer Bankmann im wilhelminischen Deutschland* (Hamburg, 1971), 68.

[63] ZStA-Potsdam, Auswärtiges Amt, Abt. IIE, Eisenbahnen . . . Nr 15326, p. 29. Consul Beselin to Foreign Office, Feb. 15, 1888.

Great Venezuelan Railroad would not flourish unless it acquired "free access to the ocean," that is, unless it purchased the "foreign undertakings" at either end of its tracks.[64] Disconto rejected Peyer's concerns as coming from someone "insufficiently knowledgeable in the details of the project." It did, however, admit that the original engineering estimates had been woefully inaccurate: tunnel length had increased from the projected 1,000 to 3,400 meters; earth removal had jumped from an estimated 1 to 2.5 million cubic meters; and steel for bridges and viaducts had tripled to 3,000 tons. Moreover, the British Central Railroad had been less than cooperative in moving supplies from the ports to the construction sites.[65]

On a more positive note, the project fulfilled the promise that it would stimulate German industry. The press at home proudly noted that some 50,000 tons of German building materials had been transported to Venezuela between 1888 and 1894. Steel rails, wheels, and axles had come from Krupp. Passenger and freight cars had been supplied by Zypen & Charlier in Cologne-Deutz. Steel ties, which could be produced faster than Venezuelan hardwood ties, had been purchased from Dortmund Union, while locomotives had been made by the Sächsische Maschinenfabrik (formerly Richard Hartmann) in Chemnitz; both of these purveyors were largely owned by Disconto. This material, estimated at 8 million Mark, had been shipped through Hamburg in German bottoms. The *Tägliche Rundschau* in Berlin lauded the Great Venezuelan Railroad as "a showpiece of German diligence and German *Kultur* and German industry."[66]

To be sure, it was that and much more. Partly because of the extremely hilly terrain between Las Adjuntas and Las Tejerias—which reminded one observer of the Rocky Mountains—partly because much of the area was prone to earth slides, and partly because of the Teutonic thoroughness with which the line was built, construction

[64] ZStA-Potsdam, Auswärtiges Amt, Abt. II, Handel . . . mit Venezuela, vol. 16, p. 81. Peyer to Chancellor von Caprivi, June 14, 1891.

[65] Ibid., vol. 16, pp. 70-71. Disconto to Foreign Office, June 27, 1891. See also Sievers, *Venezuela und die deutschen Interessen*, 63.

[66] *Tägliche Rundschau*, Nr 108, May 8, 1892; also the *Kölnische Zeitung*, Nr 207, Mar. 11, 1894.

costs, originally set at 154,000 Mark per kilometer by Engineer Müller, eventually ended up at 345,000 Mark per kilometer. No less than 215 bridges and viaducts as well as 89 tunnels were required.[67] The Norddeutsche Bank alone had to come up with 1 million Mark per month from its cash reserves to cover its share of the costs. Worst of all, Venezuela was unable to pay the seven-percent guarantee for the line. In addition to being plagued by countless domestic revolts, the country simply could not generate sufficient income to meet its pledges.[68] Instead of the seven-percent guarantee, the Great Venezuelan Railroad received only one-half of one percent throughout much of the 1890s; overall revenues from the line declined from a high of 2.7 million Bolívars in 1891 to 1.75 million in 1900.[69] As a result, Caracas rapidly fell behind its financial obligations in every respect. Finally, the railroad was top-heavy, with administrators receiving excessively high salaries of 4,000 Bolívars per month as well as costly housing and other fringe benefits.[70]

As a result of this experience with the Great Venezuelan Railroad, General Joaquín Crespo in December 1892 issued a new, highly restrictive railroad law which ended the practice of issuing ninety-nine-year leases, awarding guarantees on expected returns, and granting contractors building subsidies.[71] A clause in the new law stipulating that all financial disputes were to be submitted to Venezuelan courts and were under no circumstances to become the "ob-

[67] See the report, *Die Disconto-Gesellschaft 1851 bis 1901*, 128. Schinckel, *Lebenserinnerungen*, 235, placed construction costs at 62 million Mark by 1894. See also Henry Wulff, *Norddeutsche Bank in Hamburg 1856-1906* (Berlin, 1906), 21-22; Walter Otto, *Anleiheübernahme-, Gründungs- und Beteiligungsgeschäfte der deutschen Grossbanken in Übersee* (Berlin, 1910), 125-27; and A. Vale, "The Great Venezuelan Railway," *The Railway Magazine*, 9 (July 1901), 38-43.

[68] Under a law of 1873, Venezuela set aside forty percent of its customs revenues to meet outstanding debts; 13/100th of this amount was to go to foreign creditors. AA-Bonn, Venezuela 1, vol. 4. Department of State (Washington) to Foreign Office (Berlin), Mar. 31, 1883.

[69] See Hewitt, "Venezuela and the Great Powers," 148; and Münch, *Adolph von Hansemann*, 275.

[70] ZStA-Potsdam, Auswärtiges Amt, Abt. II, Handel . . . mit Venezuela, vol. 17, pp. 75-80. Minister von Kleist to Chancellor von Caprivi, Dec. 21, 1892.

[71] See *Gaceta oficial*, Nr 5660, December 3, 1892.

ject of international reclamations" greatly addled both Disconto and the Norddeutsche Bank. Schinckel joined Hansemann in April 1893, effectively to use this clause in order to prevent Berlin from negotiating a formal trade treaty with General Crespo.[72]

The grand opening of the Caracas to Valencia spur of the railroad took place on February 1, 1894, amidst a great deal of ceremony. Wilhelm II dispatched the schoolship *Stein* to honor the occasion. Caracas held a gala opera performance and formal reception for the railroad's personnel. For the first time ever, a commander of a foreign warship—Captain Wintersheim of the *Stein*—received the Bust of Bolívar Second Class, while three other German officers were awarded lower grades of the same decoration; Wilhelm II, not to be outdone, granted Venezuela's Foreign Minister, P. Ezequiel Rojas, the Royal Order of the Crown First Class. At 6:30 a.m. on February 1, one flag-and-flower-bedecked train left Caracas, while another concurrently left Valencia. They were to meet at La Victoria, where a grand reception was planned for 350 official guests. Unfortunately, the celebration quickly lost its intended lustre. For some unexplained reason, General Crespo cancelled at the last moment. Minister von Kleist became ill and likewise excused himself. A mud slide delayed the meeting at La Victoria, while the return trip to Caracas was rudely interrupted by the discovery of a freight car sitting directly across the tracks. Worst of all, the railroad had failed to invite the influential German community at Caracas to both opera and reception, with the result that the Caracas Germans boycotted a tea held at the German mission. Count von Kleist sadly reported "dissension within the [German] colony" to Berlin.[73] It was perhaps an omen of things to come.

To be sure, the Great Venezuelan Railroad remained on uneasy

[72] ZStA-Potsdam, Auswärtiges Amt, Abt. IIu, Handelsvertragsverhandlungen mit Venezuela Nr 12573, pp. 72-77. Disconto and Norddeutsche Bank to Foreign Office, Apr. 18, 1893.

[73] AA-Bonn, Venezuela 1, vol. 11, Kleist to Foreign Office, Feb. 5, 1894; ZStA-Potsdam, Auswärtiges Amt, Abt. II, Handel . . . mit Venezuela, vol. 18, pp. 59-61, Kleist to Chancellor von Caprivi, Feb. 5, 1894; and ZStA-Potsdam, Auswärtiges Amt, Abt. II, Entsendung deutscher Kriegsschiffe Nr 22442, pp. 57-63, Kleist to Caprivi, Feb. 5, 1894.

footing with the Caracas regime for much of the 1890s. In June 1894, Wilhelm Baron von und zu Bodman, the acting German minister at Caracas, informed Chancellor von Caprivi that the railroad treated its Venezuelan employees with condescension, and that it displayed an equal lack of consideration and tact in its dealings with the Venezuelan authorities. The latter spoke openly of a "mounting Germanization" on the part of the Great Venezuelan Railroad. When a locomotive ran over and killed a Venezuelan taking his siesta on the tracks and the government jailed the locomotive driver, the railroad protested by immediately curtailing all rail services.[74] Carl Plock, the former Prussian engineer who was now a director with the railroad, was so derogatory in his remarks concerning Venezuela and its people that Caracas early in 1895 rescinded an earlier offer to make Plock a consul *ad honorem* at Berlin.[75] Obviously, the railroad and the Venezuelan government were rapidly becoming disenchanted with each other.

Early in 1895, Adolph von Hansemann of the Disconto Bank personally intervened in the affairs of the Great Venezuelan Railroad. Indeed, Hansemann had long nurtured ambitions in railroading: some years earlier, for example, he had tried to get a concession to build a line in Rumania, but had lost out to the Austrian State Railway. As the son of a Rhinelander, Hansemann attested that he had agreed to finance the Venezuelan project mainly to help the slumping German steel industry get back on its feet.[76] Fearing that the project might not survive its growing pains, Hansemann approached the Comptoir National d'Escompte in Paris with a proposal to set up an international banking syndicate to revitalize the Great Venezuelan Railroad. When this effort failed because France demanded that its outstanding debts in Venezuela be regulated beforehand by General Crespo, Hansemann resorted to more drastic action. In April

---

[74] ZStA-Potsdam, Auswärtiges Amt, Abt. II, Handel . . . mit Venezuela, vol. 18, pp. 79-80. Bodman to Caprivi, June 27, 1894.

[75] ZStA-Merseburg, Auswärtiges Amt, Konsulate der Republik Venezuela in Preussen Nr 952, vol. 4. Bodman to Chancellor von Hohenlohe-Schillingsfürst, Feb. 2, 1895.

[76] Münch, *Adolph von Hansemann*, 273.

1895, he forced a merger between Disconto and the Norddeutsche Bank, whereby the latter received two-thirds of the face value of its holdings in Disconto stock; the 20 million Mark thus gained by Disconto's financial sleight of hand was used to tide the railroad over its troubles.[77] Unfortunately, Maximilian Harden's *Zukunft* got wind of the merger and cautioned its readers not to buy Disconto stock; the assets of Disconto, Harden warned, were being "buried and coffined" in Venezuela![78] A public panic promptly ensued on the Berlin Bourse, and only Hansemann's great drive and forceful personality allowed Disconto to weather the storm.[79] This notwithstanding, the resulting Disconto public loan issue of 50 million Bolívars for Venezuela in 1896 remained undersubscribed.[80]

Despite the fact that Hansemann in 1896 relieved Venezuela of its seven-percent guarantee, the railroad did not prosper. By the summer of 1897, the Foreign Office in Berlin was apprised of this fact through its Embassy in Washington: interest payments on the 1896 loan had not been met; General Crespo refused to pay for use of the railroad by his troops; the land promised the line on both sides of the tracks had not been released by Caracas; and Disconto had failed to "connect the German railroad to the sea" by purchasing the British-owned spur from Valencia to Puerto Cabello. The report ended with an urgent plea for further capital. "May German engineers and Ger-

[77] Schinckel, *Lebenserinnerungen*, 235; Poidevin, *Les Relations économiques et financières*, 72-73; Wulff, *Norddeutsche Bank*, 17; Otto, *Beteiligungsgeschäfte der deutschen Grossbanken*, 126-27.

[78] Münch, *Adolph von Hansemann*, 352; and *Die Zukunft*, vol. 10 (Berlin 1895), 476. The Venezuelan government in 1896 stood 7.4 million Bolívars in arrears on its loan guarantee. See also W. Däbritz, *David Hansemann und Adolph von Hansemann* (Krefeld, 1954), 120.

[79] Hugo Rachel, Johannes Papritz, and Paul Wallich, eds., *Berliner Grosskaufleute und Kapitalisten* (Berlin, 1967), III, 285, claim that Hansemann ran Disconto as a "barely veiled autocracy." See also Rohrmann, *Max von Schinckel*, 72ff.

[80] For the negotiations, see the *Berliner Tageblatt*, Nr 475, Sept. 17, 1896. Wilhelm II awarded the Venezuelan negotiator, Dr. Bruzual Serra, the Order of the Crown Second Class for his efforts. The capitalization of 60 million Mark placed the Great Venezuelan Railroad ahead of the German-financed Shantung Railroad (54 million Mark capital) in size. J. Riesser, *Zur Entwicklungsgeschichte der deutschen Grossbanken mit besonderer Rücksicht auf die Konzentrationsbestrebungen* (Jena, 1906), 114.

man banks always unite overseas to Germany's honor and profit rather than to throw their work and capital away on foreign undertakings." The Wilhelmstrasse partly met this plea in 1896 by including photographs and other exhibits of the Great Venezuelan Railroad in the Berlin Exhibition held that year.[81] However, capital did not flow to Venezuela, and Hansemann in 1897 had to raise the capital fund of the railroad to 60 million Mark, or six times the original estimate. What the Foreign Office dubbed the "Baghdad Railroad of South America" continued to drain the cash reserves of Disconto at an alarming rate.

Above all, Venezuela persistently proved unable (or unwilling) to meet its heavy foreign railroad obligations. Caracas had contracted for no less than forty-eight lines between 1853 and 1892; ten were completed, three partially finished, and the rest abandoned without payment or indemnity. Only the British line that connected the capital to La Guayra proved to be a profit-maker, and by 1895 Caracas owed foreigners at least 6 million Bolívars in direct railroad debts.[82] General Cipriano Castro's revolt in 1898 only plunged the country into further chaos and forced it to halt all payments on the Disconto loan.

The commander of the German cruiser *Geier*, Lieutenant Commander Hermann Jacobsen, in March 1898 sent Berlin a detailed report of conditions in Venezuela in general, and of the Great Venezuelan Railroad in particular, that aptly summarized the situation. According to Jacobsen, General Crespo had robbed the country blind according to the well-established Haitian tradition: "Prendre l'argent de l'Etat, ce n'est pas voler" (Take the state's money, it is not stealing). Coffee prices had tumbled from sixty to twenty-four Mark per *quintal*. Cash for commerce was almost nonexistent. Consumer goods were exorbitant by German standards. The Venezuelans were proving once again that they were unable to govern themselves. With regard to Disconto's railroad, Jacobsen was blunt and critical, terming the project "failed speculation." The line had cost

[81] ZStA-Potsdam, Auswärtiges Amt, Abt. IIE, Eisenbahnen . . . Nr 15331, pp. 74-85. Embassy Washington to Foreign Office, July 10, 1897.

[82] See Sullivan, "Rise of Despotism in Venezuela," 32-33, 59.

too much to build, and "profits in no way stand in relation to costs." Jacobsen accorded the Great Venezuelan Railroad "sole responsibility" for its present misery. Most damning of all, he seriously questioned whether it deserved "the strong support on the part of the German government that it has partly enjoyed in recent years." The commander cautioned Berlin against future support. "It seems to me, that here the special interests of a company have received preferential treatment, even though they run counter to the general interests of enhanced German trade." Turning to the future, Jacobsen saw relief for Venezuela alone through foreign intervention. "Only under the protection or in the possession of a European state can Venezuela be transformed into one of the richest commercial and industrial states" in South America.[83]

Lieutenant Commander Jacobsen's report raised many of the major issues central to German-Venezuelan relations in this era. Periodic revolts, corruption, and mismanagement had plunged the land into financial and commercial chaos. The railroad's costs had far exceeded possible returns in passenger and freight rates, yet the very size and nature of the investment had made it an object of national honor and prestige. It may or may not have been a "showpiece" of German industry, engineering, banking, and *Kultur*; it most decidedly was a shining example of Berlin's new-found *Weltpolitik*. Whether it deserved official support from the imperial government was a decision that would be dragged out over the course of the *castrista* revolution from 1898 to 1902, and one that will be dealt with in subsequent chapters. The issue whether a "European state," such as, say, Germany, needed to extend its "protection" over Venezuela or even to "possess" it likewise emerged as a topic for debate in Germany around the time of Jacobsen's report. Finally, what Friedrich Katz termed the "discovery" of South America by the various pressure groups in Germany—most notably the Pan-German League, the

[83] AA-Bonn, Venezuela 1, vol. 14. Jacobsen to Commanding Admiral, Mar. 6, 1898. The German consul at Puerto Cabello, P. Krause, termed the railroad's performance "an utter calamity." ZStA-Potsdam, Auswärtiges Amt, Abt. II, Jahresberichte des Kaiserlichen Konsulats in Puerto Cabello Nr 54115. Krause to Foreign Office, Apr. 15, 1898.

Navy League, and the Colonial League—brought forth a flood of articles, brochures, and books dealing with the so-called "mission of *Deutschtum* in South America" by the turn of the century. At the heart of that "discovery" stood Reich support for German schools, churches, and nationals overseas, including Venezuela.

CHAPTER II

THE GERMAN COMMUNITY: *DEUTSCHTUM* AS A TROJAN HORSE?

At the end of the nineteenth century, a small but influential group of writers in Germany demanded that the Reich establish closer contact with and provide financial support to the German element (*Deutschtum*) overseas. The latter was seen as a vital component in a policy of informal imperialism: Germany, lacking colonies of any commercial significance, had no choice but to use its nationals abroad as secular missionaries who would bring about a commercial orientation of their adopted lands toward the Reich. Moreover, the Germans overseas could become conduits through which German culture and learning as well as armaments sales and military training missions could permeate South America. The proponents of directed German emigration to those areas where German settlements already existed—rather than to the United States, where the immigrants were forever "lost" to the Reich—euphemistically touted the German element in the outer world as pioneers of a Greater Germany. To be sure, they evidenced a tendency toward the emotional and the irrational; their advocacy of a mystical nationalism and a mythical *Deutschtum* oftentimes stood in stark contrast to Berlin's official policy toward South America. Yet their highly visible efforts to tie the Germans living overseas (*Auslandsdeutsche*) closer to the fatherland through aid for schools and churches as well as through directed emigration in time made South America in general and Venezuela in particular focal points of popular as well as official attention.[1]

Wilhelm Sievers, Professor of Geography at Giessen University, became Germany's leading authority on Venezuela on the basis of

---

[1] See Fritz Fischer, *War of Illusions: German Policies from 1911 to 1914* (New York, 1975), 28; Ian L. D. Forbes, "German Commercial Relations with South America, 1890-1914" (diss., University of Adelaide, 1975), 40, 288ff.

two extensive trips to that country around the turn of the century. His findings, published in three separate books, greatly shaped German views of "Little Venice" until the Great War. According to Sievers, Venezuela was a land dominated by "mixed breeds" that made up fully ninety percent of the population: mulattos (Afro-Caucasoid), mestizos (Caucasoid-Amerindian), and zambos (Afro-Amerindian). Negroes, who had come to Venezuela in the sixteenth and seventeenth centuries, accounted for five percent of the populace while Caucasians and Amerindians comprised two percent each; only the Spanish remained "racially pure." Sievers estimated the "German" population in Venezuela at 1,200, including about 200 Austrian and Swiss nationals; 500 of these Germans resided at Caracas and about 300 at La Colonia Tovar. Sievers observed that Venezuela was in a state of decline despite its "slumbering wealth," and this was due to other factors than just its wanton miscegenous racial composition. Posing the rhetorical question why even Africa was more progressive than Venezuela, the professor detected the root cause "in the predominance of the Romance element in this part of the world." All other factors "were of secondary importance." Sievers saw a distinct parallel between the decline of the "Romance element" in Venezuela and in Europe (France, Italy, Portugal, Spain), "which in the long run cannot remain on the same [high] level as the Germanic" element. In the combination of "unfortunate racial mixtures" and the worldwide decline of the "Romance element," Sievers spied Germany's future opportunities: South America, he argued, "is the only part of the world whose future has not yet been decided." The "three world empires" of Great Britain, Russia, and the United States—to be joined, he hoped, by Germany—would vie for domination of this continent. But as the United States historically was South America's "natural enemy" and as Russia would most likely seek a "free hand" in Asia rather than in South America, Sievers predicted a future struggle between Germany and Britain for control of Spain's former holdings in the New World.[2]

[2] Wilhelm Sievers, *Südamerika und die deutschen Interessen* (Stuttgart, 1903), 20, 75, 91-94; Sievers, *Venezuela und die deutschen Interessen* (Halle, 1903), 75-79, 84; Sievers, *Venezuela* (Hamburg, 1921), 13ff. See also Magnus Mörner, *Race Mixture in the History of Latin America* (Boston, 1967).

have found fault with Claude Lévi-Strauss' concept of "tropical culture-lag."

Conversely, the few Venezuelan diplomats who occasionally represented their nation at the Berlin Court often did not enhance their country's esteem in the eyes of their hosts. One celebrated case in September 1891 helped shape German perceptions of Venezuela's leadership elite. Consul General Martin Zuloaga y Tovar, a relative of the former Venezuelan President, Manuel Felipe de Tovar, who in 1843 had granted German immigrants land from his estates near La Victoria, was arrested by the Berlin police for disorderly conduct. According to Prussian authorities, Zuloaga appeared almost every night at the fashionable Café Bauer on Unter den Linden "with women of questionable repute," generally causing a disturbance and frequently resorting to fisticuffs that resulted in his forceful expulsion from the café. On other occasions, Zuloaga had been seen in the foyer of the Central Hotel—again, in the company of "questionable" females—so drunk that he could not negotiate the stairs to his room. At the Hotel National, Zuloaga had refused to pay his bills of up to 900 Mark per night—about the annual wage of a German industrial worker—and, when confronted by the management, had resorted to assaulting the waiters. Prussian police reports made great play of the women who always accompanied Zuloaga in Berlin, "including the famous Bertha Rother," apparently a rather well-known Berlin companion.[11] Eventually, the Venezuelan diplomat was asked to leave the country.

Official German views of the New World took on a more serious and more precise nature after the appointment of Alfred von Tirpitz to the Navy Office. Tirpitz studiously collected information on the *Deutschtum* overseas with the assistance of the Foreign Office in order to impress the Reichstag with the need to fund a larger navy, and hence we owe much of our statistical knowledge concerning the German presence in South America to the admiral's efforts. These findings and their intended use will be dealt with in detail in later chap-

[11] Zentrales Staatsarchiv (ZStA) Dienststelle Merseburg, Auswärtiges Amt Nr 951, Die Konsulate der Republik Venezuela in Preussen, vol. 3. Berlin Police President to Chancellor Leo von Caprivi, Sept. 5, 1891. See also Gerhard Bry, *Wages in Germany 1871-1945* (Princeton, 1960), 51.

ters; for the time being, a brief general overview must suffice. In 1904, for example, the Navy Office listed over 100,000 *Auslandsdeutsche* and eleven Consulates in South America (see Table II). According to Tirpitz's compilations, there existed 530 German village schools in Brazil, 35 in Chile, 30 in Argentina, 5 in Paraguay, 2 each in Uruguay and Venezuela, and 1 each in Peru, Mexico, and Guatemala.[12] Of these roughly 600 village schools, about two-thirds were operated and funded by Protestant religious organizations. Albert Ballin's Hamburg-America Line offered thirty-percent fare discounts for teachers and pastors going overseas, and the Foreign Office in Berlin administered special "Funds for the Enhancement of German Schools and Educational Purposes Abroad" (see Table III).[13] In addition, private individual donors also gave generously toward maintaining the *Deutschtum* overseas through such schools: just before 1910, for example, Bruno Baron von Schröder, head of his family's Hamburg-based banking house in London, gave Wilhelm II 1 million Mark for "support of German schools abroad"; con-

TABLE II

AUSLANDSDEUTSCHE AND CONSULATES IN SOUTH AMERICA

Country	Reich Citizens	Reich Nationals	Consulates
Argentina	25,000	100,000	11
Brazil	8,627	131,500	24
Chile	4,300	5,000	19
Paraguay	916	815	1
Uruguay	854	252	3
Peru	—	535	11
Colombia	203	345	11
Ecuador	134	—	3
Venezuela	500	1,000	8

[12] See the compilation, "Die Entwicklung der deutschen Seeinteressen im letzten Jahrzehnt," Nov. 30, 1905, in ZStA-Merseburg, Reichskanzlei Nr 950, Flottengesetz, pp. 189-338.

[13] Figures from Jürgen Hell, "Die Politik des deutschen Reiches zur Umwandlung Südbrasiliens in ein überseeisches Neudeutschland (1890-1914)" (diss., East Berlin, 1966), 192.

TABLE III
FUNDS FOR THE ENHANCEMENT OF GERMAN SCHOOLS AND
EDUCATIONAL PURPOSES ABROAD

Year	Amount of Support (in Mark)	Number of Schools
1880	60,000	21
1893	100,000	31
1899	300,000	131
1910	900,000	361
1913	1,100,000	511

currently, Ambassador von Waldthausen at Buenos Aires contributed 200,000 Mark for similar purposes.[14] Chancellor Bernhard von Bülow in 1905 noted that Argentina and Brazil received one-fifth of the total Reich support of 500,000 Mark per annum for overseas schools, which drew the Emperor's ire as constituting insufficient succor: "One should strive more vigorously to support school facilities in South America before one reclines, self-satisfied, in one's lounge chair."[15]

To be sure, neither the German presence nor the support that it received from Berlin were great in Venezuela when compared to the ABC states of Argentina, Brazil, and Chile. However, fond historical remembrances combined with nostalgia to accord the Venezuelan case special meaning and consideration. Publicists in Germany rekindled tales of legendary El Dorado treasures in southwestern Venezuela, and reminded their readers of the Welser and Fugger presence in the New World three hundred years earlier. Hanseatic traders were celebrated as the vanguard of a much greater future German economic and financial presence in South America. Above all, the travels of Alexander von Humboldt in Venezuela a century earlier, published in the thirty-volume classic, *The Personal Narrative of Travels in the Equinoctial Regions of America*, served as a reminder to Germans of their legacy in that part of the world. As Wil-

---

[14] ZStA-Merseburg, Königliches Geheimes Civil-Cabinet Nr 21871, Die Kirchen- und Schulangelegenheiten der Süd-Amerikanischen Staaten, pp. 129a, 129i.

[15] Cited in Kannapin, "Die deutsch-argentinischen Beziehungen," 249.

liam Pierson put it, the memory "of this illustrious guest and sincere interpreter of Hispanic-American civilization" was "transmitted as a heritage from father to son." In Venezuela, Arístides Rojas (1826-1894) in his famous *Lecturas históricas*, gave eloquent expression to the close bond between his country and the great German explorer and scientist:

> Humboldt, and always Humboldt! . . . For us, Venezuelans, Humboldt is, not only the great scientific figure of the nineteenth century, but also, the friend, the teacher, the painter of our land, the generous heart that knew how to sympathize with our misfortunes, to share our glories, and to eulogize our triumphs.[16]

Surely, here was a memory that deserved to be preserved as well as a link that seemed to tie the past to the present for the advocates of German *Weltpolitik* in the 1890s.

The advocates of *Deutschtum* in Berlin proudly touted the presence of a large German settlement in Venezuela known as La Colonia Tovar. This far more than the German merchants' colony in Venezuela would be the pedestal upon which *Deutschtum* could be raised. In April 1843, about 370 German immigrants from the Kaiserstuhl region of the Upper Rhine in Baden had arrived in Venezuela to settle a hilly estate near the Río Tuy promised them by Count Martin de Tovar, and granted them as a donation nine years later by Dr. Manuel Felipe de Tovar. Most of the *Badenser* were of low social status, in the main, impoverished farmers, artisans, and day laborers; nearly ninety percent were Catholic. In 1851, about ninety Protestants from Hesse and Mecklenburg joined them, but many of these soon left the colony for Caracas. The Tovar settlers lived in virtual isolation for the first fifty years of the colony's existence. A special "Colony Law" forbade marriage with the indigenous population; transgressors were punished by immediate expulsion from Tovar. And in order to protect the members against possible inbreeding and its accompanying diseases, such as epilepsy, mental illness, and

---

[16] William W. Pierson, Jr., "Foreign Influences on Venezuelan Political Thought, 1830-1930," *Hispanic American Historical Review*, 15 (February 1935), 9.

deafness, the ruling elite promulgated an "endogamy postulate," according to which no member of the colony could marry a cousin of first, second, or third generation. In the long run, of course, this postulate was unenforceable, but the Colonia hoped that infusions of fresh blood through new German settlers would ward off the dangers associated with inbreeding. Those who nevertheless insisted on marrying closely related cousins usually had to endure the degrading custom whereby the elders placed straw bundles on the marriage altar to denote that the couple was as dumb as donkeys! Marriage was demanded of all who wished to remain at Tovar.[17]

La Colonia Tovar barely managed to eke out a living. The first harvest in September 1843 consisted mainly of wheat, oats, rye, and barley sufficient to feed its residents. The hilly and rugged 1,600-hectare donation proved inhospitable to the planting of Kaiserstuhl grapes, and in time the settlers turned more and more to the cultivation of coffee, which became the main cash crop. However, poor harvests and local revolts constantly plagued the settlement. As a result, the Tovar Germans rigorously continued to avoid all possible contacts with the outside world, including their fellow countrymen at Caracas and Maracaibo. A sawmill and a ceramic tile plant assisted their desired autarky.

To be sure, neither the Germans at Tovar nor those at Caracas added to Venezuela's cultural or spiritual life. The former preferred isolation; the latter chased profits. Major outside intellectual influences that shaped Venezuelan thought likewise did not emanate from Germany, but rather from France and the United States.[18] In the main, the Germans at Caracas devoted their free time to the German Club (125 members), the local chapter of the German Navy

---

[17] The discussion of the German colony is taken mainly from Conrad Koch, *La Colonia Tovar: Geschichte und Kultur einer alemannischen Siedlung in Venezuela* (Basel, 1969), 92-97, 117. See also Hermann Ahrensburg, *Die deutsche Kolonie Tovar in Venezuela* (Jena, 1920); Günther Leichner, "In Venezuela liegt ein Schwarzwalddorf: Hundertjährige Isolation," *Globus* (Munich, 1971), 4; and *Handbuch des Deutschtums im Auslande* (Berlin, 1906), 324.

[18] The exception being Dr. Adolf Ernst of Leipzig University, who introduced the doctrine of positivism while teaching at the Central University in Caracas after 1874. See William M. Sullivan, "The Rise of Despotism in Venezuela: Cipriano Castro, 1899-1908" (diss., University of New Mexico, 1974), 679.

League (100 members), a German Benevolent Aid Society, and a German Glee Club. The community even established its own medical care plan as well as insurance agencies.[19] There apparently existed little desire or need for either a German school or a German church for much of the nineteenth century.

This situation began to change only slowly around the time of German unification. In 1869, a Protestant theology student named Fritze visited Valencia and taught a small group of German children. Upon leaving Venezuela, he recommended to the German mission at Caracas that "Protestant affairs in this land be put on a firm footing."[20]

Minister Werner von Bergen took up the call with alacrity. In February 1870, he informed Chancellor Otto von Bismarck that especially Germans of low social status in "this unhappy land" had no recourse but to send their children to Catholic institutions or to leave them "in utter demoralization." Bergen instructed Bismarck that a Protestant church would be "a moral necessity for the future growth of the small German colony" as well as a matter "of national honor" for the new Reich. The minister requested the sum of 1,000 Thaler per annum to cover the pastor's salary and a one-time donation of 8,000 Thaler in order to build a church at Caracas. A special "Comité of the North German Confederation" had been founded on February 9 to oversee the project, and the Comité, in fact, had already approached the Lutheran High-Consistory (*Evangelischer Ober-Kirchenrat*) in Berlin with a plea for financial assistance "in this Catholic part of the world."[21] It estimated that there were forty German Protestant families in Caracas; thirty Protestant fathers had married

[19] ZStA-Potsdam, Auswärtiges Amt, Abt. II, Jahresberichte des Kaiserlichen Konsulats in Caracas Nr 54117, pp. 53-65. Director Knoop of the German railroad to Hohenlohe-Schillingsfürst, Feb. 15, 1900. See also *Handbuch des Deutschtum im Auslande*, 324.

[20] Evangelisches Zentralarchiv (EZA) Berlin, Evangelischer Ober-Kirchenrat (EOK), Die allgemeinen kirchlichen pp. Verhältnisse in Venezuela, Venezuela No. 1, 1879ff., vol. 1. Fritze to EOK, Apr. 1, 1869.

[21] EZA-Berlin, EOK, Die Gründung einer deutschen evangelischen Gemeinde zu Caracas in Venezuela, E.O. IV Venezula No. 6, vol. 1. Bergen to Bismarck, Feb. 24, 1870.

Catholics, and sixty families had not undergone marriage at all.[22] The German Foreign Office supported the request in principle as a means of "strengthening the German element in those parts of America," but made no funds available, as it believed that the Germans at Caracas had shown little inclination to date to fund a church. The Protestant Gustav-Adolf Foundation in Leipzig, on the other hand, agreed to seed the project with a pledge of 500 Mark for five years.[23] The naval chaplain of the *Niobe*, then visiting La Guayra, enthusiastically supported these endeavors as a means "to conserve the German nationality" in Venezuela.[24]

Bergen's overly zealous efforts coincided with the Blue (Conservative) Revolution in Venezuela, and most German merchants quickly abandoned the church project as they scampered to secure their goods in the face of revolutionary violence. In fact, many of the older established *Hanseaten* resented Bergen's aggressive attempts to recruit them for the church and were not sorry to see the envoy depart at the height of the revolution. Bergen's successor, Minister Friedrich von Gülich, in September 1871 bluntly informed Bismarck that "the majority of the local Germans" opposed the undertaking, not in principle but in light of Bergen's coercive funding efforts.[25] Gülich's pessimistic prognosis was shared by the naval chaplain of the *Luise*, who tersely reminded Bismarck that the Germans at Caracas remained unwilling to make any financial sacrifices for a church. Protestant baptisms and marriages continued to be performed by naval chaplains aboard visiting German warships.[26]

Indeed, Berlin from the start suspected not only that the German merchants at Caracas were at best lukewarm toward the establishment of a Lutheran church, but that the country was too prone to violence to offer a German church decent prospects for stability and

[22] Ibid., vol. 1. Comité to High-Consistory, Feb. 17, 1870.

[23] Ibid., vol. 1. High-Consistory to Prussian Ministry of Ecclesiastical Affairs and Education, May 19, 1870.

[24] Ibid., vol. 1. Pastor Büttner to High-Consistory, May 18, 1871.

[25] Ibid., vol. 1. Gülich to Foreign Office, Sept. 5, 1871.

[26] Ibid., vol. 1. Minister Peyer to Bismarck, including Pastor Aly's report, Feb. 3, 1882. See also the reports for the visits of the ships *Freya* (Pastor Mohl) in 1884, and *Nymphe* (Pastor Heims) in 1885, in ibid.

growth. Erwin Stammann, the German minister at Caracas, in 1877 and again in 1888 warned Bismarck that although Guzmán Blanco had returned to power, the "boundless demands of the colored element" in Venezuela would soon plunge the country into "chaos and racial warfare."[27] Perhaps remembering the recent Commune in Paris, which had greatly troubled Bismarck, Stammann raised the fear that a "Communist spirit" dominated Venezuela. "It will now probably turn into a struggle between the proletariat and those of property, and hence the Venezuelan of property as well as the foreign merchant see only a bleak future."[28] Berlin apparently concurred, cautioning the government of Bavaria that "the worst was to be feared from the Communist character of the revolt" in Venezuela.[29] The Reich dispatched the schoolship *Nymphe* to Venezuela at the end of 1879 in order to monitor this "Communist spirit."

The revolt of 1879, like so many before it, quickly blew over, and in 1883, Prince Heinrich of Prussia, the Emperor's brother, undertook a highly successful visit to Venezuela. Its people welcomed the prince with great warmth and charm while the German colony wined and dined him.[30] Given this turn toward happier relations, Bismarck in September 1886 finally agreed to the demands of the Pan-German and Colonial leagues that some sort of survey of Reich nationals overseas be undertaken. Minister Otto Peyer at Caracas responded in April 1887: using the official Venezuelan census of 1881, the envoy set the number of "Germans" in Venezuela at 1,171 among a total foreign element of 34,916 people. Peyer placed the number of Germans in the Federal District at 458. While he could not estimate the ratio between Catholics and Protestants, the diplomat suggested that the former were in the majority as many Protestants who had come to Venezuela had concluded "mixed marriages" in which the "Catholic part dominated," especially once children were involved.

---

[27] AA-Bonn, Venezuela 1, vol. 2. Stammann to Foreign Office, July 1, 1880.

[28] AA-Bonn, Venezuela I.C.61, vol. 5. Stammann to Minister von Bülow, Apr. 28, 1877.

[29] Bayerisches Hauptstaatsarchiv-Munich, Abt. II: Geheimes Staatsarchiv, MA 80023, Die politischen Verhältnisse der Verein. Staaten von Venezuela, p. 27. Prussian Embassy to Bavarian Foreign Ministry, Feb. 10, 1879.

[30] AA-Bonn, Venezuela 1, vol. 4. Stammann to Bismarck, Feb. 10, 1883.

Like all his predecessors since Minister von Bergen, Peyer instructed Bismarck that the roughly 200 German Protestants in Caracas had expressed no desire at all for a fulltime Lutheran pastor. Naval chaplains continued to perform the needed baptisms and marriages; about thirty of the former had been conducted between 1882 and 1886. Finally, Peyer cautioned that since the Lutherans in Caracas were of modest means, they would probably not be able to raise the 9,000 Mark per year required for a permanent pastor.[31]

This pessimistic picture changed drastically in 1892-1893 with the arrival of the new German Minister, Dr. Friedrich Count von Kleist, and his wife Leonie, the former Countess von Kospoth. Kleist, the scion of ancient Prussian nobility that dated to around 1300, owned estates at Wendisch-Tychow in Pomerania, and both he and his wife were active in the local Pietist movement. Not surprisingly, both brought their Protestant vigor to Venezuela, where they were determined to establish not only a German church but also a German school. The Gustav-Adolf Foundation in Leipzig and the High-Consistory in Berlin at once offered to renew their earlier pledges of financial support for the *Deutschtum* in Venezuela. Germany's Foreign Secretary, Adolf Baron Marschall von Bieberstein, reversed his agency's previously negative appraisal of the project, viewing it now as precious "support for the *Deutschtum* in Venezuela." Failure to establish a firm Protestant footing in Caracas, the argument suddenly ran, would seriously "damage Germany's prestige" in Venezuela.[32]

The Kleists moved quickly: on January 4, 1893, a small group of Lutherans at Caracas elected Count von Kleist to head a special committee entrusted with founding a Protestant "iron church" in the

[31] EZA-Berlin, EOK, Venezuela No. 6, vol. 1. Peyer to Bismarck, Apr. 15, 1887. Peyer had earlier reported that there were also 3,206 Dutch, 2,186 French, 4,041 British, 3,237 Italian, and 179 United States nationals in Venezuela. See ZStA-Potsdam, Auswärtiges Amt, Abt. II, Nachrichten der Kaiserlichen Konsulate im Staate Venezuela Nr 33371, pp. 174-76. Peyer to Bismarck, Jan. 26, 1882.

[32] EZA-Berlin, EOK, Venezuela No. 6, vol. 1. Prussian Ministry of Ecclesiastical Affairs and Education to High-Consistory, May 17, 1893. See also Gustav-Adolf Stiftung (Erfurt) to High-Consistory, Dec. 1, 1892; and High-Consistory to Foreign Office, Dec. 31, 1892, in ibid.

capital, to be tied organizationally to the older Prussian *Landeskirche*. The German colony immediately pledged 10,000 Bolívars
per year to support the undertaking. Birthday greetings to Wilhelm
II on January 27, 1893, ceremoniously concluded the founding efforts.[33]

Count von Kleist next turned to the High-Consistory in Berlin in
order to find a suitable Lutheran pastor. The choice would not be an
easy one. Kleist demanded a person who was "liberal" in his theology and hence inclined to avoid theological conflicts "in this totally
Catholic land." Moreover, the candidate would have to be single as
life in Caracas was dear. The pastor would also have to be of good
social background, possess impeccable manners, and be musically
talented as well as "pedagogically inclined," because he would have
to serve as teacher in the school that was projected to be built adja-
cent to the church.[34] Thereafter, Kleist set about the business of
raising funds: the Germans at Puerto Cabello pledged 1,170 Bolívars per annum, those at Valencia 1,150, those at Ciudad Bolívar
about 1,000, and those at Maracaibo and La Victoria a further
1,000. The Gustav-Adolf Foundation came through with 1,500 Mark
for the pastor's salary as well as 500 Mark per annum for five years
for the building fund. Kleist at once detected a new spirit among the
Germans in Venezuela, who were now determined "to strengthen
their sense of [German] nationality" and their affinity to the new Bis-
marckian Reich "also in spiritual terms."[35] The Prussian Ministry of
Ecclesiastical Affairs and Education gave its full support to Kleist's
endeavors, noting with satisfaction that whereas the Germans at Caracas had for twenty years refused to support a Protestant church,
they had now pledged 14,000 Bolívars per annum for that purpose.[36]

Countess von Kleist, for her part, left no stone unturned in behalf
of church and school. She persuaded the Queen of the Netherlands,
whose diplomatic affairs her husband conducted at Caracas, to give

---

[33] See the founding charter of Jan. 4, 1893, in ibid., vol. 1. 1 Bolívar was valued
at 0.80 Mark.

[34] Ibid., vol. 1. Kleist to High-Consistory, Jan. 5, 1893.

[35] Ibid., vol. 1. Kleist to High-Consistory, Apr. 28, 1893.

[36] Ibid., vol. 1. Prussian Ministry of Ecclesiastical Affairs and Education to High-
Consistory, July 17, 1893.

1,000 Bolívars to the project. Wilhelm II was cajoled into giving 500 Mark from his private funds, and the state of Hesse agreed to make future contributions in behalf of its nationals in Venezuela. Both the Hamburg-America Line and the British Central Railroad in Venezuela agreed to transport building materials free of charge. General Joaquín Crespo offered to rent out a special salon in one of his Caracas residences to be used as interim church and school, and in addition "granted" land estimated at 16,000 Bolívars for a building site near the old German cemetery. The High-Consistory in Berlin pledged another 1,000 Mark for the building fund, but it declined "on principle" to undertake a special collection and lottery at home to support the project. Well satisfied, Countess von Kleist reported to Berlin that "the Protestant faith has been secured here once and for all."[37]

Pastor Georg Ramin of Berlitz arrived in October 1893, and held his first service on New Year's Day, 1894, in the rented salon of the Compañía de Aguas before a packed house of 120 Germans. The German Glee Club "Harmonia" sang for the congregation, and Empress Augusta Victoria presented the church with a special Bible and painting for the pulpit bearing an inscription from Joshua 4:18.[38] Pastor Ramin promised to visit the Germans at Puerto Cabello and Valencia every three months, and those at Maracaibo and Ciudad Bolívar once a year.[39]

The Kleists' dream for a German school also matured. Martha Jaerschke of Dresden on May 15, 1894, welcomed her first class of twenty-three children; a later class included two of President Crespo's sons. The curriculum was divided into a lower level for children aged between six and nine with instruction in German, Spanish, and

[37] Ibid., vol. 1. Countess von Kleist to High-Consistory, Jan. 6, 1894.

[38] "And when the priests bearing the ark of the covenant of the Lord came up from the midst of the Jordan, and the soles of the priests' feet were lifted up on dry ground, the waters of the Jordan returned to their place and overflowed all its banks, as before."

[39] EZA-Berlin, EOK, Venezuela No. 6, vol. 1. Countess von Kleist to High-Consistory, Jan. 6, 1894; First Annual Report, Protestant Congregation for Venezuela 1895, in ibid.; and Pastor Ramin's First Report to High-Consistory, Sept. 29, 1894, in ibid. Both the Hamburg-America Line and the Great Venezuelan Railroad regularly contributed to the church.

arithmetic; a middle level for those aged ten to twelve, with instruction also in geography, history, and French; and an upper level for those aged thirteen to fifteen, with further instruction in religion. Tuition ranged from 24 Bolívars per month for the lower level, to 36 Bolívars for the middle level, and 48 Bolívars for the upper level. Non-German parents had to make a one-time donation of 100 Bolívars to the building fund. Classes were set at between twenty-four hours per week in the lowest, twenty-eight hours in the middle, and thirty-four hours in the highest level. By 1895, the *colegio aleman* boasted 72 students (52 boys), of whom 43 were German nationals, 24 were Venezuelan, 2 French, 2 Swiss, and 1 American.[40]

Perhaps because many of its settlers were Catholic, La Colonia Tovar escaped the Kleists' attention. The colony had no priest or teacher in its first half-century. In fact, a Catholic priest who had agreed to accompany the group had died during the Atlantic crossing. As a result, the colonists technically "lived in sin," as neither baptisms nor marriages were performed by clergymen. Illegitimate births became common, and some members of the community even turned to idolatry. Given the lack of a German teacher, the settlers soon lost their Alemannian dialect, and their spoken language degenerated into a mixture of Upper Rhenish German and Spanish. Illiteracy rose rapidly from five percent among the original settlers to forty-three percent by the early 1890s.[41] One German publication termed the Tovar Germans to be "a chapter of the lost *Deutschtum*."[42] Wilhelm Wintzer, publisher of the *Rheinisch-Westfälische Zeitung*, blamed their cultural neglect squarely upon Reich authorities: "The fate of this German village justifiably shows the misery of the total lack of planning [by Berlin officials] that forces our *Volksgenossen*, then as now scattered by the wind, to cultivate the land for foreigners."[43] And Professor Sievers of Giessen University, visiting Tovar in 1892-1893, informed his countrymen that the colony was in

---

[40] Ibid., vol. 1. Countess von Kleist to High-Consistory, Apr. 7, 1894; and First Annual Report, German school 1895, in ibid.

[41] Koch, *La Colonia Tovar*, 146. See also the detailed report by Karl Aretz to High-Consistory, EZA-Berlin, EOK, Venezuela No. 6, vol. 6, dated October 1935.

[42] *Mitteilungen des Vereins für das Deutschtum im Ausland*, Nr 45, June 18, 1909.

[43] Wintzer, *Der Kampf um das Deutschtum*, 52.

dire straits: coffee plantations were "badly maintained," houses were "not at all well kept," graves were "neglected," and contacts with the Reich "non-existent." He concluded that the settlement would be denied a bright future unless the Reich began to offer material support.[44]

Sievers' plea was partly answered in 1894 when, more than fifty years after La Colonia Tovar had been founded, Wilhelm Baron von und zu Bodman became the first German minister in Venezuela to visit it. A fellow *Badenser*, Bodman was well received at Tovar. He informed the settlers that they had lost their German citizenship because they had not appeared at any German consulate within ten years of the founding of the German Empire to claim it; their children born at Tovar had automatically received Venezuelan citizenship. The time was now at hand, Bodman counseled them, to be "renaturalized" as full members of Bismarck's creation. Thirty-eight families encompassing 287 people duly agreed to the request to establish closer ties "with the fatherland" and with all things "German," but both the Foreign Office in Berlin and the Ministry of the Interior in Baden in 1895 without reason given refused to "renaturalize" the Tovar Germans.[45] They thereafter returned to isolation for another decade.

To be sure, Countess von Kleist's claim that "the Protestant faith has been secured here once and for all" proved to be far removed from reality. Church attendance in Caracas declined once the initial euphoria of its opening had subsided. Nor did further fund-raising parallel the initial successes. Both the High-Consistory and the Emperor refused the Countess permission to initiate a lottery in Germany in behalf of the church, with the result that Leonie von Kleist not only threatened to return the Bible sent out by the Empress, but also to convert to Catholicism! Her husband pointedly reminded Wilhelm II that the church was a "piece of *Deutschtum* [designed] not only to honor God but also to raise the level of love and loyalty to Emperor and Reich" in Venezuela.[46] And when the Kleists left Ca-

[44] Sievers, *Zweite Reise in Venezuela*, 146.

[45] Koch, *La Colonia Tovar*, 150-51; Wintzer, *Der Kampf um das Deutschtum*, 52.

[46] EZA-Berlin, EOK, Venezuela No. 6, vol. 1. Prussian Ministry of Ecclesiastical Affairs and Education to High-Consistory, Feb. 6 and Sept. 29, 1897; ZStA-Merse-

racas in 1895, both church and school were deprived of their main supporters. Pastor Ramin informed Berlin in September 1896 that the entire project was now widely denounced by the Germans in Venezuela "as a piece of vanity on the part of the Countess von Kleist." Attendance at church fell to no more than thirty souls each sabbath. The Caracas Lutherans reverted to their former slovenly spiritual ways, constantly complaining:

> Church starts too early, at 10 a.m., when one really sleeps best. In addition, the room is unsuited for services, the chairs are tasteless and small, the pastor is too young, the sermons are too long.[47]

The Maracaibo Germans objected that the pronounced Lutheran tone of instruction at the school was alienating their Catholic friends, and soon withdrew financial support from both school and church.[48]

Above all, the Kleists' successor, Baron von und zu Bodman, re-affirmed Minister Peyer's earlier position that the Caracas colony supported church and school "very passively." Bodman estimated that two-thirds of the German men in Caracas were Catholic; the rest had Catholic wives. All resented the Protestant school. Worse yet, several of the more affluent backers of the project were threatening not to renew their financial pledges once the original three-year commitment ended. Finally, the property "granted" the church by General Crespo turned out to be owned by German merchants, none of whom were willing to turn it over to the church. It was also in the less desirable lower part of the city, far removed from the capital's center. Last but not least, Bodman informed Berlin that Pastor Ramin had managed to alienate virtually the entire German merchant colony with his "impersonal and imperious manner." If matters contin-

---

burg, Civil-Cabinet Nr 21871. Count von Kleist to the Court of Wilhelm II, Nov. 11, 1896, and Feb. 9, 1897. Kleist at the time had retired to his estate at Wendisch-Ty-chow.

[47] EZA-Berlin, EOK, Venezuela No. 6, vol. 1. Pastor Ramin to High-Consistory, Sept. 13, 1896.

[48] Ibid., vol. 1. Consul F. W. Birtner (Maracaibo) to Count von Kleist, Dec. 27, 1895.

ued on their present course, Bodman warned that both church and school would wither within two years.[49] In short, the showpiece of *Deutschtum* in Venezuela was on the brink of failure.

Pastor Ramin shared Bodman's bleak prognosis—albeit, from a radically different perspective. In April 1896, he informed the High-Consistory that his call was in deep trouble. The so-called "better elements" among the Caracan Germans refused to come to church, save at Christmas and on January 27 (the Emperor's birthday); usually, no more than thirty worshippers turned out each Sunday. The choir "Harmonia" often interrupted the service with loud proclamations (alleluias?) of support for the German Social Democratic leader August Bebel, and Ramin suggested that it rename itself "Discordia." The merchants chased profits and ignored spiritual matters. Administrators of the German-owned Great Venezuelan Railroad constantly quarreled with the merchants in Caracas, while their workers were devoted mainly to beer. Even the old German colony at Tovar had split along religious lines, with the small group of Protestants from Hesse and Mecklenburg leaving the Catholic majority from Baden for the friendlier atmosphere of the capital. With regard to the school, only sixteen of its eighty students were Protestant. Instruction in religion was resented, and the Caracan Germans accused Ramin of seeking to spread *Deutschtum* throughout Caracas.[50] Above all, Pastor Ramin lamented that Bodman's successor, Count von Rex, adamantly refused to support the church. In fact, at the very moment that he declined to make a financial contribution to the church, Rex managed to raise 4,000 Bolívars for a grand ball to be held at the German Club in Caracas. The Kleists' legacy was being squandered through disinterest and disunity.[51]

Ramin failed to inform his superiors in Berlin that he had, in fact, engaged Rex in a bitter feud concerning leadership of the church. Count von Rex apparently felt that as head of the German mission at Caracas, he was not only the secular but also the spiritual head of the German colony in Venezuela. At least the Reich nationals in the

---

[49] Ibid., vol. 1. Minister von Bodman to Chancellor zu Hohenlohe-Schillingsfürst, Mar. 1, 1895.

[50] Ibid., vol. 1. Ramin to High-Consistory, Apr. 16, 1896.

[51] Ibid., vol. 1. Ramin to High-Consistory, Sept. 8, 1896.

capital agreed, and continued to look upon the envoy as head of both mission and church.

The escalating conflict was defused in November 1900, when Ramin was replaced by the more conciliatory Pastor Paul Schneider. The new clergyman simply avoided contact with the *colegio aleman* and fully recognized its "non-confessional" nature. No other course of action was possible, Schneider argued, as otherwise the Catholic clerics in Caracas would have manned the barricades.[52] On the other hand, Schneider shared Ramin's views that the Caracan Germans were "utterly indifferent" toward religion in general and the Protestant church in particular. Couples in "mixed marriages" continued to raise their children in the Roman faith. German merchants came to church primarily in order to celebrate the Emperor's birthday; none appeared for communion. By the time of his death in December 1902, however, Schneider at least could claim two victories: Alfred Blohm finally agreed to join the church, and Wilhelm II in May 1902 officially welcomed the Caracas church into the fold of the old Prussian *Landeskirche*.[53]

By now, the German school had drifted away from the Protestant church and even from the German colony in Caracas. Two-thirds of the 140 students enrolled at the *colegio aleman* were Catholic and Venezuelan, and the executive committee that ran the school was firmly in the hands of the Catholic majority. The Foreign Office in Berlin took note of this development, and restricted its support to the thirty or forty children of German nationals who went to the school; the amount of the educational subsidy came to 4,000 Mark per annum, the same as Berlin gave to the German school at Rio de Janeiro.[54] Not even the lobbying activities of the "Society for the *Deutschtum* in Overseas" or the "General German School Society for

[52] Ibid., vol. 2. Pastor Schneider to High-Consistory, Mar. 13, 1901.

[53] Ibid., vol. 2. Schneider to High-Consistory, Dec. 12, 1901; and ibid., vol. 2, Wilhelm II to High-Consistory, May 2, 1902.

[54] Ibid., vol. 2. Prussian Ministry of Ecclesiastical Affairs and Education to High-Consistory, Feb. 5, 1902. The subsidy was eventually increased to 6,000 Mark in 1903. Berlin annually spent about 400,000 Mark to support German schools overseas at this time. See EZA-Berlin, EOK IV, Generalia No. 7a. Reichsschulfonds.

the Preservation of the *Deutschtum* in Overseas" could prompt the Wilhelmstrasse to raise its support.[55]

Of course, the financial plight of the German church could not be blamed entirely on the lack of religious fervor among the Caracan Germans or the failure of the Reich government to grant it greater largess. The fact of the matter is that the *Deutschtum* in Venezuela had fallen on hard times. Cipriano Castro's bid to seize power in 1898-1899 as well as the ensuing civil war plunged the country into bitter internecine strife as well as commercial anarchy. Many Hamburg firms recalled their employees. Church attendance dwindled to about a dozen steady parishioners. The school lost many of its remaining German students. Donations to both church and school were off fully 1,000 Bolívars per year after 1900. The High-Consistory in Berlin consequently chose not to fill the pastoral office at Caracas between 1902 and 1904.[56] Not even a German-language newspaper, the *Deutsche-Zeitung*, founded in November 1899 partly in order to rally the German community in the capital, met with success; its publisher, W. Luebker, a former teacher at the German school, had to cease publication in April 1900 for lack of support.[57] And the Reich's participation in the international blockade of Venezuela late in 1902 deeply split the German colony in Venezuela: while most merchants favored the action, the powerful *casa* Blohm opposed it. Castro, for his part, used the Anglo-German-Italian intervention to arouse anti-foreign sentiment in Venezuela, and instructed newspapers close to him, such as *El Avisador, Los Ecos del Zulia*, and *El Ciudadano* at Maracaibo as well as *Letras y Numeros* at Puerto Cabello, to attack German nationals.[58] The latter reacted

[55] *Handbuch des Deutschtums im Auslande*, 526. This compilation of the Germans abroad became the premiere publication of the "Allgemeiner deutscher Schulverein zur Erhaltung des Deutschtums im Auslande."

[56] EZA-Berlin, Kirchenbundesamt CVII Venezuela 8, Das deutsche Kirchenwesen in Venezuela, insbesondere die deutsche ev. Gemeinde in Caracas. High-Consistory to General Synod, 1903.

[57] AA-Bonn, Venezuela 1, vol. 16. Dr. Schmidt-Leda to Hohenlohe-Schillingsfürst, Jan. 22, 1900; and ibid., vol. 17. Schmidt-Leda to Hohenlohe-Schillingsfürst, Apr. 16, 1900.

[58] See AA-Bonn, Deutschland No. 126 No. 2i, Die Kontinentale Korrespondenz, vol. 3. Minister Alfred Pelldram's report on the Venezuelan press, Aug. 26,1903.

by lying low, and even the normally indefatigable Countess von
Kleist was forced to curtail her efforts in behalf of the *Deutschtum* of
Venezuela, readily seeing that the blockade was doing great damage
to the Germans in Caracas.[59]

The heated tempers of 1902-1903 eventually gave way to business
as usual. Castro, who had once worked for the German house of
Breuer, Möller & Co. in the coffee trade out of Maracaibo, adopted
a generally favorable attitude toward the German merchants and in
time learned to separate their sentiments from those of the Berlin
government. He confided to Minister Giesbert von Pilgrim-Baltazzi
that he greatly admired the Germans because they, unlike their
other European counterparts, quickly assimilated themselves in
Venezuela, learning the Spanish language, settling in Venezuelan
cities, and marrying "the daughters of the land."[60] The President
also harbored great admiration for the *colegio aleman* with "its children in military uniforms," who seemed to thrive on a pseudo-mili-
tary "drill." Castro as late as 1906 assured Baron von Seckendorff
that he nurtured great respect for the German merchants; the *Andino*
reiterated his earlier views that German nationals "most easily amal-
gamated themselves insofar as the sons of Germany settle perma-
nently here, marry natives, and adopt the customs of the land."[61] In
light of this restored favorable attitude toward Germans in general,
the High-Consistory in Berlin in April 1904 decided to send out yet
another Lutheran pastor for the German church in Caracas.

The choice of Wilhelm Voigt proved to be most unfortunate. Dog-
matic in his theology, unbending in his self-righteousness, and rab-
idly anti-Catholic, Pastor Voigt set out to reform the German colony
at Caracas. The clergyman used the Protestant publication *Die
Wacht* to solicit funds for the Caracan congregation on the basis of
an anti-Catholic crusade that rekindled the passions of Bismarck's
erstwhile *Kulturkampf* (cultural struggle) against the Roman curia

[59] ZStA-Merseburg, Civil-Cabinet Nr 21871, pp. 85-90. Kleist to the Court of Wilhelm II, Nov. 28, 1902.

[60] ZStA-Merseburg, Ministerium für Handel und Gewerbe, Handels- und Schiffahrtsverhältnisse mit der Republik Venezuela CXIII-17, No. 22. Pilgrim-Baltazzi to
Chancellor von Bülow, July 25, 1901.

[61] AA-Bonn, Venezuela 1, vol. 31. Seckendorff to Bülow, May 16, 1906.

and the German Catholic Center Party in the 1870s and 1880s. Five months after his arrival in Venezuela, for example, Voigt called upon Lutherans in the homeland to assist his campaign against what he termed "the negative Catholicism" that he witnessed in Venezuela. According to Voigt, the Roman church even encouraged "the not infrequent mixed marriages" between German Protestants and Venezuelan Catholics in the hope and expectation that the husband would convert and the offspring be raised Catholic.[62] By January 1906, Pastor Voigt complained to the High-Consistory that "good German character" was being "ruined" in such "mixed marriages" as German men who took local wives were in the process turned into less desirable "Venezuelans." The pastor accused the German merchants of seeking to maintain their commercial eminence "through a highly undignified accommodation" with President Castro. Neither Protestant church nor German school was able to retard this process of degeneration. "Disunity" had become a byword for the Germans at Caracas. Still worse, the British, whose colony in the capital consisted only of "niggers from Trinidad and Barbados," were about to build a fine chapel in Caracas. Voigt demanded that he be appointed official chaplain of the German mission—and thereby placed on the Reich's payroll—in order to give his position enhanced prestige. Biting the hand that he hoped would feed him, Voigt accused the Berlin government of treating the Protestant church in Caracas "like a stepchild," of not recognizing that it was in the forefront of "a good deal of national work" in Venezuela. The caustic epistle closed with the observation that only a well-endowed Lutheran church could unite the feuding German nationals in the capital.[63]

Voigt's pleas did not go unanswered. The *casa* Blohm donated 1,000 Mark, and various Protestant groups in Bavaria collected 400 Mark for the pastor's troubled church. Countess von Kleist unsurprisingly redoubled her efforts, selling Venezuelan coffee to her friends to raise an additional 1,500 Mark and writing a book on Ven-

[62] See *Die Wacht*, vol. 1, No. 25, Sept. 17, 1904.

[63] EZA-Berlin, EOK, Venezuela No. 6, vol. 2. Voigt to High-Consistory, Jan. 19, 1906

ezuela that netted 200 Mark in royalties.[64] She even sought permission to hold special art sales and theater performances in order to fund her favorite project.[65] But it was not enough. The congregation began to cover its annual deficits by dipping into the 20,000-Bolívar building fund that the Kleists had left behind. Pastor Voigt in desperation applied for a post with a German telegraph office in Caracas in order to augment his meager salary.[66] Blohm gave 3,900 Mark so that a "worm-eaten" altar could be replaced, and the High-Consistory increased its direct support from 500 to 2,600 Mark per annum.[67] The German government, by contrast, offered no direct aid, prompting Voigt to castigate its failure to recognize that the church was "a very important and significant factor in the preservation of the *Deutschtum* in Venezuela."[68]

The Foreign Office in Berlin, obviously sensitive to these charges, called upon its envoy in Venezuela to address the matter of the Lutheran church—as well as the Tovar colony. Baron von Seckendorff replied in July 1906 by first listing the customary complaints concerning the lack of religious conviction among the Germans at Caracas as well as their economic setbacks during the recent revolutionary troubles. The diplomat then went into the "deeper reasons" behind the church's failure: the congregation had been founded, not by feelings emanating from within it, but through the "impractical and badly-thought-out labors of a woman." Specifically, Countess von Kleist had failed to realize that with the completion of the Great Venezuelan Railroad many of its German employees would return home. As naval chaplains could easily perform the requisite bap-

[64] EZA-Berlin, Kirchenbundesamt, Venezuela 8. Bavarian High-Consistory to Berlin Consistory, Jan. 26, 1906; and Voigt to High-Consistory, Report for April 1905 to March 1906. See also EOK, Venezuela No.6, vol. 2. Voigt to High-Consistory, Sept. 18, 1906.

[65] ZStA-Merseburg, Civil-Cabinet Nr 21871, pp. 85-90. Kleist to the Court of Wilhelm II, Nov. 28, 1902.

[66] EZA-Berlin, EOK, Venezuela No. 6, vol. 2. Voigt to High-Consistory, Dec. 10, 1906; and Baron von Seckendorff to Chancellor von Bülow, Dec. 3, 1906.

[67] EZA-Berlin, Kirchenbundesamt, Venezuela 8. High-Consistory to Voigt, Dec. 15, 1908; and Voigt's Ninth Report, April 1909 to March 1910, to High-Consistory.

[68] EZA-Berlin, EOK, Venezuela No. 6, vol. 3. Voigt to High-Consistory, May 11, 1909.

tisms and marriages, there really existed no need for a permanent church. Moreover, the Kleists had greatly exaggerated the alleged "spiritual neglect" of the German colony. The High-Consistory, Seckendorff averred, should have permitted the church to die a natural death in 1902. Instead, Pastor Voigt had launched a Protestant crusade that had alienated not only Venezuelan and German Catholics, but also the Lutheran community at Caracas; many among the latter had been outraged by Voigt's anti-Catholic tone and had laid down their church offices in protest. As a result, attendance was down to between four and eight persons, and many Sundays no one came at all. The church annually lost 4,000 Bolívars and was on the brink of bankruptcy. In concluding, the envoy again stressed that the church "had been forced upon" the Caracan Germans by the Kleists.[69] Two years later, Seckendorff once more lectured Berlin on the "absolute lack of church interest" among the *Hanseaten* in Venezuela.[70]

Pastor Voigt remained undaunted. He complained that Seckendorff's successor, Dr. Edmund Rhomberg, was Catholic.[71] He again railed against the British for building a fine church for their "niggers from the West Indies," thereby stressing the obvious contrast to the rich German merchants who refused to support a church. In fact, Voigt denounced the latter as wolves in sheep's clothing, utterly devoid of religious feeling and undeserving of the name "German colony."[72] Worst of all, the Reich was now sending out immigrants from the lowest social strata; the workers at the German-owned glass plant in Caracas especially were internationalist scum (*vaterlandslose Gesellen*, the Emperor's favorite term) who tarnished the very name "German." Not even the celebration of the Emperor's birthday went by without "shameful" Social Democratic demonstrations.[73]

Voigt's final report from Venezuela was a composite of all the bit-

[69] Ibid., vol. 2. Seckendorff to Bülow, July 11, 1906.

[70] Ibid., vol. 3. Seckendorff to Bülow, Aug. 21, 1908.

[71] EZA-Berlin, Kirchenbundesamt, Venezuela 8. Voigt to High-Consistory, Report for April 1908 to March 1909.

[72] EZA-Berlin, EOK, Venezuela No. 6, vol. 3. Voigt to Gustav-Adolf Foundation, Mar. 27, 1908; Voigt's annual report dated Jan. 21, 1907.

[73] Ibid., vol. 3. Voigt's annual report dated January 1908.

terness that he had developed in seven years at Caracas. The *colegio aleman* was dominated by Venezuelan Catholics. The Lutheran church had for two years suffered under a "Catholic envoy." Venezuela itself was on the brink of economic ruin as President Juan Vicente Gómez and his "camarilla of thugs" robbed the country blind. The racial mixture of the land—"white Caucasians, black Africans, and brown Americans"—was a failed melting pot wherein each race contributed only its worst traits. It was a dismal balance sheet for seven years "on outpost duty."[74] Interestingly, Minister Dr. Rhomberg at about the same time informed Chancellor Theobald von Bethmann Hollweg that the Gómez regime was greatly impressed with the modern German educational system, "a world marvel of the modern Germany."[75]

As previously noted, Seckendorff also undertook an investigation of La Colonia Tovar at the request of the Foreign Office. In fact, in 1906 he became only the second German minister to do so. Successive German ministers to Venezuela after Baron von und zu Bodman had not bothered to visit the colony—not even in answer to Admiral von Tirpitz's repeated requests of 1897, 1901, and 1904 for "more detailed information" on German nationals abroad. In the main, the reports submitted by the mission at Caracas simply stated that Tovar housed about fifty to sixty families of approximately 350 people, most of whom lived "in poor circumstances." The report of 1897 alone noted that their request for "renaturalization" had been denied.[76] Seckendorff in 1906 could report that the opening of the Great Venezuelan Railroad, which tangentially touched the colony at La Victoria, and the need to cultivate outside markets for the coffee trade, had slowly brought the residents into closer contact with the outside world. Deeply shocked by the widespread illiteracy of the residents, Minister von Seckendorff offered to recruit a teacher

---

[74] Ibid., vol. 3. Voigt's annual report dated Jan. 15, 1911. See also Wilhelm E. Voigt, *Auf Vorposten: Ein Zeugnis deutscher evangelischer Arbeit im Auslande in Predigten und Reden* (Berlin, 1909).

[75] AA-Bonn, Venezuela 1, vol. 37. Rhomberg to Bethmann Hollweg, Apr. 23, 1910.

[76] See the reports for these years in ZStA-Potsdam, Auswärtiges Amt, Abt. IIu, Bedeutung der deutschen Seeinteressen im Auslande Nr 3168.

for the colony from Germany, to be paid from special educational funds administered by the Foreign Office. It was not to be. Wilhelm Ruh, head of the Tovar Germans, steadfastly refused to receive a German teacher, fearing that this would jeopardize the colony's independence as well as his own authority within it. [77]

But the matter of a priest and/or schoolmaster for the colony would not go away. It was solved in 1908 in an unexpected manner: Pastor Finström, a missionary of Swedish descent who spoke German, was recruited at La Victoria to head Tovar's predominantly Catholic congregation. Finström was a self-styled "Protestant free-thinker," who continued to observe Catholic ritual while preaching mainly from Protestant theological writings. He set out rigorously to rid the colony of its two major evils, drunkenness and gambling. Unfortunately, the choice of Finström did not sit well with either the Catholic archbishop or the German minister at Caracas, and both joined forces in 1915 to force Tovar to accept a Catholic priest named Franz Busert. [78]

Indeed, the last two years before the Great War brought a fresh attempt on the part of the German minister at Caracas, Adolf von Prollius, to revive the Protestant church there as well. In August 1912, Prollius informed Chancellor von Bethmann Hollweg that the older and more affluent Germans were dying out, that their young replacements were financially unable to support the church. Presbyterians, especially, from the United States were flocking to Venezuela and proselytizing among the lower social ranks; one such "denomination" had in fact built a splendid new church across the street from the German mission. The affluence of the Presbyterians stood in sharp contrast to the poverty of the Lutherans. Prollius was most concerned that the German church was going under just when the eyes of the world would be turned to the region for the opening of the Panama Canal. That a centerpiece of *Deutschtum* such as the Lutheran church could be allowed to perish would certainly have great impact upon the Reich's prestige in South America. Finally, Prollius came up with a novel plan to put the church on firm financial footing:

[77] Koch, *La Colonia Tovar*, 152-53.
[78] Ibid., 154.

if the Emperor or the Empress could be persuaded to make a one-time donation of 20,000 Mark, to be invested with Blohm & Co. at six percent, the annual interest of 1,200 Mark—coupled with existing support from parishioners, High-Consistory, and the Gustav-Adolf Foundation—would cover the current annual deficit of 3,200 Mark.[79] The new pastor, Friedrich Reifenrath, seconded the envoy's concerns over the missionary zeal of the Americans—in this case, the Baptists—and further supported the call for greater German efforts in Venezuela on the eve of the Canal's opening.[80] Pastor Voigt, in retirement, also sounded the alarm, urging Berlin to invigorate its efforts in Venezuela in order to head off mounting Anglo-American economic activity there.[81]

The High-Consistory in Berlin endorsed Prollius' plan, and Pastor Reifenrath in March 1914 officially requested 30,000 Mark from Wilhelm II. The pastor reminded the monarch that the Lutheran church in Caracas was the only Protestant institution in the "Catholic triangle" of Mexico City—Rio de Janeiro—Lima, and that it was his "holy mission" to shepherd the young German merchants, teachers, engineers, and craftsmen in Venezuela through the pitfalls of "spiritual sterility and syphilis."[82] A German publication, *Die Post*, in January 1914 informed its readers that the church's membership had fallen from 520 in 1894 to about 60 in 1913. Yet it deserved full support as it constituted a German "cultural monument," "cultural accomplishment," and "cultural power" in South America.[83]

Minister von Prollius in April 1914 echoed these views. He lectured the Chancellor, saying that it was the Reich's "national duty" to support the church, which had helped to unify the German colony at Caracas and to strengthen its love of the fatherland. German na-

[79] EZA-Berlin, EOK, Venezuela No. 6, vol. 3. Prollius to Bethmann Hollweg, Aug. 27, 1912.

[80] EZA-Berlin, Kirchenbundesamt, Venezuela 8. Reifenrath to German Evangelical Church Council, Sept. 16, 1912.

[81] EZA-Berlin, EOK, Venezuela No. 6, vol. 3. Voigt to High-Consistory, Jan. 23, 1912.

[82] Ibid., vol. 3. High-Consistory to Bethmann Hollweg, Apr. 14, 1913; Reifenrath to Wilhelm II, Mar. 27, 1914, in EZA-Berlin, Kirchenbundesamt, Venezuela 8.

[83] See *Die Post*, January 6, 1914.

tionals in the capital had contributed not only toward the great Venezuelan centenary celebration of 1911, but also toward German collections such as the Zeppelin Donation of 1908, the National Air Donation of 1912, and the Kaiser Wilhelm II Anniversary Donation of 1913. The German school, Prollius argued, now received between 8,000 and 10,000 Mark per annum from the Wilhelmstrasse; conversely, 1,200 Mark per year for the church was not asking too much. Finally, the envoy argued that the "national German point of view" alone demanded succor for the church. Put another way, its demise after only two decades "would undoubtedly be viewed by Venezuelans as well as other foreigners as a sign of weakness on the part of the *Deutschtum* overseas." Prollius again contrasted the penury of the Lutheran church that served Caracas' social elite to the munificence of the Presbyterian church that attended to the needs of the capital's "lower colored classes." It would be a "shame" and a "painful irony," Prollius implored Bethmann Hollweg, were the only German church in the greater Caribbean area to go under just when the United States was about to celebrate the opening of its isthmian canal. Wilhelm II, the "Patron of German Protestants Overseas," surely would not permit that to transpire.[84] In the meantime, the *casa* Blohm pledged 2,000 Mark for three years to help tide the church over its troubles until a decision was reached by the imperial government.[85] The Foreign Office, apparently impressed with both the secular and the spiritual reasoning behind the request, lent its support to the undertaking, but the outbreak of war in Europe precluded final action.[86]

There are two interesting postscripts to the story of the German

[84] EZA-Berlin, EOK, Venezuela No. 6, vol. 4. Prollius to Bethmann Hollweg, Apr. 25, 1914. Concurrently, Prollius and the Germans at Caracas gave Venezuela a bacteriological laboratory from Ernst Leitz in Germany for the new *sala* Koch designed to honor the centenary of Simón Bolívar's entry into Caracas in 1813. AA-Bonn, Venezuela 1, vol. 40. Prollius to Bethmann Hollweg, Apr. 8, 1914.

[85] EZA-Berlin, Kirchenbundesamt, Venezuela 8. High-Consistory to Reifenrath, Nov. 12, 1914, concerning the grant made by the brothers Alfred and Otto Blohm of Hamburg.

[86] EZA-Berlin, EOK, Venezuela No. 6, vol. 4. Foreign Office to High-Consistory, Nov. 17, 1914. See also ZStA-Merseburg, Civil-Cabinet Nr 21871, p. 154. Foreign Office to Prussian Civil-Cabinet, July 21, 1914.

churches at Caracas and Tovar. The Great War caught Pastor Reifenrath of the Caracan Lutheran church on vacation in Germany, and in November 1914 he volunteered to serve as chaplain with the Eighth Army Corps. Wounded in action, Reifenrath was awarded the prestigious Iron Cross First Class and returned to Venezuela only in 1926. Defeat, revolution, and inflation prevented the Foreign Office throughout the period of the Weimar Republic from making any financial contribution to the Protestant church at Caracas. The German mission there laconically lamented that "here also, the war has not brought about a revitalization of the religious spirit."[87] And in April 1933, Pastor Heinrich Rode of the Caracan Lutheran congregation caused a stir when he refused to receive Dr. Otto Boelitz of the German Lutheran Synod, who was making a goodwill tour of South America, "because Dr. Boelitz is hardly moving in spirit with the new thoughts of the present German government." Indeed, Pastor Rode went out of his way to inform Berlin that the economic ills of both Germany and Venezuela were due "primarily to despicable Jewish elements and their cohorts."[88] Rode obviously was "in spirit with the new thoughts" of the German government of Adolf Hitler.

The Tovar postscript is also interesting. Father Franz Busert, who, it might be remembered, had been forced upon the colony in 1915 by the Catholic archbishop of Caracas and the German minister to Venezuela, Prollius, upon his arrival at Tovar denounced the presence of the "Reformation" there and dedicated himself to drive it out. Busert expressed outrage over what he termed the "spiritual neglect" of the German settlers, demanded that the "fallen" Catholics return to the Roman faith, and ordered them to avoid all contacts with Protestants. He was duly driven from the colony.[89] In 1917, Prollius managed to persuade a Benedictine friar, Paul Dobbert, to accept the post at Tovar. The German government pledged nearly 4,000 Bolívars for both a church and a school; Venezuela gave 4,500 Bolívars; and the Tovar residents raised nearly 8,000 Bolívars for the project. Dobbert recruited two teachers, Egon Galler and Al-

[87] EZA-Berlin, EOK, Venezuela No. 6, vol. 4. German Mission (Caracas) to Foreign Office, Mar. 29, 1920.

[88] Ibid., vol. 6. Rode to High-Consistory, Apr. 10, 1933.

[89] Koch, *La Colonia Tovar*, 156.

fredo Jahn, and the school was opened for about sixty children. Galler, a native of the Black Forest, spoke the local Alemannian dialect and made great strides in education, while Dobbert introduced the planting of vegetables and orchards. However, Dobbert's successor, an Austrian clergyman and teacher named Clemens Brandner, was so intent on preserving the *Deutschtum* of the colony and so extraordinarily "unlike a priest" in his personal behavior, that he was eventually expelled from Tovar literally at the point of a shotgun barrel.[90] Minister von Prollius, in turn, denounced the refractory Tovar Germans, accusing them of "unworldly stupidity," of "religious neglect," of constituting a "spiritually retrogressive population," and of evidencing "a sad impression of physical decay—through inbreeding."[91]

A final chapter in the religious history of La Colonia Tovar began in May 1934, when Heinrich Ruh requested a clergyman for the settlement, in the process recording his satisfaction over Germany's recent regeneration. "That was done by God; namely, through His dear servant, Adolf Hitler."[92] And in October 1935, Tovar's newly appointed priest, Karl Aretz, noted with great glee that American Baptists, who had recently recruited over 100 families at the settlement, had asked to join the German Christian movement of Reich Bishop Ludwig Müller. To strengthen their case, the Baptists proudly flew the Nazi swastika banner in their church at Tovar![93] Aretz's brother, Richard, in the meantime had organized a chapter of the Hitler Youth at the colony.

The Tovar Germans had proved to be a great disappointment to the advocates of the cultivation of Reich contacts with the *Deutschtum* overseas. Touted as direct links in the chain that led from Welser and Fugger to Humboldt, the residents of the colony had studiously

[90] Ibid., 160-63.

[91] Prollius' reports on the colony cited in ibid., 171.

[92] EZA-Berlin, EOK, Venezuela No. 6, vol. 6. Ruh to High-Consistory, May 21, 1934.

[93] Ibid., vol. 6. Karl Aretz to High-Consistory, October 1935. For Müller and the German Christians, whose slogan ran, "The Swastika on our breasts, and the Cross in our hearts," see J. S. Conway, *The Nazi Persecution of the Churches 1933-45* (New York, 1968).

avoided all interaction with fellow Germans at Caracas and Maracaibo for as long as possible. Attempts to "renaturalize" them failed. Not a single settler had bothered to call at a single consulate within ten years of the founding of the Reich to claim citizenship therein. Endeavors to provide them with German priests and teachers were largely resented as outside intrusions. Marriages with Venezuelans, which were common among other Germans in Venezuela, were avoided well into the 1920s, and even then only about ten percent of such "mixed marriages" took place—with the customary penalty of expulsion from the settlement. No new immigrants were attracted to the colony after 1851: the doubling of the settlement's population to 610 by 1917 was due solely to births at Tovar.[94]

Nor had the German nationals at Caracas and Maracaibo proved to be overseas conduits for the extention of *Deutschtum* in Venezuela. Mainly interested in commerce and profits, they would have made perfect models for Gustav Freytag's classic novel, *Soll und Haben*. The *Hanseaten* supported the two most obvious expressions of *Deutschtum*, a German church and a German school, only once, namely, at the urging of the Count and Countess von Kleist in 1893-1894. Both before and after, they evidenced no desire whatsoever for spiritual or educational assistance from Berlin, as documented in the countless reports from the German mission at Caracas. The *Auslandsdeutsche* at Maracaibo, Valencia, Ciudad Bolívar, and La Victoria after 1894 refused to make any financial commitment to either church or school. Throughout Venezuela, the German merchants sought to accommodate themselves with Venezuelan authorities and customs. As noted especially by Cipriano Castro, they learned the Spanish language, adopted Venezuelan customs, married "the daughters of the land," often became Catholics and raised their children in the Roman faith, and generally sought to avoid any action—be it German national or Protestant—that might have offended their hosts. If anything, the German participation in the international blockade of 1902-1903 deeply divided the merchants and prompted them thereafter to seek even greater "accommodation" with Presidents Castro and Gómez.

---

[94] Koch, *La Colonia Tovar*, 170-73.

At no time did the German nationals either at Caracas or Tovar constitute a "Trojan horse" whereby the Reich could gain influence in Venezuela. Friedrich Katz's generalization that the Germans in South America "rarely assimilated" with the indigenous population and that "most often" they "displayed great disdain for their new homeland"—as discussed in the Introduction—stands in need of revision in the Venezuelan case. Especially the *Auslandsdeutsche* at Caracas, Ciudad Bolívar, Maracaibo, Valencia, and La Victoria underwent both acculturation and assimilation. Those at Tovar, on the other hand, underwent acculturation without miscegenation.[95] In fact, their isolation was encouraged by Venezuelan authorities: although the colony's males were legally liable for military service, Caracas never bothered to enforce the law. A good number of the original settlers had, indeed, left Baden, Hesse, and Mecklenburg specifically in order to avoid military conscription. Repeated attempts by German diplomats and naval doctors to muster them for possible service in the fatherland doubtless encouraged the male immigrants to appreciate their new homeland and to leave the old behind, both literally and figuratively.

[95] I follow the use of these terms as defined by Mörner, *Race Mixture in the History of Latin America*, 5: namely, acculturation as the mixture of cultural elements, and assimilation as the absorption of an individual or a people into another culture. I have also used the term "miscegenation" in its strictly technical sense, the mixture of races, without any pejorative intent.

CHAPTER III

THE BLOCKADE 1902-1903:
MOTIVATION AND HESITATION

At first glance, Germany's participation in the international blockade of Venezuela perhaps comes closest to a classic case of late-nineteenth-century "imperialism," of "big business" coercing the government to take action against a foreign power in order to collect outstanding debts. The pleas for government intervention by the Disconto Bank, the Great Venezuelan Railroad, Berlin Beton- und Monierbau, the German-Venezuelan Sulphur Company, the Orinoco Asphalt Company, the Hamburg Board of Trade, and numerous German merchants in Venezuela speak for themselves. The Social Democratic leader, August Bebel, in the Reichstag denounced the blockade as having been undertaken at the behest of Krupp and Disconto. And the list of *dramatis personae* offers two prime examples of the "bourgeois-capitalist" nature of the undertaking: Chancellor Bernhard von Bülow, whose mother was a daughter of the Hamburg merchant house Rücker, and Foreign Secretary Oswald von Richthofen, a past Commissioner of the Egyptian *Caisse de la Dette*.[1]

The blockade will be examined in this chapter primarily in order to ascertain the relationship between the demands for armed intervention by German entrepreneurs either at home or in Venezuela and the decision of the Bülow government late in 1902 to institute a formal blockade along with Great Britain and Italy. The specific claims submitted to the Caracas government fall into several broad categories: contract impairment, destruction of property, and non-payment of services rendered. With regard to the German claims, contract impairment primarily affected banking and industry concerns in the Reich; destruction of property and non-payment of serv-

---

[1] See Alfred Vagts, *Deutschland und die Vereinigten Staaten in der Weltpolitik* (New York, 1935), II, 1525, 1608.

ices mainly devolved upon German merchants in Venezuela. The Great Venezuelan Railroad submitted claims in all three categories. Finally, it should not be overlooked that seven other foreign creditors throughout much of the 1890s and 1900s pressed Caracas to honor its debts: the United States, Belgium, France, the Netherlands, Spain, Mexico, and Sweden-Norway.

In fact, the history of Venezuela from the first reign of Antonio Guzmán Blanco in 1870 until the departure of Cipriano Castro in 1908 was one of civil wars, foreign invasions, fiscal chaos, and occasional foreign blockades. Venezuela severed ties with France in 1881, 1895, and again in 1906; with the Netherlands from 1875 until 1895; with Belgium in 1895; and with Great Britain basically from 1873 until 1897. It was invaded no less than twenty-two times by Colombia between 1859 and 1901. And six bloody internecine squabbles between 1892 and 1902 forced Venezuela to endure 437 military engagements at a cost of 20,000 lives and 680 million Bolívars; nearly eighty percent of the country's cattle was consumed, while the national debt doubled to over 200 million Bolívars.[2] Despotic *caudillism* obviously did not enhance Venezuela's international reputation, much less its credit.

It is perhaps ironic in light of later events that for much of the period after German unification, Berlin's envoys assumed the role of "honest brokers" at Caracas. As early as the fall of 1875, Erwin Stammann, the German minister in "the city of roses," informed his government of an impending Dutch blockade of Venezuela and advised the Wilhelmstrasse "that this will ruin German trade, but will not restore to the Netherlands the prestige that it has long lost here."[3] Nevertheless, Germany carefully remained neutral in the Dutch-Venezuelan dispute, which had arisen over alleged Dutch assistance to a rebel group in the state of Coro via Curaçao; on the one hand, Berlin rejected Guzmán Blanco's suggestion that Venezuelan ships

[2] See William M. Sullivan, "The Rise of Despotism in Venezuela: Cipriano Castro, 1899-1908" (diss., University of New Mexico, 1974), 1, 4, 37, 57, 61, 163, 204, 214, 655.

[3] Zentrales Staatsarchiv Potsdam (hereafter ZStA), Auswärtiges Amt, Abt. II, Handels- und Schiffahrtsverhältnisse mit Venezuela, vol. 5b, pp. 155-56. Stammann to Foreign Office, Aug. 13, 1875.

be placed under German protection, yet, on the other hand, supported Venezuelan efforts at mediation at The Hague. Above all, Chancellor Otto von Bismarck warned his envoy at Caracas "to desist from any action that could be construed as support for one side or the other."[4]

Again, when a civil war in October 1880 damaged the property of German merchants, especially at Maracaibo, where they dominated the Venezuelan as well as Colombian coffee trade, Bismarck kept calm while France and the United States rushed warships to Venezuela to protect their nationals. He complimented his representative for "not having lost total impartiality," and admonished Stammann also in the future "to avoid all appearances" that the Reich took even " a theoretical partisanship" of one side or the other.[5] Twelve years later, Germany again officially represented The Hague at Caracas owing to further conflict over the role of Dutch traders (and smugglers) operating out of Curaçao.[6]

But German-Venezuelan relations began to sour by 1895. Arthur Count von Rex, Berlin's new minister at Caracas, ran afoul of the government of General Joaquín Crespo, which stated that while it fully recognized its financial obligations concerning the Great Venezuelan Railroad, it nevertheless felt that the seven-percent guaranteed rate of return on capital investment was too great a burden for the primitive Venezuelan economy to bear. And when Foreign Minister Lucio Pulido tried to sidestep the financial crisis by requesting additional German immigration, Rex countered by charging that Caracas "was doing absolutely nothing" to further the German colony at Tovar. He even accused Crespo's government of denying Tovar's German nationals additional land "even though the colony is sur-

[4] Ibid., vol. 7, pp. 122-27. Foreign Office memorandum for the Admiralty, Feb. 18, 1876.

[5] Auswärtiges Amt Bonn (hereafter AA), Venezuela 1, Allgemeine Angelegenheiten Venezuelas, vol. 2. Count Limburg-Stirum to Stammann, Nov. 13, 1880. See also Tennessee State Archives, Manuscript Division, "Eugene H. Plumacher Memoirs 1877-1890," Accession Nr 442, Box I, Ch. XI, 236-40, and Box II, Ch. XVI, 332, for reports on Maracaibo.

[6] AA-Bonn, Venezuela 6, Die Wahrnehmung Niederländischer Interessen durch Deutschland. Minister von Kleist to Chancellor von Caprivi, Aug. 31, 1892.

rounded by large state-owned tracts of jungle."[7] Three years later, Rex remonstrated that Crespo as well as his successor-designate, Ignacio Andrade, were forcing German merchants to contribute more than 280,000 Bolívars toward their war against the insurgent General José Manuel Hernández.[8]

At the root of the worsening relations between Berlin and Caracas lay Venezuela's inability (and unwillingness) to honor mostly guaranteed interest and loan payments on several major industrial undertakings financed by German entrepreneurs at hefty rates, and its dilatory handling through local courts of claims submitted by German nationals as a result of years of domestic revolts with their accompanying ravages and requisitions. The early history of several of these German undertakings was taken up in Chapter One; these issues will now be addressed in light of attempts to move the Berlin government to come to the aid of German financial interests in Venezuela.

One of the first German concerns to fall out with Caracas was the Slaughterhouse in the Federal District. Contracted between Bruzual Serra and Karl Henkel of Hamburg and approved by General Crespo in October 1896, the facility was estimated to cost 2.25 million Bolívars. It received the usual favorable terms: free land and water, relief from all import duties for its machinery, and tax-exemption from state and local levies. The Governor of the Federal District, Juan Vicente Gómez, in turn, received a monopoly on supplying it with livestock. Henkel quickly ran out of funds and when Caracas demanded that a deep-freeze facility be added, sold out part of his interest in the Slaughterhouse to the Aktiengesellschaft für Beton- und Monierbau in Berlin. The Venezuelan government failed to live up to its pledge to pay construction costs every fifteen days—half in gold, half in paper—and in 1898, Beton- und Monierbau refused to open the completed plant until all construction costs had been covered.[9]

[7] AA-Bonn, Venezuela 1, vol. 13. Count von Rex to Chancellor zu Hohenlohe-Schillingsfürst, Apr. 5, 1895.

[8] Ibid., vol. 14. Rex to Hohenlohe-Schillingsfürst, Mar. 14, 1898.

[9] ZStA-Potsdam, Auswärtiges Amt. Abt. II, Handel . . . mit Venezuela, vol. 19, pp. 75-82. Beton- und Monierbau to Foreign Office, Dec. 21, 1896. The Slaughter-

The Berlin firm appealed to the Reich's minister at Caracas as well as to the Wilhelmstrasse for assistance in pressing its claims.

The major claimant was the Great Venezuelan Railroad. In its annual business report for 1894, it listed its assets as consisting of 179 kilometers of track from Caracas to Valencia as well as eighteen locomotives, thirty-one passenger, eight baggage, twenty-nine cattle, and 115 freight cars; on the debit side of the ledger, Caracas was 4.86 million Bolívars in arrears on construction costs, 345,820 Bolívars in interest, and 567,000 Bolívars on the guaranteed rate of return at seven percent. Added to this total of 5.77 million Bolívars were damage claims of 1.85 million Bolívars stemming from the revolution of 1892 as well as 17,960 hectares of land that the government had promised but to date had refused to turn over to the company.[10] In order to head off a financial impasse—with the railroad declining to operate its line and the Venezuelan government refusing to make any payments—General Crespo and the Disconto Bank in the spring of 1896 reached an accord: Disconto freed Caracas from its guarantee of seven percent on the 44 million Mark capital, while Crespo undertook to refinance his share of the costs in the amount of 33 million Bolívars at five percent interest. This money, borrowed from Disconto, was to be used to satisfy the reclamations from 1892 set at 1.85 million Bolívars as well as to guarantee the railroad monthly payments of 250,000 Bolívars. The loan was eventually raised to 50 million Bolívars, of which 36 million were turned directly over to the Great Venezuelan Railroad. And as the loan was not fully subscribed on the German market, it is highly unlikely that Crespo received the full 14 million Bolívars promised. It was estimated that with payments on the capital of one percent per annum, the line would amortize in about thirty-six years.[11]

house was for both cattle and hogs and included extensive holding pens, gardens, and administrative buildings.

[10] ZStA-Potsdam, Kolonialwirtschaftliches Komitee Nr 346, Grosse Venezuela Eisenbahn-Gesellschaft Hamburg 1894-1914, pp. 3-8. *Geschäftsbericht* of 1894, submitted June 1895.

[11] Ibid., pp. 9-12; also, George W. F. Hallgarten, *Imperialismus vor 1914: Die Soziologischen Grundlagen der Aussenpolitik Europäischer Grossmächte vor dem Ersten Weltkrieg* (Munich, 1963), I, 562. The railroad accordingly raised its capital shares

This complicated paper shuffling, of course, did not alter the fact that the railroad was not a viable economic concern, and by the end of 1897 Caracas was again two months behind in payments on the 50 million Bolívars loan at five percent.[12] By the end of the next year, Venezuela was reduced to paying only one-half of its monthly obligations.[13] The Foreign Office at Berlin now entered the picture, and in November 1898 advised Admiral Eduard von Knorr that it would be "desirable to show the flag" off Venezuela in order "to further the negotiations" between Disconto and Caracas for payment on the 1896 loan.[14] On Christmas Day 1898, the Wilhelmstrasse again asked Knorr to dispatch a warship to La Guayra in order to impress Venezuela with the need to honor its fiscal commitments.[15] The schoolship *Moltke* was sent to the port in January 1899, but to little effect: Caracas remained ten monthly installments, or 2.5 million Bolívars, in arrears, and the railroad reported in October 1899 that its line had been closed continuously for forty days owing to domestic revolts that had destroyed bridges, tracks, and telegraph lines.[16]

By the turn of the century, Venezuela was in a full-blown financial crisis. The railroad was owed over one-half million Bolívars in transport costs for government troops; no payments had been made on the 1896 loan since April 1898; and Caracas had also halted payment on the reclamations stemming from the civil war of 1892.[17] All in all,

---

from 25 to 60 million Mark on Feb. 18, 1897. See also *Berliner Börsen Courier* of June 30, 1896, for the details of the refinancing. The German minister at Caracas, Count von Rex, reported that Crespo referred to the "noble nación alemana" at a state dinner, and that the general was inclined "to accord Germans first rank in the nation's economic affairs." AA-Bonn, Venezuela 1, vol. 14. Rex to Hohenlohe-Schillingsfürst, Apr. 30, 1896.

[12] AA-Bonn, Venezuela 1, vol. 14. Prollius to Hohenlohe-Schillingsfürst, Nov. 10, 1897.

[13] Ibid., vol. 15. Schmidt-Leda to Hohenlohe-Schillingsfürst, Nov. 21 and Dec. 28, 1898.

[14] ZStA-Potsdam, Auswärtiges Amt, Abt. IIs, Entsendung deutscher Kriegsschiffe Nr 22456, pp. 16-18. Foreign Office to Knorr, Nov. 8, 1898.

[15] Ibid., p. 132. Foreign Office to Knorr, Dec. 25, 1898.

[16] ZStA-Potsdam, Auswärtiges Amt, Abt. IIE, Eisenbahnen in Central- und Südamerika Nr 15333, p. 78. Great Venezuelan Railroad (Knoop) to Foreign Office, Feb. 15, 1900.

[17] ZStA-Potsdam, Kolonialwirtschaftliches Komitee Nr 346, pp. 37-38.

Venezuela owed about 208 million Bolívars on foreign loans, revolutionary damage claims, and internal obligations. The business climate was so depressed that financiers preferred either to invest their monies abroad or to squander them on luxury goods. The government was unable to provide any liquid assets for investment to stimulate the economy, needing every *centimo* it possessed in order to meet interest and back payments.

Against this dismal fiscal background there appeared on the scene in 1899 "the greatest international nuisance of the twentieth century," Cipriano Castro. Contemporary as well as later verdicts generally agree in evaluating Castro's character. Giesbert von Pilgrim-Baltazzi, the German minister at Caracas, in July 1901 described Castro as a "megalomaniac" who fervently desired to restore *La Gran Colombia*, and who frequently compared himself to Napoleon Bonaparte (*el cabito*, the little corporal).[18] A successor, Baron von Seckendorff, five years later depicted Castro as "a cunning Indian" of rather "small stature" and ordinary facial features; however, "one can at first sight detect the brutality" of the man. The German diplomat compared Castro to the poisonous Upas tree, "whose fragrance kills."[19] Eugene H. Plumacher, the American consul at Maracaibo, was of similar opinion, noting that Castro and his *Andino* following were what one would term "mountain trash" in Plumacher's adopted Tennessee. The loquacious consul saw "no hope for this poor downtrodden country." "Ruin and perdition" were at hand. Castro had "found 11 Centavos in the Treasury" upon seizing power. "There is absolutely nothing left to steal. His predecessors attended to all that." Nor did the future look bright. "We live upon a volcano and never know what the next day may bring."[20]

Recent scholars concur. Clyde Hewitt described the "Lion of the

[18] ZStA-Merseburg, Ministerium für Handel und Gewerbe, Handels- und Schiffahrtsverhältnisse mit der Republik Venezuela, CXIII-17 Nr 22, vol. III. Pilgrim-Baltazzi to Chancellor von Bülow, July 25, 1901.

[19] AA-Bonn, Venezuela 1, vol. 31. Seckendorff to Bülow, May 16, 1906.

[20] Tennessee State Archives, Manuscript Division, "Plumacher Papers," Accession Nr 70-76, folder 8, "Correspondence, 1901-1907." Letters to Morton B. Howell, Nashville, Apr. 27 and Nov. 15, 1902, as well as July 4, 1903, Aug. 30, 1906, and June 25, 1907. Hereafter cited as "Plumacher Papers."

Andes" as a leader with "no concept of justice," as "tyrannical and wantonly cruel," as a despot whose "dictatorship is relieved only by a revolting efficiency in dealing with dissatisfaction at home and a shocking cleverness at stalling off foreign creditors."[21] William Sullivan stressed Castro's obsession to take up the mantle of Simón Bolívar and to recreate *Gran Colombia* consisting of Venezuela, Colombia, Ecuador, Nicaragua, and several other Central American states. According to Sullivan, Castro's mania for Bolívar (and Bonaparte) prompted him every afternoon to ride a white horse through the El Paraiso section of Caracas in order to make a grand impression.[22] Edwin Lieuwen viewed Castro as "probably the worst of Venezuela's dictators."[23] Finally, Robert Gilmore saw in Castro the triumph of the *Andinos*, of the Táchirenses *caudillos* who used their private guards in order to capture power from the traditional oligarchies that had ruled Caracas for so long. And, despite his uplifting slogan, "New Men, New Ideas, and New Methods," Castro in fact delivered more of the same old disorder, robbery, and "rustling operations." Castro, in turn, was "transformed by the Caracan gang into a montage of all the vices."[24]

Surprisingly, the German community in Venezuela at first nurtured great expectations from a Castro regime—due no doubt to the fact that the President had at one time worked in the coffee trade for the Hamburg house of Breuer, Möller & Co. These expectations were to be bitterly disappointed in short order. Already in October 1899, the German-owned railroad was forced to transport Castro's troops on credit; German merchants at Valencia were forced to make "voluntary" contributions to the President. In November, Castro forces shelled German houses at Puerto Cabello, including that of H. G. & L. F. Blohm, which were all flying the imperial German flag. Twenty-nine Reich nationals at the port thereupon complained

---

[21] Clyde Eaton Hewitt, "Venezuela and the Great Powers, 1902-1909: A Study in International Investment and Diplomacy" (diss., University of Chicago, 1948), 19.

[22] Sullivan, "Rise of Despotism in Venezuela," 218, 401.

[23] Edwin Lieuwen, *Petroleum in Venezuela: A History* (Berkeley/Los Angeles, 1954), 8.

[24] Robert L. Gilmore, *Caudillism and Militarism in Venezuela, 1810-1910* (Athens, Ohio, 1964), 26, 87, 119.

to Wilhelm II that two German schoolships had taken no action to halt the bombardment by the warships *Galicia* and *Velasquez*, and petitioned the Emperor in the future to take measures to protect German nationals.[25] Wilhelm II passed the petition on to both the Chancellor and the Secretary of the Navy Office. Interestingly, the German navy firmly rejected the pleas of the Puerto Cabello Germans for protection. Vice Admiral Otto von Diederichs of the Admiralty Staff brusquely deemed the petition to be "without basis," while Admiral Alfred von Tirpitz of the Navy Office insisted that the merchants be censured for having "attacked the navy unjustly."[26] Berlin apparently was not ready to resort to "gunboat diplomacy."

Unfortunately, conditions in Venezuela deteriorated rapidly. In November 1899, Castro closed the Orinoco River to all international traffic, and the next year shut down the Zulia-Catatumbo system, thereby depriving Colombia of the opportunity to ship its coffee out via Maracaibo. The latter act greatly damaged Hamburg merchants who controlled much of Maracaibo's coffee trade. Unsurprisingly, these merchants turned to the Hamburg Senate and especially to the Board of Trade (Handelskammer) for succor. As early as December 1899, Senator Max Schinckel, head of the Norddeutsche Bank and hence a junior partner in the Great Venezuelan Railroad along with Disconto, had attempted to persuade the Senate to turn to Berlin for aid against Castro.[27] The Senate at once formed a committee to study the matter. In the meantime, both Hamburg and Berlin received numerous other requests for aid. Guillermo Wenzel, a German rancher near Ciudad Bolívar, lost cattle valued at 24,751 Bolívars on his *hato* "La Vergareña" to the "wild hordes, which one calls troops in Venezuela."[28] Theodor Heuer, a merchant, complained that he had

[25] AA-Bonn, Venezuela 1, vol. 16. Schmidt-Leda to Hohenlohe-Schillingsfürst, Oct. 6, 1899; Consul Gosewisch to Schmidt-Leda, Sept. 30, 1899; German Colony (Puerto Cabello) to Wilhelm II, Nov. 16, 1899.

[26] Ibid. Diederichs to Foreign Office, Jan. 10, 1900; Tirpitz to Foreign Office, Mar. 1, 1900.

[27] Handelskammer Hamburg (hereafter HkH), Commerzbibliothek, Protokoll der Handelskammer 1899, vol. Q.7., pp. 632ff. See also the Board of Trade's evaluation of political and economic conditions in Venezuela in its *Jahresbericht* 1900, and 1901.

[28] Staatsarchiv Hamburg (hereafter StA), Sen. Kom. f.d. Reichs- und auswärtigen

been bilked out of "several hundred thousand Bolívars" when President Castro's family simply seized his Compania Anonima Fabrica de Ciharillos.[29] The house of Breuer, Möller & Co., which had once employed Castro, asked restitution in the amount of 69,804 Bolívars, while another Hamburg firm, van Dissel & Co., sought nearly 20,000 Bolívars in damages. Karl Henkel, who had originally contracted for the Slaughterhouse in Caracas, demanded payment of 112,240 Bolívars; the Orinoco Asphalt Company—which will be taken up in more detail shortly—submitted a request for 33,658 Bolívars; Minlos, Witzke & Co. asked for 22,509 Bolívars in damages incurred at Maracaibo; and Christern & Co. at Lübeck handed in a claim double that amount. Berenberg, Gossler & Co. at Puerto Cabello sought damages well in excess of 1 million Bolívars.[30] In addition, Hermann Richter, a farmer, asked for nearly 100,000 Bolívars in claims, while four German firms that ran the Lake Maracaibo and River Catatumbo Navigation Company demanded 645,000 Bolívars from Castro for prohibition of trade.[31] The Mariara Plantation Society even took its paltry request for 2,537 Mark to the Wilhelmstrasse.[32] More seriously, the Venezuela Plantation Society sought satisfaction from the German government for the murder of its manager, Adam Rüssel.[33] Finally, the Bremen Senate also became involved in the reclamations when the trading firm of H. H. Meier &

Angel. P. II. Politik-7/94, Jahrgang 1894, Politische Lage der Vereinigten Staaten von Venezuela. Guillermo Wenzel to Foreign Office, Aug. 10, 1905.

[29] Ibid., Ältere Registratur, C I d 173, Forderungen Hamburger Firmen gegen die Regierung von Venezuela 1899-1913. Foreign Office to Hamburg Senate, Dec. 22, 1913.

[30] Ibid., P.II. Politik-7/94, Schadenersatzforderungen gegen die Venezolanische Regierung. Foreign Office to Hamburg Senate, June 13 and July 29, 1904; Christern & Co. to Foreign Office, May 20, 1904; Pelldram to Foreign Office, July 14, 1903; Hamburg Board of Trade to Senate, Mar. 12, 1903. See also, Hildegard von Marchtaler, *Chronik der Firma Van Dissel, Rode & Co. Nachf. Hamburg gegründet 1893 und deren Vorgänger in Venezuela gegründet 1852* (Bremen, n.d.), 52.

[31] Hewitt, "Venezuela and the Great Powers," 87, 182.

[32] StA-Hamburg, P.II. Politik-7/94, Schadenersatzforderungen gegen die Venezolanische Regierung. Foreign Office to Hamburg Senate, July 13, 1908.

[33] Ibid. Pilgrim-Baltazzi to Chancellor von Bülow, Nov. 1, 1902. See also the *Frankfurter Zeitung*, Nov. 10, 1902, for the Rüssel case; the *Leipziger Tageblatt* on Nov. 14, 1902, set the Great Venezuelan Railroad claim at 2.75 million Bolívars.

Co. asked it to lobby Berlin for an end to Castro's blockade of the Orinoco River.[34]

Armed with this mounting evidence, the Hamburg Board of Trade decided to approach the Wilhelmstrasse for assistance against Castro. While the Senate continued to study the matter, the Handelskammer on December 2, 1899, formally petitioned Berlin to send "large warships" to La Guayra at once. It reminded the Foreign Office that substantial German investments and trade were at stake, and reported that the Great Venezuelan Railroad had suffered work stoppages as well as track damage at the hands of Castro. It even recommended that Berlin ask Britain and the United States to join a possible intervention in Venezuela. And, to bolster its case, the Board of Trade had its petition signed by Hamburg's leading entrepreneurs, including Albert Ballin of the Hamburg-America Line, the Hamburg managers of the Deutsche Bank, Dresdner Bank, Norddeutsche Bank, Vereinsbank, Commerz & Disconto Bank, M. M. Warburg, and the Great Venezuelan Railroad. Nor were the signatures of the principal Hamburg-owned Venezuelan concerns— save the house of Blohm—missing: Mariara Plantation Society, Venezuela Plantation Society, and the Brewery Puerto Cabello & Valencia A.G.[35]

The ball was now in Berlin's court. Hamburg's economic and financial elite had demanded state intervention in its behalf. The Under Secretary of the Foreign Office, Oswald Baron von Richthofen, received Hamburg's plenipotentiary, Dr. K. Klügmann, within twenty-four hours of receipt of the petition—only to reject the demand for state help. Richthofen at once detected the motivating force behind the petition: "One is of the opinion at the Foreign Office that the Hamburg Board of Trade has taken these steps in behalf of the Norddeutsche Bank at the urging of the Disconto Bank." Moreover, the Under Secretary lectured Klügmann that "slight damage" to railroad tracks "should not cause great surprise during a revolu-

[34] Staatsarchiv Bremen, 3-A.3.V. Nr 99, Senats-Registratur, Reklamationen Deutschlands gegen die Vereinigten Staaten von Venezuela. Bremen Board of Trade to Foreign Office, Nov. 7, 1902; Senats Protokolle, Nov. 11, 1902.

[35] StA-Hamburg, P.II. Politik-7/94, Die politische Lage der Vereinigten Staaten von Venezuela. Petition by the Handelskammer to the Foreign Office, Dec. 2, 1899.

tion." And when Klügmann inquired whether a similar request might be better received at a later date, Richthofen cleverly suggested that "this might be of use in support of the Navy Bill" then being prepared for the Reichstag for the following year.[36] Obviously, the Wilhelmstrasse was not interested in pulling Disconto's chestnuts out of the fire.

Perhaps feeling that it had been shunted off to a "junior" bureaucrat, the Board of Trade next turned to Foreign Secretary von Bülow, only to be told again that no action was being contemplated against Castro. At best, Bülow was willing to request that the Emperor direct three schoolships then in the West Indies to call on Venezuelan ports.[37] More, he would not do. The Hamburg Senate took note of Berlin's reluctance to engage in "gunboat diplomacy," and on December 4 lectured the Board of Trade in the future not to take such matters directly to the imperial government without first clearing them with the Senate.[38]

Bülow in May 1900 turned to Admiral von Tirpitz in order to ascertain whether a gunboat might not be available for duty in South America. He reminded the Navy Secretary that German claims against Venezuela stood at about 6 million Bolívars and that no resolution was in sight. While recognizing that ship visits to Venezuelan ports were beneficial to German prestige as well as to the practical matter of mustering German nationals for possible military service at home, the Foreign Secretary nevertheless counseled Tirpitz that the only available overseas cruiser, the *Vineta*, drew too much water to do any good in Venezuela's shallow rivers.[39] In the end, no action was taken.

Pressure, however, continued on Berlin to assume an active role against Castro. The Great Venezuelan Railroad in late 1900 stepped

[36] Ibid. Klügmann to Senator Dr. Burchard, Dec. 3, 1899.

[37] Ibid. Klügmann to Burchard, Dec. 10, 1899.

[38] StA-Hamburg, Senat Cl. VI No 16°, Vol. 1, Fasc. 17, Venezuela-Varia, Eingabe der Handelskammer an das Auswärtige Amt um Schutz der deutschen Interessen während der Wirren in Venezuela. Auszug aus dem Protokoll des Senats, Dec. 4, 1899.

[39] ZStA-Potsdam, Auswärtiges Amt, Abt. II, Handels- und Schiffahrtsverhältnisse mit Venezuela, pp. 125-30. Bülow to Tirpitz, May 4, 1900.

up the pace of its demands for succor from the Berlin government. Director G. Knoop in November reported to Disconto that "the prestige of the German Reich has been severely damaged here" by the inability of German ships "showing the flag" off Venezuela to force the issue. Only "the most energetic representation by the Reich" could turn the tide: the "inactive" presence of warships merely convinced Castro that both Berlin and the German claimants were willing "to suffer indefinitely."[40] Early the next year, Knoop cabled Berlin that "Castro wishes to and will force a confrontation with a foreign power. The man is suffering from megalomania." Knoop suggested that it was high time that Europe showed "this unimportant, more or less uncivilized land" that it could not "insult the Great Powers and lead them around by the nose."[41] Bolder yet, Knoop informed Disconto that Venezuela "did not fear in the slightest any action by the German government." The recent recall of the *Vineta* was celebrated by Castro "as a great diplomatic triumph."[42]

Indeed, President Castro seemed to have taken just such an attitude toward the foreign powers. In January 1902, he created a three-man Junta for the Examination and Qualification of Credits, which immediately rejected over eighty percent of the 16 million Bolívars in claims standing against Castro. Moreover, the President refused to recognize any reclamations from before May 1899, when he had come to power.[43] Predictably, Germany, Great Britain, the United States, Spain, Italy, and the Netherlands refused to recognize the legitimacy of the Commission. The United States Secretary of State, John Hay, sent the warships *Hartford*, *Scorpion*, and *Buffalo* to La Guayra, while Berlin followed with the *Vineta*, *Gazelle*, and *Falke*. Castro ignored the move, and Minister von Pilgrim-Baltazzi warned Berlin that "the situation is daily growing worse."[44]

Still, Germany refused to intervene in Venezuela, preferring in-

[40] AA-Bonn, Venezuela 1, vol. 17. Knoop to Disconto, Nov. 26, 1900.

[41] Ibid. Knoop to Great Venezuelan Railrod (Berlin), May 28, 1901. See also the *Berliner Tageblatt*, No. 265, May 28, 1901.

[42] AA-Bonn, Venezuela 1, vol. 20. Knoop to Disconto, Apr. 15, 1902.

[43] Sullivan, "Rise of Despotism in Venezuela," 317-18.

[44] ZStA-Potsdam, Auswärtiges Amt, Abt. IIs, Entsendung deutscher Kriegsschiffe Nr 22468, p. 148. Pilgrim-Baltazzi to Foreign Office, Sept. 19, 1901.

stead to follow the path of negotiation. As early as April 1900, its representative had called at the *casa amarilla* to demand that Castro honor past contractual obligations to the Great Venezuelan Railroad. In July 1901, Pilgrim-Baltazzi even suggested to Castro that German claims be submitted to arbitration, only to be informed by Foreign Minister Eduardo Blanco that such action would be seen as an infringement upon Venezuela's sovereignty. The diplomat attempted to discuss the matter with Castro in the summer of 1901, only to be put off by a combination of empty promises and boastful threats.[45]

By now, the Wilhelmstrasse was taking a more pessimistic view of the Venezuelan situation. In July 1901, it expressed the fear "that serious complications with this republic [Venezuela] are not to be ruled out." It noted that neither the claims of the Great Venezuelan Railroad nor those of German nationals in the amount of 2 to 3 million Bolívars were being recognized by Castro, "and that possibly more forceful pressure" needed to be applied against Venezuela. Again, however, Richthofen, now Foreign Secretary, would only ask the Emperor to send a warship to Venezuela in order to "show the flag." Above all, he wished to avoid a larger naval demonstration, as this would require an emergency budget and hence trigger debate in the Reichstag.[46]

Minister von Pilgrim-Baltazzi took note of the new sense of urgency at Berlin and in September 1901 drafted a clever report on Venezuelan conditions, designed to appeal to both Bülow and Richthofen. Knowing well that Richthofen had been a past Commissioner on the Egyptian *Caisse de la Dette*, the envoy suggested that foreign creditors establish a parallel international financial supervisory board for Venezuela. For Bülow's benefit, he hinted that the British representative at Caracas, W.H.D. Haggard, had raised the possibility that Berlin and London join forces against Castro. Pilgrim-Baltazzi also appended a general overview of Venezuela's chaotic economic situation by the *casa* Blohm, and a plea by Consul Albert Lentz of the house of Leseur, Römer & Baasch at Puerto Cabello

[45] See Hewitt, "Venezuela and the Great Powers," 51-54.

[46] ZStA-Potsdam, Auswärtiges Amt, Abt. IIs, Entsendung deutscher Kriegsschiffe Nr 22468, pp. 11-12. Foreign Office memorandum, July 24, 1901; and pp. 163-65, Richthofen to Prince zu Eulenburg und Hertefeld (for Wilhelm II), Oct. 2, 1901.

that Berlin uphold the *Deutschtum* of Venezuela and its "German school, German church, German health insurance, German Benevolent Aid Society, and German Navy League."[47] Perhaps impressed with Pilgrim-Baltazzi's brief, the Wilhelmstrasse instructed him on the last day of the year formally to present Castro with a list of claims amounting to 1.7 million Bolívars. However, no armed intervention was yet contemplated, and the Foreign Office was careful to exclude the claims of the Great Venezuelan Railroad from its demands, preferring instead to concentrate only on the revolutionary damage reclamations by German nationals in Venezuela.

To be sure, Berlin by now had every right to press the claims of its nationals against Castro. But Foreign Secretary von Richthofen continued to have doubts about the feasibility of armed intervention. In December 1901, he informed Pilgrim-Baltazzi that a show of force would only strengthen Castro's hand domestically.[48] The following month, he bluntly informed the Saxon plenipotentiary in Berlin, Karl Adolf Count von Hohenthal und Bergen: "But Venezuela simply has no money; it is in no position to meet our financial demands or to fight a war with us." There was precious little that an industrialized European power could do against this primitive state. "Even the seizure of territory is precluded as this would immediately involve us in a conflict with the United States."[49] And to the Bavarian plenipotentiary, Hugo Count von und zu Lerchenfeld-Köfering, he expressed his firm belief that Castro would not risk war with Germany over the damage claims. "War is being waged at this moment only in the press."[50]

The slightest effort by Castro to meet Venezuela's financial obligations would probably have calmed the situation in 1902. Unfor-

[47] AA-Bonn, Venezuela 1, vol. 18. Pilgrim-Baltazzi to Chancellor von Bülow, Sept. 27, 1901.

[48] Ibid., vol. 18. Richthofen to Pilgrim-Baltazzi, Dec. 27, 1901.

[49] Sächsisches Hauptstaatsarchiv, Dresden, Gesandschaft Berlin Nr 258, Politische Angelegenheiten. Report to Minister von Metzsch (Dresden), Jan. 6, 1902.

[50] Bayerisches Hauptstaatsarchiv Munich (hereafter BHStA), Abt. II: Geheimes Staatsarchiv, MA III 2680, Bayerische Gesandschaft in Berlin, Geschäftsberichte 1902. Count von Lerchenfeld to Foreign Minister Count von Crailsheim (Munich), Jan. 4, 1902.

tunately, the President grew confident in his self-assumed role as defender of the Americas against Europe and probably counted on the United States to enforce the letter of the Monroe Doctrine against Berlin and London. As a result, German firms in Venezuela continued to bombard the Wilhelmstrasse with ever more dire predictions of impending ruin. The Hamburg-based Orinoco Asphalt Company was one of these. In 1900 it had purchased seven concessions amounting to 3,000 hectares at Pedernales, Pesquero, and Isla de Plata for 350,000 Bolívars in order to extract asphalt from the liquid oil reserves of the Orinoco region. Within a year, the firm was employing 135 workers and producing thirty tons of asphalt per day; its capitalization had increased to 1 million Mark. However, the *anticastrista* revolution threatened its operation, and Dr. Alfred Scharfenorth, the firm's head, appealed to the German minister at Caracas for naval protection. Dr. Schmidt-Leda agreed at once, and advised Berlin that the fields showed great promise and deserved additional German capital. Curiously, the Foreign Office at Berlin deleted this sentence when it passed the request on to the Prussian Ministries of the Interior and Trade and Commerce.[51] Richthofen apparently was unwilling to assist German overseas firms in attracting capital through the Foreign Office.

The German navy, on the other hand, appreciated the Pedernales fields. Lieutenant Commander Musculus of the *Falke* informed the Admiralty Staff not only that the Hamburg-America Line had shown "great interest" in the operation, but that a noted geologist, Professor Dr. Zuber, had placed the fields on the same level as those in the Caucasus and the Carpathians.[52] Count Oriola of the *Gazelle* likewise predicted "a great future" for the Orinoco Asphalt Company, comparing it to the great Baku finds, and suggested to Wilhelm II that it might prove a worthy future "competitor for North American and Russian petroleum."[53] Lieutenant Commander Eckermann of

[51] ZStA-Potsdam, Reichsamt des Innern, Handelssachen Venezuela Nr 5441, pp. 21-22. Schmidt-Leda to Chancellor von Bülow, Jan. 9, 1901.

[52] AA-Bonn, Venezuela 1, vol. 20. Musculus to Admiralty Staff, Apr. 21, 1902.

[53] ZStA-Potsdam, Auswärtiges Amt, Abt. IIs, Entsendung deutscher Kriegsschiffe Nr 22472, pp. 5-9. Count Oriola to Wilhelm II, June 20, 1902. Lieuwen, *Petroleum in Venezuela*, 6-7, states: "Until the twentieth century, petroleum was of no economic

the *Panther* shared these prior assessments and urged the monarch to mobilize additional capital for the company.[54]

Of greater importance yet was the Deutsch-Venezolanische Schwefelgruben A.G., which worked sulphur pits near Carúpano, with a capitalization of 2 million Mark. Based at Cologne, the firm had started work late in 1899, and with the financial support of the Schaffhausen'scher Bankverein was building a seventeen-kilometer aerial cable system to transport the sulphur from the pits to the port. But the Venezuelan civil war had interrupted its semi-monthly shipments of materials from Germany, and the German-Venezuelan Sulphur Company in January and February 1901 appealed to Berlin for naval protection, pointedly reminding the Wilhelmstrasse that the United States had already sent warships to Carúpano to safeguard its nationals.[55] In this case, Richthofen concurred with the need to "show the flag repeatedly at Carúpano." The *Vineta* duly arrived in the port by mid-March, and the Company noted that "German prestige" had been "greatly enhanced" as a result.[56]

Indeed, Richthofen's position seemed to be changing on the matter of applying force against Venezuela. Count von Lerchenfeld noted early in 1902 that Richthofen was prepared to press the case against Castro because "the Reich's prestige demanded satisfaction." Still, the Foreign Secretary feared that the costs of any naval action "would be totally out of proportion to the [size] of the de-

importance to Venezuela." The Spanish had seen oil oozing from the earth at Lake Maracaibo as early as 1499, while Alexander von Humboldt in 1799 spoke of oil seeps at Cumaná; however, the great Royal Dutch Shell oil strike at Maracaibo came only on Dec. 14, 1922.

[54] AA-Bonn, Venezuela 1, vol. 22a. Eckermann to Wilhelm II, Oct. 20, 1902. See also, Hewitt, "Venezuela and the Great Powers," 172.

[55] AA-Bonn, Venezuela 1, vol. 19. Report by Lieutenant Commander Franz of the *Moltke*, Dec. 23, 1901; ZStA-Potsdam, Auswärtiges Amt, Abt. II, Handels- und Schiffahrtsverhältnisse mit Venezuela, pp. 120-23. German-Venezuela Sulphur to Foreign Office, Jan. 30, 1901, and Feb. 21, 1901. See also, Hewitt, "Venezuela and the Great Powers," 173.

[56] ZStA-Potsdam, Auswärtiges Amt, Abt. IIs, Entsendung deutscher Kriegsschiffe Nr 22466, p. 124. Foreign Office to Admiralty Staff, Feb. 25, 1901; and ibid., Nr 22467, p. 120. James Schaeffer to Schmidt-Leda, Mar. 29, 1901.

mands" being made. Moreover, Lerchenfeld reported to Munich that Admiral von Tirpitz was opposed to naval intervention because the claims against Castro were "insignificant," and because Venezuela's notorious inability to meet its fiscal obligations did not bode well for any accords that might result from such action.[57] Friedrich Baron von Holstein of the Foreign Office noted a similar lack of action, not only by Tirpitz, but also by Vice Admiral von Diederichs of the Admiralty Staff, Rear Admiral Gustav von Senden-Bibran of the Navy Cabinet, and General Hans von Plessen of the Military Cabinet. Chancellor von Bülow stood alone in December 1901 and January 1902 in calling for a naval blockade of Venezuelan ports—either with or without British participation. The matter was decided by Wilhelm II, who opted to await the outcome of the Venezuelan civil war.[58] Above all, not a single one of these leaders in any document raised the issue whether the Reich ought to commit its forces in the service of "big business"; in all deliberations, only matters of prestige and honor were debated.

Bülow's plans for a "pacific" blockade of Venezuela received two shots in the arm early in 1902. In May, the London Council of Foreign Bondholders was being asked by many of its members who held shares in the Disconto loan of 1896 to exert pressure upon Prime Minister Arthur James Balfour's government to seize the Venezuelan customs houses "for the service of all Venezuelan bond issues held by European subjects." Adolph von Hansemann, head of the Disconto Bank, at once took up their cause as being "urgently desirable."[59] And in Venezuela, General Luciano Mendoza brought the civil war home to the Germans of Barquisimeto by seizing their homes and stores, collecting "protection" monies, and requisitioning their food and wine. Minister von Pilgrim-Baltazzi at once de-

[57] BHStA-Munich, Abt. II: Geheimes Staatsarchiv, MA III 2680. Lerchenfeld to Crailsheim, Feb. 5, 1902.

[58] Norman Rich and M. H. Fisher, eds., The Holstein Papers (Cambridge, 1963), IV, 244-46, diary entry for Jan. 11, 1902. The original is in AA-Bonn, Nachlass Friedrich von Holstein, Tagebücher, vol. 80.

[59] AA-Bonn, Venezuela 1, vol. 20. Atlas Trust Co. to Disconto Bank, Apr. 23, 1902; Disconto Bank to Atlas Trust Co., Apr. 30, 1902.

manded restitution of 200,000 Bolívars from Castro within three days.[60] Count Oriola of the *Gazelle* suggested to Wilhelm II that the Venezuelan fleet be seized, that a "pacific" blockade of the Venezuelan coast be undertaken, and that the customs houses at La Guayra and Puerto Cabello be occupied. "Personally, I am convinced that one can only accomplish something with the Venezuelans if one acts energetically against them, [if one] not only shows them one's teeth, but also proves to them that one knows how to bite with them."[61]

Yet, Wilhelm II was still not convinced of the need for force. In July 1902 he ruled only that a diplomatic protest be lodged with Castro in the case of the Barquisimeto Germans. Vice Admiral Wilhelm Büchsel, about to replace Diederichs at the Admiralty Staff, also cautioned against "overdrawing the bow." He was, however, willing "perhaps to contemplate a larger [naval] action in the fall."[62] The Emperor agreed, dispatched the gunboat *Panther* to Venezuela, and later that summer instructed his representative at Caracas to halt further negotiations with Castro.[63]

The fact that Germany was now willing to "contemplate a larger [naval] action in the fall" had precious little to do with the constant barrage of demands for intervention by German entrepreneurs and merchants, but rather with the highly confidential negotiations that were underway between Berlin and London throughout the summer and fall of 1902. While these will be taken up in Chapter Seven, suffice it to say that Chancellor von Bülow kept his diplomatic cards so close to his vest that the Bavarian government as late as November 27, 1902—that is, five days after Bülow had cabled his envoy at Caracas to inform Castro of the Anglo-German blockade—was still in the dark concerning the Chancellor's intended course of action—

[60] Ibid., vol. 21. Pilgrim-Baltazzi to Foreign Office, July 16, 1902, and to Under Secretary von Mühlberg, Aug. 8, 1902.

[61] Ibid. Count Oriola to Wilhelm II, July 28, 1902.

[62] Ibid. Mühlberg to Heinrich von Tschirschky und Bögendorff (for Wilhelm II), July 18, 1902.

[63] Ibid. Tschirschky to Foreign Office, July 19, 1902. See also ibid., vol. 20. Richthofen to Pilgrim-Baltazzi, June 26, 1902.

which, it might be pointed out, would require Bavarian support in the Federal Chamber (Bundesrat).[64]

In December 1902, Chancellor von Bülow summarized all German claims against Castro in a lengthy memorandum for both houses of parliament and the federal states. He listed first and foremost the damages sustained by German nationals during the revolutions of 1898-1900 in the amount of 1.7 million Bolívars as well as those during the most recent *anticastrista* revolt of well over 3 million Bolívars. And for the first time he included in the list of demands that the imperial government had carefully studied and approved, the claims of Karl Henkel and the Berlin Aktiengesellschaft für Beton- und Monierbau in the amount of 820,000 Bolívars as well as those of the Great Venezuelan Railroad (7.5 million Bolívars). Obviously, Castro's dilatory handling of the wide range of German reclamations had convinced Berlin of the need to lump them together as it set out on the blockade. Over and over, the document stressed the primary motivation behind the action: "to protect the Reich's prestige in Central and South America," to preserve its "dignity," and to counter the impression that it was willing to leave its nationals to the "arbitrariness of foreigners."[65]

At the last moment, the apparently unified front of German claimants was rudely shattered by the most powerful German merchant house in Venezuela: G. H. & L. F. Blohm of Hamburg. Its Hamburg chief, Georg Blohm, a close relative of the Blohms of the mighty Blohm & Voss shipyard in Hamburg which was eventually to build many of Tirpitz's dreadnought battle-cruisers, counseled restraint and arbitration. While the *casa* Blohm had as recently as August 1902 been quite willing to seek a German naval presence on the Or-

[64] BHStA-Munich, Abt. II: Geheimes Staatsarchiv, MA III 2680. Bavarian military attaché (Berlin) to Munich, Nov. 27, 1902; and AA-Bonn, Venezuela 1, vol. 22a. Bülow to Pilgrim-Baltazzi, Nov. 22, 1902.

[65] See Bülow's lengthy *Denkschrift* of Dec. 8, 1902, to the Reichstag, Verhandlungen. Stenographische Berichte, X. Legislaturperiode, II. Session, document 786. It is based upon a detailed report by the German minister at Caracas to Bülow, Sept. 27, 1901, in AA-Bonn, Venezuela 1, vol. 18; and upon a Foreign Office tally of Jan. 19, 1902, in ibid., vol. 19.

inoco River in order to raise Castro's blockade of Ciudad Bolívar,[66] it nevertheless did not desire foreign intervention on a grand scale. Georg Blohm presented the Hamburg Board of Trade, the Senate, and the Berlin Foreign Office with a memorandum stating his objections, especially, to a joint Anglo-German blockade. On December 11, 1902, he rushed to Berlin to make his case at the Foreign Office, only to be shunted off to Dr. Johannes Kriege, head of its legal department. Not satisfied, Blohm sought out the Hanseatic plenipotentiary at Berlin, Dr. Klügmann, and with him hurried to the Reichstag in order to discuss the pending action with Foreign Secretary von Richthofen. The latter declined to receive Blohm because he stood in opposition to the views of all the other German merchants in Venezuela.[67]

In the memorandum, Blohm lamented what he termed the Reich's "rather sudden" decision in favor of a blockade with Britain. Britain was particularly hated in Venezuela owing to its past border disputes with Caracas over Guiana and because it had recently taken the island of Pato, off northeastern Venezuela, which Castro claimed. In addition, Castro's opponent, General Manuel Antonio Matos, seemed to be favored by the British colony at Trinidad. Blohm also noted that London was lobbying long and hard to force Castro to lift a special thirty-percent surcharge on all imports from the Antilles, which would greatly benefit British traders at Trinidad. Hence, Anglo-German cooperation in the blockade would eventually benefit the British. Above all, Blohm stressed that Castro was in no position to meet the excessive foreign demands: the government currently owed creditors 11.55 million Bolívars against assets of only 9 million Bolívars; the Banco de Venezuela at Caracas was in even more dire straits, having on hand a mere 33,000 Bolívars cash against a statutory reserve of 990,000 Bolívars. "The land is completely exhausted." Merchants in the interior of the country, who were completely at the mercy of the populace's goodwill, would suffer from

[66] StA-Hamburg, P.II. Politik-7/94, Die politische Lage der Vereinigten Staaten von Venezuela. Blohm to Foreign Office, Aug. 22, 1902.

[67] Ibid., P.II. Politik-7/94, Eingabe der hies. Firma G. H. & L. F. Blohm zu der Reclamation Deutschlands gegen Venezuela. Klügmann to Lord Mayor Burchard, Dec. 11, 1902.

Castro's obvious recourse of whipping public fervor to feverish heights against the foreigners. Finally, Blohm pointedly recommended that the "fatherland" occasionally take the precarious position of its nationals overseas into closer consideration when formulating foreign policy. Not armed might, but "benevolent influence," would work best with Castro.[68]

Blohm's pleas went unheeded. Had the Bülow government opted for the blockade primarily out of financial concerns, that is, debt collection, Blohm might have been heard; he could offer little for an action based on national prestige and foreign policy considerations (joint action with Britain). Even Hamburg distanced itself from Blohm. While Klügmann considered the petition to have been "cleverly designed," he nevertheless distanced himself from it, both personally and in the name of the Senate.[69] A further appeal by Blohm to the Handelskammer to back his position in light of the fact that the blockade was being circumvented by British "smugglers" operating out of Trinidad, while German merchants were being strangled by it, fell upon deaf ears. Perhaps still smarting from the Senate's rebuke in December 1899 for directly approaching the Wilhelmstrasse, the Board of Trade rejected Blohm's plea.[70] A final attempt to move the Senate to act in his behalf likewise failed.[71] Embittered, Georg Blohm refused to accept his reelection to the executive committee of the Handelskammer in December 1903.[72]

The Anglo-German-Italian blockade was short-lived. Castro initially arrested all foreigners and sequestered their property, but he quickly realized the futility of a protracted blockade when the United States refused actively to come to his aid. He asked Herbert W. Bowen, the American envoy at Caracas, to work with Berlin and London to end the blockade: on February 13, 1903, Castro agreed

[68] Ibid. The document was given to the Hamburg Senate on Dec. 13, 1902.

[69] Ibid. Klügmann to Burchard, Dec. 21, 1902.

[70] Ibid. Blohm to Hamburg Board of Trade, Dec. 27, 1902; and Board of Trade to Blohm, Jan. 16, 1903.

[71] Ibid. Auszug aus dem Protocoll der Deputation für Handel und Schiffahrt, Jan. 6, 1903.

[72] HkH, Commerzbibliothek, Protokoll der Handelskammer 1903, vol. U.7., pp. 382-85. Sessions on Dec. 18 and 22, 1903.

in the Washington Protocols to pay Germany 140,000 Bolívars immediately as well as a further 1,578,815 Bolívars in five monthly installments. Seventy-three individual claims by German nationals against Venezuela were submitted to the International Court of Justice at The Hague, which eventually awarded 2 million of the 7.4 million Bolívars sought by Reich nationals. In order to meet the grand total of 39 million Bolívars that he agreed to honor, Castro levied a thirty-percent war tax against all imports as well as heavy duties against major exports.[73] And while Chancellor von Bülow at first feared that submitting the German claims to the International Court might set a "dangerous precedent," he was greatly relieved when Castro had made the final payment to Germany by July 1907.[74]

The two major German enterprises in Venezuela profited from the blockade—one by design, the other despite the blockade. The Great Venezuelan Railroad was fully confirmed in its claims of 10,542,881 Bolívars on the 1896 Disconto loan and 594,863 Marks in damages from the revolutionary upheavals since 1899.[75] Thereafter, it was business as usual. In June 1906, it persuaded Castro to refinance the old five-percent loan in the form of a much more advantageous Diplomatic Debt at three percent with Disconto, to be guaranteed by the customs revenues of the major Venezuelan ports.[76] The casa Blohm also prospered. As early as December 5, 1902, it had offered Castro a private loan of 2 million Bolívars in case he opted to pay off the most pressing German claims. Moreover, Blohm financed Ambassador Bowen's mediation in 1903. And when the Venezuelan Congress in April 1903 passed a new law on the rights of aliens which denied exequators to persons in the consular service who were actively engaged in trade, Blohm was conspicuously exempted. Moreover, a new thirty-percent surcharge on goods coming in from Trin-

[73] Sullivan, "Rise of Despotism in Venezuela," 349, 372.

[74] AA-Bonn, Venezuela 1, vol. 23. Bülow to Metternich, Jan. 9, 1903.

[75] ZStA-Potsdam, Kolonialwirtschaftliches Komitee Nr 346, Grosse Venezuela Eisenbahn-Gesellschaft Hamburg 1894-1914, pp. 49-52, Geschäftsbericht 1902; and pp. 53-56, Geschäftsbericht 1903. The settlement was reported in detail in the Südamerikanische Rundschau, No. 4, July 1, 1904.

[76] ZStA-Potsdam, Kolonialwirtschaftliches Komitee Nr 346, pp. 61-64, Geschäftsbericht 1905.

idad (Britain) and Curaçao (the Netherlands) worked to Blohm's advantage and averted its chief's worst fears of December 1902.[77] In 1907, Castro returned exequators to the German consuls Theodor Gosewisch at Valencia and Eduard von Jess at Maracaibo, both merchants, while Minister von Seckendorff received the Bust of Bolívar, Second Class.[78] On the other hand, both the Orinoco Asphalt Company and the German-Venezuelan Sulphur Company were reported to be in "dire circumstances" just one month after the blockade. Two years later, the Great Venezuelan Railroad sold its Mariara Plantation at no gain.[79]

French and United States firms, many of which had supported either General Matos or Castro's Colombian foes, suffered at the hands of the vengeful dictator. In the summer of 1904, Castro demanded 50 million Bolívars in damages from the New York and Bermudez Company, a subsidiary of the National Asphalt Company, and 42 million Bolívars from the Compagnie Française de Cables maritimes; in January 1906, the *caudillo* occupied the French cable company's facilities at La Guayra.[80] Not until 1912 did Venezuela pay off its obligations to French nationals under the Washington Protocols of 1903.[81] Unsurprisingly, United States Assistant Secretary of State Francis B. Loomis in 1905 confided to the German Ambassador, Hilmar Baron von dem Bussche-Haddenhausen, "that it had been a mistake to back Castro at the time of his conflict with Germany, England, and Italy, and to assist him in mediating the dispute."[82] Consul Plumacher, in slightly less diplomatic language,

[77] See Sullivan, "Rise of Despotism in Venezuela," 359, 420-23, 426; and Vagts, *Deutschland und die Vereinigten Staaten*, II, 1632-33.

[78] AA-Bonn, Venezuela 1, vol. 32. Seckendorff to Bülow, May 21, 1907.

[79] ZStA-Potsdam, Reichsministerium des Innern Nr 5441, p. 91. Pelldram to Bülow, Dec. 18, 1903; and ZStA-Potsdam, Kolonialwirtschaftliches Komitee Nr 346, pp. 61-64, *Geschäftsbericht* 1905. Dated June 25, 1906.

[80] AA-Bonn, Venezuela 1, vol. 27. Pelldram to Bülow, July 22 and July 29, 1904. See also Sullivan, "Rise of Despotism in Venezuela," 451, 589, 591. New York and Bermudez eventually agreed to pay Castro $130,000 in damages.

[81] AA-Bonn, Venezuela 1, vol. 39. Prollius to Chancellor von Bethmann Hollweg, Mar. 5, 1913.

[82] Ibid., vol. 29. Bussche (Washington) to Bülow, Sept. 27, 1905.

shared that view: "We made a hell of a mess of it when we interfered with the Blockade Powers."[83]

Indeed, Castro had emerged as a folk hero and as the incarnation of national unity. The blockade may even have had the effect of artificially prolonging his hold on power. Above all, the international situation greatly favored him. Berlin fell out not only with the United States but also with Great Britain over the blockade, as will be shown in later chapters. The Reich soon confronted France in Morocco, Russia in the Balkans, and Britain through a heated naval race in the North Sea. Europe divided into two hostile blocks, the Triple Alliance and the Triple Entente. Neither France nor Britain would likely undertake armed action in the Americas in the face of President Theodore Roosevelt's harsh reaction in 1902-1903. Nor would they deploy major forces overseas, leaving Europe to Wilhelm II. The wily Castro was no doubt aware of the changed international scene and used it to his advantage.[84]

In the long run, the great "losers" turned out to be overall German economic interests in Venezuela. Both the Mariara Plantation Society and the Venezuela Plantation Society had to be liquidated. "German agricultural interests are no longer substantial in this country," Minister Adolf von Prollius reported in June 1912 as he took stock of Germany's position in Venezuela for Chancellor Theodor von Bethmann Hollweg. With regard to mining, British, American, and Canadian firms dominated the fields. The Orinoco Asphalt Company of Hamburg had fallen to an American concern, the Caribbean Petroleum Company, in 1904. Nor did other industries fare better: the German-Venezuelan Sulphur Company was never heard from again; a German glass factory as well as a cement plant had been taken over by Venezuelans because "very few proficient entrepreneurs could be recruited in Germany for Venezuela"; a German-financed meat packing facility at Barrancas on the Lower Orinoco had been bought out by a French firm; and British packers dominated the frozen-meat

---

[83] "Plumacher Papers," folder 8, "Correspondence 1901-1907." Letter to Morton B. Howell, Nashville, July 27, 1905.

[84] See Sullivan, "Rise of Despotism in Venezuela," 588.

trade at Puerto Cabello. London-based companies also owned the wool and textile mills of Caracas.

Only the house of Blohm, which Prollius described as "an economic power" in the land, had survived the blockade unscathed. Other Hamburg merchants continued at Caracas, Maracaibo, and Ciudad Bolívar in modest fashion. While the Hamburg-America Line had increased its direct service with Venezuela to two round trips per month, the Great Venezuelan Railroad, the largest in the land, was not prospering. Prollius noted that it "has not expanded its tracks in nearly twenty years through even the smallest of side spurs." Especially disconcerting was that President Juan Vicente Gómez, an ardent rancher, was transforming what Alexander von Humboldt had called the "garden" of Lake Valencia from coffee and sugar plantations into cattle ranges, thereby depopulating it and depriving the railroad of passenger traffic as well as coffee and sugar freights. By contrast, the British-owned line from Puerto Cabello to Valencia and the Central Railroad were paying annual dividends of seven percent and expanding into the fertile Tuy Valley and Yaracuy. British firms also operated the Caracas streetcar and telephone systems.

Prollius noted that while President Gómez had restored peace and economic order and was about to pay off the last of the 39 million Bolívars debt incurred under the Washington Protocols of 1903, German interests in Venezuela did not present "a very happy picture." No new merchant houses had been established. Industrial concerns had been liquidated in great measure after 1903. Both Blohm and the Great Venezuelan Railroad were economically "passive," making no effort whatsoever to "expand their influence." Saddest of all, German capital no longer flowed to Venezuela. Although a solid European financial institute was desperately needed in Caracas, not a single German bank had opened a branch office in Venezuela. It was a great pity, Prollius concluded, that "Germany does not take a more active part in raising the slumbering treasures" of Venezuela.[85]

[85] StA-Hamburg, Sen. Kom. f.d. Reichs- und auswärtigen Angelegenheiten, Ältere Registratur, C I d 173, Die wirtschaftliche Lage Venezuelas. Prollius to Beth-

German consular reports fully supported these generalizations. The Puerto Cabello-Valencia Brewery, built in 1896 at a cost of 1 million Mark, had been dismantled five years later and sold to the Cervecería Nacional at Caracas; German interest in the latter was but one-fifth of the 1.5 million Bolívars capitalization.[86] The frozen-meat exporting plant at Puerto Cabello, started with machinery brought out from Germany in the amount of 700,000 Bolívars, had by 1909 fallen to British entrepreneurs.[87] The Caracas glass plant, built in 1905 at a cost of 600,000 Bolívars with German machinery and under German ownership, had fallen to Venezuelan investors.[88] Rhenish steel firms had been indecisive about investing in Orinoco iron-ore fields, with the result that the Canadian-Venezuelan Ore Co. of Halifax had gained the right to mine the fields up to 80,000 tons per year.[89] Late in 1908, President Castro had granted Wilhelm Jagenberg, a German financier in Caracas, the right to construct a hydroelectric dam on the Mamo River in order to bring electric power to Caracas and La Guayra, but despite the fact that Castro personally invested 850,000 Bolívars in the undertaking, Jagenberg had been unable to attract German financing for the plant.[90] The meat-packing plant on the Orinoco River, contracted to Dr. Dude of Chemnitz at a cost of 1.2 million Mark and slated to process 100,000 head of cattle per year, was finally scaled down to a capacity of 25,000 per year, and lack of German financing eventually forced

mann Hollweg, June 29, 1912. See also, Bundesarchiv-Koblenz, R85/145, Eisenbahnen in Venezuela, for the report by Prollius. It is interesting to compare this favorable analysis of Gómez's Venezuela with an earlier evaluation by the German minister at Caracas, assuring Chancellor von Bülow: "An era Gómez would hardly be of long duration." Gómez in fact ruled until 1935. AA-Bonn, Venezuela 1, vol. 34. Seckendorff to Bülow, Sept. 25, 1908.

[86] ZStA-Potsdam, Auswärtiges Amt, Abt. II, Jahresberichte Valencia Nr 54118, pp. 4-9. Consul Gosewisch to Foreign Office, Mar. 10, 1901.

[87] ZStA-Potsdam, Auswärtiges Amt, Abt. IIu, Jahresberichte Valencia Nr 4871, pp. 16-18. Gosewisch to Bethmann Hollweg, Mar. 18, 1910.

[88] ZStA-Potsdam, Reichsamt des Innern Nr 5441, Handelssachen Venezuela. Seckendorff to Bülow, Dec. 7, 1906.

[89] ZStA-Potsdam, Auswärtiges Amt, Abt. II, Jahresberichte des Konsulats La Guayra Nr 4873, pp. 41-46. Consul Müller to Bethmann Hollweg, Feb. 17, 1912.

[90] ZStA-Potsdam, Reichsamt des Innern Nr 5441, p. 142. Seckendorff to Bülow, Aug. 14, 1908.

Dude to sell out to French packers. This was an especially hard blow for German interests, as the main producer of cattle would be Venezuela's foremost cattle baron, President Gómez.[91] Above all, German businessmen had lost the competitive edge to their North American counterparts. Consul George Becker at Caracas reported in 1913 that while German imports continued along traditional lines—linens, stockings, cotton and wool garments—United States firms were taking over the market for machinery. American contractors not only sold their wares cheaper, but they arrived with them in Venezuela, installed them, and explained their operation and servicing to the natives.[92] Without question, the Americans had learned from the "Made in Germany" alarm of 1896 and were now beating the Germans with their own tactics.

The great dreams of German exploitation of Venezuela of just two decades ago had been dashed. At least in the German case, one can agree with John Lombardy that the international blockade "showed the inexperience and lack of subtlety of these North Atlantic imperialists [!] in the exercise of their new ability and in the protection of their Venezuelan interests."[93] Another North Atlantic "imperialist," the United States, in the future would display much greater "experience" and "subtlety."

In conclusion, it is relatively easy to ascertain why Germany hesitated so long to take action against Castro. Venezuela's tropical climate limited naval action to the winter months, from November through March. Germany's lack of overseas cruisers and coaling stations made it absolutely necessary that it undertake even a "pacific" blockade with a major naval power such as Britain. Finally, the refusal of the largest merchant house in Venezuela, H. G. & L. F. Blohm, to support armed intervention obviously raised concern in Berlin about the desirability of such drastic measures in the future.

[91] Ibid., p. 167. Rhomberg to Bethmann Hollweg, Dec. 26, 1909. President Gómez invested 100,000 Mark in the plant and offered an equal amount of credit for cattle purchases.

[92] ZStA-Potsdam, Auswärtiges Amt, Abt. IIu, Jahreshandelsberichte Caracas Nr 4819. Becker to Bethmann Hollweg, Jan. 7, 1913.

[93] John V. Lombardy, *Venezuela: The Search for Order, the Dream of Progress* (New York/Oxford, 1982), 205.

Indeed, Blohm's ability to live and flourish within even the chaos of despotic *caudillism* lends credence to Ronald Robinson's thesis of "outer world collaboration" as a major component of European "imperialism."

The matter of motivation, on the other hand, is more difficult to pinpoint. Germany was a semi-absolutist state without responsible government. Hence, we have no Cabinet records to track the discussions that led to the blockade. Likewise, deliberations with Wilhelm II were confidential in nature and only the results recorded. Petitions for intervention by interested concerns were duly filed by the Foreign Office, often without comment or response. Motivating factors, therefore, need be gleaned from a multiplicity of diplomatic, economic, and naval documents. As already noted, Wilhelm II, Admirals von Tirpitz and von Diederichs, General von Plessen, and several other naval leaders, opposed the blockade for technical reasons as well as cost. Foreign Secretary von Richthofen on several occasions bluntly refused to undertake a naval expedition at the beck and call of the Norddeutsche Bank and Disconto. Chancellor von Bülow, the major proponent of a "pacific" blockade, until December 1902 refused to include the financial claims of banks and industry in his demands. German naval commanders off Venezuela, such as Lieutenant Commander Eckermann of the *Panther*, Count Oriola of the *Gazelle*, Lieutenant Commander Musculus of the *Falke*, and Commodore Scheder of the *Vineta*, flooded Berlin with action reports motivated in large measure by prestige and national honor.[94] Joseph Schumpeter might well have termed it "atavism."

Indeed, "irrational" factors such as prestige, honor, and dignity seem to have been primary motivators especially for Wilhelm II and Bülow—along with the diplomatic and strategic advantage of undertaking an operation with Great Britain in an area where the United States considered itself to be the hemispheric guardian. In November 1902, Count von Lerchenfeld, Bavaria's diplomat at Berlin, reported to his superiors that the blockade was being undertaken by the Bülow government for two reasons: "to raise the Reich's pres-

[94] See, for example, Eckermann's report to Wilhelm II of Nov. 25, 1902, in AA-Bonn, Venezuela 1, vol. 22b.

tige" and to "conduct a joint operation with England."[95] Therewith, the percipient Lerchenfeld had hit the nail on the head.

Chancellor von Bülow delineated his reasons for undertaking the armed action against the refractory Castro in the Reichstag on March 19, 1903. Bülow dismissed "glory" and "territorial expansion" as motivating factors. In addition, he denied that Germany wished to play "executor of every aleatorial business venture that some German undertakes somewhere in the world." Nor was the blockade the result of an "*ad hoc*" adventurism, but rather a carefully thought-out "future warning" to other nations that they could not toy with the honor and prestige of the Reich. "Our prestige and the honor of our flag," he informed the deputies, played a decisive role. And while Bülow regretted the recourse to armed force, he nevertheless felt that Castro had left Berlin no other alternative. "We still have not discovered a method of washing the fur without getting it wet."[96] The Chancellor declined to enlighten the Reichstag as to why Germany had undertaken the blockade with Britain as a partner. Nor did he offer any insight into his government's stance on the Monroe Doctrine. *Die grosse Politik*, after all, was a prerogative of the Crown, to be exercised in its name by the Chancellor, as stated in the Federal Constitution of 1871. In the final analysis, one can probably agree with the verdict rendered on Berlin's overseas policy by another "imperialist," General Lothar von Trotha, Governor of German South-West Africa, at the very moment that German warships were blockading Venezuela: "It was neither political because we lacked the enthusiasm, nor economic because initially we lacked the capital. . . . It was simply pure speculation."[97]

[95] BHStA-Munich, Abt. II: Geheimes Staatsarchiv, MA III 2680. Lerchenfeld to Crailsheim, Nov. 30, 1902. See also Lerchenfeld's reports to Crailsheim of Dec. 29, 1902, and Feb. 18, 1903, stressing that the initiative for the blockade had come from London. Ibid.

[96] Reichstag, Verhandlungen. Stenographische Berichte, X. Legislaturperiode, II. Session, 287. Sitzung, vol. 10, p. 8719 C, D.

[97] Bundesarchiv-Koblenz, Nachlass Schwertfeger Nr 574, comment of December 1902. The most recent treatment of the German presence off Venezuela is Willi A. Boelcke, *So kam das Meer zu uns: Die preussisch-deutsche Kriegsmarine in Übersee 1822 bis 1914* (Frankfurt, 1981), 113-14.

CHAPTER IV

THE MILITARY ADVISORS' GAME

Nothing smacks more of classical imperialism than the dispatch of military advisors, instructors, or missions by a developed, modern state to a backward, underdeveloped state. The very mention of the term "military advisors" usually raises eyebrows or brings smirks to the corner of one's mouth during casual discussions. And not without cause: the role of Gurkhas and Cubans, Frenchmen and Germans, Americans and Soviets over the last century around the globe has badly tarnished the image of such "advisors."

Latin America was a good case in point for German soldiers of fortune even before they could boast of a country of their own. Military adventurers came to South America as early as the Welser period: in 1527, Johann von Ampués arrived at Coro, the second oldest Spanish settlement in the hemisphere, and one year later Ambrosius Dolfinger (also known as Ehinger) landed with 400 mercenaries and miners near Coro; soon thereafter, Dolfinger-Ehinger became Statthalter of Coro and dominated the slave trade out of Maracaibo. His fellow "conquistadores" Georg Hohermuth (Jorge de Spira), Nikolaus Federmann, and Philipp von Hutten (Felipe de Urre) ventured as far inland as Bogotá in search of treasure after they had been disappointed in the pearl beds at Cabo de la Vela.[1] But these were largely individual undertakings, devoid of official backing, and the entire Welser project, as previously noted, ended in abject failure by the middle of the 1550s.

Simón Bolívar also counted a German military presence among his followers. Friedrich Rauch, Johann von Uslar, and Otto Philipp

---

[1] See *Handbuch des Deutschtums im Auslande* (Berlin, 1906), 323; Percy Ernst Schramm, *Deutschland und Übersee: Der Deutsche Handel mit anderen Kontinenten, insbesondere Afrika, von Karl V. bis Bismarck* (Braunschweig/Berlin/Hamburg/Kiel, 1950), 21; Wilhelm Sievers, *Zweite Reise in Venezuela in den Jahren 1892/93* (Hamburg, 1896), 60.

Braun (nicknamed "Mariscal de Monte Negro") actively fought for the great Libertador. Uslar was instrumental in the battle of Cara-bobo in June 1821 that liberated Venezuela from royalist forces, and later commanded the elite Guardia del Libertador. Braun cam-paigned in Venezuela in 1820, entered Bolívar's Guardia as major in 1823, and in 1839 led the army to victory against Argentina at Junga Salta. A copy of F. W. von Steuben's *Regulations for the Order and Discipline of the Troops of the United States* in Spanish transla-tion was found preserved in Otto Philipp Braun's papers.[2] Perhaps the first genuine military "advisor," as Fritz Epstein has suggested, was Colonel Johann Heinrich von Boehm, who sought to reorganize Portuguese troops in Brazil in the second half of the nineteenth cen-tury; he would be followed in Brazil by others such as Wilhelm Bor-mann. And in Costa Rica in the 1870s, one of the Counts zur Lippe toiled to revamp that nation's armed forces.[3] Still, none of these "military advisors" can be regarded as much more than an enter-prising military adventurer, seeking personal fortune and fame.

A new era in European-South American military relations was ushered in by the mission of Captain Emil Körner to Chile in 1885 at the request of General Emilio Sotomayor of the Chilean Military School. The Chilean envoy to Germany, Guillermo Matta, had ini-tially sought out Jacob Clemens Meckel for the post, but when Meckel opted instead for Japan, both Emperor Wilhelm I and Field Marshal Helmuth von Moltke recommended Körner, who had been a classmate of Paul von Hindenburg and Colmar von der Goltz at the Prussian Kriegsakademie, to the Chileans. The Emperor apparently had been impressed by Chile's performance against Peru in the Pa-cific War of 1879-1883, and desired to see the Prussian military sys-tem transplanted to South America via Chile. Thus, official backing of the highest order accompanied Körner's mission to Chile. As is well known, Körner eventually transformed Chile's military estab-lishment into the "Prussia of South America" and its officers into consummate *germanofilos*. The existing Escuela Militar was reor-

[2] Fritz T. Epstein, "European Military Influences in Latin America" (ms., Library of Congress, 1941), pp. 18, 21; Kurt von Borcke, *Deutsche unter fremden Fahnen* (Berlin, 1938), 268-75.

[3] Epstein, "European Military Influences," 20-23.

ganized along the lines of the Kadetten-Anstalt at Lichterfelde; a school for noncommissioned officers was created (Escuela de Clases); South America's first general conscription law was enacted in 1900; a Chilean General Staff was established and, after October 1895, commanded by Körner; and an Academia de Guerra patterned after the Kriegsakademie in Berlin was officially opened in 1887. Another German mission in 1895 brought no fewer than thirty-seven European officers to Chile—one of the largest military missions ever to serve in South America. Conversely, between 1896 and 1905, forty-two Chileans went to Germany for military instruction at Spandau, Charlottenburg, Jüterbog, and Hanover. By the beginning of the Great War, the number of Chilean officers trained in Germany had risen to about 150.[4]

Perhaps equally important, the Chileans quickly became German surrogates in South American military matters. Early in the twentieth century, Colombia, Bolivia, and Paraguay sent their officers to train at the Military Academy in Santiago de Chile, while Chilean officers undertook reform of the armies of Colombia, Ecuador, and El Salvador. Körner's army regulations for Chile were adopted in 1902 by Bolivia, Ecuador, Guatemala, Colombia, and Paraguay. The Escuela Militar both in Quito and in Bogotá was commanded by Chilean officers in the first decade of the twentieth century.[5]

---

[4] Ibid., 115-23; Borcke, *Deutsche unter fremden Fahnen*, 294-98; Gerhard Brunn, "Deutscher Einfluss und Deutsche Interessen in der Professionalisierung einiger Lateinamerikanischer Staaten vor dem 1. Weltkrieg (1885-1914)," *Jahrbuch für Geschichte von Staat, Wirtschaft und Gesellschaft Lateinamerikas*, 6 (1969), 281-85; Jürgen Schaefer, *Deutsche Militärhilfe an Südamerika: Militär- und Rüstungsinteressen in Argentinien, Bolivien und Chile vor 1914* (Düsseldorf, 1974), 21ff., 114ff.; John J. Johnson, *The Role of the Military in Underdeveloped Countries* (Princeton, 1962), 108; Edwin Lieuwen, *Arms and Politics in Latin America* (New York, 1960), 32-33; Frederick M. Nunn, "Emil Körner and the Prussianization of the Chilean Army: Origins, Process and Consequences, 1885-1920," *Hispanic American Historical Review*, 50 (May 1970), 300-22; Frederick M. Nunn, *Yesterday's Soldiers: European Military Professionalism in South America, 1890-1940* (Lincoln, 1983), especially chapter four.

[5] Brunn, "Deutscher Einfluss," 290; Lieuwen, *Arms and Politics*, 32-33; Epstein, "European Military Influences," 56, 136; Nunn, *Yesterday's Soldiers*, 111-12.

Perhaps impressed with Don Emilio's efforts in Chile and ever fearful of the military intentions of that country, President Julio A. Roca of Argentina in August 1899 instructed his War Minister, Pablo Riccheri, to request a German military mission, especially to revamp the moribund Escuela Superior de Guerra as well as to overhaul the Argentinean cadet school (Colegio Militar). Argentina selected as its ambassador to Berlin General Lucio Mansilla in order to underscore the importance of the military request, but Mansilla was frustrated when his first choice as head of the mission, General Colmar von der Goltz, declined the invitation. However, Goltz recommended a former General Staff officer, Colonel Alfred Arent, to the Argentines, and Arent as well as four other officers duly sailed for Buenos Aires. They reorganized the Escuela Superior de Guerra in 1900 along Prussian lines, with German officers and professors dominant on its staff. By 1906, Argentine officers were attending military studies in Germany, with anywhere from thirty to sixty officers per annum visiting the Reich; conversely, about thirty German officers were active in Argentina between 1900 and 1914. Among the latter was Captain Wilhelm Faupel, one of the first German instructors at the Colegio Militar and destined to become Adolf Hitler's ambassador to Francisco Franco's Spain in 1938. The Argentines by 1907 had adopted German war doctrine, having translated Prussian/German artillery, cavalry, and infantry manuals into Spanish. That same year, the old General Staff transformed itself into the *gram estado mayor*, which Frederick M. Nunn has termed a "creole *grosser Generalstab*."[6] That Arent never accumulated the military and political influence of his counterpart in Chile, Körner, was due in part to his difficult personality as well as to the residual suspicion of German advisors in a land that until then had largely relied upon France for military succor. In fact, Körner's direct role in the Chilean civil war of 1891 provides the sole example of such blatant po-

[6] Nunn, *Yesterday's Soldiers*, 123-24; Borcke, *Deutsche unter fremden Fahnen*, 310-14; Brunn, "Deutscher Einfluss," 285, 295; Epstein, "European Military Influences," 138-42; Schaefer, *Deutsche Militärhilfe*, 76ff.; Warren Schiff, "The Influence of the German Armed Forces and War Industry on Argentina, 1880-1914," *Hispanic American Historical Review*, 52 (August 1972), 436-55.

litical meddling by any member of a German military mission to South America.[7]

On a much less successful level than in either Chile or Argentina, German military instructors were also engaged in Bolivia. Before the turn of the century, Colonel Max Josef von Vacano, a retired Prussian army officer, had headed the Escuela de Guerra in La Paz, but his tour of duty did not enjoy formal sanction from Berlin. In fact, by 1901 French influence dominated Bolivia—until 1910, when the head of the Bolivian Army, General José Manuel Pando, requested about two dozen German officers to come to La Paz in order to reform the Bolivian General Staff and to establish a cadet school along the Prussian Lichterfelde model. Major Hans Kundt eventually managed to establish an *estado mayor general* on the lines of the Prussian General Staff and to revamp the Bolivian cadet school.[8] Bolivia thus joined Chile and Argentina in accepting the old Roman maxim attributed to Vegetius, *si vedes pacem, para bellum* (if you want peace, prepare for war), and its renewed hostilities with Peru and Paraguay seemed to offer no choice but to prepare for conflict. Yet as in Argentina, the Kundt mission never gained political influence in the altiplano republic owing to Bolivia's domestic socio-political turbulence.

The German successes in Chile, Argentina, and Bolivia, combined with the reputation of German arms since the Franco-Prussian War of 1870-1871, also attracted other potential clients in South America, some of whom had been considered solidly in the French camp. Although Brazil's best fighting units, the São Paulo *força pública*, had been trained by France and equipped by Schneider-Creusot, Marshal Hermes da Fonseca, the Brazilian war minister who had attended German army maneuvers in 1908, persuaded Foreign Minister Rio Branco to turn to Berlin for military instructors. By 1910-1911, no fewer than twenty-six Brazilian officers were sent to Germany for military instruction, with another twenty-eight following in 1914. But, in the final analysis, domestic political strife in the

---

[7] Nunn, *Yesterday's Soldiers*, 103.

[8] Ibid., 304-305 n. 40; Epstein, "European Military Influences," 149; Borcke, *Deutsche unter fremden Fahnen*, 298-307; Schaefer, *Deutsche Militärhilfe*, 98-112.

National Congress obfuscated Hermes da Fonseca's desire to have a German military mission overhaul his nation's armed forces.[9] Nor could the Brazilians have guessed that Emperor Wilhelm II considered the dispatch of any German officers to be "difficult" because they would have to be placed "on an equal [social] rung with black and colored" officers.[10]

The mounting requests for German military instructors by South American states also strained relations among the various German federal armies by 1910. Both Saxony and Bavaria learned of the requests for about twenty officers each by Bolivia and Brazil in August, and the Bavarian military plenipotentiary, General Ludwig von Gebsattel, at once informed his government in Munich that it was imperative for Bavaria to participate "in the interest of the prestige of the Bavarian Army."[11] In fact, Georg von Hertling, head of the German Center Party, informed General Kress von Kressenstein, the Bavarian war minister, that foreign powers need only apply directly to Munich for instructors; Hertling dismissed Prussian insistences that the Emperor's prior approval was required as being "incompatible with the military sovereignty of the Bavarian Crown."[12] But when word was leaked to the Bavarians that Prussia was about to dispatch eighteen officers to Bolivia and that the matter had been handled as "a very private undertaking" in Berlin, General von Gebsattel informed his superior in Munich that this was just another indication that the Prussians reserved all such desirable military plums for their own officers.[13] His Saxon counterpart in September 1910 bitterly complained to the Foreign Office in Berlin that the matter of foreign military missions was all too often simply handed to the

[9] Epstein, "European Military Influences," 172-73; Nunn, *Yesterday's Soldiers*, 132-33; Frederick M. Nunn, "Military Professionalism and Professional Militarism in Brazil, 1870-1970: Historical Perspectives and Political Implications," *Journal of Latin American Studies*, 4 (May 1972), 35-36.

[10] Bayerisches Hauptstaatsarchiv Munich (hereafter BHStA), Abteilung IV, MKr 1951, Übertritt deutscher Offiziere in ausserdeutsche Armeen als Militärinstrukteure, p. 122. General Moritz von Lyncker, Prussian Chief of the Military Cabinet, to the Bavarian War Minister, General Horn, Aug. 25, 1910.

[11] Ibid., p. 122. Gebsattel to Horn, Aug. 25, 1910.

[12] Ibid. Hertling to Kress von Kressenstein, Nov. 23, 1912.

[13] Ibid., p. 165. Gebsattel to Horn, Nov. 17, 1910.

Prussian War Ministry by the Wilhelmstrasse "without regard for the other allied governments" in Dresden, Munich, and Stuttgart. Nor did the Saxon military plenipotentiary fail to remind his government of the great impact that such military missions would have upon the "domestic economy"; one needed to cease looking at military missions as being "purely in the military sphere."[14]

These German family squabbles were unknown to the South Americans, who merely increased their requests for military instructors. Paraguay joined the rush in 1913-1914, when President Eduardo Schaerer formally requested twelve to fourteen German officers to reform his army; four of the instructors arrived before the outbreak of the Great War. That same year, Ecuador instructed its consul in Hamburg to approach the Berlin government for yet another military mission, but once again European events in the summer of 1914 interrupted all negotiations.[15]

Generally speaking, then, by the eve of the Great War, Chile, Argentina, and Bolivia were solidly in the German camp, while Peru alone remained with the French. Germany's surrogate, Chile, was actively engaged in revamping the armies of Bolivia, Colombia, and Paraguay, while Brazil, Paraguay, and Ecuador, were leaning toward future German military missions.[16] Hence, it is hardly surprising that Venezuela also attempted to join the rush for German instructors early in the twentieth century.

In fact, the imperial German government had routinely received annual reports on the Venezuelan army of about 1,800 men from its minister at Caracas, Otto Peyer, at least since 1887. The Foreign Office in Berlin duly filed these without comment until 1889, when Peyer reported an increase of 1,000 men in the size of the army as well as a quantum leap in the highest rungs of the officer corps to 151 generals, including seventeen *generals en chef.* The Wilhelmstrasse drily noted: "Thus, one general for every twenty-two men!

---

[14] Sächsisches Hauptstaatsarchiv Dresden (hereafter SHStA), Aussenministerium Nr 4732, Übertritt sächs. Offiziere im Militärdienste des Auslandes 1907-22, Sept. 28, 1910.

[15] Epstein, "European Military Influences," 186, 194.

[16] See the appraisal by Emil Körner, "Die südamerikanischen Militärverhältnisse," *Deutsche Kultur in der Welt,* 1 (1915), 189ff.

And an officer for every three to four men!"[17] The following year, Peyer reported a further increase of more than 100 generals; in 1892, he noted a virtual doubling of the size of the army to 5,760 men, armed with Remington rifles and trained according to the Spanish tactics of the Marques del Duero.[18] Peyer's successor, Dr. Friedrich Count von Kleist-Tychow, that same year adopted the new imperial tone then fashionable in Berlin when he described the Venezuelan army as consisting of "hordes that have been honored by the name soldiers. [They], including their so-called officers, are creatures who recognize no law and who live primarily from robbery and plunder." Kleist reminded Berlin "that the country is only half-civilized, even including those circles which fancy themselves as being educated."[19]

A similar prognosis reached Wilhelm II a decade later from the captain of the gunboat *Panther*, Lieutenant Commander Eckermann. The latter graphically described a military action between government troops and insurgents at Cumaná as "a delightful piece of theatre . . . much as German youths play their beloved game of cops and robbers." Defenders as well as attackers showed "great personal pluck" as they ran wildly through the town, firing their aged Mauser 71/84 rifles without ever taking aim, whooping loudly, and deploying the only functioning cannon at will and in all directions. Several shots eventually reached the decks of the *Panther*, which was not taking part in the engagement and whose crew had to be sent below decks as a result.[20]

Robert Gilmore's study of *Caudillism and Militarism in Venezuela* basically substantiates these contemporary reports. The number of officers in the Venezuelan army dramatically increased from about 600 in 1883 to more than 10,000 a decade later. By 1897, there were no less than 12,529 officers in the army, of whom a mere 595

[17] Zentrales Staatsarchiv Potsdam (hereafter ZStA), Auswärtiges Amt, Abt. IIIb, 31935, Nachrichten über Heer und Marine in Venezuela, pp. 14, 17. Peyer to Bismarck, Apr. 26, 1889.

[18] Ibid., 25-26. Peyer to Caprivi, Apr. 2, 1891.

[19] Auswärtiges Amt Bonn (hereafter AA), Venezuela 1, Allgemeine Angelegenheiten Venezuelas, vol. 8. Kleist to Caprivi, June 17, 1892.

[20] Ibid., vol. 22b. Eckermann to Wilhelm II, Nov. 17, 1902.

were on active duty. In the years of anarchy between 1890 and 1903, there was a 900 percent rise in the number of *caudillos*, many of whom simply regarded revolution as a shortcut to "meat and drink." The title of general, one contemporary noted, was nothing more than "a synonym for señor." And military commissions during that turbulent decade climbed from 1,300 to over 12,000.[21]

To be sure, there were several attempts made to enhance the military effectiveness of the Venezuelan army. President Joaquín Crespo in 1896 reorganized the army into three separate entities: a presidential guard, an army of the line consisting of 3,600 men, and a militia or supernumerary force on active duty; in all, about thirteen battalions of infantry, cavalry, and marines. The Artillery School, founded in 1895, was converted into a general military academy two years later, but it remained largely a paper creation. Indeed, after two unsuccessful starts in 1897 and 1898, President Cipriano Castro in July 1903 formally founded a Venezuelan military academy, but it took another seven years before the Academia Militar opened its doors in 1910. Castro in 1904 ended the practice of giving commissions to all *caudillos* who had supported the winning side and instead based promotion on time in grade and the passing of examinations.[22] The Reich's minister in Caracas, Alfred Pelldram, that same year informed his government of Castro's decree that the army would henceforth consist of twenty battalions of infantry, eight batteries of artillery, and one battalion of marines for a total of 6,000 infantry, 1,600 artillery, and 600 marines. And in an attempt to prevent the soldiers from developing an affinity toward the local population, all twenty battalions were to be rotated in station every six months.[23]

The reforms notwithstanding, the German army throughout the period either ignored the Venezuelan army or, on the few occasions when it took note of that force, ranked it near the bottom of its lists of foreign armed forces. Semi-official publications such as the *Militär-Wochenblatt*, the *Neue Militärische Blätter*, and the *Internationale Revue über die Gesammten Armeen und Flotten* in the main ig-

[21] Robert L. Gilmore, *Caudillism and Militarism in Venezuela, 1810-1910* (Athens, Ohio, 1964), 65.

[22] Ibid., 154-56.

[23] AA-Bonn, Venezuela 1, vol. 27. Pelldram to Bülow, Aug. 11, 1904.

nored South America in general and Venezuela in particular, preferring to concentrate on those areas where German instructors were most evident, such as the Balkans, Turkey, and Japan.[24] The Great General Staff, for its part, evaluated the Venezuelan army in 1906 and again in 1913-1914; both prognoses were highly negative. The earlier estimate noted the utter lack of theoretical planning by the Venezuelan army, the limitation of formal training to "several drill sessions and a bit of watch duty," and the total lack of "shooting practice and active field duty." Officer recruitment, the General Staff noted, "ensues at the pleasure of whichever ruler happens to be in power." The militia, for its part, was "neither militarily trained nor adequately supplied with weapons and munitions; its value is equal to zero." Finally, the German staffers observed that the Venezuelan army "cannot be considered a serious opponent for a European power."[25] The later study concurred. It depicted Venezuela in 1913-1914 as a "disorganized state in a hot climate with predominantly colored population," with an army largely consisting of "mercenary troops" armed with aged Mauser 71/84 rifles and antiquated artillery pieces. Its final verdict was utterly devastating: "Absolutely inferior and without importance."[26] General Emil Körner in 1915 informed his readers at home that the reform efforts of the Chilean instructors headed by "Colonel Mac Gill" had made progress only among the cadets enrolled at the Academia Militar.[27]

Obviously, the quality of troops in Venezuela, both officers and enlisted men, left much to be desired, and hence Venezuela had repeatedly approached the Reich for assistance in upgrading its armed forces. The earliest documented request for German military advi-

[24] See Nunn, *Yesterday's Soldiers*, 67-68.

[25] BHStA-Munich, Abt. IV, Generalstab 320, Mittel u. Südamerikanische Staaten 1905-1914. Report of February 1906 by Section 2, Division 9, of the Great General Staff in Berlin.

[26] Ibid., report dated 1913-1914.

[27] Körner, "Die südamerikanischen Militärverhältnisse," 189ff. I am indebted to Professor Frederick M. Nunn of Portland State University for confirming Colonel Samuel McGill's role in Venezuela sometime before the Great War; apparently, McGill was in charge of cadet training, military instruction, and served on the Venezuelan "general staff." See Samuel McGill, *Poliantea: Memorias del Coronel McGill* (Caracas, 1978).

sors came in July 1896, when Foreign Minister P. Ezequiel Rojas asked in behalf of President Crespo for an instructor in artillery and infantry tactics. The German envoy in Caracas, Arthur Count von Rex, favored the Venezuelan initiative, seeing therein "a further enhancement of German influence, respectively also of German trade, and last but not least because the German instructors will naturally draw the requisite war materials from Germany." German officers, Rex averred, should be accorded the rank of general and be accountable for their actions only to the Venezuelan War Ministry; a monthly salary of 1,500 francs would suffice for a bachelor, 2,000 francs for a married man, in addition to 7,000 francs travel money. But Rex cautioned that "any and all social contact with local officers as well as enlisted men, who are usually colored, would be impossible for a German officer."[28] The Foreign Office, the War Ministry, and the Emperor in Berlin agreed to honor the Venezuelan request for two instructors for two-year tours of duty, but General Crespo in January 1897 rescinded his invitation owing to "the present [dire] financial situation." He did, however, promise to renew the request at a later date.[29]

There, the matter rested for a decade. In the meantime, the Venezuelans were content simply to engage German free-lance "instructors" on an individual basis, as was the case with a certain Prussian Colonel von Ehrnberg, who headed the Artillery School founded in 1895, and with Wolfgang Iren von Carlowitz, a Saxon officer who since 1898 had labored to reform the Venezuelan artillery.[30] The Germans, of course, could hardly be expected to be enthusiastic about an army that in 1901 consisted of only 4,000 men but a staggering aggregate of 11,365 officers of various sorts: four *generals en chef* including the president and war minister, twenty-eight other

[28] ZStA-Potsdam, Auswärtiges Amt, Abt. IIIb, 29085, Deutsche Militärinstrukteure in Venezuela, pp. 4-7. Rex to Hohenlohe-Schillingsfürst, July 8, 1896.

[29] Ibid., pp. 11-12, 14-15, 18-19. Foreign Office to War Ministry, Aug. 12, 1896; War Minister Bronsart von Schellendorf to Hohenlohe-Schillingsfürst, Sept. 25, 1896; and Rex to Hohenlohe-Schillingsfürst, Jan. 8, 1897.

[30] AA-Bonn, Venezuela 1, vol. 15. Minister Dr. Schmidt-Leda to Hohenlohe-Schillingsfürst, May 30, 1899. The minister reported the presence of 29 *generals en chef*, 1,364 generals, and 1,381 colonels in the Venezuelan army.

"*generals en chef*" nominated by the president, 1,439 generals, 1,462 colonels, 2,300 majors, 3,230 captains, 2,300 lieutenants, and 1,000 sub-lieutenants (*alféreces*).[31]

The situation brightened somewhat in the summer of 1908. With the Academia Militar under construction, President Castro requested two German military instructors to train the fifty "sons from better families" whom Castro sought annually to enroll at the Academy. But the German minister to Caracas, Baron von Seckendorff, was extremely wary of the request, not only on account of Castro's intransigent behavior during the international blockade of 1902-1903, but also with a view toward the *Andino*'s worsening relations with the United States; any German assistance to Castro could endanger the existing "cordial relations" between Berlin and Washington.[32] In light of this, the Venezuelans appealed directly to the Wilhelmstrasse for military instructors, but the Foreign Office in August 1908 termed the request "undesirable" owing to Castro's current policy of brinkmanship vis-à-vis the United States, France, and the Netherlands. However, the German diplomats requested that the Prussian War Ministry base its rejection on "other than political grounds."[33]

General Karl von Einem, the Prussian War Minister, informed Chancellor Bernhard von Bülow in September 1908 that, given the Reich's present political alignment in Europe, he could spare no instructors for Castro; retired officers, who alone were eligible for overseas duty, would probably decline such an invitation from the tropics, while Wilhelm II would not permit any active officers to resign in order to go to Venezuela. The Caracas government was apprised of the decision later that month.[34]

The Venezuelans, however, were most persistent. The new Military Academy, at first patterned after West Point to honor one of the Point's graduates, Francisco Alcantara, was about to enroll its first class and was in dire need of professional instructors. Accordingly,

[31] Epstein, "European Military Influences," 44.

[32] AA-Bonn, Venezuela 1, vol. 33. Seckendorff to Bülow, July 4, 1908.

[33] Ibid. Foreign Office to War Ministry, Aug. 20, 1908.

[34] Ibid., vol. 34. Einem to Bülow, Sept. 25, 1908; Foreign Office to Venezuelan envoy, Sept. 29, 1908.

Caracan diplomats in the spring of 1910 once more approached Berlin for an official training mission. Once again, that request ran up against a highly negative evaluation of the Venezuelan military by the German envoy in Caracas. Minister Rhomberg informed Berlin in March 1910 that one could scarcely speak of a Venezuelan army. Conscription "existed only on paper." The concept of "national defense" was not even in circulation. Venezuela's forces consisted only of "battalion hordes" deployed primarily "to protect the ruler *against* the country and its revolutionary lust." Moreover, only "the lowest strata of society" were "pressed" into military service; at other times, so-called "enlistment" was reserved as "punishment for obstinate, odious individuals." Rhomberg went out of his way to inform Berlin that the "low niveau" of the Venezuelan officers precluded any formal education on their part, and that such officers were without "social rank." The titles of "captain" and "colonel" were meaningless, and there were more generals than soldiers. "Given this milieu, the endeavors of German military instructors would run up against a complete lack of understanding. The matter must therefore rest, given such utter lack of prospects." Even the best German efforts would be doomed to failure, given the typical Venezuelan "conceit and arrogance" as well as their ingrained "ill-bred nature to resist anything that is related to discipline." Indeed, Venezuelans were attracted not to "sober work" and to the "attainable," but ever to "glittering façades" and the "impossible." Rhomberg concluded that, at best, Venezuela might be allowed to dispatch several officers for tours of instruction in Germany, or to seek German help to establish "a military prep-school, a kind of cadet school."[35] It was the lengthiest evaluation of the Venezuelan military ever penned by a German diplomat in Caracas, and it remained the basis for all future German military dealings with Venezuela.

The Venezuelans once more responded by going over the head of the German minister in Caracas: Dr. Santos A. Dominici, the Republic's envoy in Berlin, formally requested two German military instructors from the Wilhelmstrasse in April 1910. The request was

[35] Ibid., vol. 39. Rhomberg to Bethmann Hollweg, Mar. 5, 1910.

denied. Foreign Secretary Wilhelm Baron von Schoen simply did not wish to waste his energy on the mounting number of such requests from South America, especially at a time when the Reich seemed encircled by a hostile European coalition; he commented caustically upon the "presénce du grand nombre de demandes pareilles qui lui sont recement [sic] parvenues."[36]

The Venezuelans thereafter tried yet another approach, asking the Foreign Office in August 1910 whether young Venezuelan officers could enroll, officially or privately, at the Military Academy in Berlin. Alfred von Kiderlen-Wächter, the new State Secretary of the Foreign Office, asked Rhomberg whether this request constituted but the first of many more to come, a development that "would unquestionably be undesirable." Kiderlen-Wächter reminded his envoy in Caracas of Baron von Schoen's earlier refusal to send advisors there owing to the great number of similar requests already on hand. Rhomberg concurred, recommending that Venezuelans not be sent to the Kriegsakademie, either as official or as private students.[37] The matter came to a rest when the new War Minister, General Josias von Heeringen, ruled against the Venezuelan request "for military reasons."[38]

Undaunted, the Venezuelan regime of President Juan Vicente Gómez, who had ousted Castro late in 1908, tried yet another approach. In August 1911, the German envoy to Chile, Friedrich Carl von Erckert, informed Chancellor Theobald von Bethmann Hollweg that Venezuela had formally requested a Chilean military mission. Erckert reminded the Chancellor that Chile had responded positively to earlier requests for military advisors by Bolivia, Colombia,

---

[36] Ibid., vol. 37. Dominici to Schoen, Apr. 14, 1910; War Minister to Chancellor, Apr. 25, 1910; Schoen to Dominici, Apr. 29, 1910.

[37] ZStA-Potsdam, Auswärtiges Amt, Abt. IIIb, 29044, Erlaubnis für Venezolaner zum Eintritt in diesseitige Militär- Erziehungs- und Lehranstalten, sowie zur Dienstleistung bzw. Information bei diesseitigen Truppenteilen und der Kaiserlichen Marine, pp. 2-5. German legation in Caracas to Kiderlen-Wächter, Aug. 1, 1910; Kiderlen-Wächter to Rhomberg, Aug. 7, 1910; Rhomberg to Bethmann Hollweg, Sept. 26, 1910.

[38] Ibid. Heeringen to Foreign Office, Oct. 31, 1910.

El Salvador, Honduras, and Paraguay, and that in each case Chile had placed weapons orders for the new clients in Germany.[39] Adolf von Prollius, the Reich's new minister in Caracas, soon got wind of the Venezuelan initiative, and in December 1911 reported to Berlin that while the Military Academy in Caracas ("more correctly, a cadet school") had been opened the previous year and that while some progress had been made there by the Chilean Colonel Samuel McGill, an officer of British descent, "the unmilitary disposition of the Venezuelan youth" worked against formal military training; the locals instead preferred to enroll in potential revolutionary armies in order thereupon to parade around as "generals." Prollius again reminded Bethmann Hollweg that the "highest social elements" in Venezuela avoided service with the armed forces, with the result that the army's officers were mainly "uneducated coloreds." Given these "hideous" local conditions, neither German nor Chilean instructors would find fertile ground in Caracas.[40] Nor did it further the Venezuelan cause when the German envoy to Peru, Wilhelm Count von Hacke, informed Bethmann Hollweg in March 1912 that the Venezuelans had sent seven officers to the French-oriented Escuela Militar in Lima.[41]

Indeed, this action by the Venezuelans greatly annoyed the Germans. General von Heeringen in May 1912 tersely informed the Wilhelmstrasse that he would consider future requests for military instructors only from states "which are of special interest to us militarily and economically," and which "have bound themselves to send their officers for military training only to us and to accept none other than German instructors."[42] Heeringen obviously had the Venezuelan delegation to Peru freshly in mind.

In the meantime, the ubiquitous Chilean Colonel McGill was moving ahead with his military reforms in Caracas. Minister von Prollius optimistically reported to Bethmann Hollweg in July 1912

[39] AA-Bonn, Venezuela 1, vol. 39. Erckert to Bethmann Hollweg, Aug. 24, 1911.
[40] Ibid. Prollius to Bethmann Hollweg, Dec. 4, 1911.
[41] Ibid. Hacke to Bethmann Hollweg, Mar. 26, 1912.
[42] ZStA-Potsdam, Auswärtiges Amt, Abt. IIIb, 29044, p. 10. Heeringen to Foreign Office, May 7, 1912.

that McGill had made progress with the "badly neglected Venezuelan armed forces," and that the Inspector-General of the Venezuelan army, General Félix Galavís, a close friend of President Gómez, was an ardent admirer of the Prussian/German military system. Indeed, in a complete reversal of form, Prollius went on to detail how a newly formed military commission (Escuela de Aplicacíon) had managed to upgrade existing barracks and to establish routine exercise and shooting drills. General conscription was being enacted on the Chilean-German model. New uniforms "on the Prussian model and even the spiked helmet" (*Pickelhaube*) had been adopted at least for the elite 1,500-man Caracas garrison to replace the former "tasteless French uniforms"; German field grey was on order. Although the army was still mainly equipped with ancient Mauser 71/84 rifles, new weapons for its twenty-five battalions would be ordered from Berlin in the near future. And while Caracas for the moment still insisted on sending officers to Peru for instruction, that situation would be drastically altered in 1913, when Venezuelans would be sent to Chile instead. In short, Venezuela now deserved "the right to acquire our sympathetic interest" as reforms were being undertaken "according to the German example and preference given to German purveyors." Prollius requested that Venezuelan officers be permitted to come to Berlin for instruction, and promised that military purchases, "while minimal to date," would be greatly increased in the future. "Since Germany's activity here has been almost exclusively of a commercial nature, any extension of that influence into all other spheres, however small or indirect, would be most welcome."[43]

This abrupt about-face by its envoy in Caracas apparently caught the Foreign Office in Berlin off stride. Without comment, the Wilhelmstrasse in August 1912 reversed its former negative stance on the matter and recommended to the Prussian War Ministry that Prollius' request that Venezuelans be allowed to attend the Kriegsakademie be granted.[44]

Kiderlen-Wächter's request arrived at the War Ministry at a most

---

[43] Ibid., pp. 11-12. Prollius to Bethmann Hollweg, July 26, 1912.
[44] Ibid., p. 13. Foreign Office to Heeringen, Aug. 24, 1912.

unpropitious moment. General von Heeringen was hard-pressed in the Reichstag by the Right, which accused him of dragging his feet on projected armaments increases, and by the Left, which denounced any and all military increases as these would have to be paid for by further rises in indirect taxes on consumer products, for the Reich could levy no direct taxes of its own. Moreover, General Helmuth von Moltke the Younger, Chief of the General Staff, had presented the War Ministry with a demand for an increase in the peacetime strength of the army of about 300,000 men. The request, largely drafted by Colonel Erich Ludendorff, head of the Mobilization and Deployment Division of the General Staff, came at a time when Heeringen was pressing for enhanced production of heavy artillery, military aircraft, and machine-guns. The navy's share of the 831 million Mark budget would amount to three dreadnoughts and two light cruisers. These material demands, coupled with the knowledge that Russia's Great Program of armaments production was scheduled for completion in 1916-1917 as well as the pending French army proposal to lengthen conscription duty by twelve months, weighed heavily upon the War Minister's mind. Venezuela was thus a trivial inconvenience.

General von Heeringen on September 21, 1912, brusquely rejected Kiderlen-Wächter's request. "It is not in the interest of Prussian troops to increase this burden [of military missions] by extending it to a new state when it entails a diminution of various [domestic] military matters in favor of our foreign policy and our industry."[45] In short, Prussian/German military preparedness in Europe came first; foreign affairs and commerce were of secondary importance. Thus instructed, the Foreign Office in October lamely informed Prollius that further Venezuelan requests could be considered only "when other, important reasons for it could be established."[46] For the time being, Berlin could only agree to sell Venezuela what equipment it might require for its military reform program. And in 1913 Caracas formally invited a Chilean military mission to undertake the reform

[45] Ibid., p. 14. Heeringen to Foreign Office, Sept. 21, 1912.
[46] Ibid., pp. 15-16. Foreign Office to Prollius, Oct. 1, 1912.

of its armed forces.[47] Fritz Epstein has argued that Berlin viewed the Chilean mission as a transitional stage, preparing the ground for an eventual German mission; perhaps Colonel McGill could make the "battalion hordes" receptive to sophisticated European military instruction.[48]

But even this might be overly optimistic. General von Heeringen's position of September 1912, of course, was an expression of Germany's worsening military posture on the Continent, and little appeared on the horizon to temper that bleak appraisal. The Prussian War Minister as well as the Chancellor concurred in the need to press every available recruit into service, and to supply the army with the latest weaponry. Foreign states could at best be granted what the German army did not need.

Yet that had not always been the case. The Essen armaments giant Krupp had for much of the nineteenth century dominated—if not monopolized—the South American weapons market, along with lesser firms such as the Deutsche Waffen- und Munitionswerke and the Rheinische Metallwarenfabrik (Ehrhardt). Indeed, in its 1912 centenary publication, Krupp claimed that it was the official purveyor of fifty-two non-German armies, including eighteen in the American hemisphere.[49]

The vast extent of Krupp sales to South American states can be gauged from a highly confidential report that Gustav Krupp von Bohlen und Halbach passed on to Admiral Prince Heinrich, the Emperor's younger brother, who was about to depart on a goodwill tour of several South American republics in February 1914. Krupp estimated that Chile had made about a dozen major purchases in Essen between 1872 and 1912, or a total of 784 cannons; in the first decade of the twentieth century, these artillery purchases had come to 31.4 million Mark. The largest orders had been recorded in 1880 (77 guns), 1895 (102 field and alpine guns), 1898 (166 cannons), 1901 (73 guns), and 1910 (144 cannons and howitzers).[50] The last order

---

[47] John J. Johnson, *The Military and Society in Latin America* (Stanford, 1964), 70.
[48] Epstein, "European Military Influences," 200-01.
[49] Ibid., 223.
[50] AA-Bonn, Preussen 1 Nr 3 Nr 3, Seine Königliche Hoheit der Prinz Heinrich

was placed in the neighborhood of 50-60 million Mark. For Brazil, Krupp listed nineteen orders between 1871 and 1912 for a total of 710 guns; purchases since 1901 alone had totaled 44 million Mark. Past orders had included 108 cannons in 1881, 201 in 1894, 70 in 1908, 60 in 1909, and 108 in 1912; the latter two purchases were for modern 7.5cm rapid-fire artillery.[51] And Argentina had placed sixteen orders with Krupp between 1864 and 1911 for an aggregate of 1,427 guns; again, orders for the first decade of the twentieth century came to 40 million Mark. And while earlier purchases had been relatively modest—66 guns in 1880 and 72 in 1896—Argentina in 1898 bought 351 artillery pieces of various calibers, and in 1909 followed with 457 new 7.5cm rapid-fire field guns. In addition, Buenos Aires had also ordered six torpedo-boats, of which two (*Catamarca* and *Jujuy*) had already been delivered.[52]

Nor had the Reich fared badly in the small-arms trade. In fact, by the 1890s, Mauser rifles from the Deutsche Waffen- und Munitionsfabriken had virtually swept American Remington and French Gras rifles from the field. And Mauser maintained its share of the market. In October 1907, Bolivia bought 5,000 Mauser rifles as well as bayonets and ammunition for 649,200 Mark. Brazil followed in May 1908 with an order for 50,000 rifles and 10,000 carbines from the same firm. Ecuador in August 1909 purchased 25,000 "Rifles 88" from Georg Grotstück in Berlin as well as 10 million rounds of ammunition. And in 1912 Chile acquired a further 50,000 carbines and 30 million rounds of ammunition.[53] Finally, even the smaller German purveyors managed to get a piece of the action: before 1911, Chile had purchased alpine artillery and howitzers from Ehrhardt for

---

von Preussen, vol. 13. Krupp to Lieutenant von Tyszka (for Prince Heinrich), Feb. 26, 1914. Krupp listed sales for the years 1872, 1879, 1880, 1889, 1890, 1894, 1895, 1898, 1901, 1910, 1911, and 1912.

[51] Ibid. Major sales were recorded in 1871, 1872, 1873, 1874, 1875, 1880, 1881, 1882, 1893, 1894, 1896, 1899, 1901, 1904, 1905, 1908, 1909, 1911, and 1912.

[52] Ibid. Again, major sales were listed for 1864, 1867, 1873, 1880, 1883, 1884, 1889, 1890, 1892, 1895, 1896, 1898, 1903, 1909, 1910, and 1911.

[53] ZStA-Potsdam, Auswärtiges Amt, Abt. IIu, 2950-51, Waffenlieferungen deutscher Firmen an fremde Regierungen (Amerika), pp. 12-18, 46, 62, 66, 75.

about 16 million Mark, while Ecuador in November 1911 ordered eight batteries of alpine artillery for 3.5 million Mark from the same firm in Düsseldorf.[54]

Overall, then, German armaments sales to South America were a lucrative undertaking. Gerhard Brunn estimates that Krupp alone sold artillery valued at 115.4 million Mark to Argentina, Brazil, and Chile in the period 1901-1913. It is little wonder that Krupp in 1914 requested not only Prince Heinrich but also Rear Admiral Hubert von Rebeur-Paschwitz, who was about to head a naval tour of South America, to do all in their power to further the firm's cause there. Small-arms sales had also been profitable: by 1913, carbines and pistols constituted Brazil's second most important trade commodity with the Reich, and the armies of Ecuador, Paraguay, and Uruguay were also equipped with Mauser rifles. The only limit to continued sales seemed to be the ability of South American states to pay for them. Krupp, for example, in June 1913 refused Paraguay a modest credit of one million Mark, arguing that outstanding bad debts on the part of several Balkan states and Chinese provinces in the range of 30-40 million Mark had forced the Essen concern to be more circumspect in extending weapons credits.[55]

Of course, German armaments sales to Venezuela paled in comparison with those of the ABC states. One of the first major purchases made by Caracas in December 1891 clearly revealed Berlin's ranking of Venezuela: the Prussian War Ministry agreed to the sale of forty-eight artillery pieces from "existing reserves of horse-drawn artillery," seeing therein an excellent opportunity "to sell this inferior material in a most advantageous manner."[56] In short, Venezuela could purchase whatever the Reich considered to be superfluous and antiquated weaponry.

In the summer of 1893, Count von Kleist, the German minister in Caracas, personally mediated the sale of 30,000 Mausers and 7.5 million rounds of ammunition to Venezuela through the firm of Au-

[54] Ibid., pp. 84-85, 90.

[55] Ibid., pp. 92-94; Brunn, "Deutscher Einfluss," 335.

[56] AA-Bonn, Deutschland 121, Nr 19 secr., Angelegenheiten der Deutschen Armee: Verkauf von Waffen, vol. 2. Prussian War Ministry to Caprivi, Dec. 28, 1891.

gust Schriever in Düsseldorf; the weapons were to come from Saxon army surplus stocks. Schriever felt confident that the Foreign Office would not object to the sale, owing to "presently heavily engaged German commercial interests" in Venezuela. And while the Reich undertook no guarantee concerning the quality of the rifles, Venezuela, for its part, had to agree not to resell the arms to a third party.[57] Kleist's assistance proved decisive, and the minister could report the safe arrival of the first 6,000 Mausers in September 1893; the Saxon government agreed to deliver a further 18,000 guns in the near future.[58] Only the Prussian War Ministry refused to get involved in sales to Venezuela because of an internal decision to leave such surplus sales to private brokers.[59] Nor should it be overlooked that while the Venezuelans were sold the ancient Mauser 71/84 rifles, the obviously more important regimes in Turkey, Spain, Sweden, Brazil, Chile, and Mexico were offered the most recent "Modell 93" weapons.[60] This notwithstanding, Kleist was ecstatic over the sales and even held out the prospect that General Crespo might purchase three warships in Germany in the near future.[61]

In March 1896 Crespo again turned to Germany for 10,000 Mausers. His agent in Hamburg, Moritz Magnus, Jr., assured the Wilhelmstrasse that Crespo was fervently pro-German, and that the planned purchase of the light cruiser *Olga* had foundered, not on lack of goodwill, but on lack of cash.[62] In a parallel appeal for arms to the Prussian War Ministry, Magnus reminded that office of Crespo's past purchase of 30,000 rifles and closely linked the new sales to overall German interests in Venezuela:

[57] Ibid., vol. 2. Schriever to Foreign Office, July 20, 1893.

[58] Ibid. Kleist to Caprivi, Sept. 14, 1893; and ibid., vol. 3, Foreign Office to Venezuelan Consul F. G. Vollmer (Hamburg), July 25, 1893.

[59] Ibid., vol. 2. War Minister Bronsart von Schellendorf to Caprivi, Nov. 22, 1893.

[60] *Die Geschichte der Ludw. Loewe & Co. Actiengesellschaft Berlin: 60 Jahre Edelarbeit 1869 bis 1929* (Berlin, 1930), 33.

[61] AA-Bonn, Venezuela 1, vol. 11. Naval attaché London (Gülich) to Foreign Office, Oct. 24, 1893.

[62] AA-Bonn, Deutschland 121 Nr 19 secr., vol. 3. Magnus to Foreign Office, Mar. 23, 1896.

One could indirectly provide German interests [there] great protection by agreeing to this expressed request [for Mausers] as 85 million [Mark] of German capital is tied down alone in the Great Venezuelan Railroad and as German commerce is most actively conducted in this land.[63]

The War Ministry concurred, for whatever reasons, and in July 1896 approved the sale. At a later date, the Imperial Navy Office agreed to provide Clemens Müller Co. in Hamburg with twenty-eight naval guns as well as ten Krupp rapid-fire 10.5cm cannons for resale to Venezuela.[64] Apparently well pleased with this turn of events, Wilhelm II in 1897 awarded General Crespo the Grand Cross of the Order of the Red Eagle. Count Rex quickly pressed the advantage by selling Crespo 1,000 Mauser 88 cavalry carbines for his "llano shepherds," whom Crespo apparently sought to transform "into a sort of mounted bodyguard" for his retirement years.[65]

The years of revolution and anarchy that accompanied the reign of Cipriano Castro not surprisingly fueled Venezuela's hunger for guns. Already in September 1900, Castro sought to purchase 10,000 Mauser 71/84 rifles from Germany through August Loh Sons in Berlin.[66] At first, the Wilhelmstrasse raised concerns on account of Venezuela's reputation for being a most reluctant payer of outstanding debts, as many Reich firms had recently discovered. Alfred von Hellfeld, Loh's director, countered by suggesting that Castro might sweeten any armaments deal by placing orders in German shipyards for several cruisers.[67] On another level, José Cecilio de Castro, special Venezuelan agent in Germany, hinted to the Foreign Office that Caracas might redirect its armaments purchases either to France or to Austria. De Castro left the Wilhelmstrasse with the impression that

[63] Ibid. Magnus to War Ministry, Mar. 19, 1896.

[64] Ibid. Consulado General de Venezuela en Alemania to Foreign Office, June 1, 1898; Imperial Navy Office to Foreign Office, June 14, 1898.

[65] AA-Bonn, Venezuela 1, vol. 14. Rex to Hohenlohe-Schillingsfürst, Apr. 7, 1897.

[66] AA-Bonn, Deutschland 121, Nr 19 secr., vol. 4. Loh Sons to Foreign Office, Sept. 1, 1900.

[67] Ibid. Foreign Office memoranda of Sept. 3 and 5, 1900.

Germany was at that very moment contemplating "some action against Venezuela"; the special agent apparently got the same message from the Disconto Bank. Any German attempt to force Venezuela to honor her outstanding debt, De Castro warned the Wilhelmstrasse, "would only drive it into the arms of the United States."[68] De Castro's actions prompted the Foreign Office to coordinate its policies with those of the Imperial Navy Office, and in the end both agreed to sell Venezuela the requested 10,000 Mausers; the Admiralty Staff, also consulted on the matter, caustically commented that Castro "would find little pleasure in these fragile repeater rifles."[69] A later attempt by Venezuela to bypass Berlin and to purchase rifles directly from the Saxon government failed because Dresden had none to sell.[70]

Indeed, the German government was well aware of Castro's mounting problems with Colombia in general, and with his attempt to revive *La Gran Colombia* at the expense of Bogotá in particular. The Wilhelmstrasse was thus in danger of becoming embroiled in the Venezuelan president's *folie de grandeur*.[71] It did not have long to wait: on September 10, 1901, Castro asked for 10,000 Mauser rifles and 3 million rounds of ammunition through the firm of Ferd. Kugelmann in Hamburg.[72] Obviously unbeknown to Castro, Colombia had eight days earlier contracted with his bitter enemy, the Berlin Disconto Bank, for an equal number of rifles from the Deutsche Waffen- und Munitionsfabriken. And while Venezuela would again be offered the antiquated Mauser 71/84 rifles, Colombia would instead get the latest Mausers, originally intended for sale to the Boers in South Africa.[73] The Wilhelmstrasse initially hoped to escape any

[68] Ibid. Foreign Office memorandum of Sept. 8, 1900.

[69] Ibid., memorandum dated Sept. 11, 1900.

[70] SHStA-Dresden, Gesandschaft Berlin Nr 1130, Waffen Ausfuhr. Saxon Legation Berlin to Saxon War Ministry, Aug. 20, 1901.

[71] See Miriam Hood, *Gunboat Diplomacy 1895-1905: Great Power Pressure in Venezuela* (London, 1983), 159ff., for the border dispute between Colombia and Venezuela, which she dates back to 1833.

[72] AA-Bonn, Deutschland 121, Nr 19 secr., vol. 5. Kugelmann to Foreign Office, Sept. 10, 1901.

[73] Ibid., vol. 5. Foreign Office memorandum dated Sept. 3, 1901, based upon in-

possible conflict of interest by agreeing on September 16 to sell weapons to *both* sides so long as no formal state of war existed between Caracas and Bogotá.[74] It was not to be. Instead, the Colombian sale would quickly develop into an international *cause célèbre*.

It was an open secret that Colombia backed the *Libertadora* insurgency of General Manuel Antonio Matos, an erstwhile Castro backer, and that the Castro forces had received an almost total defeat near Ríohacha late in 1901. Not surprisingly, Foreign Secretary Oswald Baron von Richthofen became suspicious of arms sales to Colombia, and as early as April 1902 inquired in Brussels and London whether "foreign capital had a hand in the matter."[75] The German ambassador to Brussels, Nicolas Count von Wallwitz, quickly reported that the Colombian vessel *Ban Righ*, brazenly renamed the *Libertador*, had been loaded with 1,000 cases of rifles and 4,000 cases of ammunition, and that it was bound for General Matos, son-in-law of former President Guzmán Blanco. Moreover, Colombian consuls in Brussels and London had provided the ship with bogus registry papers—as well as with one case of French perfume and forty-one cases of French wine for the arduous cross-Atlantic trip.[76] On April 11, the Wilhelmstrasse received official confirmation from its naval attaché in London, Carl von Coerper, that the *Ban Righ* was indeed Colombian and bound for Matos.[77] Yet there was nothing that the Germans could do at this late date: the *Ban Righ* eventually steamed in Caribbean waters without unloading its arms for Matos, and was finally repurchased from Matos by Colonel Rafael Reyes of Colombia for $75,000. In the opinion of the German minister in Caracas, Alfred Pelldram, the *Ban Righ* adventure had been funded by a United States firm, Bermudez Asphalt, in the hope that the weapons would help tumble Castro from power.[78] In the meantime, the

---

formation received from Alexis Riese, Director-General of the Deutsche Waffen- und Munitionsfabriken.

[74] Ibid. Foreign Office to War Ministry, Sept. 16, 1901.

[75] AA-Bonn, Venezuela 1, vol. 19. Richthofen's inquiry is dated Apr. 4, 1902.

[76] Ibid. Wallwitz to Bülow, Apr. 8, 1902.

[77] Ibid. Coerper to Tirpitz, Apr. 11, 1902.

[78] Ibid., vol. 26. Pelldram to Bülow, Mar. 30, 1904.

bloody Matos insurgency continued unabated, and the country lost about 12,000 lives in more than 210 pitched battles.

Berlin took note of Castro's miserable plight and for reasons not entirely clear decided that its best course was to assist the *Andino* against the rebels. Giesbert von Pilgrim-Baltazzi, the acting German minister in Caracas, in May and again in June 1902 warned the Reich that the Matos insurgency was daily growing and that Colombia was about to invade the country. On both occasions, Pilgrim-Baltazzi pleaded with the Foreign Office to expedite arms shipments to Castro.[79] And apparently with success: 7,000 Mausers arrived for Castro in July 1902, and another 15,000 in November 1903.[80] That same fall, August Loh Sons managed to wheedle another 5,000 Mauser 71/84 rifles out of the Wilhelmstrasse for Castro.[81]

The *Andino* apparently appreciated the lessons he learned from the Anglo-German-Italian naval blockade of 1902-1903, for in April 1904 he set out to fortify his major ports. In addition to creating a Navy Shooting School on the old troopship *Zamora*, Castro purchased eight French Schneider-Canet coastal defense guns for La Guayra and Puerto Cabello, and engaged as many French instructors to train the Venezuelans in handling the 15cm guns.[82] Unfortunately, the Venezuelans were unable properly to mount the guns or to sight them, and in the absence of expert local artificers not a single practice round could be fired throughout the summer of 1904. In the end, Castro became disappointed with the French, as only one of the promised eight instructors ever arrived in Venezuela.[83]

Therefore, it is not surprising that Castro turned once again to Germany for his weapons needs. Minister Pelldram estimated that in 1904 alone Germany had sold 30,000 rifles and 15 million rounds of

[79] Ibid., vol. 20. Pilgrim-Baltazzi to Bülow, May 31, 1902; and AA-Bonn, Deutschland 121 Nr 19 secr., vol. 5. Pilgrim-Baltazzi to Bülow, June 21, 1906.

[80] AA-Bonn, Venezuela 1, vol. 21. Count von Oriola of *Gazelle* to Wilhelm II, Aug. 28, 1902; ibid., vol. 25. Pelldram to Bülow, Dec. 3, 1903.

[81] AA-Bonn, Deutschland 121, Nr 19 secr., vol. 5. Loh Sons to Foreign Office, Aug. 27, 1903, and Foreign Office to Loh Sons, Aug. 29, 1903.

[82] AA-Bonn, Venezuela 1, vol. 26. Pelldram to Bülow, Apr. 2 and 14, 1904.

[83] Ibid., vol. 27. Pelldram to Bülow, Sept. 15 and Nov. 5, 1904.

ammunition to Venezuela.[84] In March 1906 Kugelmann in Hamburg arranged the sale of another 5,000 Mausers to Castro.[85] And in August 1908 Georg Grotstück in Berlin sought to sell Castro several older warships, none of them of German make; however, in return for assistance in this matter, Castro hinted not only at the possible purchase of two German cruisers, but also at lucrative future contracts for modern artillery guns and ships. The matter once more came to nought: the Foreign Office in October informed Navy Secretary Admiral Alfred von Tirpitz that it considered German ship sales to Castro "impractical" because of the President's continuing troubles with the United States and the Netherlands over outstanding debts.[86] In other words, Berlin was not interested in coming between Castro and his overseas creditors so soon after the international blockade of 1902-1903.

There was a "cloak-and-dagger" postscript to the issue of German armaments sales to Venezuela that would have made Inspector Clouseau proud. Baron von Seckendorff informed Chancellor von Bülow in November 1908 that President Castro was on his way to Berlin to be treated for an abscess on his kidneys by Dr. James A. Israel.[87] Rumors, fueled by the London press, abounded at once in Caracas that Castro had been received by a military guard of honor and that a military band had saluted him with the Venezuelan national anthem. Moreover, wags in Caracas had it—again from "reliable sources" in the London press—that Castro had already purchased 50,000 rifles, Krupp artillery, six warships, and engaged military instructors for a pending return to Venezuela.[88] And the United States government apparently let it be known that it would prefer that

[84] Ibid. Pelldram to Bülow, July 22, 1904.

[85] AA-Bonn, Deutschland 121 Nr 19 secr., vol. 6. Kugelmann to Prussian War Ministry, Mar. 15, 1906.

[86] AA-Bonn, Venezuela 1, vol. 34. Minister von Seckendorff to Bülow, Aug. 21, 1908; Schoen to Tirpitz, Sept. 15, 1908.

[87] Ibid., vol. 35. Seckendorff to Bülow, Nov. 19, 1908.

[88] Ibid. Seckendorff to Foreign Office, Dec. 18 and 24, 1908. The Foreign Office noted "base lies" and "infamous calumny" on the reports. State Secretary von Schoen on Dec. 30, 1908, cabled Seckendorff that Castro had "attempted nothing political, had purchased neither rifles nor cannons, nor warships, nor instructors." Ibid., vol. 35.

Berlin ignore Castro's presence—a request bitterly rejected by the Wilhelmstrasse on account of Washington's erstwhile support of Castro in 1902-1903 during the blockade.[89] The *Andino*, for his part, settled comfortably into the thirty-four-room Princess Suite at the Hotel Esplanade and, according to the *Berliner Tageblatt*, a steady diet of 60-80 Mark wines and 120 Mark cognacs.[90] But official Berlin kept its distance and advised Wilhelm II not to receive Castro.[91] General Juan Vicente Gómez seized the opportunity to take over the government in Caracas, and requested that the Germans place Castro under constant police surveillance.[92]

Castro recovered from the renal operation and from 1909 to 1913 set out on an international odyssey that took him from Dresden to Bordeaux, from Martinique to Spain, and from France to Ellis Island, New York. All the while, rumors concerning a possible *castrista* restoration abounded. Castro's alleged agents in Germany were constantly under surveillance. Minister Prollius cabled Chancellor von Bethmann Hollweg from Caracas in March 1911 that "the megalomaniacal tyrant" Castro had hooked up with Tello Mendoza, his brother Carmelo, and General Manuel Hernandez (*El Mocho*) in Hamburg in order to purchase guns and ships for a triumphant return.[93] And while the *Neue Hamburger Zeitung* carried the banner headline, "Castro The Flying Dutchman," that city's secret police found no evidence that Castro had bought either weapons or ships.[94]

[89] Ibid., vol. 35. State Secretary von Schoen to Ambassador von Sternburg (Washington), Dec. 22, 1908. "We have not forgotten that America stood beside Castro when we had legitimate complaints against him."

[90] *Berliner Tageblatt*, No. 10, Feb. 8, 1909.

[91] AA-Bonn, Venezuela 1, vol. 35. General von Lyncker to State Secretary von Schoen, Dec. 15, 1908. The heads of the Emperor's Military Cabinet, Household, and Foreign Office all concurred that a formal reception would "accord too much honor" to Castro.

[92] SHStA-Dresden, Aussenministerium Nr 2039, Politische Verhältnisse in Venezuela, p. 5. Christian Count Vitzthum von Eckstädt to Karl Adolf Count von Hohenthal und Bergen (Dresden), Feb. 22, 1909.

[93] ZStA-Merseburg, Kgl. Pr. Gesandschaft Hamburg Nr 344, Mittel- und Südamerika 1911-1918, pp. 10-11. Prollius to Bethmann Hollweg, Mar. 16, 1911.

[94] Ibid., p. 5. Lord Mayor Burchard to Foreign Office, Jan. 7, 1911; *Neue Hamburger Zeitung*, June 18, 1911.

In Dresden, rumors spread that Castro had secretly shipped guns to his supporters in Colombia under the guise of "sewing machines."[95] Renewed police activity revealed that the *Andino* had contacted a former German merchant active in Venezuela, Wilhelm Langelott, with the promise that should he be "reelected" president, he would offer the Reich a coaling station in Venezuela.[96] As late as November 1913, German agents in Hamburg reported that Castro had shipped 120 cases of "copper nails," that is, bullets, to his men in Colombia.[97] And at the very moment that Castro was in the United States, detained on Ellis Island, it was rumored in Berlin that H. Mahillon of Paris, alias "Monsier Spirkel," was secretly buying up more than 4,000 Mauser rifles for Castro.[98] Obviously, Cipriano Castro was good copy, and journalists simply would not let the rumor mills be shut down.

General Gómez apparently was satisfied with German assurances that these rumors were without basis, for in July 1914 he welcomed Minister Prollius' help in bringing an artillery salesman from the Rheinische Metallwaren- und Maschinenfabrik (Ehrhardt) to La Guayra.[99] Little came of the mission as Germany that month faced much more pressing problems in Europe. The outbreak of the Great War thus ended a chapter in German armaments sales and military missions to South America.

One final aspect of "the military advisors' game" is the indisputable link between the instructors and weapons sales. For the East German Marxist school of historians on South America, formerly led by Friedrich Katz and his pupils Jürgen Hell, Manfred Scharbius,

[95] SHStA-Dresden, Aussenministerium Nr 4702, Waffen- und Munitionsverkauf ins Ausland 1895-1928, p. 142. Saxon government to Foreign Office (Berlin), May 16, 1913.

[96] Ibid. Wilhelm Langelott's statement to Dresden police, July 12, 1913.

[97] Ibid., p. 168. Memorandum of Dresden Hauptzollamt, Nov. 4, 1913. Langelott described Castro as being "full of mistrust, vindictive and easily angered" on account of his "Indian origins." Ibid., p. 156.

[98] AA-Bonn, Deutschland 121, Nr 19, secr., vol. 8. Venezuelan Embassy to Foreign Office, Dec. 23, 1912; ibid., vol. 9. Deutsche Waffen- und Munitionsfabriken to Foreign Office, Jan. 3, 1913.

[99] AA-Bonn, Venezuela 1, vol. 40. Rheinische Metallwaren- und Maschinenfabrik to Foreign Office, July 6, 1914; Foreign Office to Prollius, July 17, 1914.

Ingrid Uhlich, and Klaus Kannapin, the role of German instructors from Körner to Kundt to Arent clinches the argument that Imperial Germany flagrantly exploited South American states for its armaments industry. Gerhard Brunn of West Germany basically agrees, arguing that the instructors played a decisive role at least in the ABC states in this regard.[100]

Indeed, the Wilhelmstrasse in an undated position paper, most likely penned in 1910, was keenly aware of the intimate connection between military advisors and armaments sales. The Foreign Office divided South American states into two categories: those, like Mexico and Peru, which could count upon a reliable police to quell domestic unrest; and those, like Argentina and Chile, which could undertake offensive military operations with their armies. What united all was a common fear of the United States and its aggressive policy in South America.[101] The resulting desire to seek military instructors in Europe necessarily narrowed the field to France and Germany; likewise, weapons purchases could be placed primarily with Schneider-Creusot or Krupp. The Wilhelmstrasse argued, on the one hand, that both the German victory over France in 1870-1871 and the "bad experiences" of South American states with French instructors had given the Reich the edge in this field; armaments sales, on the other hand, continued to undergo vicious competition, especially after 1884, when France repealed its prohibition on foreign weapons sales. "The fact that Germany by and large won this competition as well is attributable first and foremost to German instructors." The Wilhelmstrasse credited military instructors with the extensive Chilean artillery order of 1909 encompassing 200 cannons valued at 20 million Mark, and acknowledged that German officers had been in-

[100] Brunn, "Deutscher Einfluss," 330-34. Willi A. Boelcke, *Krupp und die Hohenzollern in Dokumenten: Krupp-Korrespondenz mit Kaisern, Kabinettschefs und Ministern 1850-1918* (Frankfurt, 1970), 184, lists the following Krupp ties to official Berlin: Chancellor von Bülow's brother for many years headed Krupp's Berlin office; a brother of the Prussian Minister of Public Works was employed as an engineer at Krupp-Essen; and the brother of the general responsible for armaments debates in the Reichstag in 1913 sat on Krupp's board of directors.

[101] AA-Bonn, Deutschland 121, Nr 19 secr., vol. 7. Foreign Office paper of 1910 (date based on internal evidence).

strumental in persuading the Santiago regime not to hold a planned competition between Krupp and Schneider-Creusot. In a similar manner, German instructors had been decisive between 1907 and 1909 in persuading Argentina to order 360 cannons valued at 35 million Mark from Krupp as well as 100,000 Mauser rifles from the Deutsche Waffen- und Munitionsfabriken. Brazil, which the Foreign Office saw engaged in a deadly duel with Argentina "for supremacy in South America," ordered 7 million Mark artillery and 3.5 million Mark rifles from Germany mainly because the incoming President, Hermes da Fonseca, was an admirer of German military instructors. Uruguay, Paraguay, and Bolivia were about to follow the example of the ABC states; Peru alone remained solidly in the French camp. Finally, the Foreign Office noted that these developments were but part of a much larger picture:

> The fact that as many South American states as possible employ German officers as instructors is of great importance not only for our armaments industry, but also for the strengthening of *Deutschtum* and general commercial relations in these lands. Without question, Germany will gain an advantage in commercial competition in South America if German influence can take root there as a result of our officers, [of] purchases of our armaments, and adoption of our military regulations.

This classic expression of imperialism in the military sphere unfortunately did not conform to reality. Quite apart from German fears that officers sent to South America would be tainted by the "low social niveau" of their counterparts there, General von Einem's decision of 1908 that the Reich simply could spare no overseas instructors at a time when it was hard-pressed by foreign powers on the Continent laid bare the physical limitations of "the advisors' game." This position was confirmed in 1910 by the head of the Foreign Office, Baron von Schoen, and again later that same year by General von Heeringen, the new chief of the Prussian War Ministry. Indeed, Heeringen's terse comment two years later, that Germany could spare instructors only for states "which are of special interest to us militarily and economically," once more underlined the limitations placed upon military advisors. And Krupp's refusal in 1913 to ex-

tend a modest credit of one million Mark to Paraguay spoke little of
the company's commitment to "the strengthening of *Deutschtum*" in
South America as envisaged by the Wilhelmstrasse. Company profits rather than patriotism seemed paramount in Essen. In short, the
very real physical limits placed upon German "imperialists" both in
the War Ministry and in private industry by the eve of the First World
War stood at odds with the classic model of "the military advisors'
game."[102]

[102] I put forth such a tenative conclusion in an earlier piece, "German Imperialism
and South America before the First World War: The Venezuelan Case 1902/03," in
Russland-Deutschland-Amerika: Festschrift für Fritz T. Epstein zum 80. Geburtstag
(Wiesbaden, 1978), 125-26.

CHAPTER V

GERMANY, VENEZUELA, AND THE PANAMA CANAL: THE ELUSIVE QUEST FOR A GERMAN NAVAL BASE IN SOUTH AMERICA

A major aspect of classic imperialism is the penetration of foreign markets by European merchants and the concomitant need to "protect" that trade with the armed might of the mother country. In the case of South America, it was often a matter of the flag following trade, of naval protection for men and money following commerce only at a later date. Indeed, Spain had formally prohibited European competition in its South American empire, but Hanseatic merchants, working through Cadiz, the main clearing house in Spain for goods bound for the New World, managed to operate illicitly alongside their fellow English "smugglers." At times, *Hansa* merchants worked hand-in-glove with the British, and soon developed their own secret trade routes directly from Central Europe to South America. As a result, Silesian linen exports to South America, for example, more than doubled to nearly 10 million Thaler in the two decades prior to 1800. In time, *Hansa* merchants flagrantly ignored the Spanish trade prohibition and opened direct routes to South America. After the Wars of Independence, these merchants at first acted as junior partners of the British, but the new South American states quickly spied a chance to play one European power off against another by inviting Hamburg houses, especially, to found consulates in Bahia, Rio de Janeiro, Mexico, Port-au-Prince, Montevideo, Lima, and Buenos Aires by the 1820s and 1830s.[1] Formal trade

---

[1] See Ingrid Uhlich, "Die Politik des deutschen Kaiserreiches und der Grossmächte in Peru von 1871 bis zum Beginn des 1. Weltkrieges" (diss., East Berlin, 1971), 7-9.

treaties were concluded by Hamburg with Brazil in 1827, with Mexico in 1832, with Venezuela in 1837, and with Ecuador in 1842. By the mid-1840s, there were no less than ninety-eight German firms active in the trade with South America, of whom sixty-seven belonged to the Hanseatic cities. And as early as 1849, Hamburg's consul in Venezuela had decried the lack of naval power, "the only means by which one can attain the respect of the local government and populace."[2]

Yet, as previously noted, Hanseatic traders managed by and large to assimilate with the indigenous populations and to get along with the various sorts of South American rulers. The fact that the *Hanseaten* lacked a unified nation obviously contributed to the absence of any "gunboat diplomacy" on their part. But even German unification in 1871 did not alter this state of affairs as Chancellor Otto von Bismarck was not about to expend either men or money on building a merchant—much less a naval—fleet. It was only the advent of Wilhelm II's ascension to power in 1888 and the appointments of Bernhard von Bülow to the Foreign Office and Alfred von Tirpitz to the Navy Office a decade later that a new era of *Weltpolitik*, or global strategy, was ushered in. The new leaders trumpeted the need to show the flag in order to "protect" the Reich nationals and their investments in South America as well as to flaunt their new-found power, both economic and naval, before established and potential trading partners. Two technological developments brought a great urgency to the matter of a German naval base in South American waters off Venezuela by the turn of the century: the rush to lay the world's first submarine cable connecting the homeland with the far world, and the determination of the United States to complete the isthmian canal across Panama, the rights to which Washington acquired in 1903 by less than savory means.

It therefore became imperative for planners in Berlin to plant the German flag somewhere in the Caribbean basin. Such a *Stützpunkt* could serve as an anchor in the projected German cable network,

[2] Percy Ernst Schramm, *Deutschland und Übersee: Der Deutsche Handel mit den anderen Kontinenten, insbesondere Afrika, von Karl V. bis zu Bismarck* (Braunschweig/Berlin/Hamburg/Kiel, 1950), 54-55, 418.

could provide a coaling station for both merchant and naval vessels, and could serve as a center from which to harass the eastern terminus of the canal, when completed, in case of war. For a matrix of reasons, ranging from national prestige to maritime strategy, Berlin became interested in the western American hemisphere in general and in Venezuela in particular, owing to its geographical location.

Venezuela did not get off on good footing with the new German state. The schooners *Franz* and *Marie Sophie* of the nascent North German Confederation were boarded and detained at Maracaibo in 1869, and the German envoy at Caracas, Werner von Bergen, at once demanded a formal apology in the form of a twenty-one-gun salute, reparations to the parties concerned, and a special customs houses reserve of fifteen percent to assure such payments. To back these demands, Werner persuaded Berlin to assemble a small naval squadron consisting of the vessels *Arcona*, *Meteor*, and *Niobe* under Lieutenant Eduard von Knorr off Venezuela. Caracas agreed to these terms in March 1870, and a triumphant Werner reminded his government that the appearance of German warships was "of discernible value for our general political relations" with Venezuela.[3]

This incident remained an isolated case for as long as Bismarck ruled in Berlin. The Iron Chancellor desired no conflict either with the United States or with Great Britain on the high seas; South America hardly troubled him at all. German diplomats quickly stepped into line. In April 1872, the German Chargé d'affaires in Caracas, Gülich, warned against showing the flag too often, and bravely informed the Foreign Office: "My basic attitude concerning the German Reich's relationship to Venezuela can be summed up in the words: il ne faut pas compromettre l'armée pour une sentinelle perdue."[4] Two years later, when the Venezuelan President, Antonio Guzmán Blanco, offered Max Baron von der Goltz of the *Augusta* a coaling station off Curaçao "in order to have a friendlier neighbor

[3] Auswärtiges Amt Bonn (hereafter AA), Venezuela I.C. 61, Schriftwechsel mit der Kaiserl. Minister-Residentur zu Caracas sowie mit anderen Missionen und fremden Kabinetten über die inneren Zustände und Verhältnisse Venezuelas 1869-1875, vol. 1. Foreign Office memorandum of May 29, 1870; and Foreign Office to Wilhelm I, May 30, 1870.

[4] Ibid., vol. 1. Gülich to Foreign Office, Apr. 18, 1872.

there," and when the Admiralty in Berlin displayed the slightest interest in the matter, Bismarck seized the opportunity to lecture his colleagues that all such offers were to be "decisively rejected," now as before.[5] And when Guzmán Blanco repeated the offer to Erwin Stammann, the new German minister in Caracas, the envoy was similarly instructed "firmly to reject all such offers."[6]

Incredibly, the Venezuelan president continued to press the matter. In May 1875, Guzmán Blanco asked Stammann again whether Germany might not wish to seize Curaçao; "one need not concern oneself with the Monroe Doctrine," he flippantly assured Stammann. The Venezuelan leader even resorted to flattery, confiding to the envoy "that in the matter of the *Kulturkampf*" against the Catholic Church and the Center Party in Germany, "I stand completely on the side of Prince Bismarck as I also want to liberate my country from the Roman bonds."[7] And as late as 1879, in the wake of yet another rumor concerning a possible German purchase of Curaçao, this one emanating from Paris, Friedrich Baron von Holstein, the *éminence grise* of the Wilhelmstrasse in Berlin, informed the Reich's envoys in Caracas and Paris that Germany "very unequivocally" rejected all such offers of "colonies in America." Holstein especially informed the representative to France, Chlodwig Prince zu Hohenlohe-Schillingsfürst, "that a misunderstanding *mola fides* on the part of Venezuela today is unthinkable." The baron closed his epistle to Paris with a stern reminder "that we here are not conducting colonial policies, and especially desire no acquisitions in America."[8] Clearer diplomatic language is hardly imaginable. Indeed, the studied cau-

[5] Ibid., vol. 1. Goltz to Admiralty, Nov. 22, 1874; and ibid., vol. 2. Foreign Office to Admiralty, Jan. 24, 1875.

[6] Zentrales Staatsarchiv Potsdam (hereafter ZStA), Auswärtiges Amt, Abt. II, Die Handels- und Schiffahrtsverhältnisse mit Venezuela, vol. 5a, p. 127. Foreign Office to Admiralty, Jan. 24, 1875.

[7] AA-Bonn, Venezuela, I.C. 61, vol. 2. Stammann to Bülow (Foreign Office), May 14, 1875. The Foreign Office simply passed Guzmán's offer on to the Dutch government on Jan. 8, 1877. ZStA-Potsdam, Auswärtiges Amt, Abt. II, Handel . . . mit Venezuela, vol. 9.

[8] AA-Bonn, Venezuela 1, Allgemeine Angelegenheiten Venezuelas, vol. 1. Holstein to Hohenlohe-Schillingsfürst, Apr. 8, 1879; see also Foreign Office to Stammann, Feb. 12 and Aug. 31, 1874.

tion of the Germans reached such heights that in February 1880 the commander of a German schoolship (Lieutenant Commander Matthesen) downright refused to come to the assistance of German nationals who claimed to be endangered by a local rebellion on the Orinoco River; fearing that such action might be misconstrued as interference in Venezuelan domestic matters, the officer lamely argued that "my primary mission is to train my sea cadets."[9]

The cautionary German position in matters concerning South America underwent a basic transformation with the coronation of Wilhelm II in 1888 and the "dropping of the pilot," Bismarck, two years later. The new ruler routinely ordered German warships to South America in order to show the flag in the hope that such action might enhance the international reputation of his "boys in blue,"[10] and "strengthen the prestige of German nationals"[11] overseas. On a more practical level, such visits were also used to baptize the offspring of German nationals and to register their elder sons for possible induction into one of the various German federal armies. This feverish activity regularly brought German warships to Puerto Cabello and La Guayra throughout the decade of the 1890s: the *Nixe* in 1890-1891, *Moltke* in 1891, *Gneisenau* in 1892-1893, and *Arcona* in 1891, *Nixe*, *Stosch* and *Stein* in 1893-1894, *Stosch* and *Moltke* in 1894-1895, *Gneisenau* in 1897, and *Moltke* again in 1899.[12] Venezuela thus became a principal training ground for future German admirals.

At the other end of South America, the Chilean civil war, in which the German military instructor Emil Körner in 1891 openly fought on the side of the insurgent Congressionalists, reminded the Reich

[9] ZStA-Potsdam, Auswärtiges Amt, Abt. II, Handel . . . mit Venezuela, vol. 11, pp. 3, 5. Matthesen to Foreign Office, Feb. 29 and Mar. 2, 1880. The Admiralty on Apr. 8, 1880, formally apologized to the Foreign Office for Matthesen's lack of action. Ibid., vol. 11, p. 28.

[10] ZStA-Potsdam, Auswärtiges Amt, Abt. IIs, Entsendung deutscher Kriegsschiffe Nr 22431, pp. 100-01. The Emperor's marginal comments on a report from the German Embassy in Portugal to Chancellor von Caprivi, Apr. 6, 1891.

[11] ZStA-Potsdam, Auswärtiges Amt, Abt. Ib, Reisen Kaiserlicher Kriegsschiffe, p. 6. Goltz to Captain von Erhardt, Mar. 18, 1891.

[12] ZStA-Potsdam, Auswärtiges Amt, Abt. IIs, Entsendung deutscher Kriegsschiffe Nr 22447, pp. 126-28.

all too painfully that it did not yet possess a maritime force able to protect its nationals. The destruction of two German ships in Chilean waters prompted Hamburg merchants to petition Berlin for the stationing of German warships on that continent in order to correct the present "depressing and shameful impression" of weakness. In March 1891, the *Hamburgischer-Korrespondent* publicly demanded "a South American station for our fleet." And while Chancery, Navy Office, High Command, and Foreign Office bickered over the details and funding involved in sending a squadron of ships to Chile, Wilhelm II settled the matter in April by ordering the Reich's Far East Squadron (*Leipzig, Alexandrine, Sophie*) to steam to Valparaiso. It is interesting to note that Wilhelm undertook this drastic action mainly for reasons of international prestige; he informed Chancellor Leo von Caprivi that he was sending the warships "because in addition to England and America, even France is represented there by a squadron."[13] Appearances were evidently as important as substance. The matter of a permanent naval station in South American waters eventually foundered, owing to lack of funds. A plan by Gustav Baron von Senden-Bibran, head of the Navy Cabinet, to keep six cruisers constantly circling the globe as mobile troubleshooters was caustically dismissed by Alfred von Kiderlen-Wächter of the Foreign Office as rendering Germany "incapable of resistance and *à la merci* of foreign intrigues, especially those of the Americans."[14]

The need to protect German nationals in South America grew in quantum leaps and gave authorities in Berlin numerous headaches. Late in 1892, for example, the *Frankfurter Zeitung* took the government to task for its inability to protect the 100 German nationals in Puerto Cabello during a local revolt on August 22, 23. The paper

---

[13] Ibid., Nr 22430, pp. 91-96. Goltz to Marschall von Bieberstein, Feb. 17, 1891. The request by Hamburg merchants is in ibid., Nr 22430, pp. 97-98, dated Feb. 16; while the Hamburg newspaper report is in ibid., Nr 22431, p. 46; and Wilhelm II to Chancellor von Caprivi, Apr. 4, 1891, ibid., Nr 22431, pp. 80-81. See also Alfred Vagts, *Deutschland und die Vereinigten Staaten in der Weltpolitik* (New York, 1935), II, 1649; Ernst Baasch, *Die Handelskammer zu Hamburg 1665-1915* (Hamburg, 1915), II, 370-71; and Ekkehard Böhm, *Überseehandel und Flottenbau: Hanseatische Kaufmannschaft und deutsche Seerüstung 1879-1902* (Düsseldorf, 1972), 38-46.

[14] ZStA-Potsdam, Auswärtiges Amt, Abt. IIs, Nr 22432, p. 186. Kiderlen-Wächter to Foreign Office, July 28, 1891.

informed its readers that the Reich nationals had to turn to French and Spanish ships for succor, and that the German vessel *Arcona* did not arrive until August 29, "thus precisely 6 days too late." It found the incident to be "a great moral defeat for the Germans" of Venezuela.[15] Perhaps with this chastisement in mind, Berlin acted with alacrity in December 1893, when the Great Venezuelan Railroad requested the presence of two warships, *Stein* and *Stosch*, for its planned opening of tracks in February 1894.[16] That same winter, the ships *Arcona* and *Alexandrine* protected German nationals and trade off the coast of Brazil.

German naval commanders stationed in South America over the years bombarded Berlin with suggestions for seizing naval bases such as the Ilha d'Agua in the Bay of Rio de Janeiro, Coiba and Affnera southwest of Panama, the Corn Islands off Nicaragua, and Gorgona Island off Colombia, to name but a few. Reich authorities, in turn, became alarmed at the growing number of these "suggestions," and in 1891 and again in 1896 had to negotiate the procedure for handling these among Navy Office, Foreign Office, and Chancery.[17] Moreover, lack of available ships—especially given Tirpitz's later obsession with deep-draft battleships that were of little use off South American ports—grew acute. In November 1895, Adolph Woermann, Germany's second most prominent shipowner after Albert Ballin, inquired at the Chancery in his official capacity as head of the Union of Hamburg Shipowners concerning the accuracy of recent newspaper reports that Germany was about to establish a permanent naval base in South America. Woermann enthusiastically endorsed such a project and reminded Chancellor zu Hohenlohe-Schillingsfürst of past naval impotence during the Chilean troubles in 1891 and of Hamburg's petition for warships in South American waters.

[15] *Frankfurter Zeitung*, Nr 277, Oct. 3, 1892.

[16] ZStA-Potsdam, Auswärtiges Amt, Abt. II, Handel . . . mit Venezuela, vol. 18, pp. 33-35. Kleist to Caprivi, Dec. 9, 1893, with the Emperor's approval noted in the margin. In the end, the Reich could spare only the *Stein*. Ibid., vol. 18, pp. 39-40, Goltz to Marschall von Bieberstein, Jan. 13, 1894.

[17] ZStA-Potsdam, Auswärtiges Amt, Abt. IIs, Entsendung deutscher Kriegsschiffe Nr 22467, pp. 28, 30-31. Memoranda by Marschall von Bieberstein, Jan. 29, 1891, and Chancellor zu Hohenlohe-Schillingsfürst, May 23, 1896.

Woermann then lectured the Chancellor on Hamburg's growing trade with Central and South America—one-sixth of all exports, or 218 of 1,214 million Mark, and one-fourth of all imports, or 415 of 1,566 million Mark—and specifically pointed out that Germans had built the Great Venezuelan Railroad and owned vast tracts of Venezuelan land. German prestige would suffer greatly, however, if it became known that the Reich was unable to finance a permanent naval presence in these waters. Finally, Woermann noted that of the 3,084 roundtrip sailings from Hamburg in 1893, Central and South America had accounted for 2,467 (or eighty percent) of these. He concluded his report by formally requesting a constant German naval presence in South American waters.[18]

The Foreign Office passed Woermann's request on to Admiral Friedrich von Hollmann with the comment "utterly desirable." But Eduard von Knorr, the navy's commanding admiral, in February 1896 informed the Wilhelmstrasse that the navy lacked the personnel to staff a cruiser in South American waters, that no officers or men could be spared for such from the Home Fleet, and that no ships could be detached from the Far East Squadron for the American hemisphere.[19]

This nagging lack of men and ships surfaced again in October 1897 in the wake of unrest in Guatemala that threatened German nationals. Wilhelm II angrily cancelled the proposed dispatch of a schoolship there as "a political or military action" because such a vessel could not hope to "press" German demands energetically and forcefully. "It is imperative that the showing of the flag is meant in earnest." The monarch took the opportunity to blame Germany's present "embarrassment and shame" over the lack of sufficient overseas cruisers on the Reichstag.[20] And when the Great Venezuelan Railroad in December 1897 requested two German warships in order

---

[18] Ibid., Nr 22471, pp. 62-64. Woermann to Chancellor zu Hohenlohe-Schillingsfürst, Nov. 15, 1895.

[19] Ibid., Nr 22447, pp. 66-67. Foreign Office to Admiral von Hollmann, Dec. 13, 1895; ibid., pp. 91-92, Knorr to Foreign Office, Feb. 7, 1896.

[20] Ibid., Nr 22451, p. 97. Prince zu Eulenburg to Chancellor zu Hohenlohe-Schillingsfürst, Oct. 1, 1897.

to impress Caracas with the need to meet its financial obligations under the auspices of a general loan of 1896, Admiral von Knorr could offer only the 1,600-ton unprotected cruiser *Geier*.[21] Reality was once more at odds with desire.

German diplomats overseas continued to request warships at an alarming rate. This practice reached its ludicrous apex in December 1897, when the German minister in Haiti asked Berlin for two warships in order to pressure President Simon Sam into reversing the conviction of an alleged German national, Emil Lüders, on charges of having accosted a Haitian policeman. Count Schwerin demanded an official apology as well as an indemnity of $30,000 to offset Lüders' original fine of $500. The ships *Stein* and *Charlotte* duly accomplished their task off Port-au-Prince on December 6, and the German acting minister in Caracas, Adolf von Prollius, informed Chancellor zu Hohenlohe-Schillingsfürst that this "energetic action" had made a "great impression" in Venezuela. His chief, Arthur Count von Rex, in February 1898 celebrated the arrival of the *Geier* at La Guayra, even though he admitted that there existed absolutely no need whatsoever for the ship's presence.[22]

The bizarre Haitian incident notwithstanding, German diplomats in South America on every occasion continued to lament the lack of a permanent naval presence there. A permanent base, so the argument ran, alone could guarantee the timely arrival of warships in a hemisphere constantly racked by civil disturbances and rebellions. It found a sympathetic listener in the new State Secretary of the Navy Office, Alfred von Tirpitz, who asked that each and every request for a German warship be reported directly to him "on the one hand because it is a yardstick for the necessity to maintain a naval presence overseas, which is especially dear to my heart, and on the other hand because it can be effectively exploited for the navy in its parliamen-

[21] Ibid., Nr 22452, pp. 91-93, 99. Foreign Office to Admiral von Knorr, Dec. 25, 1897; and Knorr to Foreign Office, Dec. 31, 1897.

[22] AA-Bonn, Venezuela 1, vol. 14. Prollius to Hohenlohe-Schillingsfürst, Dec. 18, 1897; Rex to Hohenlohe-Schillingsfürst, Feb. 11, 1898. See also Charles Callan Tansill, *The Purchase of the Danish West Indies* (Baltimore/London/Oxford, 1932), 378ff.; Vagts, *Deutschland und die Vereinigten Staaten*, II, 1708ff.

tary dealings."[23] In other words, the greater the clamor for warships from abroad, the better the chance for parliamentary approval of more ships.

In fact, Tirpitz proved most adept at getting "more ships." Masterfully exploiting what he termed "spiritual massage," the admiral popularized the need for a fleet through translations of naval yarns, information tours by active officers, inspections of ships by Reichstag deputies, lectures on the need for maritime power by eminent German university professors, sermons from the pulpit on navalism, and serialization in domestic journals of works such as Alfred Thayer Mahan's *Influence of Seapower Upon History*. And whereas his predecessor, Albrecht von Stosch, had denounced Hamburg patricians as "a society of egoists," Tirpitz instead courted them with flattery and had their lord mayors routinely christen overseas cruisers.

Hamburg's elite, for its part, responded in kind. The venerable Union of Hamburg Shipowners, headed by Ballin and Woermann, informed the Reichstag in 1897 that Germany was becoming increasingly dependent upon her overseas trade and that its protection "was of eminent practical importance for the economic life of the entire nation." The Union's epistle argued that "the Reich's overseas prestige" could only be enhanced through "the repeated energetic dispatch of German warships and, if necessary, through their forceful yet responsible intervention" in behalf of beleaguered Reich nationals.[24] One year later, when the Foreign Office asked its representatives abroad to mobilize German nationals to support the fleet, Hamburg merchants were largely responsible for the fifty-two petitions—including those from all South American states save one—that duly arrived.[25] Apparently influenced, the Reichstag in April 1898 passed the First Navy Bill, which called for a fleet of 19 battle-

[23] ZStA-Potsdam, Auswärtiges Amt, Abt. IIs, Entsendung deutscher Kriegsschiffe Nr 22453, pp. 44-45. Tirpitz to Bülow, Jan. 21, 1898.

[24] Verein Hamburger Rheeder to Foreign Office, Mar. 10, 1897, cited in Uhlich, "Politik des deutschen Kaiserreiches," 157. For Tirpitz's "spiritual massage," see Holger H. Herwig, *"Luxury" Fleet: The Imperial German Navy 1888-1918* (London, 1980), 40ff.

[25] Böhm, *Überseehandel und Flottenbau*, 132-35.

ships, 8 armored cruisers, 12 large and 30 light cruisers. Adolph Woermann was rewarded for his efforts in this behalf with the Royal Order of the Crown, Second Class.[26]

Wilhelm II, in typical hyperbole, informed the *Hansa*'s ambassador to Berlin: "Navigare necesse est, vivere non est necesse."[27] Tirpitz, on the other hand, realized that construction of a symmetrical battle fleet was the task of an entire generation, and likened his overall plan to "the patient laying of brick upon brick." Those who grew impatient over what they perceived to be the slow pace of naval building were lectured that one could not divide "the bearskin" until "the bear is killed."[28]

But the timetable went awry. The onset of the Spanish-American War early in 1898, "*which came politically too early for him,*" forced Tirpitz's hand.[29] Washington's thinly veiled desire to annex Cuba convinced Tirpitz that "the last chance" had come to acquire St. Thomas and Curaçao. The dramatic 14,000-mile journey of the *Oregon* from the Pacific Ocean to Cuba convinced naval planners in Washington of the need to intensify their plans to construct a canal across Central America (Hay-Pauncefote Treaty 1900, 1901), and thereby further alarmed Tirpitz. At the least, he informed the Wilhelmstrasse in March 1898, German warships would have to be sent to the West Indies at once "to show that we, too, must have a say in that region."[30]

Alleged German designs on the Caribbean region had been rumored in the United States press throughout the 1890s. As early as April 1895, the *New York Herald* had informed its readers that the presence of German warships off Venezuela, disguised as an effort to collect outstanding debts for the Rothschilds and Krupp, was in reality an attempt to seize Margarita Island as a base from which to

[26] Ibid., 102.

[27] Ibid., 83. In 1893, Wilhelm II had informed Ambassador Friedrich Krüger: "Believe me, our future lies with the water."

[28] See Herwig, *"Luxury" Fleet*, 34ff.

[29] Bundesarchiv-Koblenz, Nachlass Bülow, Nr 22, pp. 255-59. Tirpitz to Bülow, Mar. 16, 1898.

[30] Ibid. See also Ursula Schottelius, "Das Amerikabild der deutschen Regierung in der Ära Bülows, 1897-1909" (diss., Hamburg University, 1956), 13.

operate against the projected isthmian canal in Nicaragua or Panama.[31] Two months later, the *Washington Post* took note of Germany's immense capital investment in Venezuela, which "is to be protected by the establishment of a naval station" there.[32] The *Berliner Neueste Nachrichten* reported the story, but lamented that it knew nothing of such an "extremely desirable acquisition." The paper assured its readers that the Monroe Doctrine would "not cause the slightest problems" in the case of Margarita Island.[33] And the *Hannoverscher Courier* likewise reported that the *Post*'s allegations "unfortunately" were untrue. "Unfortunately—because the possession of a naval base in Central American waters would undoubtedly be of great value to Germany, and one could simply pass over the howl concerning the Monroe Doctrine" that was sure to be raised in the United States over this.[34]

On a more official level, the German Embassy in Copenhagen as early as February 1896 had passed on to Berlin a suggestion by the Danish Foreign Minister, Baron Reetz-Thott, that Denmark might be interested in trading its Caribbean possessions; Alfred von Kiderlen-Wächter, the German ambassador, quickly mentioned North Schleswig as "bait." Professor Ernst von Halle of Marburg University, a semi-official spokesman for the Navy Office, took the notion up with alacrity, suggesting that a German purchase of St. Thomas, especially, was "more than necessary." For more than a century, he informed the Foreign Office, German merchants had dominated the trade with Central America and Venezuela; the planned isthmian canal made a German naval base in the region "absolutely necessary." In the end, the project foundered on the monarch's opposition. "I will not sell my subjects out for a few islands. What Wilhelm I has conquered, I will firmly hold on to."[35]

[31] Clipping from April 14, 1895, in AA-Bonn, Venezuela 1, vol. 12.

[32] *Washington Post*, June 16, 1895.

[33] *Berliner Neueste Nachrichten*, June 16, 1895.

[34] *Hannoverscher Courier*, June 21, 1895.

[35] AA-Bonn, Dänische Besitzungen in Amerika 1, Dänisch-West-Indien, vol. 1. Kiderlen-Wächter to Hohenlohe-Schillingsfürst, Feb. 20, 1896; Halle to Foreign Office, July 10, 1896; Kiderlen-Wächter to Hohenlohe-Schillingsfürst, Sept. 1, 1896, with the Emperor's marginal comments.

The sinking of the *Maine* in February 1898 apparently altered that casual attitude. On March 10, 1898, the German Embassy in Washington sent Berlin an urgent prognosis on the "strategic importance of a shipping canal through Central America." The report cited Captain Mahan at length to the effect that only United States control of Cuba and several other Caribbean islands could assure Washington security for the Atlantic approaches to the canal; Hawaii, on the other hand, could safeguard the Pacific sea lanes. While Germany could never aspire "exclusively to control the canal and its approaches," it could nevertheless play a decisive role in the region by "acquiring one or more independent, militarily strong positions" in the area. Both the growing United States trade with its southern neighbors and the constant threat posed to German nationals by the political tumult of the "semi-civilized" South American states left Berlin with no choice but to find sufficient funds to realize a naval station in the Caribbean Sea—even at the risk of thereby challenging the Monroe Doctrine. An added bonus in acquiring especially St. Thomas was that the island could serve as anchor for the projected German world cable that would run from Germany to West Africa, across that continent and on to New Guinea and Samoa, and finally to South America, which alone could "emancipate" Germany from its present reliance upon British cables. The report concluded by raising the prospect of a future German "chain of maritime coaling stations" from Wilhelmshaven to St. Thomas, from there to the Galapagos Islands and Samoa, and finally to the German colony of Kiaochow in China. "The first ship that passes through the isthmian canal will accord this [design] great practical importance."[36] Tirpitz fully concurred with the prognosis, and that same month informed State Secretary von Bülow that without the immediate acquisition of

[36] AA-Bonn, Amerika, Generalia Nr 12, Projekt eines Schiffahrtskanals durch Mittelamerika (Panama resp. Nicaragua-Kanal), vol. 1. German Embassy (Washington) memorandum originally drafted Mar. 1, 1898. The position paper was most likely penned by the military attaché, Count G. Adolf von Goetzen. See Vagts, *Deutschland und die Vereinigten Staaten*, II, 1493-94. On the matter of the world cable, see Paul M. Kennedy, "Imperial Cable Communication and Strategy, 1870-1914," *English Historical Review*, 86 (October 1971), 740-52.

St. Thomas and Curacao, the Reich would lose its South American markets forever.[37]

Germany's quest for a naval base in the Caribbean region was thereby moved to center stage. In April 1898 the High Command of the Navy asked the Foreign Office whether it might not be feasible to purchase one of the Dutch islands in the West Indies, as a recent report from the commander of the *Geier* had recommended.[38] And late in August, the German minister to Santo Domingo, Michahelles, informed Bülow that President Ulisses Heureaux had offered Germany a coaling station on his island "out of fear of the Americans." The Reich's ambassador to Washington, Theodor von Holleben, at once warned that such a project would "make the worst conceivable impression" in the United States and instead advised "dilatory handling" of the matter. Wilhelm II once more ended the possible purchase of a naval base in the West Indies with an eye toward the Republic: "Oh, sweet innocence. I shall not fall into that trap."[39]

Thereafter, German interest in the Caribbean returned to the Danish West Indies. In December 1898 Captain Walter Christmas Dirckinck von Holmfeld and his German partner, Rear Admiral Zirzow, approached Berlin with a scheme to purchase St. John for the Navy Cabinet as a private undertaking. The price was set at $500,000, with Dirckinck-Holmfeld pocketing fully one-fifth as commission. Tirpitz at once seized the bait, warning that the United States was "the Phoenix" of the region.[40] But Bülow, undoubtedly aware of probable United States opposition to such an undertaking, informed Tirpitz that he viewed the project as being "inopportune";

---

[37] Cited in Otto-Ernst Schüddekopf, *Die Stützpunktpolitik des Deutschen Reiches 1890-1914* (Berlin, 1941), 58. See also Wolfgang Petter, "Die Stützpunktpolitik der preussisch-deutschen Kriegsmarine 1859-1883" (diss., Freiburg University, 1975).

[38] AA-Bonn, Deutschland 167, Kolonien und Flottenstützpunkte, vol. 1. High Command of the Navy to Foreign Office, Apr. 25, 1898.

[39] Ibid., vol. 1. Michahelles to Foreign Office, Aug. 30, 1898; Holleben to Foreign Office, Aug. 31, 1898; Bülow to Wilhelm II, Sept. 2, 1898, with the Emperor's marginal notes. See also Tansill, *Purchase of the Danish West Indies*, 397-98.

[40] Ibid., 406ff.; Böhm, *Überseehandel und Flottenbau*, 155-56. For Tirpitz's comment, "But the United States is the Phoenix," see Wilhelm Deist, *Flottenpolitik und Flottenpropaganda: Das Nachrichtenbureau des Reichsmarineamtes 1897-1914* (Stuttgart, 1976), 170.

however, he would pursue it if the Navy Office considered it "pressingly necessary" from the military point of view. This, Tirpitz refused to commit to writing. Instead, he instructed Captain August von Heeringen, a trusted aide, to seek out Ballin in Hamburg and to inquire whether the shipowner could not simply purchase the island privately, and later transfer it to the Reich. Ballin argued that St. Thomas, where his Hamburg-America Line already owned coaling depots and large tracts of land, might be a more suitable target for Germany; but, when pressed on the matter of St. John, Ballin agreed "with a heavy heart but out of patriotism" to undertake the purchase due to its "great national interest."[41]

In May 1899 Bülow again inquired at the Navy Office whether the purchase of St. John was of absolute necessity. The crafty Tirpitz replied that such an acquisition constituted not a military but a political act, and that it therefore rested in Bülow's domain. He slyly suggested that the entire issue "came down to whether the Foreign Office intended to pursue an active policy in America in the future, when we are finally strong at sea (for example, planned direction of German emigration to South America)." The Pan-Germans joined Tirpitz in the clamor for the Danish West Indies, but Bülow, slippery as ever, evaded the question and shelved the issue for the time being.[42] Obviously, Bülow was not about to commit the government to adventures in the American hemisphere in writing to Tirpitz.

But Bülow had not reckoned with Albert Ballin, who was not about to abandon his role in *die grosse Politik*. Ballin now tacked a different course, and in September 1899 proposed to Bülow that Germany assume a major role in the construction of the Central American canal, now resurrected by a new French financial consortium (Compagnie nouvelle du Canal de Panama) and staffed by Ger-

---

[41] AA-Bonn, Dänische Besitzungen in Amerika 1, Dänisch-West-Indien, vol. 2. Bülow to Tirpitz, Feb. 3, 1899; Ambassador von Metternich (Hamburg) to Foreign Office, Mar. 1, 1899. See also Böhm, *Überseehandel und Flottenbau*, 155-56; Frank Bernard Herschel, *Entwicklung und Bedeutung der Hamburg-Amerika Linie* (Berlin, 1912), 66, 81; and Kurt Himer, *Die Hamburg-Amerika Linie: Im Sechsten Jahrzehnt ihrer Entwicklung 1897-1907* (Hamburg, 1907), 53, 123.

[42] AA-Bonn, Dänische Besitzungen in Amerika 1, Dänisch-West-Indien, vol. 2. Bülow's memorandum on the issue, dated May 27, 1899.

man engineers. After reminding the Foreign Secretary that he privately had—albeit unsuccessfully—attempted over the past year to interest German bankers in such an undertaking, Ballin again pressed the issue by warning the Foreign Office that the canal would constitute "a tremendous economic and political weapon in the hands of the Americans." Above all, the canal question was of "paramount importance for Germany's overseas interests."[43] In order to make quite certain that Bülow could not simply consign this letter to the files, Ballin sent a copy to Tirpitz at the Navy Office.

The admiral reacted with alacrity. That very summer, he had been counseled by the commander of the *Geier*, Lieutenant Commander Hermann Jacobsen, stationed in American waters, that the Panama canal issue was to Germany "what the Suez Canal in its time was to England." Jacobsen minced no words: "It is of the utmost importance for Germany, strategically and commercially, to assure itself of a leading role in this undertaking, which is extraordinarily crucial for world traffic."[44] Tirpitz was of one mind with the commander, and in October 1899 lectured Bülow on the pivotal importance of the canal. The "strategic value" of the proposed waterway simply could not be overestimated, "given our interest in Pacific and American regions, especially in case of war." Germany's "multifaceted economic relations" with South American states rendered such a future clash with the United States "unquestionably assumable." Both now and in the future, Germany could never count upon "benevolent" treatment from Washington. In case of war, the Americans would not hesitate to close the canal to German traffic; thereafter, they would continue to harass German commerce even in peacetime. Given the Reich's late arrival on the world scene, it had no alternative but to assume "a strategic offensive" in Pacific and American waters, yet closure of the isthmian canal would preclude any "offensive operations" in the region. Such action by the Americans would confront the Germans with two choices: "to fight for possession of the canal, which would entail a detrimental marshalling of forces for an interim

⁴³ AA-Bonn, Amerika. Generalia 12, vol. 1. Ballin to Bülow, Sept. 2, 1899; Vagts, *Deutschland und die Vereinigten Staaten*, II, 1495-96.

⁴⁴ ZStA-Potsdam, Auswärtiges Amt, Abt. IIs, Entsendung deutscher Kriegsschiffe Nr 22460, pp. 89-105. Jacobsen to Wilhelm II, June 15, 1899.

operation," or to continue to use the much longer sea routes through the Suez Canal and around Cape Horn. The latter choice was clearly out of the question. And in much more forceful terms than Ballin had used the previous month, Tirpitz warned Bülow that Germany's "growing overseas interests" could be safeguarded only through a growing number of well-fortified naval bases which, in turn, would be threatened if the United States could safely shuttle its fleet from one ocean to the other through the canal. The *Oregon*'s journey had obviously made an impression upon the admiral.

Tirpitz next turned to what a later German general (Franz Halder) would call "dreaming in continents."[45] South America, he informed Bülow, was on the verge of forming a united front against the United States, and the heart of the southern Pan-American alliance would be "the formation of a common South American fleet." This force could, in case of the expected clash with the United States, be combined with Germany's ships in the Pacific and the Far East in order to harass the western shores of the United States. The latter would be crippled without the canal, as its fleet would probably be based on Atlantic ports. And, finally, Tirpitz trotted out his favorite shibboleth, namely, that Germany's "alliance value" would be greatly enhanced were it to become a major partner in the canal.[46] Participation in an international canal consortium, as recommended by Ballin, then, was a safe way to further German overseas interests, to protect existing markets, to offer other powers an attractive alliance partner, and to provide the future "South American fleet" a reliable partner against the United States. It was a small price to pay for such grand *Weltpolitik*.

Indeed, Tirpitz was at that moment riding the crest of the wave of navalism. With Britain embarrassingly tied down in South Africa against the Boers and with the United States out of favor in South America for the brutal manner in which it had acquired Panama from Colombia, the moment seemed opportune for Germany to make

---

[45] Franz Halder, *Kriegstagebuch* (Stuttgart, 1962-64), III, 455. Entry for June 12, 1942, concerning a plan by German and Japanese admirals to divide the world at a line running north and south at 70° longitude.

[46] AA-Bonn, Amerika. Generalia 12, vol. 1. Tirpitz to Bülow, Oct. 29, 1899. See also Vagts, *Deutschland und die Vereinigten Staaten*, II, 1497-99.

progress in its quest for world power status. To buttress his claims to "a place in the sun," Tirpitz had convinced Bülow to mount a gigantic effort to ascertain what fiscal interests the Reich did, indeed, have overseas. Every envoy and consul in even the remotest corners of the world was ordered in 1899-1900 to submit a detailed list of German investments around the globe. The results were published in June 1900, and for South America suggested holdings of 570-600 million Mark in Argentina, 350 million Mark in Brazil, 270-300 million Mark in Chile, 253 million Mark in the five republics of Central America, and about 200 million Mark each in Mexico, the West Indies, and Venezuela.[47] Obviously impressed, the Reichstag that same month passed the Second Navy Bill, doubling the size of the fleet to 38 battleships, 20 armored and 38 light cruisers. A spokesman for the Navy Office brazenly asserted: "If we wish to promote a powerful overseas policy and to secure worthwhile colonies, we must be prepared first and foremost for a clash with England and America."[48]

State Secretary von Bülow and the Wilhelmstrasse were not quite as enthusiastic as the German admirals concerning a confrontation with the United States in the Western Hemisphere. Baron von Holstein repeatedly rejected the navy's demands for a base in the Gulf of Mexico as being "in opposition to the Monroe Doctrine," and as late as January 1900 had vetoed a joint demand by the Navy Office and the Pan-German League for the acquisition of the Danish Virgin Islands.[49] Bülow, true to form, obfuscated on the issue for more than a year, and finally tackled it by instructing his staff to probe the legal ramifications of German involvement in the canal issue in light of existing German trade agreements with states in the region and of international maritime law. By late February 1901, Bülow, now Chancellor, was forced to take a stand as Tirpitz, who had been summoned to instruct Wilhelm II on the issue, demanded clarifica-

---

[47] AA-Bonn, Deutschland 167, vol. 3. Navy Office memorandum, "Die deutschen Kapitalanlagen in überseeischen Ländern," June 1900.

[48] See Volker R. Berghahn, "Zu den Zielen des deutschen Flottenbaus," *Historische Zeitschrift*, 210 (1970), 70; Herwig, *"Luxury" Fleet*, 43.

[49] Norman Rich and M. H. Fisher, eds., *Die Geheimen Papiere Friedrich von Holsteins* (Göttingen, 1956), I, 176.

tion. In two memoranda, the Foreign Office concluded that the United States would not only build the canal—as outlined in the Hay-Pauncefote agreement of February 5, 1900—but also fortify it, as prohibited by treaty but demanded by the Senate. The sole possible *entré* into the canal issue for Germany, the Wilhelmstrasse noted, was to approach Washington with the suggestion that the Reich's trade and friendship agreements with Nicaragua of February 4, 1896, accorded her a voice in the "free and unfettered" movement of ships in the region—provided, of course, that the canal was constructed in Nicaragua. Should Washington reject such an approach, there was nothing else to be done; international law did not "exclude one nation from controlling an inter-oceanic canal exclusively."[50] In short, as things now stood, the canal was purely an American matter.

To make matters worse for the navy, Ambassador von Holleben informed Chancellor von Bülow in November 1901 that the United States was prepared to purchase the Danish West Indies at the urgings of Admiral George Dewey. Wilhelm II was irate. He blamed America's expansion in the wake of its victory over Spain upon British weakness and Germany's lack of a fleet due to "the decade-long stupidity of the Reichstag."[51] But the monarch's mood improved considerably in March 1902, when the German representative at Batavia cabled that the Dutch might be prepared to sell Germany some islands in the West Indies after all. Wilhelm II quickly grasped this slender straw and instructed his Admiralty Staff to prepare a position paper on the matter.

In what was to become one of the last great memoranda on the Caribbean, the Admiralty Staff of Otto von Diederichs on May 26 enthusiastically endorsed the purchase of the Dutch islands off the coast of Venezuela. German capital investment of 200 million Mark in Venezuela dictated the need for a naval presence there at all times. While conceding that American acquisition of St. Thomas and St. Croix was "only a question of time," the Admiralty Staff pressed for the immediate purchase of Curaçao and its superb harbor Willem-

[50] AA-Bonn, Amerika. Generalia 12, vol. 2. Memoranda dated Feb. 20 and 21, 1901, by Drs. Rücker-Jenisch and Schauenburg-Herrlisheim of the Foreign Office.

[51] AA-Bonn, Dänische Besitzungen in Amerika 1, Dänisch-West-Indien, vol. 3. Holleben to Bülow, Nov. 25, 1901, with the Emperor's marginal notes.

stad. "The strategic importance of a German naval station on Curaçao is readily obvious with an eye toward the isthmian canal question." The very last chance for Germany to set foot in the Caribbean
basin was at hand; even Captain Mahan had suggested as much in
an article in the *Atlantic Monthly*. Diederichs considered the matter
of such extreme urgency that he asked the Foreign Office to probe
whether Germany ought not attempt to make the matter more palat-
able to the United States by proposing to surrender its "interests in
Colombia and Guatemala." And to show that Tirpitz did not have an
exclusive on "dreaming in continents," Diederichs even envisaged
German acquisition of Dutch Guiana, or Surinam, as "a demarcation
line at which the United States influence and expansionism in South
America had to make a halt." At the very least, the Foreign Office
needed to be instructed to do all in its power for "economic as well
as military reasons" to keep Dutch possessions in the Western Hemisphere out of the hands of the United States.[52]

The Reich's envoy in Washington, Holleben, once more poured
cold water over these naval aspirations. He informed Bülow in June
1902, "with my deepest sorrow," that any and all German territorial
acquisitions in the Western Hemisphere were out of the question as
long as Theodore Roosevelt, the biggest defender of the Monroe
Doctrine, was in the White House. Chancellor von Bülow quickly
passed Holleben's views on to the Admiralty Staff, adding that such
purchases were also out of question under all future American presidents.[53]

Unfortunately, Wilhelm II chose to ignore this sane advice. Instead, he had taken the opportunity of launching the Hamburg-
America Line's *Prinzessin Viktoria Luise* in June 1901 to remind his
audience "that our future lies with the water." Specifically, the ruler
suggested that the new Germany take up the mantle of the erstwhile
Hanseatic League, which had been forced to abandon its overseas
mission owing to the absence "of the supportive and protective

[52] AA-Bonn, Niederländische Besitzungen in Amerika Nr 2, vol. 1. Admiralty
Staff to State Secretary Oswald Baron von Richthofen of the Foreign Office, May 26,
1902. Also Vagts, *Deutschland und die Vereinigten Staaten*, II, 1504-05.

[53] AA-Bonn, Niederländische Besitzungen in Amerika Nr 2, vol. 1. Holleben to
Bülow, June 28, 1902; Bülow to Admiralty Staff, July 15, 1902.

power of the Empire." Wilhelm assured all those present that he cherished every single merchant who went out into the wide world "in order to find a place where we can drive in a nail and hang our armor on it."[54] His brother, Admiral Prince Heinrich, in preparing for a goodwill mission to the United States in January 1902, openly expressed his desire "to bring something concrete back from this trip." Baron von Holstein was mortified to learn from intimate sources that Heinrich planned to demand from Roosevelt "a German sphere of influence in South America." Holstein, who feared that this would send German-American relations "to the freezing point," managed at the last moment to dissuade the prince from such a potentially disastrous undertaking by threatening to call a Crown Council to deal with the issue.[55]

What had gone wrong with the quest for *Weltpolitik*? The high hopes of 1898-1899 had somehow faded into the dismal prospects of 1902-1903. The German acquisition of one of the Danish or Dutch islands in the West Indies had not come to pass. And the isthmian canal would be built without German participation or influence. In fact, the Caribbean was fast becoming not a German, but an "American lake." On both a global and a South American level, Tirpitz's master plan was at odds with reality. The simple truth was that events would not conform to his expectations.

Alfred von Tirpitz had come to the Navy Office in 1897 not merely with a promise to wring "more ships" from the Reichstag, but with a grand scheme to elevate Prussia/Germany from a first-rate land power to a first-rate maritime power. In his maiden speech in parliament in December of that year, he had bluntly stated that the navy had become "a question of survival" for Germany; failure to develop maritime power would lead first to economic and then to political decline. In February 1899 the admiral had opined that in the coming century power shifts in Asia and South America would require a

[54] ZStA-Potsdam, Reichskanzlei, Allerhöchste Kundgebungen Nr. 810, p. 18. The Emperor's speech was on June 18, 1901.
[55] Bundesarchiv-Koblenz, Nachlass Bülow, Nr 111, Prinz Heinrich von Preussen. Holstein to Bülow, Jan. 29, 1902. See also Holger H. Herwig, *Politics of Frustration: The United States in German Naval Planning, 1889-1941* (Boston/Toronto, 1976), 74.

mighty German fleet as the fulcrum of "our entire foreign policy." In crude social Darwinistic terms, Tirpitz had depicted the "Romance" nations such as Spain, Portugal, and France to be in a state of decline. The British Empire was in its last throes, and the main issue of the twentieth century would be the contest to determine which nation—the United States, Russia, Japan, or Germany— would take up the British "inheritance." To the Emperor he had promised "a great overseas policy." Failure to accept the challenge would relegate Germany "to the status of a poor farming country." And Bernhard von Bülow was of similar mind, at least initially, in demanding that Germany obtain her rightful "place in the sun." In a celebrated speech, the Chancellor reduced the future to a simple formula: "In the coming century the German people will become hammer or anvil."[56]

But Tirpitz fully knew that a fleet would take a generation to complete, and hence he needed a period of international calm until about 1920-1921, when Germany could take her place among the world's foremost naval powers. The "gigantic liquidation" of the British Empire could then proceed. Yet, as already suggested, events had rendered this timetable obsolete. Both the Japanese and the Americans expanded at a much faster pace than Tirpitz had envisaged; there could be no simple "holding action" until the 1920s. What islands remained unclaimed, regardless of how desolate or barren they were, became important to naval planners on the lookout for coaling stations or cable anchors. The Spanish-American War, which had almost led to a confrontation between German and American naval squadrons in the Philippines, had taken the Germans by surprise. The resulting American acquisition of Guam, Hawaii, Wake Island, Cuba, Puerto Rico, and the Philippines ("a gift from the Gods"), compounded by Washington's right to construct the canal across Central America, panicked Tirpitz into risking an early confrontation with the United States. Especially in the southern American hemisphere, where great German capital investments were at stake, Berlin simply could not afford to stand back and let

---

[56] These arguments are summarized in Herwig, *"Luxury" Fleet*, 35ff.; and *Politics of Frustration*, 38ff.

the United States drive it from its markets. And if the German fleet was truly to become a global force, it would need some sort of secure base in the Caribbean area from which to harass the canal's traffic as well as to protect German interests in Central and South America— James Monroe's "insolent dogma" notwithstanding.

Venezuela and its offshore islands thus became a focal point of these aspirations. Long an object of trade for Hanseatic merchants, Venezuela had also become a settlement colony for farmers from Baden in the 1840s (La Colonia Tovar); the Great Venezuelan Railroad was second only to the planned Berlin-Baghdad rail link in size and prestige; offshore islands such as Margarita appeared ideal for use as a German naval base; the domestic socio-economic turmoil seemed to demand some sort of foreign intervention; and the advantageous geographical location of the country near the projected isthmian canal made it attractive to naval planners in Berlin. In short, might this not be the place to "drive in a nail" on which Wilhelm II could "hang his armor"?

Indeed, the anarchy that accompanied the rule of President Cipriano Castro resulted both in a spate of requests for German warships on the part of the Reich's envoys to Caracas and in numerous recommendations by ship commanders in the region that Berlin seize especially Margarita Island, off Cumaná, as a *point d'appui*. As early as March 1898, Lieutenant Commander Jacobsen of the *Geier* had suggested that the navy exploit the next political unrest "to force Venezuela to cede the entire island group of Los Roques, Orchilla, Tortuga, Cubagna, and Marguerita" to Germany as security to hold against the outstanding claims of the Great Venezuelan Railroad Society.[57] Intensifying civil warfare late in 1899 brought new requests for the presence of German cruisers off Venezuela, but the official paper of the Hamburg Stock Exchange lamented that only the ancient training vessels *Nixe*, *Moltke*, *Stosch*, and *Charlotte* were available; it would be 1903, at the earliest, before the Reich could spare overseas cruisers for American waters under the aegis of the Second

[57] AA-Bonn, Venezuela 1, vol. 14. Jacobsen to Commanding Admiral, Mar. 25, 1898.

Navy Bill.[58] The Berlin press echoed these sober sentiments, and the *Berliner Tageblatt* in November 1899 bitterly complained that protection of Reich nationals and their holdings existed "only on paper" owing to "the lack of cruisers."[59]

Yet even the presence of these antiquated sailing ships off Venezuela was reported in the world press as evidence of alleged German designs on the region. The *New York Sun* in January 1900 ran the banner headline: "Signs that the Kaiser is about to squeeze Venezuela. Belief that old debts due to German bankers will be made an argument for seizing the island of Margarita, of great strategical value, in the Caribbean." The *New York Herald* and even the *Novoe vremia* in St. Petersburg published similar reports of German designs on Margarita Island.[60]

President Castro's decision not to honor Venezuela's foreign debts or claims arising from the many civil wars brought that country of otherwise infinitesimal importance to the forefront of *die grosse Politik* by 1900. The Great Venezuelan Railroad, which was especially hard-hit by the *Andino*'s refusal to meet even interest payments, in March 1900 sought to involve Berlin in its plight by cabling the Foreign Office that the Cabinet in Caracas—with the single exception of Foreign Minister Andueza Palacio—was willing to turn Margarita Island over as a naval base in lieu of outstanding interest payments. Castro's fiscal obfuscation brought Baron von Holstein at the Wilhelmstrasse to the end of his patience by April: "It might be well to give the navy a free hand" in Venezuela, he suggested, that is, to mount a naval demonstration off the Venezuelan coast. Moreover, Holstein argued that "German claims against Venezuela and Colombia are so important that the greatest possible naval presence on the northern coast of South America (and West Indies) appears desirable."[61] Foreign Secretary von Bülow largely concurred, and in May

[58] *Hamburgische Börsen Halle*, Nr. 455, Sept. 28, 1899.

[59] *Berliner Tageblatt*, Nr 599a, Nov. 25, 1899. See also the *Vossische Zeitung*, Nr 571, Dec. 6, 1899.

[60] AA-Bonn, Venezuela 1, vol. 17. *New York Sun*, Jan. 28, 1900; *New York Herald*, May 3 and May 30, 1901; *Novoe vremia*, May 7, 1901.

[61] AA-Bonn, Venezuela 1, vol. 17. Director Knoop to Berlin, Mar. 30, 1900;

1900 informed the Admiralty Staff that "all seems to point to a ca-
tastrophe" in Venezuela. He was already eyeing "military measures"
against Castro, whose regime he estimated to be about 6 million Bolívars (4.8 million Mark) in arrears in payments to German firms.
Bülow reminded Vice Admiral von Diederichs that Reich holdings
in Central America stood at 1,000 to 1,200 million Mark, with a further 1.75 to 2 billion Mark invested in South America.[62] But the nagging lack of suitable warships for overseas duty was again under-
scored in December 1900, when Wilhelm II wished to send the
cruiser *Vineta* to Brazil "to protect Germans and their property"
there during a civil disturbance, only to discover that the *Vineta* had
already been lying off Venezuela for more than a year, without apparent effect on Castro.[63]

The year 1901 brought bloody warfare to Venezuela and mounting
frustration to Berlin. German leaders were reminded on numerous
occasions of their inability to pressure Castro. In October, for example, Vice Admiral von Diederichs informed the new State Secretary, Oswald Baron von Richthofen, that he could not fulfill a Foreign Office request to dispatch warships to Maracaibo; the navy
could spare only two torpedo-boats, which were utterly unsuited for
the task and which could therefore only embarrass Germany if deployed. Diederichs felt certain that the current unrest in Venezuela,
Colombia, Argentina, and Uruguay was due to "Pan-American
machinations," fueled by the United States and designed to drive
Germany out of South America. However, he again cautioned
against frittering away what little "military (maritime) means" Germany had at its disposal by rushing single and unsuitable vessels to
the various trouble spots.[64] And when some sailors from the *Vineta*
became embroiled with a shore patrol in Puerto Cabello, both Bülow
and Tirpitz warned against immediate naval retaliation because most

---

ZStA-Potsdam, Auswärtiges Amt, Abt. IIs, Nr 22463, p. 110, Holstein's memorandum dated May 2, 1900.

[62] AA-Bonn, Deutschland 138, Die Kaiserlich deutsche Marine, vol. 17. Bülow to
Diederichs, May 4, 1900.

[63] Ibid., vol. 18. Richthofen (Foreign Office) to Wilhelm II, Dec. 16, 1900, with
the monarch's marginal comments.

[64] Ibid., vol. 20. Diederichs to Richthofen, Oct. 10, 1901.

of the valuable targets on land belonged to foreigners, and especially to Germans.[65] The limits of "gunboat diplomacy" were all too evident.

Tirpitz, for his part, attempted to put the lack of suitable overseas cruisers in the best possible light by brazenly assuring both Emperor and Chancellor that he could dispatch two torpedo-boats to Venezuela at once—despite Vice Admiral von Diederichs' advice to the contrary—but that this "was not desirable at the moment as it would demonstrate to the Americans *ad oculis* how German torpedo-boats could reach the American coast" undetected. United States realization of the immense range of these craft—in reality, at best about 1,000 sea miles—would only cause alarm.[66] The Emperor accepted this absurd contention and blamed the "pathetic" lack of overseas cruisers, not on the architect of the battle fleet, Tirpitz, but rather upon the Reichstag's "sins of dereliction of the past twenty years." The present inability to pressure Castro by way of a naval demonstration only served to remind him "how pathetic our navy still is." Time alone would improve matters. "How completely different my aspirations and policies would be in Central and South America if the *cruiser* squadron could—as it should *de facto et de jure*—suddenly appear off Venezuela."[67] Was the monarch becoming aware of the global shortcomings of Tirpitz's master plan?

Germany's participation, along with Great Britain and Italy, in the blockade of Venezuela in 1902-1903, taken up in detail in another chapter, brought the warships *Vineta*, *Stein*, *Moltke*, *Panther*, *Stosch*, *Falke*, and *Gazelle* to the Caribbean region. While Ambassador von Holleben went out of his way to assure the State Department "that under no circumstances do we consider in our proceedings the acquisiton or the permanent occupation of Venezuelan property,"[68] the Foreign Office in Berlin remained sufficiently suspicious of Castro's pledge to honor all foreign debts that it main-

[65] AA-Bonn, Venezuela 1, vol. 18. Bülow to Wilhelm II, Oct. 15, 1901.

[66] AA-Bonn, Deutschland 138, vol. 20. Bülow to Wilhelm II, Oct. 15, 1901.

[67] Ibid. Wilhelm II added this note to the end of the letter from Bülow, Oct. 15, 1901.

[68] AA-Bonn, Venezuela 1, vol. 19. Holleben to State Department, Dec. 11, 1901.

tained two warships off Venezuela throughout 1903. It considered this to be necessary not only "to put pressure on President Castro," but also "with an eye toward public opinion in Germany."[69] Once more, appearance and prestige were ranked above reality and substance.

Not surprisingly, the blockade of Venezuela and the hostile American reaction it engendered made the Wilhelmstrasse extremely sensitive toward the United States in general and the Monroe Doctrine in particular. State Secretary von Richthofen in August 1903 vetoed a planned visit to eastern seaports by the *Vineta* "for political reasons," that is, for the ship's role in the recent blockade.[70] He would have been even more alarmed had he known that the *Vineta* was being sent to Newport, Boston, Cape Cod, Martha's Vineyard, Block Island, and Long Island in order to scout these sites as possible landings in a contingency war plan that Germany was then developing against the United States (Operations Plan III).[71] That same year, Richthofen instructed Vice Admiral Wilhelm Büchsel, the new head of the Admiralty Staff, that it was not desirable to send the gunboat *Panther*, of Maracaibo fame, to Ciudad Bolívar to celebrate the Kaiser's birthday "in the face of the unsilenceable suspicions regarding our South American policy" that existed in many quarters.[72] And when the navy resurrected the proposal in 1904, the Venezuelans blocked it by arguing that the harbor was too shallow for the gunboat.[73]

It apparently never dawned upon the Admiralty Staff that the *Panther*'s presence in American waters acted, in the words of Ambassador Speck von Sternburg, "as the proverbial red rag to a bull." In April 1906 Sternburg warned against a planned visit of the ship

[69] AA-Bonn, Deutschland 138, vol. 23. Richthofen to Büchsel, Mar. 4, 1903.

[70] ZStA-Potsdam, Auswärtiges Amt, Abt. IIs, Nr 22476, p. 9. Richthofen to Admiralty Staff, Aug. 28, 1903.

[71] See Holger H. Herwig and David F. Trask, "Naval Operations Plans between Germany and the United States of America 1898-1913. A Study of Strategic Planning in the Age of Imperialism," *Militärgeschichtliche Mitteilungen*, 2/1970, 24-25.

[72] AA-Bonn, Venezuela 1, vol. 25. Richthofen to Büchsel, Nov. 29, 1903.

[73] ZStA-Potsdam, Auswärtiges Amt, Abt. IIs, Nr 22476, pp. 153ff.

to the United States, as this would "rekindle the deep-rooted mistrust" against Germany's "aggressive South American policy."[74] In November, the envoy again requested that the *Panther* be kept out of American waters, as its very name served only to remind Americans of alleged German designs on the Western Hemisphere.[75]

That these designs were not without foundation was made abundantly clear by the continued clamor for a German presence in South America. In 1902, for example, Wilhelm Wintzer, editor of the *Rheinisch-Westfälische Zeitung*, published a book entitled *Der Kampf um das Deutschtum*, in which he demanded "the permanent occupation of a [Venezuelan] harbor by Germany." Wintzer argued not only that this was "unavoidable," but also that it should be undertaken "despite America." Subtitled "Germans in Tropical America," the book pointed to a future clash for South America between "the Europeans and the North Americans." While Mexico and Central America would fall to the United States once the isthmian canal—"the American North Sea-Baltic Sea Canal"—was built, the remaining possessions of the "Spanish race" in the Americas would fall to the stronger claimant. Hence, German occupation of a Venezuelan port was but the first step in a political dismantlement, which would see South Brazil joined to Germany. Thereafter, "the global mission of the Germanic race" would be to take control of all of Venezuela as well as Colombia, Bolivia, and Peru. "Here, too, the Germanic tree will take root, spread its branches, and bear fruit which will benefit mankind and his culture for many centuries."[76]

The Pan-Germans, at their executive congress in April 1904, gave concrete expression to Wintzer's desires. Listed as "immediate tasks" were agitation for more rapid naval building, acquisition of coaling and naval stations, support for the laying of the German world submarine cable, endorsement of an energetic colonial policy,

[74] AA-Bonn, Deutschland 138, vol. 32. Sternburg to Bülow, Apr. 4, 1906.

[75] ZStA-Potsdam, Auswärtiges Amt, Abt. IIs, Nr 22487, p. 67. Sternburg to Bülow, Nov. 30, 1906.

[76] Wilhelm Wintzer, *Der Kampf um das Deutschtum: Die Deutschen im tropischen Amerika* (Munich, 1900), 53, 77, 79, 81-82.

and the acquisition of Fernando Po, Río Oro, and Río Muni from Spain. [77]

Officials in Berlin also did their part to further German overseas aspirations. A "Central Union of German Navy Leagues in Overseas," founded in June 1898 through the Chancery with the aid of the Colonial Society, sought to organize overseas branches of the German Navy League—including those at Maracaibo and Puerto Cabello in Venezuela—to agitate in behalf of naval expansion. Its members included not only F. A. Krupp and Albert Ballin, but also Baron von Richthofen of the Foreign Office, Vice Admiral Büchsel of the Admiralty Staff, Captain August von Heeringen of the Navy Office, and many of their colleagues. [78] Even the Great General Staff of the Prussian army at times fueled American suspicions concerning German designs on the Western Hemisphere by assigning South American topics for war-game studies that often included on-site inspections. Thus, for example, a certain Captain Thewald, attached to the German Embassy in Mexico, was sent to Venezuela only three years after the international blockade in order to study "coastal defenses" with an eye toward the greater problem of "what resistance can Venezuela muster against landings by foreign powers?" [79] A German army captain inspecting gun placements at Puerto Cabello or La Guayra could hardly be mistaken for a Hamburg coffee merchant.

In the end, even such official actions could not conceal the fact that *Weltpolitik* was on the wane. Especially the hostile American reaction to the blockade of Venezuela in 1902-1903 and the resulting falling out between Berlin and London had turned that joint undertaking into a cynosure of sorts for Germany's overseas policies. Thereafter, Berlin gradually withdrew from the wider world and retreated to the Continent. The developing *entente* among Britain, France, and Russia, on the one hand, and General Alfred von Schlieffen's decision in 1905-1906 to commit Germany's future to a

[77] ZStA-Potsdam, Alldeutscher Verband Nr 43, Sitzung des Geschäftsführenden Ausschusses, 1904 Gotha, p. 40.

[78] Böhm, *Überseehandel und Flottenbau*, 181.

[79] AA-Bonn, Venezuela 1, vol. 31. General Staff to State Secretary von Tschirschky, May 22, 1906.

two-front war in Europe, on the other hand, forced Berlin to eye, not South America, but the Balkans for future expansion. Available resources lagged far behind desired expansion. Hence it is hardly surprising that by 1906, we find Vice Admiral Büchsel informing the Wilhelmstrasse in graphic terms "that the Admiralty Staff has virtually no interest whatsoever in German ships visiting ports on the eastern coast of South America." The Foreign Office, for its part, not only blocked a planned visit of the *Panther* to Venezuela that year, but informed Büchsel "that from a political point of view there is no desire for such ship visits." Moreover, the Wilhelmstrasse now espoused "no desire for the presence of a cruiser at our West American naval station." The Admiralty Staff thereupon brought the *Falke* home and sent the *Panther* to Africa.[80] In a complete change of tone from shortly before the turn of the century, the Foreign Office in 1909 asked its South American envoys to inquire of those states what regulations needed to be met before German warships could make official calls.[81] Finally, Baron von Schoen that same year instructed the Admiralty Staff carefully to check reports submitted by overseas ship commanders before passing them on to higher authority as such reports in the past had often been inaccurate or incomplete, and had only brought confusion or misinformation; again, a far cry from the time when admirals and diplomats had argued bitterly over who had first right to receive these reports and to present them to the Emperor.[82]

To be sure, this is not to imply that German activity overseas ceased or that it was abandoned altogether. To the contrary, Tirpitz's Navy Office continued to cling to the view that it was "one of the navy's most noble tasks" to "display the power of the German Empire" off the coast of all nations that counted German nationals among

[80] ZStA-Potsdam, Auswärtiges Amt, Abt. IIs, Nr 22486, pp. 146-49. Büchsel to Schoen, Nov. 22, 1906; Schoen to Büchsel, Aug. 26, 1906; Schoen to Büchsel, Nov. 26, 1906.

[81] AA-Bonn, Deutschland 138, vol. 40. Foreign Office inquiry dated simply Spring 1909.

[82] ZStA-Potsdam, Auswärtiges Amt, Abt. IIs, Beziehungen der Kaiserlich Gesandten und Konsuln zur Kriegsmarine Nr 22544, pp. 107-08. Schoen to Admiralty Staff, Oct. 20, 1909.

their population. The Venezuelan blockade had obviously not dampened the enthusiasm of the Navy Office for showing the flag "since we must pursue *Weltpolitik*."[83] And on another occasion, the Navy Office in fact welcomed any and all "embroilments" with foreign powers as being potentially "extremely advantageous." "Every such embroilment, which leads to the use of armed force, means a strengthening of *Deutschtum* not only at the immediate point of concern but also along the entire line of outposts where German nationals stand duty in the world." The Reichs-Marine-Amt went so far as to see German nationals in foreign lands as front-line soldiers. "Given the lack of overseas bases, we are forced to seek compensation therefore in the Germans overseas with regard not only to the provisioning of coal, supplies, and food, but also with regard to information and military intelligence."[84]

Nor did individual commanders of German cruisers stationed in American waters completely cease to demand that the Reich establish a naval base in the Western Hemisphere. In February 1914, for example, Lieutenant Commander Seebohm of the *Bremen* cabled Wilhelm II that with the impending completion of the Panama Canal, Germany was presented with her last opportunity to seize a base in the Caribbean. "Our vast commercial interests in the South demand the constant presence of a warship on the eastern coast of South America." And while lamenting that Germany at present possessed no "naval station in American waters," Seebohm optimistically informed the Emperor that the United States had torn up the Monroe Doctrine through its recent actions in Mexico.[85] More importantly, Rear Admiral Hubert von Rebeur-Paschwitz in June 1914 returned from an extended goodwill tour of South America along with Prince Heinrich, and suggested a radical change in the well-established practice of sending cruisers or gunboats overseas whenever diplomats requested a naval presence. "This tends to be fatiguing

[83] Navy Office memorandum dated December 12, 1904, cited in Klaus Kannapin, "Die deutsch-argentinischen Beziehungen von 1871 bis 1914 unter besonderer Berücksichtigung der Handels- und Wirtschaftsbeziehungen und der Auswanderungspolitik" (diss., East Berlin, 1968), 128-30.

[84] Ibid. Navy Office standpoint dated Oct. 30, 1905.

[85] AA-Bonn, Deutschland 138, vol. 49. Seebohm to Wilhelm II, Feb. 16, 1914.

and no longer suffices for today's Germany or for today's German fleet." Instead, the admiral, who had commanded the battleships *Kaiser* and *König Albert* as well as the cruiser *Strassburg* to South America, suggested that only "really large warships, each a piece of German soil, each a mirror of the fatherland with its crews coming from all parts and tribes of Germany," could effectively "expand German influence in the world." Rebeur-Paschwitz also returned to a theme aired by Wilhelm II in a celebrated speech in January 1896, in which the monarch had demanded the closest possible ties between German nationals overseas and the mother country.[86] The admiral in 1914 echoed these sentiments and suggested that dreadnoughts alone could accomplish that mission. Finally, Rebeur-Paschwitz argued that only capital ships "can break the ring of United States, English, and French competition that currently surrounds the South American states."[87]

Unfortunately, we shall never know what Wilhelm II thought of this proposal, for the Great War interrupted the dispatch of German warships to South American states. Suffice it to say that the old fears concerning alleged German designs in the southern American hemisphere never quite died. The Wilhelmstrasse noted in the summer of 1917, at a time when virtually all German ships had been chased from the world's oceans, that newspapers such as *Prensa* in Buenos Aires, *Mercurio* in Santiago, and *Dépêche Colonial* in Paris still occupied themselves with rumored German plans to seize Margarita Island off Venezuela—in the case of the Chilean paper, as a base for Berlin's U-boat force.[88]

In the end, Germany acquired neither a naval base in the Carib-

---

[86] See the Emperor's speech of Jan. 18, 1896, cited in Böhm, *Überseehandel und Flottenbau*, 80. "The German Empire has become a world empire. Everywhere, in the farthest parts of the world live thousands of our countrymen. German goods, German knowledge, German industry press across the ocean. German goods at sea are valued at thousands of millions [of Mark]. You, gentlemen, are duty-bound to assist me in joining this greater German empire to our homeland."

[87] AA-Bonn, Deutschland 138, vol. 51. Rebeur-Paschwitz to Wilhelm II, June 7, 1914.

[88] AA-Bonn, Der Weltkrieg Nr 24, Stellung des lateinischen Amerika zum Weltkrieg, vol. 3. *Dépêche Colonial* dated Aug. 3, 1917; *Mercurio* dated June 4, 1917; and *Prensa* dated July 1, 1917.

bean Sea nor a piece of the Panama Canal. Wilhelm II, for all his braggadocio, was never willing to confront the United States openly for St. Thomas or St. John. And the Foreign Office under Bülow obfuscated the issue as best it could because it shared the Emperor's view that the time was not ripe for a clash with the United States. With regard to the Panama Canal, Albert Ballin had to realize that the German capital market was grossly inadequate to finance even a part of the planned waterway. By and large, Wilhelm II meddled in South American affairs, as during the Chilean civil war of 1891, mainly to show his self-appointed role as *arbiter mundi*; German ships were sent out, not because they were to seize land or goods in the name of the Reich, but because the flag needed to be shown along with that of Britain and France. Prestige, pride, national ardor accounted for most of the Emperor's maritime policy in South America.

But matters had stood differently with German admirals. They, in fact, were the primary agents of Germany's "imperialistic" naval policy in the Western Hemisphere. They desired a naval base in the Caribbean as well as an anchor for their world submarine cable. They encouraged the dispatch of vessels to South American shores whenever German nationals or their holdings were imperiled. They argued that Germany must "be prepared first and foremost for a clash with England and America." They demanded that Berlin establish some control over the Panama Canal, be it through investment or purchase of an island at its eastern terminus. And they changed the basic view from the days of Bismarck, when the German minister in Caracas had cautioned that it was senseless to risk an army for a lost sentinel, to one of expansion and confrontation under the general rubric of *Weltpolitik*.

That they did so stemmed from their crude social Darwinistic belief that the British Empire was in decay, and that the main question of the twentieth century would be what nations would take part in the "great liquidation" of that Empire. But the German fleet would not be ready until the early 1920s to challenge the major sea powers, and hence planners in Berlin had hoped to be able to defer the matter until then. This plan was rudely torn up by the United States, the "Phoenix," as Tirpitz put it, in the wake of the Spanish-American

War. German admirals became almost frantic in their fear that the United States would obtain the overseas possessions of "dying" colonial powers such as Denmark, the Netherlands, Spain, and Portugal before Germany was able to contest such action. As a result, they proved willing at the turn of the century to confront the United States in the Western Hemisphere simply in order to block further expansion by Washington. Vice Admiral von Diederichs' suggestion of 1902, namely, that Germany seize Dutch Guiana as "a demarcation line at which the United States influence" in South America "had to make a halt," vividly expressed the prevailing mood of German naval planners. Tirpitz, for his part, later lamented the "sentimental civility" that Germans had generally shown toward the United States, and denounced the American navy as an "indolent" force, to be compared to that of France.[89] His views of America around 1900 as well as in retirement perhaps give best expression to the fears and envy of German naval planners—sentiments that bordered closely upon downright paranoia—concerning the United States and the Western Hemisphere. Venezuela, unimportant on the greater stage of world politics, thus became an excellent barometer by which to gauge German *Weltpolitik* during the critical years around the turn of the century.

[89] Alfred von Tirpitz, *Erinnerungen* (Leipzig, 1920), 160.

CHAPTER VI

VENEZUELA AND PRESIDENT JAMES MONROE'S "INSOLENT DOGMA"

"In the coming century we must desire at all costs a German colony of some 20 to 30 million people in South America. . . . This is impossible without warships, which provide secured maritime communications and a presence backed by force."[1] With this statement in 1900, Gustav Schmoller, Germany's most eminent economist, gave verbal expression to the fears that haunted Americans such as Theodore Roosevelt, John Hay, and Henry Cabot Lodge concerning the Reich's intentions to violate the Monroe Doctrine. Indeed, the supporters of that Doctrine in the United States constantly pointed to the presence of Reich nationals in South America in general and in South Brazil in particular as potential germ cells for just such a German "colony" south of the Río Grande. Colonists and warships, they argued, were but the most obvious manifestation of a nefarious plot in Berlin to establish a claim in the Western Hemisphere as Spain's heir. How accurate were these fears? What was the role played by German nationals in South America, and especially in Venezuela? And what was Germany's attitude toward the Monroe Doctrine?

German emigration to South America was spotty at best, ill-starred at worst. The earliest example of guided emigration stemmed from the middle of the sixteenth century, when the Augsburg patrician house of Welser had obtained the right to colonize "Little Venice" from Emperor Charles V. From 1528 to 1530, several expeditions crossed the Atlantic to what today is Venezuela under the guidance of Ulm adventurers such as Ambrosius Dalfinger, Hieronymus Sayler, Nikolaus Federmann, Sebastian Rentz, Franz Lebzel-

---

[1] Cited in W. Marienfeld, "Wissenschaft und Schlachtflottenbau in Deutschland 1897-1906," *Beiheft 2: Marine-Rundschau* (April 1957), 31-32.

ter, and Georg von Speyer. However, as has been shown in another chapter, these were by and large voyages of discovery and treasure that produced few settlements. Partly because of this, a court at Madrid in 1555 stripped the Welsers of their imperial charter, thereby effectively closing South America to Germans for the next three hundred years. Moreover, the horrendous loss of life occasioned by the Thirty Years War prompted most of the nearly four hundred petty German states after 1648 to introduce various forms of serfdom, which effectively tied their subjects to the land and denied them freedom of movement. And those who still harbored thoughts of emigration generally had to pay a substantial fee as well as a standard ten percent levy on all goods that they sought to take with them.[2]

The ravages of two decades of extended warfare engendered by the French Revolution and Napoleon Bonaparte, coupled with poor harvests and widespread starvation, eventually brought a change in German emigration policy early in the nineteenth century. Baden took the lead in removing restrictions against emigration, and in December 1803 granted its citizens the right to unfettered and untaxed emigration. In time, the press of what was considered excess population became so great in the minds of its rulers that Baden began to subsidize the exodus of farmers with state funds: almost 300,000 Mark were spent for this purpose by the government at Karlsruhe between 1840 and 1849.[3]

Modest German colonies began to spring up in South America. A German settlement was founded in the state of Bahia in Brazil as early as 1818, but soon ended in failure. Five years later, former German soldiers of fortune founded Colony São Leopoldo in Rio Grande do Sul in Brazil, followed in 1850 by the more famous Colony Blumenau in the state of Santa Catarina; smaller settlements were also established in the state of Paraná, with the result that the number of German nationals in Brazil eventually climbed to about 300,000. Nearly 100,000 Germans in time settled in Argentina,

[2] Wilhelm Mönckmeier, *Die deutsche überseeische Auswanderung: Ein Beitrag zur deutschen Wanderungsgeschichte* (Jena, 1912), 6, 229.

[3] Ibid., 48, 229.

many at the Colony Baradero and Colony Tornquist in the province of Buenos Aires, at Villa Urquiza in Entre Ríos, and along the main road between Rosario and Marcos Juárez in Santa Fé. Chile absorbed about 30,000 Reich nationals, most notably in the south along the shores of Lake Llanquihue, and a small Bavarian settlement flourished along the Puzozo River after 1857.[4] With regard to Venezuela, the most striking development came in 1843, when nearly 400 persons from the Kaiserstuhl region of Baden near Freiburg crossed the Atlantic to found a new home near La Victoria on the sprawling estate of Dr. Manuel de Tovar; Agustin Codazzi had acted as agent for the *Alemannen* in establishing what became known as La Colonia Tovar.[5]

The German nationals in South America remained, in the words of one German historian, "a body without a head." By and large, they quickly assimilated with the indigenous population, married native residents, and took pride in their new homeland. In addition, they resented the fact that Berlin continued to regard the males as liable for military service at home and frequently dispatched medical doctors on the warships that visited South America in order to muster the young men for possible conscription. Social rifts also occurred between the wealthier merchants and the artisans and craftsmen overseas. The German consul in Rio Grande do Sul greatly lamented as late as 1904 that German nationals there generally failed to support *Deutschtum* in the form of German schools, churches, and hospitals.[6] In the case of the Colonia Tovar, a combination of geographical isolation, poor harvests, and lack of support from the gov-

<hr />

[4] See Jürgen Hell, "Die Politik des deutschen Reiches zur Umwandlung Südbrasiliens in ein überseeisches Neudeutschland (1890-1914)" (diss., East Berlin, 1966), 78; Ernst Wagemann, "Die deutschen Kolonisten in Südamerika," *Schmollers Jahrbuch für Gesetzgebung, Verwaltung und Volkswirtschaft im Deutschen Reiche*, vol. 39 (Munich/Leipzig, 1915), 284-86; and Ian Forbes, "German Commercial Relations with South America, 1890-1914" (diss., University of Adelaide, 1975), 49ff.

[5] Conrad Koch, *La Colonia Tovar: Geschichte und Kultur einer alemannischen Siedlung in Venezuela* (Basel, 1969), 42ff.

[6] Wagemann, "Die deutschen Kolonisten in Südamerika," 293; Alfred Vagts, *Deutschland und die Vereinigten Staaten in der Weltpolitik*, II (New York, 1935), 1742-43.

ernment in Baden decimated their ranks and embittered the survivors against Reich institutions and authorities.[7]

The not always benevolent role of emigration brokers eventually put another halt to German migration to South America. The misuse of the so-called *parceira* system, whereby wealthy Brazilian coffee plantation owners brought impoverished German farmers over as semi-indentured tenants, prompted the Bavarian government several times to prohibit all emigration to that land in order to head off further suffering for its poor. Of far more wide-reaching importance was the decision by the Prussian Minister of Trade, August von der Heydt, to ban any and all Prussian emigration to Brazil on November 3, 1859, partly owing to the aforementioned dislike of immigration brokers, and partly owing to Heydt's fears that Prussia was losing too many of her agricultural laborers as a result. The so-called Heydt-Rescript was amended to exclude the three southern provinces of Santa Catarina, Rio Grande do Sul, and Paraná in 1896; two years later, it was revoked altogether. And while the *Reskript* effectively curtailed emigration to Brazil for nearly forty years, the ingenious Dr. Bernhard Förster, son-in-law of Friedrich Nietzsche, nevertheless managed in 1887 to found the colony of *Nueva Germania* in Paraguay; its very name, of course, suggested future dreams and aspirations.[8]

Given this background of erratic emigration patterns and the continued lack of German unification, it is hardly surprising that little attention was paid by Germans to President James Monroe's Annual Message to Congress on December 2, 1823, wherein he enunciated the principles of the Doctrine that was to bear his name. In answer to British feelers that the United States and Britain unite their efforts in order to prevent the Holy Alliance of Austria, Prussia, and Russia from reimposing Spanish rule in South America, Monroe decided to seize the initiative alone. He announced to Congress that the Western Hemisphere was no longer open to colonization by European

---

[7] *Handbuch des Deutschtums im Auslande* (Berlin, 1906), 324.

[8] Mönckmeier, *Die deutsche überseeische Auswanderung*, 16; Ernst Baasch, *Die Handelskammer zu Hamburg 1665-1915*, II (Hamburg, 1915), 316; W. Vallentin, *Das Deutschtum in Südamerika* (Berlin, 1908), 19-22; Vagts, *Deutschland und die Vereinigten Staaten*, I, 545.

powers; that the United States would regard any attempt at such colonization to be "dangerous to our peace and safety"; that the United States would refrain from intruding in European matters that did not directly concern it; and that Europe, in turn, would refrain from intruding in American matters. This "negative imperialistic formula," as Alfred Vagts has dubbed it, rested for many decades mainly upon the power of the British fleet, and it basically lay dormant until 1845, when President James K. Polk resuscitated it in order to lay claim to the Oregon Territory. And while that potential crisis was averted by the traditional British policy of assuaging the United States at the expense of Canada, the principles underlying the Doctrine would place a heavy strain upon German-American relations later in the century. German unification combined with industrial growth and commercial expansion as well as an aggressive naval posture to place the Reich, rather than France and Britain as had hitherto been the case, squarely in the way of the Monroe Doctrine and its most vociferous proponents in the United States. In fact, the German-American rivalry became so keen by the 1890s that both nations prepared contingency war plans against each other.[9] And, as Paul Kennedy has recently stated, the American "republican, materialistic, bustling way of life appeared the very antithesis to Prussian notions of monarchical authority, social deference and philosophical idealism."[10]

A very few statistics are necessary in order to give visible form to the commercial and banking explosion that took place in Germany before the turn of the century. During the decade of the 1890s, the liquid capital of major German banks almost doubled from 1,291 to 2,291 million Mark; the major Berlin banks alone in the three years from 1897 to 1900 doubled their deposit agencies from twenty-seven to fifty-three. The Reich's foreign trade increased by 66 percent between 1894 and 1904, more than that of the United States (59 per-

[9] See Holger H. Herwig and David F. Trask, "Naval Operations Plans between Germany and the United States of America 1898-1913. A Study of Strategic Planning in the Age of Imperialism," *Militärgeschichtliche Mitteilungen*, 2/1970, 5-32.

[10] Paul Kennedy, "British and German Reactions to the Rise of American Power," in R. J. Bullen, H. Pogge von Strandmann, and A. B. Polonsky, eds., *Ideas into Politics: Aspects of European History 1880-1950* (London/Sydney, 1984), 18.

cent), Britain (38 percent), France (28 percent), or Russia (23 percent). Moreover, the German merchant fleet passed the United States in terms of gross tonnage in 1884 and France in 1889; by 1901, it was second only to that of Great Britain. Albert Ballin's Hamburg-America Line—whose motto was "My Field—The World" (*Mein Feld—die Welt*)—doubled its tonnage during the last fifteen years of the past century. It is little wonder that Wilhelm II took the opportunity of the twenty-fifth anniversary of the founding of the German Empire in January 1896 to crow that Otto von Bismarck's creation had become a "world empire."[11]

While the greater part of the newly accumulated capital remained in Europe—especially the Balkans—there nevertheless took place a hefty concurrent export of money to South America. The Imperial Navy Office in 1898 calculated that of a total overseas investment of about 7,035 to 7,735 million Mark, Central America and the West Indies had received 1,000 to 1,250 million Mark, the western part of South America 370 to 420 million Mark, and the eastern part of the continent 1,000 to 1,300 million Mark—with a further 2,025 million Mark placed in the United States and Canada. Friedrich Katz claims that German investments in South America in 1913 constituted 10.5 percent of all foreign investment there.[12] Not surprisingly, the German banks scrambled around the turn of the century to establish branches in South America. As early as 1886, the Deutsche Bank had founded the Deutsche Überseebank, mainly for Argentina, and one year later the Disconto Bank and the Norddeutsche Bank united to create the Brasilianische Bank für Deutschland, with a capitalization of ten million Mark; Disconto soon thereafter also assumed a share of Ernesto Tornquist Bank in Buenos Aires. The Deutsche Bank in 1893 reformed the Deutsche Überseebank into the new Deutsche Überseeische Bank, with a capitalization of twenty million Mark and branches in Argentina, Brazil, Chile, Bolivia, Peru, and Uruguay. Two years later, Disconto absorbed its junior partner in Hamburg, the Norddeutsche Bank, and

[11] A. S. Jerussalimski, *Die Aussenpolitik und die Diplomatie des deutschen Imperialismus Ende des 19. Jahrhunderts* (East Berlin, 1954), 53-65.

[12] Friedrich Katz, *Deutschland, Diaz und die Mexikanische Revolution* (East Berlin, 1964), 90.

established the Bank für Chile und Deutschland with ten million Mark capital. Finally, in 1906 the Dresdner Bank, the Schaffhausen'scher Bankverein, and the Nationalbank für Deutschland joined forces to found the Deutsch-Südamerikanische Bank, with capitalization of twenty million Mark.[13] Among the more prominent members of German society involved in such overseas undertakings were the King of Württemberg, the Grand Duke of Sachsen-Weimar, the Duke of Sachsen-Coburg-Gotha, Prinz Heinrich XXXII of Reuss as well as his son, and the Counts Baudissin, Dönhoff, Pfeil, and Wartensleben, to name but a few.[14] As late as July 1917, Georg Simon of the "Deutscher Wirtschaftsverband für Süd- und Mittelamerika" demanded that an export bank be established for Venezuela, "which for many years has been an important market for Germany." Bernhard Dernburg, the organization's president and past director of the German Colonial Office, warned that in the future, *Weltpolitik* would have to be based not only on warships, merchants, the Navy League, and the Colonial League, but "upon the entire German *Volk*."[15] Dernburg thus clearly revealed the close interrelationship that existed between the various components that were required for a truly successful overseas policy.

Indeed, the greatest impetus for that policy came from the pressure groups that began to dominate the tone of German politics by the 1880s, namely, the Colonial League, the Pan-German League, and the Navy League. A forerunner, the Kolonisationsverein von 1849 in Hamburg, had toiled for forty years to bring even 25,000 settlers to Santa Catarina in Brazil, but a much greater effort to redirect German emigration away from North America, where it was lost to the Reich forever, toward South America in general and South

[13] See Henry Wulff, ed., *Norddeutsche Bank in Hamburg 1856-1906* (Berlin, n.d.), 5-6, 16-20; Katz, *Deutschland, Diaz und die Mexikanische Revolution*, 90; Jakob Riesser, *Die deutschen Grossbanken und ihre Konzentration im Zusammenhange mit der Entwicklung der Gesamtwirtschaft in Deutschland* (Jena, 1910), 327-28, 333, 337; Zentrales Staatsarchiv (ZStA) Potsdam, Auswärtiges Amt, Abt. IIu, Deutsche Banken in Mittel- und Südamerika 4804.

[14] Richard Lewinsohn, *Das Geld in der Politik* (Berlin, 1930), 36-37.

[15] Sächsisches Landeshauptarchiv Dresden, Wirtschaftsministerium Nr 359. Deutscher Wirtschaftsverband Süd- und Mittelamerika, n.p. Report dated July 2, 1917.

Brazil in particular was needed; had not Prince Klemens von Metternich already warned that the children of Europe not become the adults of America?[16] To this end, Professor Ernst Hasse of Leipzig University, a future leader of the Pan-German League, in October 1882 had founded the South American Colonial Society in Leipzig. Hasse demanded "private purchase" of large tracts of land in Argentina, Brazil, Chile, Paraguay, and Uruguay as "future colonial lands for unmixed German" populations. Future generations would benefit from such a farsighted endeavor; the current "glut of educated elements in Germany," especially, dictated that the Reich become active in railroad building in South America, thus securing jobs for future engineers and civil servants. Hasse was not greatly discouraged by the meager treasury of 33,107 Mark raised for such ambitious undertakings.[17] In fact, Hasse calculated that if all members paid their dues, the Society would possess 300,000 Mark, more than enough for an initial purchase of a 20,000 hectare farm and its operation for three years, estimated at 195,720 Mark. The Hamburg-South American Steamship Company even agreed to provide the Society a twenty-percent discount for all its clients. Privately, Hasse felt that the Germanic race, which alone was multiplying at a decent rate— 35 per 1,000 compared with 29 per 1,000 in Britain—would replace the Spanish in South America, just as the Anglo-Saxons had once replaced the French in North America.[18]

In time, the South American Colonial Society in Leipzig became too small a stage for Hasse, and he soon drifted first toward the German Colonial League (*Deutsche Kolonial-Gesellschaft*), founded in Frankfurt in December 1882, and later toward the Pan-German League (*Alldeutscher Verband*), founded in Berlin in April 1891; Hasse headed the latter from 1893 until 1908. It was in this capacity

[16] Vagts, *Deutschland und die Vereinigten Staaten*, II, 1639; ZStA-Potsdam, Deutsche Kolonial-Gesellschaft 903, 61 KO 1 Ausschuβsitzungsprotokolle 1886-1911, pp. 85-86. Session of 1888.

[17] ZStA-Potsdam, Deutsche Kolonial-Gesellschaft 261, Südamerikanische Colonisations-Gesellschaft zu Leipzig, pp. 7-8.

[18] Ibid., Nr 261, pp. 10b-10d, 2b; and ibid., Nr 262, pp. 5-6. Undated memorandum, probably from 1883.

that he announced: "Our future lies in South America . . . only there will we be able to found the New Germany." Hasse bluntly predicted that Germany would have to tackle the United States in order to achieve this dream.[19] Indeed, time and general conditions seemed to be working in his favor. The 1860s and 1870s witnessed another great wave of German emigration—albeit mainly to the United States as a result of rising American prosperity and the promulgation of the Homestead Act in the aftermath of the Civil War. In Germany, Chancellor von Bismarck's assault on the Catholic Church and the Center Party (*Kulturkampf*), the extension of the military draft to non-Prussian states after 1871, and the industrial depressions of 1873-1879, 1882-1886, and 1890-1895 furthered the last spurt of emigration (about 1.5 million people) from the Reich. Unsurprisingly, the German Colonial League grew rapidly during this period from 2,735 members in 1883 to 10,000 by 1885 and just over 18,000 by 1892. The Pan-Germans, for their part, increased membership from 2,000 in 1891 to more than 20,000 by the turn of the century.

The Colonial League drew a significant proportion of its members—at both the national and the local levels—from the ranks of retired naval officers. These included Vice Admirals Aschenborn, Henck, Kühne, Livonius, and Valois; Rear Admirals Hake, Lyncker, Schering, Strauch, Schleinitz, Werner, and Zirzow; as well as numerous captains and naval physicians.[20] Indeed, at its Executive Committee meeting in 1904, the League listed Rear Admiral Strauch in its presidium; its directory included Admirals Aschenborn, Kühne, and Valois; and local chapters were represented by Admirals Aschenborn (Kiel), Diederichs (Baden-Baden), Lyncker

---

[19] Cited in Hell, "Die Politik des deutschen Reiches zur Umwandlung Südbrasiliens," 109. Document from 1905.

[20] ZStA-Potsdam, Deutsche Kolonial-Gesellschaft 899, 61 KO 1 Ausschuss und Vorstandssitzungsprotokolle vom 6.12.1882-3.11.1885; and ibid., Deutsche Kolonial-Gesellschaft 903, p. 131. The Colonial League in 1882-1883 maintained 492 chapters in Germany and 19 overseas, with a total membership of 3,260 people. Jürgen Kuczynski, *Studien zur Geschichte des deutschen Imperialismus*, II (East Berlin, 1952), 123.

(Wiesbaden), and Sander (Berlin).[21] Yet another Admiral, Max Plüddemann, headed the German-Brazilian Club in Wilmersdorf-Berlin, and demanded that the Reich steer potential emigrants away from North America, "where Germans are Americanized," and toward South America, "where Germans remain German and stay in touch with their homeland."[22]

A similar sentiment was expressed by Professor Theobald Fischer at the Colonial League's annual meeting in 1883, but Johannes von Miquel, a future Prussian finance minister, warned that any large-scale acquisition of colonial land would require the support of the government.[23] Such support was hardly possible, given the spirit, if not the precise law, of the Heydt-Rescript of 1859. Moreover, Bismarck publicly voiced his opposition to any active recruitment of potential immigrants on German soil: "The promotion of emigration in *no* way lies within the realm of our state functions."[24] Indeed, when the omnipresent Professor Hasse in 1884 circulated a proposal to establish a large German colony in Paraguay in order to take charge of that nation "first economically and then also politically," Bismarck instructed the Foreign Office to advise the head of the Colonial League, Hermann Prince von Hohenlohe-Langenburg, that the government would not offer "any binding military protection" for the undertaking. Neither Adolph von Hansemann of the Disconto Bank nor Georg von Siemens of the Deutsche Bank would invest in the undertaking.[25] Alone Friedrich Krupp agreed to make available a paltry 5,000 Mark for "an expedition to South Brazil."[26]

---

[21] *Bericht über die Sitzung des Vorstandes der Deutschen Kolonialgesellschaft am 26. Mai 1904 zu Stettin* (Stettin, 1904), 3-6.

[22] ZStA-Potsdam, Deutsche Kolonial-Gesellschaft 621, Deutsche Siedlungen in Südamerika, pp. 134-35. Plüddemann to Society, May 16, 1904. See also Mack Walker, *Germany and the Emigration 1816-1885* (Cambridge, Mass., 1964).

[23] ZStA-Potsdam, Deutsche Kolonial-Gesellschaft 899, pp. 38-39. Executive Committee report, Oct. 10, 1883.

[24] Cited in Klaus Kannapin, "Die deutsch-argentinischen Beziehungen von 1871 bis 1914 unter besonderer Berücksichtigung der Handels- und Wirtschaftsbeziehungen und der Auswanderungspolitik" (diss., East Berlin, 1968), 84. Statement from September 1888.

[25] ZStA-Potsdam, Deutsche Kolonial-Gesellschaft 899, pp. 59-72, 107-10. Special Committee report of Jan. 5, 1884; Executive Committee meeting of Mar. 17,

The dream that Germany should find "its India" in South America never quite died.[27] Bismarck's fall from grace in 1890 and the founding of the Pan-German League the following year briefly breathed new life into the various South American colonization projects, but they never materialized. The hard reality remained that well over ninety percent of the 200,000 Germans who left their homeland annually in the 1880s preferred to go to the United States, not to South America. And not even the infusion of such illustrious members as King Friedrich August III of Saxony, King Wilhelm II of Württemberg, Crown Prince Wilhelm of Prussia, and Prince Regent Luitpold of Bavaria into the *Wirtschaftliches Komitee* of the Colonial League could invigorate its overseas projects.[28] In fact, Ernst Hasse's South American Colonial Society in Leipzig admitted defeat in June 1900, with fully one-half of all monies pledged still outstanding; it listed its South American assets as 46,525 hectares of land with 4,527 head of cattle and eighty-two horses valued at 206,355 Mark; against this, the Society owed 275,638 Mark. Its meeting even failed to meet quorum requirements.[29]

Finally, on April 1, 1898, the Reichstag revoked the Heydt-Rescript of 1859 and liberalized emigration somewhat: agents had to deposit a bond of 50,000 Mark with the federal government, only certain states such as those in South Brazil were targeted for emigration, and no persons eligible for military draft could be recruited.[30]

1884. The reactions of Hansemann and Siemens are in ibid., pp. 144-46. Executive Committee meeting. Nov. 20, 1884.

[26] ZStA-Potsdam, Deutsche Kolonial-Gesellschaft 928, 61 KO 1 Vorstandssitzungsprotokolle 1886-1905, pp. 17-18. Report dated Feb. 9, 1886.

[27] See the request to Wilhelm II by Richard König of Magdeburg, an agrarian economist, that Argentina be "Germanized" through emigration. "England found its India in Asia. Germany must find its India in the south of South America!" ZStA-Merseburg, Königliches Geheimes Civil-Cabinet Nr 13361, Die Südamerikanischen Staaten . . . 1873-1918, pp. 111-15.

[28] Kuczynski, *Geschichte des deutschen Imperialismus*, II, 130. See also *Die Bürgerlichen Parteien in Deutschland*, I (East Berlin, 1968), 390ff.

[29] ZStA-Potsdam, Kolonialwirtschaftliches Komitee 326, Südamerikanische Kolonisations-Gesellschaft Leipzig 1900, p. 1; *Der Tropenpflanzer*, August 1900.

[30] Mönckmeier, *Die deutsche überseeische Auswanderung*, 254-56. The revocation was greatly abetted by Adolph Woermann's ability to woo the Emperor for this undertaking.

Those males who emigrated were obliged to report to German consulates annually as part of their ongoing military obligation; failure
to do so for ten years consecutively would result in the loss of Reich
citizenship.[31] The Colonial League and the Pan-Germans vigorously
opposed this stipulation and instead demanded that citizenship be
extended "to the children of the children of emigrants." Duke Johann Albrecht zu Mecklenburg, president of the Colonial League in
1898, termed citizenship "a common bond for all Germans overseas" with the fatherland, "which cannot be underestimated for its
effect upon Germany's role in world politics."[32] As late as 1902, the
Colonial League still sought to revoke the stipulation that Reich nationals automatically lost their citizenship upon failure to report to
the local consulates; instead, it lobbied for a new law that citizenship
could only be lost "through the acquisition of foreign citizenship."[33]
The Foreign Office in December 1904, in the wake of the Venezuelan blockade, firmly came out against such recommendations, fearing that further demands for Reich protection by German nationals
in South America, where 60,000 of about 300,000 emigrants had
maintained their citizenship, would overtax German capabilities
and complicate German diplomacy "especially given the current position of the United States" in the matter.[34]

This general pattern of German colonization hopes and fears was
also evident in the Venezuelan case. As early as June 1871, the German envoy in Caracas, Gülich, warned the Foreign Office that "emigration speculators" were taking advantage of a large number of
"*kleine Leute*," that is, artisans, domestics, and farmers. An attractive brochure entitled "German Emigration to Venezuela by Glöck-
ler" had misled many Reich nationals; as Gülich put it, the brochure
"turned black into white and vice versa."[35]

[31] ZStA-Potsdam, Deutsche Kolonial-Gesellschaft 913, p. 74. Executive Committee meeting, June 14, 1898.

[32] Cited in Kannapin, "Die deutsch-argentinischen Beziehungen," 127-28.

[33] *Deutsche Kolonialzeitung*, Nr 50, pp. 506-07, dated Dec. 11, 1902.

[34] Foreign Office memorandum, Dec. 12, 1904. Cited in Kannapin, "Die deutsch-
argentinischen Beziehungen," 128–30.

[35] Staatsarchiv (hereafter SA) Hamburg, Auswanderungsamt II. A. No. 13, vol. I,
p. 20. Gülich to Foreign Office, June 3, 1871.

Three years later, the Prussian Embassy in Hamburg warned the city's lord mayor that the Caracas regime was actively recruiting "farmers, artisans, and domestics" for a country which "on account of its political, social and climatic conditions is utterly unsuitable for Germans." Chancellor von Bismarck, the envoy informed the mayor, had already ordered "careful observation" of the Venezuelan Consul General, Dr. Martin J. Sanavria, on account of his recruiting activities.[36] The Hamburg Senate, readily convinced of the accuracy of the report, in March 1874 reported to the Wilhelmstrasse that Dr. Sanavria had already recruited 100 families and chartered transportation for them to Venezuela; however, the Senate pledged to do all within its legal power to obstruct the exodus.[37] At its April meeting, the Senate expressed great concern over the activity of emigration recruiters, in this particular case C. Kümpel Jr. Concurrently, it appealed to the Prussian Interior Ministry for assistance in handling this matter.[38]

Friedrich Count zu Eulenburg, the Prussian Minister of the Interior, informed the Hamburg Senate on June 22, 1875, that he opposed all attempts to further German emigration to Venezuela. Eulenburg cited recent Italian emigration disasters in Venezuela as examples against such a practice and returned to Hamburg's position of 1871: social, political, and climatic conditions in Venezuela militated against "any and all chances" for success. In addition, Prussia's negative experiences with emigration agents for Brazil did not bode well for similar activity in behalf of Venezuela. Finally, Eulenburg informed the Senate that Prussia had already banned all publications within its borders that advertised emigration to Venezuela and had barred all such agents from its territory. He advised Hamburg to do the same forthwith.[39] The official Prussian *Amtsblatt* had duly published a stern warning against "emigration to the north coast of South America."[40]

[36] Ibid., p. 29. Prussian Embassy (Hamburg) to Lord Mayor Burchard, Mar. 17, 1874.

[37] Ibid., p. 30. Hamburg Senate to Foreign Office, Mar. 20, 1874.

[38] Ibid., p. 35. Senate protocol, Apr. 1, 1874.

[39] Ibid., pp. 57-58. Eulenburg to Hamburg Senate, June 22, 1875.

[40] *Amtsblatt*, Nr 73, Mar. 27, 1874.

Given this official action against recruited emigration to Venezuela, it is not surprising that the number of Germans there remained extremely small. Apart from the already mentioned 400 Kaiserstuhl residents at La Colonia Tovar since 1843, Germans in Venezuela reached 1,171 in the 1881 census, 1,891 in the 1891 census, and only 612 in the 1904 census, after the blockade of Venezuela. Not counting the large number of primarily Hamburg merchants, which were dealt with in Chapter One, the Germans were mainly hotel owners, restauranteurs, photographers, engineers, and railroad workers.[41] Nor were German nationals particularly numerous in other South American states: they comprised only 1.1 percent of the population of Chile, 2 percent of the population of Argentina, and 2.3 percent of the population of Brazil; even in the latter case, the 105,321 Germans who emigrated there between 1820 and 1910 constituted a mere 4 percent of the total of 2.8 million Europeans who came to Brazil during that time.[42]

Nevertheless, by the 1890s the Venezuelan government again attempted to woo German settlers to its shores. The *Hamburger Correspondent* in 1891 informed its readers that Caracas sought "to improve and to uplift the local population" by inviting German settlers there; it depicted Venezuela as the "future object of a stream of immigrants" from Germany. Land would be offered at half price, free passage across the Atlantic would be provided, no tariffs would be placed upon any and all goods brought along on the voyage, and start-up funds would be readily available to all prospective farmers, domestics, and textile workers willing to come.[43] The *Münchner Allgemeine Zeitung* in 1896 went so far as to declare Venezuela to be "the land of the future in South America." Especially since the indigenous population was "slothful by nature, avoided work, and let the Good Lord worry for them," Germans would find fertile ground to exert "a preponderant moral influence" upon Caracas' "political elite."[44]

Such unwarranted optimism was shared by few in Germany. In the

---

[41] *Handbuch des Deutschtums im Auslande* (Berlin, 1906), 325.

[42] Otto Kasdorf, *Der Wirtschaftskampf um Südamerika* (Berlin, 1916), 24, 28.

[43] *Hamburger Correspondent*, Nr 596, Aug. 25, 1891.

[44] *Münchner Allgemeine Zeitung*, Nr 115, Apr. 26, 1896.

main, German nationals preferred to work in Venezuela, not as settlers but as merchants and railroad entrepreneurs. As early as November 1885, George Wilson of the Manoa Company had offered the German government and German investors 7.2 million acres of land in the Orinoco River delta, an offer that was at once rejected by the Foreign Office in Berlin as not being worthy of consideration.[45] At the same time, a certain E. von Münster of Kent, England, offered the Reich 700,000 English acres of land in Coro (North Tocuya and Aqua Viva Estates) for 100,000 pounds sterling, claiming that Prince Heinrich of the Netherlands had agreed to purchase it earlier but that the prince's untimely death had ended all negotiations. Bismarck noted that the offer was to be passed on to the Hanseatic Embassy since he was disinterested in it in behalf of the government.[46]

Indeed, it was not until 1897 that the first German plantation society, the Venezuela-Plantagen-Gesellschaft, was formed in Hamburg with a capital of 1.05 million Mark. Its major investors, apart from the Berliner Bank, included such Hamburg patricians as F. H. Ruete, Max von Schinckel, W. M. Goddefroy, and Dr. M. Rücker-Jenisch. The Society purchased seven plantations in Venezuela: Curamata, La Toma, Bucaral, Caoma, Cataure, La Luz, and Jaguara.[47] Two years later, it raised its capital by 500,000 Mark, and in 1901 it estimated its annual planting of new coffee trees at 200,000 Mark.[48] This notwithstanding, the Hamburg Board of Trade, headed by Adolph Woermann, in 1901 denied the Society access to the Hamburg Stock Exchange because it was a limited

[45] ZStA-Potsdam, Auswärtiges Amt, Abt. II, Die Handels- und Schiffahrtsverhältnisse mit Venezuela, vol. 14, pp. 38-40. Manoa Co. to Foreign Office, Nov. 2, 1885; Foreign Office memorandum, Dec. 17, 1885.

[46] ZStA-Potsdam, Auswärtiges Amt, Abt. II, Kais. Konsulate in Venezuela 33372, pp. 28-31. Münster to Bismarck, Nov. 14, 1885.

[47] SA-Hamburg, CL VII Lit. Kᵃ No. 5, Vol. 21 Fasc. 1 Inv. 10, Handelskompagnien & Aktiengesellschaften, Gesuch der Venezuela-Plantagen-Gesellschaft. Ruete to Hamburg Senate, May 3, 1901. The financial status of these patricians was verified in Rudolf Martin, *Jahrbuch des Vermögens und Einkommens der Millionäre in den drei Hansestädten (Hamburg, Bremen, Lübeck)* (Berlin, 1912).

[48] SA-Hamburg, CL VII Lit. Kᵃ No. 5, Vol. 21 Fasc. 1 Inv. 10, German-Venezuelan Plantation Society to Hamburg Senate, Apr. 30, 1901.

company, and therefore not obligated to open its books to investors on a regular basis.[49]

The Venezuela-Plantagen-Gesellschaft prospered modestly, despite Woermann's action, and the Reich's consul in Caracas could report at the turn of the century that the Society had planted 950,000 coffee trees (of which 350,00 were already bearing beans) at its seven *haciendas* near La Guayra; its harvest for 1899 stood at 2,000 kilogram coffee. Moreover, the Society was introducing sheep and goats as well as breeding bulls on its ranches, while growing its own sugar and distilling its own brandy.[50]

In the summer of 1899, a second German plantation society, Plantage Mariara, came into being in the state of Carabobo. Its capitalization of 800,000 Mark represented the cream of Germany's entrepreneurial elite: the Great Venezuelan Railroad (Disconto Bank) with 105,000 Mark, the Disconto Bank with 130,000 Mark as well as its director Adolph von Hansemann with 50,000 Mark, the Norddeutsche Bank of Hamburg (Disconto controlled) with 50,000 Mark, M. M. Warburg with 50,000 Mark, Max von Schinckel with 25,000 Mark, and Adolph Woermann with 10,000 Mark.[51]

Despite these promising beginnings, the plantations did not prosper. The ravages of the civil war engendered by Cipriano Castro around the turn of the century obfuscated all efforts by their owners to draw either capital or labor from Germany. By the end of 1906, the Venezuela Plantation Society declared bankruptcy. An attempt to revitalize it as the Caracaya Plantation Society never got off the ground for lack of capital: just 200,000 Mark could be secured, which represented only one-half of the requisite capital. Little is known of its development, but in June 1909 Caracaya reported to the *Wirtschaftliches Komitee* of the German Colonial League that it would no longer report on its progress "as so few persons are inter-

[49] Ibid., Woermann's report, dated May 29, 1901.

[50] ZStA-Potsdam, Auswärtiges Amt, Abt. II, Jahresberichte des Kaiserlichen Konsulats in Caracas 1894-1906, Nr 54117, pp. 53-65. Report of Feb. 15, 1900. See also a report on the Society in the *National Zeitung*, Nr 571, of Oct. 5, 1902.

[51] ZStA-Potsdam, Kolonialwirtschaftliches Komitee 345, Plantage Mariara. Founding report, Hamburg, dated June 20, 1899.

ested in our Society."[52] A new Venezuelan citizenship law of April 1903, which barred all aliens from public office or political activity and which automatically granted them citizenship after two years of residence in one place, greatly dimmed all German efforts to uphold the *Deutschtum* of Venezuela.[53] In this area also, the international blockade of 1902-1903 had brought serious results for the Europeans who resided in Venezuela. Only colonial and naval enthusiasts could still run on about the fleet constituting the "physical power" and the German schools the "spiritual power" that tied the *Bundesgenossen* overseas to those at home.[54]

It is ironic that at the very moment when German colonization projects in many parts of South America were at their nadir, United States fears concerning possible German violation of the Monroe Doctrine south of the Río Grande were at their apex. This was mainly the result of the continued clamorings of the Pan-Germans and the Colonial League for colonies in the Western Hemisphere, and the support that such Utopian aspirations received from Wilhelm II. The monarch's oft-repeated assertions at the turn of the century that "South America is of no concern to the Yankees"[55] and that he would "do whatever is necessary for our navy, even if it displeases the Yankees,"[56] were grist for the mills of the American supporters of the Monroe Doctrine. Moreover, the gunboat *Panther's* violation of Brazilian sovereignty during the unrest of 1893 and its sinking of the Haitian gunboat *Crête-à-Pierrot* in 1902, which prompted Wilhelm to cable "Bravo *Panther!*" to its commander, further fueled American paranoia concerning a possible "New Germany" in South Amer-

---

[52] ZStA-Potsdam, Deutsche Kolonial-Gesellschaft 411, Caracaya-Plantagen-Gesellschaft. Letter of June 21, 1909.

[53] ZStA-Potsdam, Auswärtiges Amt, Abt. IIIb, Nr 31795, Die Fremdengesetze in Venezuela. Dr. Schmidt-Leda to Chancellor von Bülow, Apr. 22, 1901.

[54] *Das Deutschtum im Auslande*, Nr 4 (April 1902), 62-64.

[55] Auswärtiges Amt (hereafter AA) Bonn, Ver. St. v. Amerika Nr. 16, Beziehungen der Vereinigten Staaten von Nordamerika zu Deutschland, vol. 8. Holleben to Foreign Office, Feb. 12, 1900, with the Emperor's marginal comments.

[56] Ibid., Ver. St. v. Amerika Nr 5a, Militär-Angelegenheiten der Vereinigten Staaten von Nordamerika, vol. 10. Holleben to Bülow, Feb. 9, 1902, with the monarch's comments. See also Holger H. Herwig, *Politics of Frustration: The United States in German Naval Planning, 1889-1941* (Boston/Toronto, 1976), 68-69.

ica.[57] And the Pan-German propaganda that "Uncle Sam was sub-
jugating Brazil with Monroe Doctrine and lard, gunboats and
Methodist preachers"[58] combined with the founding in 1899 of a
German-Brazilian Union to bring anti-German sentiment to a fever
pitch in the United States. Nor was it overlooked in Washington that
no less than nine German consuls regularly toured South Brazil,
often incognito. Germany's role in the international blockade of Venezuela in 1902-1903 seemed to give concrete expression to these
fears. The claims of recent scholarship that Chancellor Bernhard
von Bülow basically accepted the Monroe Doctrine sometime between the Spanish-American War and the Venezuelan blockade notwithstanding,[59] the crux of the matter is that Germany never undertook the one simple step that could have effectively defused
American fears of alleged German intentions to set foot in the Western Hemisphere: *official* recognition of the Monroe Doctrine.

While a broad investigation of German attitudes toward the Monroe Doctrine since unification in 1871 clearly goes beyond the scope
of this book, a few general observations are nevertheless in order. In
one of the first official German position papers on the Doctrine, Minister Bernhard Ernst von Bülow, the father of the future Chancellor,
as early as 1876 foresaw what later came to be known as the Roosevelt Corollary of 1904. Bülow advised his envoy in Washington that
the United States probably would not be inclined "generally and in
all cases" to support South American states "in all matters of differ-
ence with a European power."[60] In other words, Bülow percipiently
envisaged the future United States role as mediator between Europe
and South America in matters of commercial or financial dispute. In-

---

[57] Vagts, *Deutschland und die Vereinigten Staaten*, II, 1684ff.; Herwig, *Politics of Frustration*, 71-72.

[58] Cited in Alfred Funke, *Deutsche Siedlung über See: Ein Abriss ihrer Geschichte und ihr Gedeihen in Rio Grande do Sul* (Halle, 1902), 77, 22.

[59] Ursula Schottelius, "Das Amerikabild der deutschen Regierung in der Ära Bülow, 1897-1909" (diss., Hamburg University, 1956), 109.

[60] ZStA-Potsdam, Auswärtiges Amt, Abt. II, Handels- und Schiffahrtsverhältnisse mit Venezuela, vol. 7, pp. 98-105. Bülow to Ambassador von Schlözer (Washington), Jan. 31, 1876.

deed, as long as Bismarck was at the helm, Germany was not inclined to challenge the Monroe Doctrine in South America because the potential risk of alienating the United States was totally out of proportion to any possible gain. During a revolt in Brazil late in 1889, for example, the Iron Chancellor not only declined to send German warships to Brazil, but went out of his way to assure the American Secretary of State, James G. Blaine, of Germany's disinterest "in Brazil in general and in the Province of Rio Grande do Sul in particular."[61]

This state of affairs changed drastically after Wilhelm II had "dropped the pilot" Bismarck. During yet another period of unrest in Brazil in 1892-1893, the Emperor adopted a more aggressive stance in South American affairs. He immediately dispatched two German warships to Brazil to safeguard German interests there and toyed with the notion of establishing Prince August von Coburg, a nephew of Dom Pedro II, on the throne. Moreover, Wilhelm desired "a closer relationship" between Rio Grande do Sul and Germany, and generally sought to "play the big man" in Brazilian affairs.[62] The new Chancellor, Leo von Caprivi, echoed these sentiments in February 1893: "We must accept the risk of a conflict with the United States; they might invoke the Monroe Doctrine against us." In fact, Caprivi was quite willing to accept such a risk for the sake of "our weapons and munitions trade with Rio."[63] Not only Right-wing newspapers such as the Pan-German *Alldeutsche-Blätter*, but even the semi-official *Kreuzzeitung* of East Elbian agrarians as well as the generally moderate *Grenzboten* fully endorsed such German aspirations in South Brazil.[64] Needless to stress, the German position on the Monroe Doctrine stood in sharp contrast to that of Great Britain, where Foreign Secretary Lord Salisbury as early as February 1896

---

[61] Cited in Vagts, *Deutschland und die Vereinigten Staaten*, II, 1675.

[62] Ibid., 1681, 1684, 1687.

[63] Ibid., 1694-95. See also Forbes, "German Commercial Relations with South America," 75; and Gerhard Brunn, *Deutschland und Brasilien (1889-1914)* (Cologne/Vienna, 1971), 43-46.

[64] See Vagts, *Deutschland und die Vereinigten Staaten*, II, 1729, 1754.

had let it be known that he was not an opponent of the Monroe Doctrine, that he accepted it "as a rule of policy."[65]

The late 1890s sharpened Germany's position vis-à-vis the Doctrine. The revocation of the Heydt-Rescript on emigration to Brazil, the rapid expansion of German industry and export trade, and the passage of Navy Bills in 1898 and 1900 did not go unnoticed in the United States. In addition, the constant complaints of German professors and publicists concerning the menace that American agricultural surpluses posed for East Elbian interests, and the host of tariffs raised by Berlin against "unhealthy" United States pork, were detrimental to the general state of German-American relations. Finally, the Emperor's highly publicized attempts to create some sort of "United States of Europe" to head off the "Yankee" danger, while repeatedly rejected in Paris and St. Petersburg, helped to exacerbate political relations between Berlin and Washington.[66]

The heart of the matter was that while Germany was rapidly outpacing Britain and France in industrial output, the growth of the United States was even more spectacular. Whereas United States manufacturing production in 1871 already stood at 45 percent of *Europe*'s total, by 1890 it had climbed to 75 percent, and by 1910 to 86 percent; future estimates projected American production to equal that of Europe by 1925.[67] Indeed, Tables IV and V, which show world manufacturing production and total industrial potential between 1880 and 1913, will illuminate the German rate of growth against British and French general declines as well as the even more spectacular American rate of growth.[68]

The United States, for its part, seemed to be on the same path of growth as Germany: undergoing industrial expansion, building a

[65] AA-Bonn, Venezuela 2, Grenzstreitigkeiten zwischen Venezuela und England, vol. 8. Hatzfeld to Hohenlohe-Schillingsfürst, Feb. 1, 1896.

[66] On this, see Herwig, *Politics of Frustration*, 18-24, 27, 34, 60-61; and Fritz Fischer, *War of Illusions: German Policies from 1911 to 1914* (New York, 1975), 30.

[67] L. L. Farrar Jr., *Arrogance and Anxiety: the Ambivalence of German Power, 1848-1914* (Iowa City, 1981), 18 n. 12, 39 n. 18.

[68] From Paul Bairoch, "International Industrialization Levels from 1750 to 1980," *Journal of European Economic History*, 11 (Spring 1982), 294, 297, 299; also Paul M. Kennedy, "The First World War and the International Power System," *International Security*, 9 (Summer 1984), 12-14.

TABLE IV
WORLD MANUFACTURING PRODUCTION, 1880-1913

	1880 %	1900 %	1913 %
Great Britain	22.9	18.5	13.6
France	7.8	6.8	6.1
Germany	8.5	13.2	14.8
United States	14.7	23.6	32.0

TABLE V
TOTAL INDUSTRIAL POTENTIAL IN RELATIVE PERSPECTIVE
(Great Britain in 1900 = 100)

	1880	1900	1913
Great Britain	73.3	**100**	127.2
France	25.1	36.8	57.3
Germany	27.4	71.2	137.7
United States	46.9	127.8	298.1

substantial surface fleet, and expanding into the wider world as a result of its successful war with Spain. Not surprisingly, one saw the
Republic in Berlin as the most dangerous rival for colonies and fleet
stations—as well as for the expected "liquidation" of the British Empire in the coming century. With every step that the United States
took beyond its continental borders, Germany reacted immediately
by charging that Washington was therewith voluntarily tearing up
the Monroe Doctrine. In March 1895, for example, when an American naval squadron stopped off at La Guayra, Wilhelm II declared
that the hour of reckoning had come. "In other words, Venezuela is
in the process of being lost [to us] under the guise of the Monroe Doctrine! This is very serious! And we must soon make up our minds
with regard to the rest of South America whether we wish to reverse
this trend."[69] The Wilhelmstrasse in October 1898 took the occasion

[69] AA-Bonn, Venezuela 1, Allgemeine Angelegenheiten Venezuelas, vol. 12. Bod-

of an offer to purchase land in the Danish West Indies in order to issue a general position paper on the Monroe Doctrine: "The Monroe Doctrine has not become an international law, to which the European nations are tied. It remains largely a question of power for the United States of North America to gain general acceptance" for the Doctrine.[70] Indeed, the very use of the term "United States of *North* America" spoke volumes for what Berlin perceived to be Washington's arrogant role in overall American matters.

To be sure, Germany was not alone in perceiving American actions in 1898 to be in conflict with James Monroe's dictum that the United States desist from interfering in non-American matters, just as Europeans were being asked to refrain from playing a role in American matters. *Punch* in London captured the feelings of many Europeans at the conclusion of the Spanish-American War with an illustration that went: " 'Pray, who are you?' says Dame Europe. 'Uncle Sam,' was the reply. 'Ah! any relation to the late Colonel Monroe?' "[71] In addition, the United States' leading role in the first two Pan-American Congresses of 1889 and 1901-1902 was largely viewed with suspicion in Europe. In Berlin, State Secretary Adolf Baron Marschall von Bieberstein in 1891 declared such developments to constitute "a serious danger" to German interests in Venezuela. "We must therefore consider it our duty to oppose this Pan-American movement, and we must use all means available to secure our place in the American market."[72] Wilhelm II became so alarmed over the "American danger" south of the Río Grande that he feverishly worked to forge a sort of "continental alliance" of European

---

man to Hohenlohe-Schillingsfürst, Mar. 17, 1895, with the Emperor's marginal comments. Five years later, Chancellor von Bülow informed the Budget Commission of the Reichstag that the United States had "abandoned the Monroe Doctrine" with its actions during the Spanish-American War. Sächsisches Hauptstaatsarchiv (hereafter SHStA) Dresden, Gesandschaft Berlin Nr. 1749, Flottengesetz 1900. Saxon Ambassador (Berlin) to State Secretary von Metzsch (Dresden), Mar. 27, 1900.

[70] AA-Bonn, Deutschland 167, Kolonien und Flottenstationen, vol. 1. Foreign Office memorandum, October 1898.

[71] Cited in Vagts, *Deutschland und die Vereinigten Staaten*, II, 1725.

[72] ZStA-Potsdam, Auswärtiges Amt, Abt. IIu, Handelsvertragsverhandlungen Deutschlands mit Venezuela 12573, pp. 2-6. Marschall von Bieberstein to Peyer (Caracas), June 16, 1891.

powers against what Admiral von Tirpitz termed "the Phoenix" America.[73] In the end, the dreams of the Pan-American movement died, owing to the great number of differences among the South American states, not the least of which was the animosity among Chile, Peru, and Bolivia over Tacna-Arica, the "Alsace-Lorraine of South America." Over time, the Wilhelmstrasse became content to let the South American republics arrange their own "Pan-American" congresses. While viewing these largely to be "political operettas," Berlin nevertheless appreciated them as their obvious *Leitmotiv* was "a feeling of insecurity with regard to the United States."[74]

Germany's public attitude toward James Monroe's *lex panamerica* was further shaped by a most unlikely source in 1897-1898: Otto von Bismarck. With no apparent concern for *die grosse Politik*, the Iron Chancellor in retirement granted the *Leipziger Neueste Nachrichten* an interview in October 1897, in which he denounced the "very extraordinary insolence" of the Doctrine. One year later, Bismarck used the start of the Spanish-American War to denounce Monroe's epistle as "a species of arrogance peculiarly American and inexcusable," as a "presumptuous idea" that even Washington had been unable consistently to interpret and apply. He accused both Great Britain and the United States of having "profited for ages from dissensions and ambitions on the continent of Europe," and closed the interview by demanding that Monroe's "insolent dogma" be revoked "in plain daylight."[75]

Bismarck's demotic views of the Monroe Doctrine combined with similar sentiments aired in the popular press to bring about in the United States what William L. Langer termed a "pathological suspicion of Germany" by the turn of the century. Men such as St. Loe Strachey, Henry White, Brooks Adams, and John Hay all shared the common fear of German intentions in the Western Hemisphere along

---

[73] Tirpitz cited in Wilhelm Deist, *Flottenpolitik und Flottenpropaganda: Das Nachrichtenbureau des Reichsmarineamtes 1897-1914* (Stuttgart, 1976), 170, dated Oct. 16, 1902.

[74] AA-Bonn, Amerika Generalia Nr 6, Berufung eines Südamerikanischen Diplomaten-Kongresses nach Caracas, vol. 1. Minister Rhomberg to Chancellor von Bethmann Hollweg, Dec. 8, 1910.

[75] Cited in Vagts, *Deutschland und die Vereinigten Staaten*, II, 1704-05.

with Theodore Roosevelt and Henry Cabot Lodge. The President, especially, believed the Kaiser to be "restless and tricky," and his country "alert aggressive, military and industrial. . . . It respects the United States only so far as it believes that our navy is efficient and that if sufficiently wronged or insulted we would fight."[76] Here was *Realpolitik* worthy of a Bismarck! Lodge, for his part, also saw "the difficulty of enforcing the Monroe Doctrine in South Brazil."[77]

Instead, the confrontation so widely and firmly expected on both sides of the Atlantic came over Venezuela in 1902-1903. As will be discussed in detail in the next chapter, it appears from the documentary evidence that the Wilhelmstrasse moved with extreme caution against the government of Cipriano Castro. The Reich's envoy in Washington went out of his way as early as the fall of 1901 to prepare the United States government for Germany's intention to force Caracas to honor its foreign debt—"without seizing a coaling station or a naval base in the West Indies."[78] President Roosevelt, in turn, assured Berlin that he favored any action designed to collect debts, "but always under the auspices of the Monroe Doctrine."[79] And to the delight of the Wilhelmstrasse, Great Britain took the initiative in bringing about an international blockade with both Germany and Italy. Much would depend, of course, upon the behavior of the naval officers off Venezuela and upon the tone of the press at home.

As was to be expected, the Pan-Germans welcomed armed action against Venezuela from the start, fearing only that British participation might force moderation upon Berlin. However, the *Alldeutsche-Blätter* rapidly became disillusioned with the international nature of the blockade and let loose a torrent of vituperative ink against the Bülow government. Above all, the paper argued that by

[76] Cited in Herwig, *Politics of Frustration*, 96; see also Howard K. Beale, *Theodore Roosevelt and the Rise of America to World Power* (New York, 1962); and Dexter Perkins, *The Monroe Doctrine 1867-1907* (Baltimore, 1937).

[77] *Selections from the Correspondence of Theodore Roosevelt and Henry Cabot Lodge 1884-1918* (New York, 1925), I, 487. Lodge to Roosevelt, Mar. 30, 1901.

[78] AA-Bonn, Venezuela 1, vol. 18. Holleben to Foreign Office, Nov. 30, 1901, and Dec. 12, 1901.

[79] Ibid., vol. 21. Quadt to Foreign Office, Oct. 7, 1902. See also Vagts, *Deutschland und die Vereinigten Staaten*, II, 1537, 1539.

even recognizing that the blockade might be of interest to Washington, the Berlin regime had recognized the Monroe Doctrine *de facto* if not *de jure*, "a highly dangerous principle." Heinrich Class, a future president of the Pan-Germans, denounced what he perceived to be German "weakness" with regard to the United States and especially the apparent recognition of Monroe's edict. Over and over, the Pan-German press denounced the apparent recognition of the *lex panamerica* and castigated Berlin's "weak-kneed" stance vis-à-vis Washington, which would only "increase the Yankees' conceit and megalomania."[80] And Ernst Hasse, in his official capacity as president of the *Alldeutschen*, took pains to denounce the Doctrine as "a highly dangerous" piece of international law, that "until now has been rejected by all [*sic*] the world." Hasse, contradicting this claim, then railed against Britain's "submissive" acceptance of the Doctrine, which threatened to transform it from "an act of policy into international law."[81]

Nor could the more moderate press resist such jingoistic attacks against the blockade. The *Hamburger Nachrichten* assaulted the Monroe Doctrine as "a piece of incredible impertinence," while the *Tägliche Rundschau* insisted that "the insolence of the United States is . . . simply unbearable." Even the semi-official *Kreuzzeitung* informed its readers that it was "preposterous" to regard American naval strength as being sufficient to "prevent German expansion in the New World if that were to assume a territorial aspect."[82] It conveniently overlooked the fact that the fourteen light craft of the European blockade forces were being shadowed by fifty-four American warships in the Caribbean Sea. Likewise, the *Hannoverscher Courier* admonished Berlin to recognize the Monroe Doctrine only above the equator, also suggesting that Washington lacked the requisite power to enforce its claims in the south. Like the Pan-Germans, it lamented the *de facto* recognition of the Doctrine off Venezuela, and reminded its readers that "in South America lie the most serious and

[80] *Alldeutsche-Blätter*, 1902 and 1903, cited in ZStA-Potsdam, "Die Haltung der Alldeutschen zu Lateinamerika 1891-1918" (ms., dated 1964).

[81] *Alldeutsche-Blätter*, Nr 1, vol. 13, p. 1. Jan. 3, 1903.

[82] Cited in Edward B. Parsons, "The German-American Crisis of 1902-1903," *The Historian*, 33 (May 1971), 447, 449-50.

delicate tasks of German diplomacy, if we are to conduct *Weltpolitik* at all." The paper closed its editorial with a dire warning that Germany simply could not avoid a future "reckoning with the Union and the Monroe Doctrine" in South America. Finally, the *Deutsche Zeitung* reminded its readers of a historical parallel: about 350 years earlier, the medieval warriors of the House of Welser had marched through Venezuela with drums beating.[83]

State Secretary Oswald Baron von Richthofen was keenly aware that the Foreign Office "could not treat German public opinion as a *quantité négligeable*," and he advised Chancellor von Bülow that the time had come for Germany officially to tackle the matter of the Monroe Doctrine.[84] Richthofen was keenly aware that Arthur James Balfour, the British prime minister, had just delivered a keynote speech before the Conservative Club in Liverpool in February 1903, stating that "the Monroe Doctrine has no enemies in this country." Balfour had even gone out of his way to assure fellow Conservatives that his government would "welcome any increase of the influence of the United States of America upon the great Western Hemisphere. We desire no colonization, we desire no alteration in the balance of power, we desire no acquisition of territory."[85] The Prime Minister's address squarely placed the ball in Berlin's court.

Chancellor von Bülow, never one to make a tough, unpopular decision when it could be avoided, reacted as before by turning to Admiral von Tirpitz. The admiral, for his part, cagily refused to define his views on the Monroe Doctrine, apparently because this could lead to loss of support from and attacks on his naval policy by the Pan-Germans, the Colonial League, and even the Navy League. Tirpitz simply suggested that the government refuse to discuss the matter, should it be brought up in the Reichstag; should that prove impossible, he recommended that the Chancellor give vague, evasive

---

[83] *Hannoverscher Courier*, Apr. 24, 1902, in ZStA-Potsdam, Auswärtiges Amt, Abt. IIs, Entsendung deutscher Kriegsschiffe 22471, pp. 38-39; Vagts, *Deutschland und die Vereinigten Staaten*, II, 1541.

[84] Cited in Vagts, *Deutschland und die Vereinigten Staaten*, II, 1602. Dated Feb. 8, 1903.

[85] *The Times*, Feb. 14, 1903. That same day, *The Daily Telegraph* summed up the speech as follows: "In a word, we accept the Monroe Doctrine in spirit and in letter."

explanations of German intentions.[86] This was a plan of action that appealed to Bülow. He informed State Secretary von Richthofen in January 1903 "that especially in the case of Venezuela, I will not go into any details" concerning Germany's attitude toward the Monroe Doctrine. If pressed, Bülow stated that he would read a few diplomatic telegrams from London, Washington, and Caracas in order to obfuscate the issue. In no event would he permit a close discussion of the Doctrine, or "how we stand with America, with England, and what we seek to accomplish."[87] In the end, Bülow was spared a decision since the matter was never raised in parliament; in the process, the German government forfeited a splendid chance officially to put to rest American fears concerning German intentions in the Western Hemisphere.

Unfortunately for Bülow, the greatest German provocation of the Monroe Doctrine was still ahead. On January 17, 1903, the gunboat *Panther* was fired upon by Fort San Carlos at Maracaibo. Because the *Panther*'s 10.5cm guns were too light to damage the ancient stone fort, Commodore Georg Scheder of the cruiser *Vineta* four days later leveled the fort with his 15cm guns in order to uphold German honor and prestige. This act, coming upon the heels of a goodwill mission to the United States by the Emperor's brother, Admiral Prince Heinrich, poisoned German-American relations. Envoy Albert von Quadt on January 23 cabled Berlin that Secretary of State John Hay was extremely "bitter" over the naval action, and that German-American relations had hit an all-time low. He lamely demanded some "technical" reasons behind the *Vineta*'s shelling of the fort.[88] These, Richthofen could not invent; indeed, on January 24 he cabled Quadt that President Castro had probably ordered Fort San Carlos to fire on the *Panther* in order to stir up the American press against Berlin.[89] President Roosevelt was not convinced by this ex-

[86] AA-Bonn, Ver. St. v. Amerika Nr 20a, Die Monroe-Doktrin, vol. 1. Tirpitz to Richthofen, Jan. 13, 1903.

[87] Bundesarchiv-Koblenz, Nachlass Oswald von Richthofen, vol. 8. Bülow's memorandum for Richthofen, Jan. 7, 1903.

[88] AA-Bonn, Ver. St. v. Amerika Nr 16, Beziehungen der Vereinigten Staaten von Nordamerika zu Deutschland, vol. 12. Quadt to Foreign Office, Jan. 23, 1903.

[89] Ibid. Richthofen to Quadt, Jan. 24, 1903.

planation: "Are people in Berlin crazy? Don't they know that they are inflaming public opinion more and more here?"[90]

In fact, the German naval action off Maracaibo also alarmed several South American states. Reports quickly came in from Chile and Ecuador that these nations were enraged over the *Vineta*'s bombardment, while the news from Argentina intimated that several South American states were contemplating sending warships to La Guayra to support Castro under the theme of "*solidaridad americana.*"[91] And from Brazil came the first hint that Argentina was attempting to issue "a general, official manifesto by the South American republics against the actions of the European powers in Venezuela." However, Karl Georg von Treutler, the German ambassador to Rio, did not think that much would come of the so-called Drago Doctrine, named for the Argentine foreign minister, as neither the United States nor Brazil would honor it. State Secretary von Richthofen concurred, pointing out to his envoy in Buenos Aires that not a single South American state, save Colombia, had lifted a finger when the United States had seized the Panamanian isthmus.[92]

Berlin reacted to all these developments by firing Ambassador Theodor von Holleben in Washington and replacing him with Hermann Baron Speck von Sternburg. It was a strange appointment. Sternburg came from the consular corps, not the diplomatic corps, and was plucked out of obscurity in Calcutta to assume what was then the most critical post in the Service.[93] Moreover, it was known that Roosevelt was pushing for his appointment, and that Sternburg was married to an American citizen—an obvious affront against Bis-

[90] Cited in Vagts, *Deutschland und die Vereinigten Staaten*, II, 1595. Dated Jan. 25, 1903.

[91] AA-Bonn, Venezuela 1, vol. 24. Michahelles (Ecuador) to Bülow, Jan. 7, 1903; Erbgraf zu Castell-Rüdenhausen (Chile) to Bülow, Jan. 8, 1903.

[92] AA-Bonn, Amerika Generalia Nr 13, Zusammenschluss der Republiken des amerikanischen Kontinents und Zusammengehen der europäischen Staaten gegen Amerika, vol. 4. Wangenheim (Argentina) to Bülow, Dec. 24, 1902; Treutler (Brazil) to Bülow, Jan. 10, 1903; and Richthofen to Wangenheim, Feb. 13, 1903. Dr. Luis María Drago served as Argentine foreign minister from 1902 until 1903.

[93] Richthofen informed Bülow on Apr. 15, 1903: "In any case, our relations with America are more and more becoming my major concern." Bundesarchiv-Koblenz, Nachlass Oswald von Richthofen, Nr 6.

marck's hallowed principle that no envoy be married to a citizen of his assigned land. Baron von Holstein of the Foreign Office was well aware that Albert Ballin thought little of Sternburg, and that the Hanseatic cities largely shared that feeling.[94] The Pan-Germans objected to Sternburg's American wife and to his apparent willingness to recognize the Monroe Doctrine, *de facto* if not *de jure*.[95] One incisive observer at Court decried Sternburg as a "lackey" and recorded Roosevelt as informing the head of the Deutsche Bank: "I hope, the Emperor does not think me stupid enough to be influenced by Specky!"[96] Apparently, only the Saxon government in Dresden was satisfied with the appointment, as finally one of its own was being considered for a high diplomatic appointment.[97] In the end, Wilhelm II headed off all discussion of the matter by having the Wilhelmstrasse draft a document reminding those concerned that such appointments came under the heading of "imperial prerogative" on the basis of Articles 11, 18, and 25 of the Federal Constitution. For its part, the Foreign Office did not think it "opportune" to discuss the political motivations behind Sternburg's appointment.[98]

"Specky" did all he could once in Washington to defuse the volatile state of German-American relations. During one of his first horseback rides with Roosevelt, Sternburg brought up the Venezuelan matter. Roosevelt bluntly informed the ambassador that while "the German warships of the blockade had seen their future oppo-

[94] AA-Bonn, Ver. St. v. Amerika Nr 16secr. Beziehungen der Ver. St. zu Deutschland, vol. 1. Sternburg to Bülow, Nov. 26, 1902, claiming that Roosevelt needed an envoy to whom he could speak "freely and confidentially" concerning a possible "cooperation between the two powers." See Holstein's memorandum of Apr. 12, 1903, in ibid., vol. 1, concerning Ballin.

[95] *Alldeutsche-Blätter*, Nr 4, Jan. 24, 1903; Nr 8, Feb. 21, 1903.

[96] Rudolf Vierhaus, ed., *Das Tagebuch der Baronin Spitzemberg: Aufzeichnungen aus der Hofgesellschaft des Hohenzollernreiches* (Göttingen, 1960), 424, entry for Jan. 7, 1903; and 444, entry for Nov. 23, 1904.

[97] SHStA-Dresden, Gesandschaft Berlin Nr 259, Politische Angelegenheiten. Saxon Ambassador (Berlin) to State Secretary von Metzsch (Dresden), Jan. 9, 1903.

[98] AA-Bonn, Deutschland Nr 135 Nr 20. Die Kaiserlich Deutsche Botschaft in Washington, vol. 1. Undated memorandum. Baroness Spitzemberg also noted the Emperor's "unbelievable arbitrariness" in forcing Sternburg's appointment. Vierhaus, ed., *Tagebuch der Baronin Spitzemberg*, 424, entry for Jan. 7, 1903.

nent in Admiral Dewey's fleet, Dewey's people had seen the German ships as their future opponent." That situation had now been remedied, and the President looked forward to a future peaceful "extension of German influence" in South Brazil especially. However, Sternburg felt that Roosevelt still did not have "*absolute* confidence" in Berlin's ability to respect the Monroe Doctrine, to which the envoy replied that "Germany did not think of territorial gain in South America."[99] A few weeks later, "Specky" reported that Roosevelt was quite willing "to return New Mexico and Arizona" to Mexico.[100] Only the American popular press continued to trumpet "the old story of Germany's desire to colonize South America and to gain coaling stations there." He summed up the press position on Germany as follows: "To show Venezuela the mailed fist, to test the Monroe Doctrine, and to give our young navy a chance to show what it could do."[101]

Sternburg would have been mortified to learn that the German Admiralty Staff was at that moment preparing its final contingency war plan against the United States, with the express aim of destroying the Monroe Doctrine and with it America's dominant position in the Western Hemisphere. Vice Admiral Wilhelm Büchsel, in presenting the final draft of "Operations Plan III" to Wilhelm II, specifically called for American "surrender of the Monroe Doctrine" in order that German industry could, with impunity, exploit economic concessions in Venezuela, Brazil, Argentina, and other South American states. Büchsel also demanded a "firm" German "position in the West Indies," to be realized through permanent possession of Culebra and Puerto Rico.[102] And the German naval attaché in Washington, Commander Erwin Schaefer, at the same time cautioned Tirpitz that "Dewey and his ilk" were utterly determined to seek an

[99] AA-Bonn, Ver. St. v. Amerika Nr 16, vol. 12. Sternburg to Foreign Office, Feb. 19, 1903.

[100] AA-Bonn, Amerika Generalia Nr 10. Bestrebungen behufs Zusammenschluss der südamerikanischen Freistaaten, vol. 1. Sternburg to Foreign Office, Mar. 13, 1903.

[101] AA-Bonn, Venezuela 1, vol. 24a. Sternburg to Bülow, Mar. 13, 1903.

[102] See Herwig and Trask, "Naval Operations Plans," 24-25.

armed confrontation with Germany at the earliest possible date.[103] And even the Bavarian government was not willing to entrust the role of mediator in the Venezuelan matter to Roosevelt for fear that this would constitute "a new triumph of the Monroe Doctrine."[104] Obviously, it would require more than a change in ambassadors for Germany to improve its relations with the United States.

President Roosevelt reacted to Sternburg's overtures, not by returning New Mexico and Arizona to Mexico, but by enunciating the so-called Roosevelt Corollary in 1904: while prohibiting European use of force in the New World, Roosevelt promised to use force, if necessary, to guarantee that Latin American states paid their debts and lived up to their treaty obligations. At least the *Frankfurter Zeitung* accepted this turn of events.[105] Wilhelm II, however, refused to accord Washington "police power" over South America. "I can never agree with such an interpretation of the Monroe Doctrine."[106] A simple recognition of the *lex panamerica* would have done quite nicely. Instead, the "big navy people" in the United States effectively exploited the Venezuelan blockade in order to wring larger naval appropriations from Congress. The Reich thereafter served as a convenient yardstick by which to measure requisite American sea power.

A final note must address what even the President's family ridiculed as his "posterity letters." On several occasions, especially during the First World War, Roosevelt took pains to assure writers such as William R. Thayer, Joseph B. Bishop, James F. Rhodes, A. A. Callisen, and Henry A. Wise Wood, to name but a few, that he had barely averted war with Germany in 1902-1903 by keeping Dewey's fleet off Culebra, ready at a moment's notice to destroy the German blockade ships; further, that his stern warnings to Ambas-

---

[103] AA-Bonn, Ver. St. v. Amerika Nr 16, vol. 12. Schaefer to Tirpitz, Mar. 30, 1903.

[104] Hauptstaatsarchiv Munich, Abt. II, Geheimes Staatsarchiv. Bayerische Gesandschaft Berlin Nr 1074, page 29. Hugo Count von Lerchenfeld to Bavarian government, Dec. 29, 1902.

[105] *Frankfurter Zeitung*, Nr 9, Jan. 5, 1905.

[106] Cited in Vagts, *Deutschland und die Vereinigten Staaten*, II, 1783, dated Dec. 23, 1904.

sador von Holleben had forced the Kaiser to cancel his desires to seize land in the Western Hemisphere as a result of the Venezuelan action.[107] While this is not the place to deal with the "posterity letters" in detail, a few comments are nevertheless in order—especially since they tend to creep into American history books even today.[108]

In a word, the "posterity letters" are unauthentic. In the first place, as Alfred Vagts pointed out nearly half a century ago, Holleben was absent from Washington at the height of the Venezuelan crisis—from December 14 to 26, 1902—and did not see the President upon his return to Washington; moreover, he was recalled to Berlin on January 3, 1903. In addition, Admiral George Dewey was likewise absent from the capital, namely, in the Caribbean Sea, and hence out of touch with Roosevelt, given the available communications of the day. Finally, the entire "Teddy-Willy" correspondence has been meticulously filed and maintained by the German Foreign Office and reveals not a single threatening note from Roosevelt to any German diplomat, from Holleben on up to the Emperor. When the Wilhelmstrasse received word in October 1917 that Roosevelt had raised the issue again in a speech in Chicago, it combed its files in order to investigate the claims, concluding laconically that "nothing exists" to substantiate them.[109] The simple truth is that Roosevelt invented them to fit the moment—namely, American entry into the First World War and his desire to play a role therein.

In fact, there existed a certain empathy between the two rulers. The voluminous "Teddy-Willy" correspondence reveals mainly letters of great flattery, in which both Roosevelt and Wilhelm II complimented each other on how well they managed their affairs against unknowing and uncaring fellow politicians. Both decried the restrictions imposed upon them by their parliaments, and both railed

---

[107] See Vagts, *Deutschland und die Vereinigten Staaten*, II, 1611ff.; Parsons, "The German-American Crisis of 1902-1903," 439ff.

[108] See, for example, Arthur S. Link, Stanley Coben, Robert V. Remini, Douglas Greenberg, and Robert C. McMath Jr., *The American People: A History*, II (Arlington Heights, 1981), 620.

[109] AA-Bonn, Ver. St. v. Amerika Nr 6 Nr 2. Personalien: Journalisten, vol. 6. Memorandum of Oct. 1, 1917. *"Nicht vorhanden!"*

against the mediocre caliber of South American leaders ("inefficient bandits"). While Roosevelt confessed the world's "thrill of admiration" over Wilhelm's "brilliant mastery" of affairs and "lofty adherence to noble ideals," the Kaiser, in turn, lauded Roosevelt as a *"man."* In fact, the Emperor lamented that the twentieth century was "sadly in want of men of your stamp at the head of great nations," but took satisfaction in the knowledge "that, thank heaven, the Anglo-Saxon-Germanic Race is still able to produce such specimen."[110] These are the authentic letters between Roosevelt and Wilhelm II. That Germany "behaved" in 1902-1903 was due in the main because it had no other options: relations with Britain were severely strained owing to the joint naval action; neither France nor Russia desired any part in a planned "continental league" against the United States; and German naval power was incapable of conducting more than a multinational demonstration off Venezuela.

One cannot help but conclude that the twin issues of German emigration to South America and recognition of the Monroe Doctrine were central to the state of German-American relations. Whatever hopes and aspirations radical organizations such as the Navy League, the Colonial League, and the Pan-Germans may have nurtured concerning a German colony, especially in South Brazil, hard reality dictated otherwise. German nationals in South America were quickly assimilated, took pride in their new lands, married into the local populace, and, much as their brethren to the north, were "lost" to the homeland. As one German scholar put it, they were a "body without a head." Moreover, Germany openly challenged the Monroe Doctrine only in the late 1890s, that is, at a time when emigration had been reduced to a mere trickle. Visions of a German "India" in South America remained just that, visions.

The great tragedy of German-American affairs is that Berlin steadfastly refused officially to recognize the Monroe Doctrine,

[110] AA-Bonn, Ver. St. v. Amerika Nr 11. Die Präsidenten der Vereinigten Staaten von Amerika, vol. 11. Roosevelt to Wilhelm II, Dec. 2, 1903; Wilhelm II to Roosevelt, Jan. 14, 1904. It is interesting to note that this documentary collection for the first time dropped the word "North" from its description of the United States of America, and that the letters came just one year after the Venezuelan blockade.

mainly out of fear that such action might be viewed as weakness and as an abandonment of *Weltpolitik* by the domestic radical Right. Chancellor von Bülow's opaque diplomacy during the Venezuelan crisis of 1902-1903 let slip the single greatest opportunity that Berlin ever possessed to assure the residents of both South and North America that it did not secretly covet colonies or bases in the Western Hemisphere. Berlin's later grudging *de facto*, if not *de jure*, recognition of the Monroe Doctrine and its willingness to refer to the United States *of America*, rather than *of North America*, came too late and was too little to reverse the tide of anti-German sentiment in the American *vox populi* well into the Great War. Venezuela, so unimportant by itself, in the final analysis proved to be a "parting of the ways," not only with regard to the United States but also with Great Britain.

CHAPTER VII

PARTING OF THE WAYS: GERMANY, GREAT BRITAIN, AND VENEZUELA AROUND 1900

Until the mid-1890s, Anglo-German relations had been amicable. Both sides shared a common goal of preventing the repeated French attempts at continental hegemony, and both sought to contain Russia within her eastern borders. The few attempts undertaken by several German states to establish overseas trade and colonies posed little threat to the British and quickly foundered. Not even German unification by Prussia in 1870-1871 endangered Anglo-German relations—Benjamin Disraeli's statement in the House of Commons that this event constituted a greater threat to the concert of Europe than the French Revolution of 1789 notwithstanding.[1] For Otto von Bismarck was content with the semi-hegemony that he had brought about for Prussia/Germany on the Continent and, as perhaps best expressed in his Bad Kissingen Decree of June 1877, thereafter sought to isolate France in order to preserve the European status quo, a goal shared by Britain under the rubric of "the balance of power." As long as Prussia/Germany desired no territorial expansion in Europe, it was a benevolent neutral in British eyes. And the few overseas possessions that Germany acquired under Bismarck in Africa and in the Pacific were, as A.J.P. Taylor observed many years ago, "the accidental by-product of an abortive Franco-German entente."[2] Above all, neither power posed a threat or offered an advan-

---

[1] See Hansard, Parliamentary Debates, House of Commons, vol. 204, column 81ff. Speech dated Feb. 9, 1871.

[2] For the *Diktat* of June 15, 1877, see Johannes Lepsius, Albrecht Mendelssohn Bartholdy, and Friedrich Thimme, eds., *Die Grosse Politik der Europäischen Kabinette 1871-1914: Sammlung der Diplomatischen Akten des Auswärtigen Amtes* (Berlin, 1922), II, 64ff. Hereafter cited as *Grosse Politik*. See also A.J.P. Taylor, *Ger-*

tage to the other: the British navy was of no use to Germany in a European land war, and the German army was of no use to the British in India or Canada. Given Bismarck's fall-back position that a strong alliance with Russia was the crux of his foreign policy, Berlin was much more concerned with St. Petersburg than with London.

Above all, in the field of overseas trade, where British and German interests might well have clashed, cooperation rather than confrontation ruled the day. London was the financial center of the world. German banks maintained branch offices there and relied upon British banks as well as insurance firms and their overseas contacts. Indeed, German world trade ran mainly through the London banks, which would pay in sterling for the raw goods purchased by their German clients, arrange shipping (largely with British carriers) to Germany either directly or through London, insure it with Lloyds, and at the end of six months request payment, plus charges, from their clients. As Paul Kennedy has suggested: "Perhaps the most persistent economic lobby for good Anglo-German relations were the financial circles in the City of London and their equivalents in Frankfurt, Berlin and Hamburg."[3]

This peaceful practice underwent change by the mid-1890s primarily because of three factors: Wilhelm II, the German fleet, and the explosive growth of German industry and trade. The Emperor throughout his life nurtured a love-hate relationship with the homeland of his mother: while adopting the Royal Navy as a model, he sought to rival it with a fleet of his own; while reveling in British rituals such as regattas, grouse hunting, and salmon fishing, he denounced "perfidious Albion" as a nation of shopkeepers more interested in profit than in honor; and while posing as Britain's one true friend in Europe, he strove to create a "continental league" against the island nation.[4] Of course, the two German Navy Bills of 1898

many's First Bid for Colonies 1884-1885: A Move in Bismarck's European Policy (London, 1938), 6.

[3] Paul M. Kennedy, The Rise of the Anglo-German Antagonism 1860-1914 (London, 1980), 302.

[4] See Jonathan Steinberg, "The Kaiser and the British: the state visit to Windsor, November 1907," in John C. G. Röhl and Nicolaus Sombart, eds., Kaiser Wilhelm II:

and 1900 posed a unilateral challenge to Britain's maritime supremacy, one that Admiral Sir John Fisher, especially, was determined
to meet and to blunt at all cost. And in terms of economic rivalry,
there was no question that Britain was losing her dominant role in
world production and trade especially to the United States and to
Germany around 1900. Whereas Britain's share of world industrial
output dropped from 32 percent in 1870 to 14 percent in 1913, that
of Germany conversely increased from 13 percent in 1870 to 16 percent during the same period. Again, Britain's portion of global trade
fell from 23 percent in 1880 to 17 percent in 1913, while Germany's
share rose from 10 percent to 13 percent in the same period.[5] The
Reich was also fast outstripping Britain in terms of population: from
49 million in 1890 to 65 million in 1910, while the British population slowly climbed from 38 million in 1891 to just 45 million in
1911; a German birthrate of 35 per 1,000 also compared favorably
with the British rate of 29 per 1,000. German coal production,
barely one-half of Britain's as late as 1890, virtually equalled British
production by 1913. And with regard to iron and steel output, Germany had passed Britain at the turn of the century. Nor did the future favor the British, given German advantages such as aggressive
entrepreneurship and salesmanship, advanced technology, broader
scientific and educational base, high level of managerial training,
high rate of investment in new plants, and concentration of financial
and industrial firms in government supported cartels.[6] All these factors combined by the late 1890s to place a heavy burden upon Anglo-German relations.

The early pattern of Anglo-German cooperation also held true for
the two nations' relations with Venezuela. Shortly after German unification, in February 1877, London informed Berlin of its standard
procedure in dealing with South American states that failed to honor
their financial obligations: four warships appeared off La Guayra in
order to impress upon President Antonio Guzmán Blanco the need

---

New Interpretations. The Corfu Papers (Cambridge, 1982), 121-41, for a recent treatment of Wilhelm II and the British.

[5] Kurt Stenkewitz, *Gegen Bajonette und Dividende: Die politische Krise in Deutschland am Vorabend des ersten Weltkrieges* (East Berlin, 1960), 13.

[6] See Kennedy, *Anglo-German Antagonism*, 293.

to meet outstanding debts.[7] Ten years later, three British warships again appeared off La Guayra in order to press London's claims for shipping damages incurred during a border dispute over British Guiana; Whitehall entrusted the Wilhelmstrasse with the lives and property of its nationals in Venezuela.[8] Continuing Anglo-Venezuelan border disputes over Guiana as well as over the Orinoco delta in 1892 and again in 1893 led London once more to seek diplomatic succor from Berlin; in fact, there was no British minister at Caracas from 1873 until 1897.[9] By 1894-1895, Germany was representing the official interests of Britain, Italy, and the Netherlands in Venezuela, with the result that Berlin raised its envoy at Caracas to the status of "extraordinary ambassador and authorized minister."[10] Only in October 1899 were London and Caracas able to negotiate their border dispute in Paris—largely in favor of the British owing to the domestic chaos experienced during the government of President Ignacio Andrade.[11]

However, storm signals were already on the horizon for the future of Anglo-German relations. The *Kölnische Volkszeitung* in January 1896 attacked Britain's obdurate claim to the Orinoco delta as well as to several Venezuelan islands as being potentially dangerous to German *Weltpolitik*. The paper pompously announced that, in British hands, the Venezuelan island of Barima would become "a South

---

[7] Auswärtiges Amt (AA) Bonn, Venezuela I.C. 61, Schriftwechsel mit der Kaiserl. Minister-Residentur zu Caracas sowie mit anderen Missionen und fremden Kabinetten über die inneren Zustände und Verhältnisse Venezuelas 1869-1875, vol. 4. Stammann to Bülow, Feb. 12, 1877.

[8] AA-Bonn, Venezuela 2, Grenzstreitigkeiten zwischen Venezuela und England (Schutz der britischen Unterthanen durch Deutschland), vol. 1. Edward Malet to Bismarck, Mar. 1, 1887.

[9] Zentrales Staatsarchiv Potsdam, Auswärtiges Amt, Abt. II, Kais. Mission in Venezuela Nr. 50964, pp. 18-20. British Vice Consul M. R. Price (Puerto Cabello) to Minister von Kleist-Tychow (Caracas), Jan. 30, 1893. See also William M. Sullivan, "The Rise of Despotism in Venezuela: Cipriano Castro, 1899-1908" (diss., University of New Mexico, 1974), 37ff.

[10] Zentrales Staatsarchiv Potsdam, Auswärtiges Amt, Abt. II, Kais. Mission in Venezuela Nr 50965, pp. 147-48. Imperial order of June 11, 1896.

[11] AA-Bonn, Venezuela 2, vol. 13. Schmidt-Leda to Hohenlohe-Schillingsfürst, Nov. 23, 1899. See also Miriam Hood, *Gunboat Diplomacy 1895-1905: Great Power Pressure in Venezuela* (London, 1983), 152ff.

American Constantinople," and the waterway of Boca de Novios "a second Dardanelles." Further, it depicted the Orinoco delta as "the gate to South America," and warned that British possession of this strategic area meant that London "would hold Venezuela in a vise grip like the claws of a lobster [hold] an oyster."[12] More ominous yet, the German military attaché to Britain, Baron von Lüttwitz, in February 1896 published an article in the semi-official *Militär-Wochenblatt* wherein he prophesied the future German claim to "world policy and sea power" and even suggested that the advent of steam and electricity had made invasion of the British Isles feasible. The article was quickly translated and published in the April 1897 issue of the *Journal of the Royal United Service Institution*. One month after Lütwitz's sensational piece, the Chief of the Admiralty Staff, Rear Admiral Otto von Diederichs, penned his first official memorandum concerning a contingency war plan against Great Britain.[13]

The Venezuelan civil strife of the 1890s kept that nation on the agenda in European capitals, and by 1892 Germany, Belgium, France, Great Britain, and Spain were plotting joint strategies against Caracas; two years later, the Italian government published a "Green Book" entitled "Venezuela: Reclami italiani" to press Rome's claims against Venezuela. And in 1898 Italy sought to enforce payment of its credits by sending a naval squadron composed of four cruisers to La Guayra.[14] Yet another bloody civil war engendered by Cipriano Castro after 1899 further exacerbated Caracas' relations with the European powers. Castro's repeated refusals to meet foreign debts—or even their interest payments—constantly raised the specter of European naval pressure upon Venezuela, which, in

[12] *Kölnische Volkszeitung*, No. 7, Jan. 4, 1896.

[13] L. Hilbert, "The Role of Military and Naval Attachés in the British and German Service with Particular Reference to those in Berlin and London and their Effect on Anglo-German Relations 1871-1914" (diss., Cambridge University, 1954), 178; P. M. Kennedy, "The Development of German Naval Operations Plans against England, 1896-1914," in Paul M. Kennedy, ed., *The War Plans of the Great Powers, 1880-1914* (London, 1979), 173.

[14] See the Foreign Office memorandum of Mar. 16, 1895, in AA-Bonn, Venezuela 1, Allgemeine Angelegenheiten Venezuelas, vol. 13; and Schmidt-Leda to Hohenlohe-Schillingsfürst, Sept. 19, 1898, in ibid., vol. 15.

turn, would call into play American determination to enforce the Monroe Doctrine.

By the turn of the century, Venezuela and South Africa strangely became intertwined focal points in Anglo-German affairs. Wilhelm II had linked both overseas territories as early as October 1895, when, in answer to a British suggestion that Germany not encourage the Dutch Boers against them in South Africa, the monarch had retorted: "We are not Venezuelans."[15] Indeed, Britain's mounting military involvement in the Transvaal and the harsh reaction that it engendered in Germany would cause Berlin and London to drift dangerously apart; and the belated effort to improve Anglo-German relations through a joint naval action against Venezuela would bring a final parting of the ways. Already in August 1898, Foreign Secretary Bernhard von Bülow had recognized the centrality of Berlin's relations with London: "I am afraid that we are standing before a fork in the road: our relations with England will either become much better or much worse."[16]

For a brief moment before the turn of the century, it seemed as though Berlin and London would take the "fork in the road" leading to better relations. Joseph Chamberlain, the Colonial Secretary, in speeches at Birmingham on May 13, 1898, and at Leicester on November 30, 1899, suggested an Anglo-German-American "natural alliance" to maintain the peace of the world. And the influential Alfred Rothschild took the unprecedented step of inviting both Chamberlain and the German Ambassador to Britain, Paul Count

[15] Cited in Kennedy, *Anglo-German Antagonism*, 219. When news arrived in Berlin three months later that President Grover Cleveland was willing to accept a British request that he mediate the Anglo-Venezuelan border dispute, Wilhelm II trumpeted that "the British have become cowards because they place the easy acquisition of money above national honor." AA-Bonn, Venezuela 2, vol. 7. Marginal comment on a report, Hatzfeld to Hohenlohe-Schillingsfürst, Dec. 26, 1895.

[16] AA-Bonn, England Nr 78 Nr 1secr. Verhandlungen zwischen Deutschland und England (und zwischen Deutschland und den Vereinigten Staaten von Nordamerika) über eine ew. Auftheilung des Kolonialbesitzes anderer Staaten, vol. 6. Bülow memorandum to Foreign Office, Aug. 20, 1898. See also George W. F. Hallgarten, *Imperialismus vor 1914: Die Soziologischen Grundlagen der Aussenpolitik Europäischer Grossmächte vor dem Ersten Weltkrieg* (Munich, 1963), I, 466ff.

von Hatzfeld, to dinner in order to expedite possible alliance negotiations.[17] *Finanzkapital* was very much on the side of peace.

Wilhelm II at first reacted enthusiastically to these overtures, assuring King Edward VII at Marlborough House on February 5, 1901,
that the "two Teutonic nations" would learn to live in peace side by
side. "We ought to form an Anglo-German alliance, you to keep the
seas while we would be responsible for the land."[18] In part, the monarch had been prompted to make this magnanimous offer out of fear
that Germany would eventually have to decide which of its two flank-
ing powers, Britain or Russia, to choose as an ally. As Wilhelm put
it while in Britain for the funeral of his grandmother, Germany could
not play the waiting game too long for fear that in the end it would
"sit between two chairs."[19] The notion that Britain would "keep the
seas" while Germany would "be responsible for the land" was one
that Adolf Hitler was to return to repeatedly in the 1930s, with no
more success than Wilhelm II; in both cases, it foundered upon the
German terms for an alliance.[20]

The background for the rapid deterioration of Anglo-German relations after Chamberlain's alliance offers must be seen in the doctrine of world empires that emerged in Germany. Historians such as
Hans Delbrück, Max Lenz, Erich Marcks, Otto Hintze, and Hermann Oncken, to name but a few, published works in which they depicted the twentieth century as the time in which British world supremacy would end, with the result that its Empire would be
redistributed among the "rising" powers of Russia, the United
States, Japan, and—it was hoped—Germany. These scholars wrote
of the existing "three world empires" of Britain, Russia, and the
United States, and expressed the firm conviction that only a "United

[17] For the German reaction to Chamberlain, see Norman Rich and M. H. Fisher,
eds., *The Holstein Papers* (Cambridge, 1963), IV, 78, Hatzfeld to Holstein, May 17,
1898; and p. 169, Eckardstein to Holstein, Dec. 2, 1899. For Rothschild, see Kennedy, *Anglo-German Antagonism*, 304.

[18] Cited in Hilbert, "Role of Military and Naval Attachés," 147-48.

[19] Cited in Willy Becker, *Fürst Bülow und England 1897-1909* (Greifswald,
1929), 208.

[20] For Hitler's "alliance offers" to Britain, see Andreas Hillgruber, *Die gescheiterte
Grossmacht: Eine Skizze des Deutschen Reiches 1871-1945* (Düsseldorf, 1980), 82ff.

States of Europe" headed by Germany could ward off especially the pending "Yankee" danger.[21] All shared the view that Britain's inability to subdue the Boer farmers in the Transvaal signalled the start of its decline as a world power. Their views were given concrete expression by Alfred von Tirpitz, State Secretary of the Navy Office, who argued long and loud that "we must run the risk" of challenging the British "or abdicate politically," and by Bernhard von Bülow, State Secretary of the Foreign Office, who announced in December 1899 that "our foreign position is brilliant."[22] Was Germany about to take her place as a "fourth world empire"?

As is well known, the splendid opportunity of 1898-1899 with regard to Anglo-German relations was squandered by Berlin. Tirpitz was at that moment preparing the Navy Bill of 1900 that would double the size of the German fleet, and he ruthlessly fanned the flames of Anglophobia in order to assure passage of the measure in the Reichstag. Baron Friedrich von Holstein of the Foreign Office opposed the timing of the British alliance feelers as he felt that time was on Germany's side and that the British would have to make greater sacrifices the longer they waited.[23] And the popular press, as Wilhelm II put it, "is awful on both sides."[24] The key to any alliance negotiations rested with the new Chancellor, Bernhard von Bülow (since October 1900).

Bülow's basic foreign policy concept, as worked through most recently by Peter Winzen, was twofold: to unite the nation behind him through a demotic Anglophobia, and eventually to seek an under-

---

[21] See Fritz Fischer, *War of Illusions: German Policies from 1911 to 1914* (New York, 1975), 30ff.; and Wilhelm Sievers, *Südamerika und die deutschen Interessen* (Stuttgart, 1903), 94.

[22] Cited in Ivo N. Lambi, *The Navy and German Power Politics 1862-1914* (London, 1984), 363, 174.

[23] See Becker, *Fürst Bülow und England*, 214. Holstein informed Bülow on Nov. 21, 1903, that he viewed foreign policy "much like photography" as neither could "tolerate daylight." AA-Bonn, Nachlass Holstein, vol. 30 (Bülow 4), p. 00060.

[24] AA-Bonn, England Nr 78 secretissima, Beziehungen Deutschlands zu England, vol. 5. Wilhelm II to Edward VII, Dec. 30, 1901. The Kaiser assured "Uncle Eddy" that in Germany the press "has nothing to say, for I am the sole arbiter and master of German Foreign Policy and the Government and Country *must* follow me, even if I have to face the musik [*sic*]!"

standing with the eastern neighbor. In other words, Bülow sought an offensive alliance with Russia directed against Britain. Such an accord would permit German expansion in South America and Russian aggrandizement in East Asia.[25] Hence it is no surprise that he effectively sabotaged all negotiations with London in 1900-1901 and actively supported anti-British sentiment as a means toward achieving national solidarity. Nor is it surprising that British statesmen such as Lord Salisbury, Lord Curzon, and Lord Rosebery as well as the popular press, ranging from the *National Review* to the *Spectator* and to *The Times*, accused Bülow of duplicity in his conduct of Anglo-German alliance negotiations.

Bülow initially opted to play a waiting game, that is, to maintain a "free hand" between London and St. Petersburg. As early as November 1899, during a state visit to Windsor, he had summed up his future policy as one of maintaining good relations with both powers on the European periphery, Britain and Russia, and awaiting future developments "with patience and composure."[26] At a later date, Bülow opined that Berlin simply had to behave "like a sphynx" until London and/or St. Petersburg arrived to solicit an alliance.[27] Wilhelm II, for his part, could never quite adhere to this course. In the spring of 1901 he bluntly informed the British military attaché, Colonel W.H.H. Waters: "Your policy of isolation will no longer do; you will no longer be able to stir up strife among the nations on the continent. . . . You will have to join one side or the other."[28] Yet, by the end of the year, he again suggested to Edward VII that both Britain and Germany "belong to the great Teutonic Race, which Heaven has entrusted with the culture of the world; for—apart from the Eastern Races—there is no other Race left for God to work His will in

[25] Peter Winzen, *Bülows Weltmachtskonzept: Untersuchungen zur Frühphase seiner Aussenpolitik 1897-1901* (Boppard, 1977), 357; and Sievers, *Südamerika und die deutschen Interessen*, 94.

[26] *Grosse Politik*, XV (Berlin, 1927), 420. Bülow's memorandum dated Nov. 24, 1899.

[27] Ibid., XVII (Berlin, 1927), 332. Bülow's notes on a report from Ambassador Paul Count von Hatzfeld, June 19, 1901.

[28] Cited in Hilbert, "Role of Military and Naval Attachés," 149.

and upon the world except us."[29] While Chamberlain could not have put it better, the German Ambassador to the Court of St. James's, Paul Count von Wolff-Metternich, openly spoke of a new "juvenile extravagance in political views" at Berlin.[30]

Germany was not permitted the luxury of time to sit back and to assume the role of Europe's arbiter. The greater the British military dilemma became in South Africa, the more hostile became the attacks of the German press upon the efficacy of the British army. Exasperated, Chamberlain in October 1901 at Edinburgh firmly rejected charges aired in the continental press concerning the "barbarity" and "cruelty" of British troops against the Boers and their families, and suggested that British measures in South Africa fell far short of the harshness displayed by other armies at other times, including that of the German forces "in the Franco-German war."[31] Chamberlain's speech brought forth a public outcry in Germany from veterans' associations, agrarian conservatives, professors, and the Pan-Germans that outdid anything to date in both tone and volume. The Colonial Secretary's attack upon the honor of the German army could not go unanswered: as Bülow had once informed his envoy in London, "questions of honor are questions of life and death."[32] And so on January 8, 1902, the Chancellor countered Chamberlain's Edinburgh speech before the Reichstag by referring to Frederick the Great, who, in dismissing an attack upon his army, had stated: "Let the man do as he likes and do not agitate yourselves, he bites on granite."[33] It was Bülow's greatest hour in the Reichstag: all parties including the Social Democrats gave him their undivided support. Liebermann von Sonnenberg of the Pan-Germans, apparently not satisfied with the Chancellor's reply, went out of his way to denounce the British army as "robber bands and packs of thieves," and Chamberlain as "the most villainous knave who ever soiled

[29] AA-Bonn, England Nr 78 secretissima, vol. 5. Wilhelm II to Edward VII, Dec. 30, 1901.

[30] Cited in Hilbert, "Role of Military and Naval Attachés," 180.

[31] See Winzen, *Bülows Weltmachtskonzept*, 371. The speech was on Oct. 25, 1901.

[32] *Grosse Politik*, XV, 454. Bülow to Hatzfeld, Jan. 6, 1900.

[33] Reichstag, Verhandlungen. Stenographische Berichte, X. Legislaturperiode, II. Session, 112. Sitzung, Jan. 8, 1902, pp. 3208-09.

God's good earth."[34] Baron von Holstein concluded that Bülow had delivered the "granite speech" purposely in order to torpedo the alliance negotiations between Berlin and London.[35]

In fact, Bülow had a multiplicity of reasons for delivering the "granite speech" in January 1902. It would improve his image as a great statesman. It would prompt the nation to close ranks behind a great national cause. It would win him back the Boer supporters whom he had alienated by refusing actively to support the Boer cause or even to receive their leader, Paul Krüger. But above all, it was a question of *prestige*. Loss of prestige at the hands of the British could lead to a loss of self-confidence on the part of the young German nation; it could seriously impair the hopes and expectations of all classes in Germany for progress and advance at home and abroad; and it could jeopardize a government that had presented itself to the nation and to the Emperor as the guarantor of Germany's drive to *Weltgeltung*.[36] Yet the price paid for Bülow's sterling theatrics was exorbitant: the Reich's envoy to London, Metternich, concluded a report to Bülow: "I wouldn't give twopence for Anglo-German relations."[37]

Indeed, Bülow's speech outraged the British. Edward VII momentarily toyed with the notion of cancelling the planned visit to Berlin of the Prince of Wales, the future King George V, to celebrate Wilhelm II's birthday on January 27. Sir Francis Bertie cabled Chamberlain from Lisbon: "The Germans are like vultures." The Colonial Secretary at once reversed his pro-German stance and declared: "The Teuton is a good hand at bluff, but our people can stand no nonsense." The conclusion of an alliance with Japan later that same January 1902 showed the world that Britain had abandoned "splendid isolation" forever in favor of firm alliances. The "new departure" by London was basically well received in Berlin, where it was argued that it would drive Britain to war with Russia in the not too distant future in order to "save" Japan from certain defeat in the Far East at the hands of the Russians. Wilhelm II optimistically ac-

---

[34] Ibid., p. 3278.

[35] *Holstein Papers*, IV, 244. Diary entry for Jan. 11, 1902.

[36] The argument is taken from Winzen, *Bülows Weltmachtskonzept*, 376, 379.

[37] *Holstein Papers*, IV, 254. Metternich to Bülow, Feb. 21, 1902.

cepted London's "new departure" as well: "The noodles seem to have had a lucid interval."[38] Above all, the Emperor remained firmly convinced that it was his sacred "duty and prerogative" to pursue *Weltpolitik* "with even the most radical means."[39]

That quest for world policy would (for one last time) bring Germany closer to Britain. As has been shown in earlier chapters, numerous companies in both nations were urging their governments to exert some form of pressure upon Venezuela to meet its financial obligations. German as well as British representatives in Caracas had for some time advised their governments to "show the flag" in order to press their cases. The Italian government as early as the summer of 1901 had approached Berlin to ascertain whether some sort of joint naval action should be taken against President Castro.[40] With the latter steadfastly refusing to meet any and all outstanding debts and with the war in South Africa decided in Britain's favor, the time seemed ripe for an international action against Venezuela. A joint venture with the British might gloss over the wounds of the verbal war engendered by the Boer War; above all, it would serve to test the resolve of the United States to enforce the Monroe Doctrine.

Chancellor von Bülow spied his chance late in 1901, and on December 30 presented Wilhelm II with a brief listing Venezuelan debts to Germans and demanding pressure upon the Castro government. Bülow stressed that Venezuela already was 6 million Bolívars (4.8 million Mark) in arrears on interest due on a 55-million Bolívars loan from the Great Venezuelan Railroad—refinanced in the amount of 33 million Bolívars by the Disconto Bank in 1896—and was responsible also for damage claims of 2 million Bolívars submitted by thirty-five German nationals in the wake of the latest civil war of 1898-1900. Moreover, he demanded protection for the 1,000 German nationals in Venezuela as well as for the overall German investments of 150 to 180 million Mark. Of particular importance was the Great Venezuelan Railroad, which had a capitalization of 60 mil-

---

[38] Winzen, *Bülows Weltmachtskonzept*, 389, 395, 397.

[39] AA-Bonn, Preussen 1, Nr 1 Nr 13, Reden S. M. des Kaisers und Königs, vol. 9. Speech of July 3, 1900, at the launching of the *Wittelsbach* in Wilhelmshaven.

[40] AA-Bonn, Venezuela 1, vol. 18. Botho Count von Wedel to Bülow, Nov. 28, 1901.

lion Mark and which had built the 180-kilometer spur from Caracas to Valencia with 20 million Mark of German rolling stock, rails, ties, and the like. German merchants, who controlled about one-third of all Venezuelan trade, managed capital assets of 50 to 60 million Mark and extended credits of an equal amount. The Chancellor above all desired pressure upon Castro to meet the damage claims of German nationals in Venezuela; the reclamations of the Great Venezuelan Railroad and the Disconto Bank were to be taken up only at a later date. Bülow fervently hoped that German actions against Castro would have a salutary effect upon public opinion, both at home and in Caracas. He was most concerned that sufficient means were available in order to prevent possible failure of the action, and recommended that Germany blockade the major ports of La Guayra and Puerto Cabello in order to prevent the export of grains. In addition, the proposed "pacific blockade" would not require a formal declaration of war, though Venezuelan warships could be seized and held as pawns. Finally, Bülow was well aware of the potential reaction of the United States against such action and assured the monarch that he had already cabled his envoy at Washington to inform the Americans "carefully and confidentially" of the impending undertaking which, in any case, would "under no circumstances include the acquisition or the permanent occupation of Venezuelan territory" by Germany.[41]

But Bülow was to be denied his international triumph against Venezuela. On January 8, 1902, Wilhelm II ruled against a blockade because its success could not be assured. Indeed, Diederichs at the Admiralty Staff had the previous day rejected the very notion of a "pacific blockade" as being "insufficiently energetic" and had instead recommended a "belligerent blockade." The ruler concurred with this prognosis and decided to await the outcome of the present civil war in Venezuela before taking any armed action. Above all, the Admiralty Staff stressed that climatic conditions in Venezuela dictated that any undertaking be carried out before April.[42] To add

[41] Ibid. Bülow to Wilhelm II, Dec. 30, 1901.

[42] Ibid., vol. 19. Foreign Office memorandum (Dr. Johannes Kriege) of Jan. 7, 1902.

insult to injury, Wilhelm II sent his decision, not to Bülow, but rather to Oswald Baron von Richthofen, the State Secretary of the Foreign Office.

Friedrich von Holstein was also greatly annoyed by this turn of events. He had basically come to the conclusion that Castro would yield only to force, and the "Grey Eminence" of the Wilhelmstrasse blamed German inaction squarely upon the State Secretary of the Navy Office. "Tirpitz has no stomach for a fight." Of course, Tirpitz had his reasons: the fleet that he was building was designed to meet the British in the North Sea, with the result that Germany did not possess sufficient overseas cruisers effectively to undertake a blockade some 5,000 miles away from its support facilities. For Holstein, the main question was "whether the Chancellor will let the Venezuela matter ride."[43]

He did not have long to wait. On January 20, Bülow again petitioned the Emperor to initiate a "pacific blockade" of Venezuela. Bülow's trump was a British suggestion that London and Berlin coordinate their efforts along the lines of a joint naval demonstration off Venezuela. Britain's wealth in overseas cruisers and bases would make the "pacific blockade" more feasible, and a joint action promised better Anglo-German relations as well as assurances against American interference. Yet Wilhelm II again declined to act, fearing not only that the British might turn such German overtures to advantage by leaking them to Washington, but also that the naval demonstration would undermine the goodwill tour of his brother, Admiral Prince Heinrich, in the United States.[44] There, the matter rested. In February 1902, the commander of the cruiser *Vineta*, Lieutenant Commander Stiege, informed the Emperor that his hopes for a victory by the insurgent General Manuel Antonio Matos were misplaced, and that the bloody internecine strife would continue unabated. Castro, whom Stiege denounced as a thief, a robber, a megalomaniac, and as a man totally devoid of moral scruples, would stay in power—largely because of his loyal *Andinos*, "a sort of an-

[43] *Holstein Papers*, IV, 245-46. Diary entry for Jan. 11, 1902.

[44] AA-Bonn, Venezuela 1, vol. 19. Bülow to Wilhelm II, Jan. 20, 1902, with the Emperor's marginal notes.

cient Roman praetorian guard." Moreover, the naval commander concurred with the Admiralty Staff that a "pacific blockade" would be utterly ineffective against this "rotten state"; only the permanent occupation of customs houses by Europeans would restore order in Venezuela. All German merchants agreed with this synopsis save the house of Blohm & Co., which Stiege accused of wishing to "fish in troubled waters" by its continued opposition to foreign intervention.[45] Not surprisingly, the April deadline for naval action passed almost unnoticed. However, the cardinal issue had been placed on the table by Bülow: joint Anglo-German measures against Venezuela.

While a great debate ensued early in 1903 both in Berlin and London concerning which government had initiated the negotiations leading to the joint naval action, with vituperative barbs hurled by both sides, it seems clear from a careful reading of the British and German documents that the government in London in fact seized the lead. Already on January 2, 1902—that is, at a time when Bülow's suggestion for naval pressure upon Castro was being rejected by the Emperor, the Admiralty Staff, and the Navy Office—F. H. Villiers, the British Under Secretary responsible for South America, inquired of the German Chargé d'affaires in London, Hermann Baron von Eckardstein, whether a "joint action" against Venezuela might not be feasible.[46] And on January 30—again, after Wilhelm II had rejected Bülow's second plea for pressure upon Castro—Sir Frank Lascelles, the British envoy to Germany, officially asked State Secretary von Richthofen "what steps are contemplated" in Berlin against Caracas. Richthofen noted that Wilhelm II did not wish to mount any action against Castro as long as his royal brother was in the United States, and added that he was as yet unclear in his own mind over the proper course to follow.[47]

Indeed, the Wilhelmstrasse sat on Lascelles' inquiry until July 1902, when it became convinced that Castro was in danger of losing to the rebels. Under Secretary Otto von Mühlberg informed Ambas-

---

[45] Ibid. Stiege to Wilhelm II, Feb. 3, 1902.

[46] Ibid. Eckardstein to Foreign Office, Jan. 2, 1902.

[47] Ibid. Lascelles to Richthofen, Jan. 30, 1902, with the latter's notes appended.

sador von Metternich in London that the German government now "thoroughly favored" a joint action against Castro with Britain, and recommended that the two powers undertake a "pacific blockade" of Venezuelan ports from December 1902 through March 1903. Mühlberg instructed Metternich "carefully and highly confidentially to ascertain" whether Britain was prepared to join in any future action against Castro with an eye toward both "our prestige in Central and South America" and a possible interpellation in the Reichstag as to why no action had yet been taken.[48] Metternich reported on July 24 that Lord Lansdowne had agreed "in principle" to joint action, but that the Foreign Secretary desired time "to think the matter over."[49] And on August 7 Metternich cabled the Wilhelmstrasse that Lansdowne was "completely prepared to undertake joint steps against the Venezuelan government," requesting only that the United States be asked to join the two European powers.[50] Mühlberg was willing to include Washington, but suggested that the relatively small American claims against Castro would probably dictate against any official naval action.[51]

London was prepared to act. On August 8, Sir Francis Bertie, now at the Foreign Office, advised the Admiralty that Lord Lansdowne "is of opinion that the time has arrived when strong measures must be resorted to for the purpose of bringing the Venezuelan Government to a sense of their international obligations." Bertie informed the Admiralty that the Germans were prepared to "take part in a joint naval demonstration" and inquired "as to the most effective and convenient manner of putting pressure on the Venezuelan Government."[52] Their Lordships replied that "there was no objection to a blockade of one or more Venezuelan ports," and asked only that the blockade be delayed until November "for climatic reasons."[53] Lans-

[48] Ibid., vol. 21. Mühlberg to Metternich, July 17, 1902.

[49] Ibid. Metternich to Bülow, July 24, 1902.

[50] Ibid. Metternich to Bülow, Aug. 7, 1902.

[51] Ibid. Mühlberg to Metternich, Aug. 14, 1902.

[52] Public Record Office (PRO) London, Admiralty I/7690, Foreign Office 1902. Bertie to Secretary of the Admiralty, Aug. 8, 1902.

[53] Ibid. Lansdowne to Lascelles, Aug. 19, 1902.

downe, in turn, informed his supporters that he was not personally disposed against Castro and that he was even willing to allow Venezuela "a moderate allowance in the matter of revolutions." However, he noted that it had over the past seventy years "indulged in the luxury of no fewer than 104 revolutions. Three revolutions in [the last] two years [seem] to be altogether unreasonable."[54]

Chancellor von Bülow was on the threshold of success. On September 1, 1902, he formally requested permission from Wilhelm II to finalize negotiations with London concerning the projected blockade. The Emperor at once gave his consent, warning only that a "pacific blockade" would require an emergency budget of 10 to 20 million Mark, while a more "serious blockade" would necessitate as much as 50 to 60 million Mark.[55] By November 12, Bülow, who was at Sandringham, could report that both Edward VII and Lansdowne were prepared to undertake joint action against Castro. But the unctuous Chancellor, while welcoming British involvement, cautioned that London's participation "might complicate our position." He slyly informed Wilhelm II that the British only hated "the German government" but not "the kaiser." Desiring above all to leave the initiative with London, Bülow recommended "patience," "tact," and "shutting one's trap"—all qualities not then in evidence in Berlin. Finally, Bülow testily reminded Tirpitz that Germany possessed but eight capital ships to thirty-five for Britain.[56]

Villiers on November 17 again stressed Britain's resolve to join Germany in the naval action, recommending that both the Venezuelan warships and customs houses be seized; further, Lansdowne still opposed a "pacific blockade," as Britain had in 1884 lodged formal protests in Paris against a similar French blockade against Formosa.[57] And in a remarkable display of amity, Baron von Richthofen

[54] *The Times*, Dec. 13, 1902. Speech before the United Club.

[55] *Grosse Politik*, XVII, 244-46. Bülow to Wilhelm II, Sept. 1, 1902; and ibid., 248, Bülow to Wilhelm II, with the monarch's marginal notes.

[56] AA-Bonn, Deutschland 137, Allgemeine Deutsche Politik, vol. 3. Bülow to Wilhelm II, Nov. 12 and 13, 1902.

[57] AA-Bonn, Venezuela 1, vol. 22a. Bernstorff to Foreign Office, Nov. 17, 1902. Lansdowne had first raised the idea of seizing the Venezuelan warships to Metternich

at once urged Bülow to treat the British offer as "bona fide," not to debate its details, but to accept it "en bloc."[58] On November 19 Lansdowne cabled Lascelles that "it would be sufficient if we were to give the United States' Government notice of our intentions without asking them to act with us in the matter."[59] At the last moment, Italy's Foreign Minister, Giulio Prinetti, fearing that his government might miss the chance to collect outstanding debts of 2.8 million Bolívars from Caracas, on December 4 requested that Rome too be included in the blockade. While neither Berlin nor London was especially keen about the Italian request, for it might delay the planned blockade, both nevertheless agreed to honor it: Germany in order to maintain good relations with its ally, and Britain in order to garner Italian "benevolence" for an expedition then being planned into Somaliland.[60] In truth, Italy like Germany desperately needed British participation in any action off Venezuela since it possessed only four overseas cruisers.[61] On December 11, 1902, Foreign Secretary von Richthofen asked the Federal Chamber (Bundesrat) to convene at once; Chancellor von Bülow, fearing that a "belligerent blockade" constituted a *de facto* if not *de jure* declaration of war against Venezuela, argued that approval by the Bundesrat was required under Article 11, Paragraph 2, of the Federal Constitution of 1871. Above all, Richthofen was most careful to explain to the representatives of the German federal states that the planned action was being under-

on Oct. 22, 1902. PRO, Admiralty I/7690, Foreign Office 1902. Lansdowne to Lascelles, Oct. 22, 1902. The Foreign Office in London also considered various other "pacific blockades" such as those by Britain in 1837 against New Grenada and in 1842-1844 against St. Juan as well as Nicaraguan ports; by Britain and France in 1845-1847 against Argentine ports; and by Britain in 1882 against Rio de Janeiro. Ibid., confidential memorandum of Nov. 28, 1902.

[58] AA-Bonn, Venezuela 1, vol. 22a. Richthofen's memorandum of Nov. 18, 1902.

[59] PRO, Admiralty I/7690, Foreign Office 1902. Lansdowne to Lascelles, Aug. 19, 1902.

[60] AA-Bonn, Venezuela 1, vol. 22a. Metternich to Foreign Office, Dec. 4 and 5, 1902.

[61] Ibid., vol. 22b. Wedel to Bülow, Dec. 16, 1902. The official Italian declaration concerning the blockade was issued at Rome on Dec. 19, 1902. See Staatsarchiv (SA) Bremen, 3-A.3.V. Nr 99, Senats-Registratur, Reklamationen Deutschlands gegen die Vereinigten Staaten von Venezuela. Richthofen to Bremen Senate, Jan. 3, 1903, with the Italian proclamation appended.

taken "upon the recommendation of the English government."[62] Four days later, the Federal Chamber granted the government's request.[63] A joint declaration of the international blockade was issued in Berlin and London on December 20, 1902.[64]

If President Castro had hoped that the European action was largely bluff, he was quickly disillusioned. On December 9—that is, eleven days before the formal blockade announcement—the German cruiser *Vineta* and the gunboat *Panther* under the command of Commodore Georg Scheder seized the Venezuelan vessels *General Crespo* and *Totumo* at La Guayra. The British squadron under Vice Admiral Sir Archibald L. Douglas thereupon captured the *Zamora* and the *23 de Mayo* in the Golfo de Paria. Within days, the remaining ships of the Venezuelan fleet (*Restaurador, Bolívar, Margarita,* and *Ossun*) were overtaken by Anglo-German warships. And when the Venezuelans refused to release the British freighter *Topaze* at Puerto Cabello, the British cruiser *Charybdis* as well as the *Vineta* on December 13 levelled Forts Vigía and Libertador guarding the port.[65]

These actions aroused "mob excitement" in Caracas. Reuter's Special Service on December 10 reported the arrest of more than 200 foreigners at Caracas in the aftermath of the seizure of the Venezuelan ships. Four days later, Reuter's announced that a throng of 10,000 persons had "called at the Yellow House" of President Castro in order to protest the Anglo-German shelling of Puerto Cabello.[66]

In Britain, one member of the House of Commons denounced the action off Puerto Cabello as "using a Nasmyth hammer in order to

[62] Ibid. Hanseatic Embassy (Berlin) to Lord Mayor Dr. Pauli (Bremen), Dec. 13, 1902.

[63] Bundesraths-Protokolle, Session 1902, 3.9. Sitzung, Dec. 15, 1902.

[64] Both declarations are in SA-Bremen, 3-A.3.V. Nr 99, Senats-Registratur, Reklamationen Deutschlands gegen die Vereinigten Staaten von Venezuela.

[65] See Holger H. Herwig, *Alemania y el bloqueo internacional de Venezuela 1902/ 03* (Caracas, 1977), 29-30. See also the lengthy report of the bombardment by Commodore R. A. Montgomerie of the *Charybdis* to Admiral Douglas. PRO, Admiralty I/ 7690, Foreign Office 1902. Dated Dec. 15, 1902, at La Guayra.

[66] PRO, Admiralty I/7690, Foreign Office 1902. Cable from Willemstad, Dec. 10, and from Caracas, Dec. 14, 1902.

crack a nut."[67] The Admiralty, for its part, regretted the scuttling of the Venezuelan vessels *General Crespo* and *Totumo* by Commodore Scheder, commenting bitterly upon the "absurdity and willfulness" of the German proceedings; their Lordships were especially concerned lest the United States place a share of the blame with London.[68] Across the North Sea, the Pan-Germans not surprisingly argued that the British could not be trusted honorably to uphold their end of the blockade. Paul Samassa, editor of the *Alldeutsche-Blätter*, was particularly upset that the British had sent more cruisers than Germany as well as a more senior naval commander.[69] Baron von Richthofen at the Wilhelmstrasse informed the Saxon plenipotentiary to Berlin that, despite the present temporary alliance, the British press was behaving "in the most despicable manner" in its handling of German blockade activities. Richthofen saw therein "proof of the fact that one hates us in England not only for political but also for economic reasons." He counseled "caution" for the future of Anglo-German relations, but suggested that the Reich "keep its powder dry."[70]

The Foreign Secretary's reference to the British press can be narrowed down to a single item: Rudyard Kipling's poem, "The Rowers," which appeared in the morning edition of *The Times* on December 22, 1902. The bard coupled events in South Africa and Venezuela in his rhyme:

> Last night ye swore our voyage was done,
> But seaward still we go;

[67] Cited in Herwig, *Alemania y el bloqueo internacional*, 32.

[68] Cited in Arthur J. Marder, *The Anatomy of British Sea Power: A History of British Naval Policy in the Pre-Dreadnought Era, 1880-1905* (New York, 1940), 465-66.

[69] *Alldeutsche-Blätter*, Nr 51, vol. 12, pp. 456-57. Dated Dec. 20, 1902. See also the articles by S. Passarge and Vice Admiral Livonius in the *Deutsche Kolonialzeitung*, Nr 52, vol. 19, of Dec. 25, 1902, wherein especially Passarge warned that United States demand for more beef would force Washington to acquire Venezuela and Colombia in the near future.

[70] Sächsisches Hauptstaatsarchiv Dresden, Gesandschaft Berlin Nr 258, Politische Angelegenheiten. Confidential report by the Saxon plenipotentiary in Berlin to Count von Metzsch in Dresden, Dec. 30, 1902.

> And ye tell us 'now of a secret vow
>   Ye have made with an open foe!

Warming up to his topic, Kipling reminded his countrymen of German insults during the recent Boer War:

> Look South! The gale is scarce o'erpast
>   That stripped and laid us down,
> When we stood forth but they stood fast
>   And prayed to see us drown.
>
> The dead they mocked are scarcely cold,
>   Our wounds are bleeding yet—
> And ye tell us now that our strength is sold
>   To help them press for a debt!

Obviously, the joint naval action off Venezuela did not find favor with Britain's most celebrated poet:

> That we must lie off a lightless coast
>   And haul and back and veer,
> At the will of the breed that have wronged
>   us most
>   For a year and a year and a year!
>
> There was never a shame in Christendie
>   They laid not to our door—
> And ye say we must take the winter sea
>   And sail with them once more?

Finally, Kipling's closing stanza was especially irritating:

> In sight of peace—from the Narrow Seas
>   O'er half the world to run—
> With a cheated crew, to league anew
>   With the Goth and the shameless Hun!

The editors of *The Times* in their afternoon edition regretted the words "open foe" in obvious reference to Germany, but otherwise stood by the views expressed by Kipling as giving vent "to a sentiment which unquestionably prevails far and wide throughout the nation."[71] Foreign Secretary Lord Lansdowne denounced "The Rowers" as "an outrage."[72] Conversely, Lord Rosebery, in a speech at the Guildhall at Plymouth, attacked the government for its "unwise" alliance with Germany, which had placed Britain in "a very dangerous position." The former prime minister reminded the nation of a similar case in 1861-1862, when Britain had joined France in a "process of debt-collecting" in Mexico only to discover "that the French had an ulterior policy of their own."[73]

Kipling's vituperative verses did not fail to have their desired effect. Wilhelm II at once realized their gravity in terms of Anglo-German relations: "It is an ill wind that blows nobody good!"[74] And Chancellor von Bülow not surprisingly decided to bring the poem before the Reichstag, denouncing Kipling as "a savage poet of great talent" who had "the audacity to inflict verbal injuries upon us."[75] His speech was met with great applause. General Alfred von Waldersee, a former head of the General Staff, spied an Anglo-American *rapprochement* in the offing and noted that the Emperor was determined to demand a new increase in the size of the German fleet in 1904.[76] Whatever benefit the original plan of a joint naval undertaking had accomplished for more cordial relations between London and Berlin was now in danger of being drowned in a tide of purple prose. The new Prime Minister, Arthur James Balfour, struggled loyally alone to adhere to the policy of cooperation with Germany off Venezuela.

Unfortunately for Balfour, events in Venezuela were to bring Anglo-German relations to their nadir early in the new year. Lieutenant Commander Eckermann of the gunboat *Panther* on January 17,

[71] *The Times*, Dec. 22, 1902, morning and afternoon editions.

[72] Cited in Alfred Vagts, *Deutschland und die Vereinigten Staaten in der Weltpolitik* (New York, 1935), II, 1573.

[73] See *The Daily Chronicle*, Jan. 17, 1903.

[74] AA-Bonn, England Nr 78, Beziehungen Deutschlands zu England, vol. 18. The Emperor's notes on a letter from R. H. Collins (Britain), dated Dec. 31, 1902.

[75] Reichstag, Verhandlungen. Stenographische Berichte, X. Legislaturperiode, II. Session, vol. 186, p. 7432b. Jan. 20, 1903.

[76] Heinrich Otto Meisner, ed., *Denkwürdigkeiten des General-Feldmarschalls Alfred Grafen von Waldersee* (Stuttgart/Berlin, 1923), III, 200. Entry for Jan. 11, 1903.

1903, engaged Fort San Carlos off Maracaibo in a firefight, only to discover that his 10.5cm guns were ineffective against the ancient stone fort. And while the Venezuelans celebrated, in grand style for several days, Eckermann's failure to reduce the fort, Commodore Scheder at once decided that the "boastful manner" in which Caracas had reacted to the *Panther*'s action demanded "energetic" retaliation: on January 21, the cruiser *Vineta* severely damaged Fort San Carlos with a bombardment of more than 100 (21cm and 15cm) shells.[77]

Scheder's actions drew loud protests from President Theodore Roosevelt and Secretary of State John Hay in Washington, while the American Admiral George Dewey ominously patrolled the Caribbean Sea with an armada of more than fifty vessels, including battleships. In Italy, Foreign Minister Prinetti lamented that the *Panther*'s action might possibly be deleterious to future negotiations with Castro, while King Vittorio Emanuele III innocently noted that "on such occasions cannons have a way of going off on their own."[78] Ambassador Adolf Baron Marschall von Bieberstein noted from Constantinople that the *Panther*'s dismal performance might adversely affect Turkish plans to purchase artillery pieces in Germany.[79]

British reaction to the German naval efforts off Venezuela was predictably glum. Ambassador von Metternich reported as early as January 19, 1903: "As long as I have known England, I have never observed such bitterness toward any other nation as now [exists] against us."[80] Nine days later, Metternich informed Berlin that both Edward VII and the Prince of Wales desired to end the Venezuelan matter as quickly as possible, which drew from Wilhelm II the barb that Edward "is losing his nerve! Grandmama would never have said

[77] Herwig, *Alemania y el bloqueo internacional*, 35-37. See also Scheder's report to Wilhelm II on Jan. 24, 1903, in Bundesarchiv-Militärarchiv Freiburg, RM 3/3301 Reichs-Marine-Amt, Ostamerikanische Kreuzerdivision.

[78] AA-Bonn, Venezuela 1, vol. 23. Ambassador Anton Count von Monts to Bülow, Jan. 25, 1903.

[79] Ibid. Marschall von Bieberstein to Foreign Office, Jan. 19, 1903.

[80] AA-Bonn, England Nr 78 secretissima, vol. 6. Metternich to Foreign Office, Jan. 19, 1903. See also Vagts, *Deutschland und die Vereinigten Staaten*, II, 1598-99.

that."[81] Early in February, Metternich ruefully noted that the royal couple as well as the Prince of Wales were "for the moment very pro-American," and that they displayed "a great antipathy against the joint action off Venezuela." Much of the public now seemed to equate the shelling of Fort San Carlos with "a desecration of the holy soil of Venezuela." Most importantly, Metternich warned that any discussion regarding which government had taken the initiative in suggesting the joint nature of the venture be avoided, as it might topple the Balfour government.[82] Chancellor von Bülow fully concurred with this fear, seeing in the fall of the Balfour government "an immediate danger" to Anglo-German relations; a successor government headed by Lord Rosebery would be "much more dangerous" for Berlin.[83]

Finally, the Venezuelan episode also set off a heated debate in the Reichstag. Ernst Hasse of the Pan-Germans demanded that the Reich in the future display less hesitancy in using "the mailed fist," while his colleague, Liebermann von Sonnenberg, even suggested that Chancellor von Bülow had acted against the wishes of the nation in joining Britain against Castro.[84] Their assessment that only the United States had reaped benefit from the undertaking was shared by the Social Democrats August Bebel and Georg von Vollmar; characteristically, Bebel denounced the blockade as an expedition undertaken at the behest of Krupp and the Disconto Bank.[85] Even the Liberal Party's spokesman, Ernst Bassermann, sounded the alarm:

[81] AA-Bonn, Venezuela 1, vol. 23. Metternich to Wilhelm II, Jan. 28, 1903, with the Emperor's notes. Edward VII informed Carl von Coerper, the German naval attaché, that especially the British press had placed his government "in a very unfortunate position." AA-Bonn, England Nr 81 Nr 1, Das englische Königshaus, vol. 11a. Coerper to Foreign Office and to Wilhelm II, Feb. 9, 1903.

[82] AA-Bonn, England Nr 78 secretissima, vol. 6. Metternich to Bülow, Feb. 4, 1903.

[83] Ibid. Bülow to Metternich, Feb. 12, 1903.

[84] Reichstag, Verhandlungen. Stenographische Berichte, X. Legislaturperiode, II. Session, vol. 186, pp. 7462ff., 7494, 8722-24. Debates on Jan. 21, Jan. 22, and Mar. 19, 1903.

[85] Ibid., pp. 7413ff., 7467ff. Debates of Jan. 21 and Jan. 22, 1903.

"We must speak softly to England before we have a navy."[86] Neither Wilhelm II nor Tirpitz could have put it more succinctly.

The conclusion of hostilities between Venezuela and the three blockading powers early in February 1903 was almost an anticlimax. On February 19, 1903, the German Federal Chamber ratified the accords which granted Germany 1.7 million Bolívars in damages, to be collected against future customs revenues at La Guayra and Puerto Cabello.[87] A later ruling at the International Court of Justice at The Hague likewise favored Germany's outstanding claims and awarded it thirty percent of customs revenues from the Venezuelan ports.[88] Wilhelm II only lamented that the International Court had not been involved in the Boer War.[89] Obviously, events in South Africa and Venezuela continued to be coupled, owing to their explosive impact upon Anglo-German relations.

As previously suggested, the events of the years 1900-1902 proved to be a watershed, or a parting of the ways for Britain and Germany. The government in London, unlike the one in Berlin, had realized at the height of the international blockade that it stood in serious danger of thereby alienating the United States. Already at the time of the *Panther*'s bombardment of Fort San Carlos, Villiers at the Foreign Office had lectured the Admiralty on the importance "to not being implicated in any violent or indiscreet action, and the desirability of matters being kept as quiet as possible."[90] Their Lord-

[86] Cited in Pauline R. Anderson, *The Background of Anti-English Feeling in Germany, 1890-1902* (Washington, D.C., 1939), 347.

[87] See SA-Bremen, 3-A.3.V. Nr 99, Senats-Registratur, Reklamationen Deutschlands gegen die Vereinigten Staaten von Venezuela. *Protokoll* of Feb. 13, 1904, and *Denkschrift* of Feb. 14, 1903. Also, Richthofen to Bremen Senate, Feb. 19, 1903, and Bülow's formal declaration of Feb. 16, 1903, that the blockade was being lifted. For formal ratification of the accords, see Bundesraths-Protokolle, Session 1903, 8. Sitzung, Feb. 19, 1903.

[88] AA-Bonn, Venezuela 1, vol. 26. Ambassador Karl von Schlözer to Foreign Office, Feb. 22 and 23, 1904.

[89] AA-Bonn, Venezuela 2, vol. 13. Bülow to Hohenlohe-Schillingsfürst, Oct. 4, 1899.

[90] PRO, Admiralty I/7696, Foreign Office 1903. F. H. Villiers to Secretary of the Admiralty, Jan. 24, 1903.

ships concurred and at once decided not to reinforce Admiral Douglas' squadron off Venezuela, as this "would certainly be misunder-
stood in the United States, however simple and reasonable the real
explanation."[91] Obviously, both Cabinet and Admiralty in London
were of one mind that the British possessions in North and South
America depended for their continued existence much more upon
United States benevolence than upon German. Indeed, Paul Kennedy has argued that Liberals such as Edward Grey and Winston
Churchill, Unionists such as Arthur Balfour and Joseph Chamberlain, and navalists such as John Fisher and Charles Beresford, as
well as newspaper editors such as Valentine Chirol and St. Loe
Strachey, to name but a few, were rapidly developing the "myth" of
an Anglo-American "special relationship"—despite the presence of
large German-American and Irish-American elements in the United
States as well as the growing Anglo-American commercial rivalry.[92]
A good number of them undoubtedly shared Bismarck's evaluation
of Wilhelm II: "The Kaiser is like a balloon. If you do not hold fast
to the string, you never know where he will be off to."[93]

If Wilhelm II needed further evidence of the bitter anti-German
sentiment that gripped the British press, he received it in December
1903 when, on the 100th anniversary of the Hanoverian "German
Legion," he brazenly commended it for its role in "saving the British
army from disaster at Waterloo" in 1815. A storm of protest erupted
at once in *The Times*, *The Standard*, *The Daily Chronicle*, *Pall Mall
Gazette*, *Spectator*, and many other publications.[94] The conclusion of
the Anglo-French *entente cordiale* the following year drove the Emperor into the depths of depression: "The situation begins ever more
to resemble that before the Seven Years War."[95] His envoy to the
Court of St. James's, Metternich, was equally pessimistic concern-

[91] Ibid. Memorandum, Senior Naval Lord, Feb. 5, 1903.
[92] Kennedy, *Anglo-German Antagonism*, 399.
[93] Cited in ibid., 405.
[94] AA-Bonn, Preussen 1, Nr 1 Nr 13, vol. 12. Speech in Hanover on Dec. 19,
1903.
[95] Cited in Hilbert, "Role of Military and Naval Attachés," 184-85.

ing the state of Anglo-German relations: "The English government has not cooperated with us since the Venezuelan affair."[96]

In short, the stakes for *Weltpolitik* were becoming too high for Germany. While Wilhelm II bravely continued to assert that Britain and the United States would "have to accept the existence of the German fleet,"[97] Foreign Secretary Heinrich von Tschirschky und Bögendorff in September 1907 presented Chancellor von Bülow with a most dour evaluation of the Reich's world policy. Tschirschky openly questioned whether Germany's "basis for the tall pyramid of our world interests" was sufficiently broad, and even suggested that Berlin "must place its eggs in foreign baskets because we lack sufficient production for good nests of our own." He fully understood the driving force behind the Reich's world policy: "No one is more aware than I of the fact that our entire *Weltpolitik*—so far as it lies outside Europe—is mainly a prestige policy, a most difficult and precarious form of politics, because our world interests surpass . . . [our] available power to enforce and to protect it." The Foreign Secretary laconically concluded: "But we can no longer go back."[98] It would be difficult to find a clearer expression of diplomatic bankruptcy. Partly because of its behavior during the Boer War and the Venezuelan blockade, Germany had fulfilled Wilhelm II's greatest fear of 1901: rabid Anglophobia, coupled with the failure to forge an alliance with Russia, had left Germany, in the Emperor's words, sitting "between two chairs."

[96] AA-Bonn, England Nr 78secr., vol. 26. Metternich to Chancellor von Bethmann Hollweg, Aug. 3, 1911.

[97] AA-Bonn, Deutschland 138, Die Kaiserliche Marine, vol. 38. Imperial marginalia on a report from the German ambassador at Lisbon to Bülow, Aug. 6, 1908.

[98] AA-Bonn, Deutschland 137, vol. 5. Tschirschky to Bülow, Sept. 4, 1907.

CONCLUSION: WHAT PRICE IMPERIALISM?

More than twenty years ago, Richard J. Hammond cautioned his fellow economic historians against what he called the "besetting sin" of "going a-whoring" after "striking and colourful first approximations."[1] The profession by and large ignored his advice. As a result, we are constantly offered a veritable flood of "theories" on imperialism, evaluations of those theories, and evaluations of the evaluations. In researching this book over the past decade, I have been queried by numerous individuals, ranging from archivists in the German Democratic Republic to historians in North America, as to what "striking and colourful first approximations" concerning imperialism I would spring on the profession. My inability instantaneously to offer my own monistic theory has been met with astonishment, disbelief, and the suspicion that I was holding back. One colleague, in fact, suggested that I not write this book unless I could come up with a novel interpretation.

Obviously undaunted, I have penned my analysis of Imperial Germany's "vision of empire" in the Caribbean region and in the process have plunged into the murky waters of the great imperialism debate. I had no other choice: if a case study is to have any validity at all, it must be tested against existing models of interpretation. To my critics, I can only riposte, like Professor Hammond before me, that I was handicapped from the start by having been exposed to R. G. Collingwood's work, *The Idea of History*, wherein the English historian postulated that "history does not consist of events causally de-

---

[1] Richard J. Hammond, "Economic Imperialism: Sidelights on a Stereotype," *Journal of Economic History*, 21 (December 1961), 596. The term "striking and colourful first approximations" stems from Professor A. K. Cairncross.

termined and scientifically comprehensible."[2] Research into various facets of the Wilhelmian period of German history has only recon-firmed that innocent finding. Nor has the emergence either of the much-heralded school of "new social history" in the United States or of the so-called school of "scientific history" (*Geschichtswissen-schaft*) in the Federal Republic of Germany prompted me to forsake Collingwood's wise counsel that "historical knowledge . . . is the discerning of the thought which is the inner side of the event."[3] In the preceding chapters, I have striven on the basis of international, multi-archival research to elucidate the "inner side" of Germany's policies and actions in Venezuela.

In the Introduction, I divided the numerous imperialism schools against which this case study must be measured into two basic cat-egories, the economic and the noneconomic; both are Eurocentric insofar as they deal almost exclusively with Europe's needs and de-sires. Moreover, I alluded to two recent rebuttals of these major schools stressing developments overseas, that is, the "peripheral" thesis of D. K. Fieldhouse and the "outer world collaboration" hy-pothesis of Ronald Robinson. Finally, I offered Friedrich Katz's analysis of the specific case of German "imperialism" in several South American states before 1914. It remains to offer some obser-vations on both these general as well as specific interpretations on the basis of my findings in this case study of German policy toward Venezuela between 1871 and 1914.

To be sure, Germany's actions in Venezuela fall within the broad definition of "imperialism." The Reich's participation in the inter-national blockade of 1902-1903 comes close to constituting a classic case of governmental intervention at the behest of capitalist entre-preneurs. The venerable Social Democratic leader, August Bebel, went so far as to term it a "collection" action undertaken at the be-hest of Krupp and Disconto. The repeated demands for armed inter-vention—or at least showing the flag—on the part of the Disconto Bank, Norddeutsche Bank, Great Venezuelan Railroad, Berlin Be-ton- und Monierbau, German-Venezuelan Sulphur Company, and

[2] R. G. Collingwood, *The Idea of History* (London, 1961), 150.
[3] Ibid., 222.

Orinoco Asphalt Company speak for themselves, as do the constant clamorings for the dispatch of warships by Reich ministers in South America. Above all, German naval officers, both at home and abroad, became the primary advocates of a "formal" imperialism. Aided and abetted by Wilhelmian pressure groups such as the Pan-German League, the Colonial League, the Navy League, and the Central Union of German Navy Leagues in Overseas, their actions greatly troubled American proponents of the inviolability of the Monroe Doctrine.

A closer examination of actual German policy, however, gives pause for reconsideration. German nationals in Venezuela never constituted a "Trojan horse" whereby German influence and power could penetrate that country. The Hanseatic traders, in fact, assimilated with the people and culture of Venezuela by learning their language, adopting their customs, attending to the needs of their local markets, and, as President Cipriano Castro put it, by marrying "the daughters of the land." They never fulfilled the hopes and dreams of the advocates of *Deutschtum* such as Admiral Alfred von Tirpitz, who once stated: "Given the lack of overseas bases, we are forced to seek compensation therefore in the Germans overseas." Nor did the Hanseatic traders at home feel "duty-bound to assist" Wilhelm II "in joining this greater German empire [overseas] to our homeland." The Reich never realized "its India" in South America; not even the more limited dreams of a *Nueva Germania* in South Brazil ever reached fruition. And Gustav Schmoller's vision of a "German colony of some 20 to 30 million people in South America," "a presence backed by force," remained just that, a vision. As one historian of the German element overseas, Ernst Wagemann, concluded, the *Auslands-deutsche* remained "a body without a head."

With specific reference to theories of economic determinism, it should be evident that Hilferding's notions concerning the dominant role of *Finanzkapital* in "imperialism" simply do not hold true in the German-Venezuelan case. Neither German banks, nor German traders, nor German insurance companies ever attained a position of dominance in South America. Neither Hamburg nor Berlin replaced the City of London as Europe's commercial clearing house for world trade. In fact, German traders abroad continued to work through the

London Merchant Bankers and to insure their cargos with Lloyds of London. The major German houses in Venezuela—Blohm and Van Dissel—financed their trade through French banking institutions such as de Neuflize & Cie. rather than through German banks at home or their affiliates in South America. They desired peace and cooperation rather than confrontation and conflict. As Paul Kennedy has aptly put it: "Perhaps the most persistent economic lobby for good Anglo-German relations were the financial circles in the City of London and their equivalents in Frankfurt, Berlin and Hamburg." Raymond Poidevin certainly would expand that statement to include the Parisian *haute banques.* And while the very real and important presence of financial factors must never be overlooked or slighted when dealing with German policies overseas, it should nevertheless be pointed out that not even the 60-million-Mark Disconto/Norddeutsche Bank investment in the Great Venezuelan Railroad conforms to the classic pattern of capital export à la Hobson: it was undertaken not to conquer new markets (neo-mercantilism) but rather to place fixed-interest securities held by German rentiers. If anything, it was a function of what one might term "depression imperialism." Disconto as well as the Norddeutsche Bank exported capital to Venezuela during the so-called "great depression" at home in order to stimulate the slumping German steel industry and thereby to regain and to maintain economic prosperity at *home* and eventually to stabilize the domestic economy. Adolph von Hansemann, Max von Schinckel, and Friedrich Krupp all attested to this function of the railroad investment—as did the Prussian and German governments. Disconto's railroad "finance capital" clearly bears out Erich Preiser's "safety valve" thesis, namely, that German capital was exported primarily in order to overcome *domestic* cyclical financial depressions.

Most importantly, it is abundantly clear that there was no official German governmental support of, nor guarantee for, the highly speculative Disconto/Norddeutsche Bank investment in the Great Venezuelan Railroad. Oswald von Richthofen of the Foreign Office made this perfectly clear in 1899 and again in 1901 by arguing that the Wilhelmstrasse would not undertake any intervention in Venezuela at the beck and call of Hansemann (Disconto) or Schinckel (Norddeutsche Bank). He bluntly informed the Hamburg Board of Trade when it attempted to lobby the Foreign Secretary for armed intervention in Venezuela in behalf of Hamburg merchants that it was not the government's business to pull Disconto's chestnuts out of the fire. And when Chancellor Bernhard von Bülow finally moved against Venezuela, he was motivated by other than economic factors. The percipient Bavarian plenipotentiary to Berlin, Hugo Count von Lerchenfeld-Köfering, in 1902 noted that Bülow finally acted against President Castro "to raise the Reich's prestige" in South America, and to "conduct a joint operation with England" designed to overcome the recent Anglo-German acrimony stemming from the Boer War in South Africa. In other words, Bülow was playing the good old European game of power politics—albeit, as Fieldhouse would put it, on the Continent's "periphery." *Die grosse Politik* rather than sales and profits constituted the prime motivating force. In the end, the Foreign Office was not a branch of Disconto.

In the realm of diplomacy and grand strategy, Germany's actions off Venezuela in 1902-1903 poisoned international relations as perhaps best evidenced in Rudyard Kipling's poem, "The Rowers." With regard to Anglo-German relations, the events of 1902-1903 proved to be a watershed, a parting of the ways. Joseph Chamberlain's overtures concerning the creation of a "natural alliance" among Britain, Germany, and the United States were rudely rejected in Berlin. Instead, Bülow sought to unite the nation behind him with a demotic Anglophobia while concurrently wooing Russia into concluding an offensive alliance. He failed miserably. Ambassador Paul Count von Wolff-Metternich in 1911 reported from London: "The English government has not cooperated with us since the Venezuelan affair." And Foreign Secretary Heinrich von Tschirschky und Bögendorff at about the same time fully conceded that Germany's means were out of proportion to its desires in the realm of overseas expansion. Neither "formal" nor "informal" empire in South America was within the realm of the attainable. "Our entire *Weltpolitik*," the diplomat confessed, "is mainly a prestige policy, a most difficult and precarious form of politics."

With regard to German-American relations, Berlin never undertook the one step that might have removed the fears and suspicions of people like Theodore Roosevelt, John Hay, Henry Cabot Lodge, and George Dewey that Germany intended to set foot in the Western Hemisphere: *official* recognition of President James Monroe's "insolent dogma." Instead, Chancellor von Bülow in 1902 frittered away what possibly may have been a last chance publicly to render Germany's official position on the Monroe Doctrine for fear of thereby alienating the domestic radical Right (Pan-German, Colonial, and Navy League supporters). Instead, his government stubbornly continued to refer to the "United States of *North* America" in official documents in order to stress Washington's northern continental limits. Vice Admiral Otto von Diederichs of the Admiralty Staff that same year spelled out this policy in concrete form when he sought German occupation of Dutch Guiana (Surinam) as "a demarcation line at which United States influence" south of the Río Grande "had to make a halt."

Not even in the realm of military training missions and armaments sales to South America was Germany able to fulfill the ambitions of the advocates of overseas extension of power. Once again, ambition and capability stood in sharp contrast to one another. While Reich advisors had gained great influence on the southern American continent, by about 1908 they had to scale down their activities as conditions at home grew more threatening (Triple Entente). War Minister General Karl von Einem in 1908, Foreign Secretary Wilhelm von Schoen in 1910, and War Minister General Josias von Heeringen in 1912, while concurring on the intimate and indisputable link between military advisors and weapons sales as well as their beneficial effect on the domestic economy, nevertheless also agreed that Germany could attend to the needs of only those countries "which are of special interest to us militarily and economically." Heeringen, especially, in his capacity as Prussian war minister, bluntly rejected a Venezuelan request for advisors and arms in 1912: "It is not in the interest of Prussian troops to increase this burden [of military missions] by extending it to a new state when it entails a diminution of various [domestic] military matters in favor of our foreign policy and our industry." It would be difficult to find a clearer rejection of the extension of European military advisors and their wares overseas from any officer, be it in London, Paris, or Washington. And while

Krupp often touted the German element abroad as conduits for Reich influence and sales, it is worth noting that the Essen firm sacrificed no profits in behalf of this expressed mission—as evidenced in its refusal to extend a modest credit to Paraguay in 1913 in lieu of cash in hand. Finally, with the sole exception of Emil Körner's participation in the Chilean civil war in 1891, not a single German advisor ever interfered directly in the affairs of a single South American nation. As Frederick Nunn has presciently observed, the very complexity of South American socio-political conditions precluded direct German involvement.

If not economic, what, then, were the motivating forces behind German "imperialism" in South America? I would suggest, along with Winfried Baumgart, emotional and "irrational" factors such as pride, prestige, national honor, showing the flag, and simply the burning desire to be part of the global order.[4] And who were the agents of this assertive German overseas posture? I would suggest first and foremost German naval officers. What Joseph Schumpeter might have termed "atavism" on the part of German ship commanders in South American waters greatly shaped the nature of the perceived threat inherent in German ambitions and actions in the New World. It was these naval commanders stationed in foreign waters who constantly bombarded Admiralty Staff, Chancery, Foreign Office, Navy Office, and the Court with demands for coaling stations and naval bases in the Caribbean basin; who demanded some form of control over the Panama Canal, preferably through seizure of an island at its eastern terminus; who desired to use the *Auslandsdeutsche* as the agents of an "informal" imperialism; and who argued that the Reich "be prepared first and foremost for a clash with England and America." In all their actions, they were motivated by a crude form of social Darwinism. To stand still meant to decline. To fail to secure foreign markets meant to stagnate economically at home. To fail to show the flag in South America meant to lose national prestige. I would suggest that the actions of German naval of-

[4] See Holger H. Herwig, "Imperial Germany," in Ernest R. May, ed., *Knowing One's Enemies: Intelligence Assessment Before the Two World Wars* (Princeton, 1984), 91ff.

ficers off Venezuela corroborate A. S. Kanya-Forstner's suggestion
that the military rather than the government "determined the pace,
the extent and the nature" of French imperialism—at least in the
Western Sudan.

Not surprisingly, Hamburg's most influential shipowners endorsed many of these expansionist desires on the part of naval officers. The Union of Hamburg Shipowners, headed by Albert Ballin
of the Hamburg-America Line and Adolph Woermann of the North
German Lloyd, frequently demanded that Berlin show the flag overseas to enhance not only trade and commerce but also "the Reich's
prestige." The Hamburg Board of Trade consistently served as their
lobby with federal authorities in Berlin. At the private level, Ballin
even agreed to a harebrained scheme to purchase an island in the
West Indies (St. John or St. Thomas) in behalf of the Navy Office. On
another occasion, he attempted to create a European financial syndicate to complete the Panama Canal in order to keep it out of United
States control. Yet once again, German wishes were out of line with
German capabilities: the domestic capital market proved woefully
inadequate to tackle such a gigantic task, and Ballin was soon forced
to abandon the project.

Nearly three hundred so-called "fleet" professors—mainly econ-
omists and historians—provided the theoretical underpinnings for
Weltpolitik. In numerous articles, brochures, books, and public lectures, they informed the nation that in order to survive Germany
needed to take its rightful place alongside the existing "three world
empires" of Great Britain, Russia, and the United States. They reiterated with gusto Lord Salisbury's notion concerning such "dying"
colonial powers as Denmark, the Netherlands, Portugal, and Spain.
Indeed, the twentieth century, so the argument ran, would witness a
"gigantic liquidation" of the British Empire, one that Germany had
fully to exploit. These academic apostles of overseas expansion did
not shrink from lacing their analyses with a good deal of crude rac-
ism, stressing the inevitable decline of "Romance" nations such as
France, Italy, Portugal, and Spain, and the concomitant rise of
"Germanic" nations such as Germany and the United States. Like
Tirpitz, they feared the United States as "the Phoenix" in the New
World. Their works were read and disseminated by members of the

teaching professions, the clergy, the press, the upper civil service—in other words, by the educated middle class that by and large viewed itself as the "liberal" or "progressive" element in German society. In fact, the *gebildete Bürgertum* provided the rank and file for the Pan-German League, the Colonial League, and the Navy League. Its members attended public lectures and sermons designed to arouse interest in overseas empire. And they lobbied the government to extend the Reich's power and prestige beyond the narrow confines of the European continent.

With specific reference to Venezuela, Germany's actions and policies in 1902-1903 revealed the very real limits of gunboat diplomacy. While successful in the short run in forcing President Castro to meet his international financial obligations, the blockade in the long run proved highly detrimental to German nationals. Alone the *casa* Blohm flourished—mainly by seeking even closer "accommodation" with Castro as well as his successor, Juan Vicente Gómez. Those German undertakings that had supported the blockade suffered greatly: Mariara Plantation, Venezuelan Plantation Society, Orinoco Asphalt Company, German-Venezuelan Sulphur Company, Puerto Cabello & Valencia Brewery, Caracas glass plant, and Barrancas as well as Puerto Cabello meat packers, all disappeared from the scene shortly after the blockade, to be replaced largely by their North American rivals. Indeed, the entire history of Blohm's intimate relationship with the various *caudillos* of Venezuela gives credence to Ronald Robinson's astute theory of "outer world collaboration" (or non-collaboration) as a crucial component of European "imperialism."

If anything, this case study involving several of the better known theories of imperialism in light of the German experience in Venezuela and South America in general should caution us against applying broad generalizations to highly complex phenomena. As a result of rampant overuse, the term "imperialism" today is virtually devoid of any precise meaning. One speaks with great dexterity of American imperialists in Honduras, British imperialists on the Falkland Islands, Chinese imperialists in Tibet, Cuban imperialists in Angola, French imperialists on New Caledonia, Russian imperialists in Afghanistan, Vietnamese imperialists in Cambodia, and the list could go on *ad infinitum*. In the German case in Venezuela, I have suggested that human factors, be they emotional or "irrational," as well as traditional European power politics, international gamesmanship, global rivalries, maritime strategy, and national idiosyncracies—all conducted under the general rubric of *Weltpolitik*—were the prime motivators. Reich nationals, military training missions, armaments sales, trade agreements, educational aid, church activities, and the dispatch of warships to show the flag were the outward symbols of Germany's drive for that cherished place in the world order. Therein, rather than in the economic domination of markets or the export of capital, lie the root causes of Berlin's restless and aggressive overseas policies beginning in the 1890s. While a case study such as this obviously cannot "prove" one theory or another, I suggest that it give cause for serious reconsideration and further study.

In concluding the German example in South America, I resort once more to the eminently sensible Richard J. Hammond: "If I were tempted to set up a rival doctrine of economic imperialism to that of Hobson and Lenin, my choice for prophet would be [Thorstein] Veblen, the apostle of conspicuous consumption."[5] I would be hard-pressed to find better examples of "conspicuous consumption" than Wilhelm II and Bernhard von Bülow.

---

[5] Hammond, "Economic Imperialism," 596. See also Thorstein Veblen, *The Theory of the Leisure Class* (New York, 1967), 68ff.

BIBLIOGRAPHY

PRIMARY SOURCES: UNPUBLISHED ARCHIVAL COLLECTIONS

I. Federal Republic of Germany

1. BUNDESARCHIV, KOBLENZ.

Personal Papers:
Fürst von Bülow: Nr 23 Wolff-Metternich
   Nr 24 Entwürfe zu Parlamentsreden
   Nr 77 Philipp Fürst zu Eulenburg
   Nr 89 Hohenlohe-Schillingsfürst
   Nr 91 Friedrich von Holstein
   Nr 99 Karl von Lindenau
   Nr 111 Heinrich von Preussen
   Nr 112 Wilhelm II
   Nr 126 Alfred von Tirpitz
Hohenlohe-Schillingsfürst: Nr 126, Nr 383, Nr 432, Nr 559, Nr 1641, Nr 1645
Oswald von Richthofen: Nr 6, Nr 8
Loebell: Nr 26
Auswärtiges Amt, Abt. II
   R85/145 Eisenbahnen in Venezuela
   R85/690 Postverhältnisse mit Venezuela
   R85/1175 Patent-, Muster- und Markenschutz in Venezuela
   R85/1593 Zoll- und Handelsverträge mit fremden Staaten. Venezuela
Auswärtiges Amt, Abt. III
   R85/5660 Massnahmen Kriegführender gegen neutrale Firmen, die Handelsbeziehungen zum Feinde unterhalten. Schwarze Listen. Nordamerika
   R85/6871 Haltung der Neutralen im europäischen Kriege 1914

2. BUNDESARCHIV-MILITÄRARCHIV, FREIBURG.

F 5175-79 Admiralstab der Marine. Unternehmungen gegen Venezuela
F 7567 Kommando der Kreuzerdivision. Anlage III, V zum Kriegstagebuch
F 7568 Kommando der ostamerikanischen Kreuzerdivision. Ganz geheime
Sachen. O.
F 7569 Admiralstab der Marine. Venezuela. SMS "Gazelle." Geheime Ak-
ten
RM2/1866 Blockade der Küste von Venezuela
RM2/2995 Reichs-Marine-Amt. Entsendung von Schiffen nach Amerika
RM3/3301 Reichs-Marine-Amt. Ostamerikanische Kreuzerdivision

3. AUSWÄRTIGES AMT, BONN. POLITISCHES ARCHIV.

Personal Papers: Bernhard von Bülow, vols. 27–35
Philipp zu Eulenburg-Hertefeld, vols. 36–40
Maximilian Harden, vols. 41–42
Alfred von Kiderlen-Wächter, vols. 55–57
Hohenlohe-Schillingsfürst, vols. 52–54
Speck von Sternburg, vol. 18
Paul von Wolff-Metternich zur Gracht, vol. 58; *Tagebücher*, vols. 71–81
Anhalt Nr 2 Nr 1. Die Herzoglich Anhaltinische Familie
Deutschland Nr 121 Nr 8. Angelegenheiten der deutschen Armee: Reisen
von Offizieren im Ausland
Deutschland Nr 121 Nr 10. Vorlagen an den Reichstag und Reichstagsver-
handlungen darüber
Deutschland Nr 121 Nr 10secr. Vorlagen an den Reichstag und die Reichs-
tagsverhandlungen darüber
Deutschland Nr 121 Nr 12secr. Angelegenheiten der deutschen Armee:
Massregeln für die Eventualität eines Krieges
Deutschland Nr 121 Nr 19secr. Angelegenheiten der deutschen Armee:
Verkauf von Waffen
Deutschland Nr 122 Nr 2g. Seine Exzellenz Herr Staatssekretär Freiherr
von Richthofen
Deutschland Nr 122 Nr 2g Nr 1. Parlamentarische Reden des Staatssekre-
tärs Freiherrn von Richthofen u. Beurtheilungen derselben in der
Presse
Deutschland Nr 122 Nr 13. Seine Exzellenz der Herr Reichskanzler Graf
von Bülow
Deutschland Nr 122 Nr 13 Nr 1. Parlamentarische Reden des Reichskanz-
lers Graf von Bülow und Beurtheilungen derselben in der Presse

Deutschland Nr 126 Nr 2i. Die Kontinentale Korrespondenz
Deutschland Nr 126 Nr 7. Die an Seine Majestät den Kaiser und König erstatteten Zeitungsberichte
Deutschland Nr 126 Nr 7a secr. Die von Seiner Majestät dem Kaiser dem Auswärtigen Amt zugesandten Zeitungsausschnitten
Deutschland Nr 126f secr. Auslandsnachrichtenstelle
Deutschland Nr 127 Nr 22. Die Gesandschaft der Vereinigten Staaten von Nordamerika in Berlin
Deutschland Nr 127 Nr 24. Die Venezolanische Mission in Berlin
Deutschland Nr 135 Nr 20. Die Kaiserlich Deutsche Botschaft in Washington
Deutschland Nr 137. Allgemeine deutsche Politik
Deutschland Nr 138. Die Kaiserliche Marine
Deutschland Nr 138secr. Die Kaiserlich deutsche Marine
Deutschland Nr 138 Nr 4. Die Frage der Zulassung fremder Offiziere zur Dienstleistung in der deutschen Marine
Deutschland Nr 167. Kolonien und Flottenstützpunkte
Deutschland Nr 169. Alldeutscher Verband
Deutschland Nr 175secr. Die Schiedsgerichts-Verträge Deutschlands

Preussen 1 Nr 1d. Seine Majestät der Kaiser und König Wilhelm II
Preussen 1 Nr 1d secr. Seine Majestät der Kaiser und König Wilhelm II
Preussen 1 Nr 1 Nr 3hh. Korrespondenz Seiner Majestät mit dem Präsidenten der Vereinigten Staaten 1900-1916
Preussen 1 Nr 1 Nr 13. Reden Seiner Majestät des Kaisers
Preussen 1 Nr 3 Nr 3. Seine Königliche Hoheit der Prinz Heinrich von Preussen
Preussen 11secr. Staats- Ministerial- und Kronraths-Protokolle

Der Weltkrieg Nr 24. Stellung des lateinischen Amerika zum Weltkrieg

England Nr 71. Militär-Angelegenheiten Englands
England Nr 71b. Die englische Marine
England Nr 73. Die englische Presse
England Nr 78. Die Beziehungen Deutschlands zu England
England Nr 78 secretissima. Beziehungen zu Deutschland
England Nr 78 Nr 1secr. Verhandlungen zwischen England und Deutschland (und zwischen Deutschland und den Vereinigten Staaten von Nordamerika) über eine ew. Auftheilung des Kolonialbesitzes anderer Staaten
England Nr 81 Nr 1. Das englische Königshaus

England Nr 81 Nr 2. Englische Staatsmänner
England Nr 93. Die auswärtige Politik Englands

Italien Nr 68. Allgemeine Angelegenheiten Italiens
Italien Nr 72a. Marine-Angelegenheiten Italiens
Italien Nr 82. Die Beziehungen Italiens zu Deutschland

Amerika Generalia Nr 6. Berufung eines Südamerikanischen Diplomaten-
Kongresses nach Caracas
Amerika Generalia Nr 7. Kirchliche Angelegenheiten in Central-Amerika
Amerika Generalia Nr 8 Nr 1. Sozialisten und Anarchisten in Süd-Amerika
Amerika Generalia Nr 10. Bestrebungen behufs Zusammenschluss der
südamerikanischen Freistaaten
Amerika Generalia Nr 11. Die Kirche in Süd-Amerika
Amerika Generalia Nr 12. Projekt eines Schiffahrtskanals durch Mittel-
Amerika (Panama resp. Nicaragua-Kanal)
Amerika Generalia Nr 13. Zusammenschluss der Republiken des ameri-
kanischen Kontinents und Zusammengehen der europäischen Staaten
gegen Amerika

Dänische Besitzungen in Amerika Nr 1. Dänisch-West-Indien

Englische Besitzungen in Amerika Nr 2. Englische Besitzungen in Südamerika

Niederländische Besitzungen in Amerika Nr 2. Niederländische Besitzungen in Westindien

Spanische Besitzungen in Amerika Nr 2. Intervention der europäischen
Mächte zu Gunsten der Erhaltung Kubas für die spanische Monarchie

Venezuela Nr 1. Allgemeine Angelegenheiten Venezuelas
Venezuela Nr 2. Grenzstreitigkeiten zwischen Venezuela und England
(Schutz der britischen Unterthanen durch Deutschland)
Venezuela Nr 3 Nr 1. Die Praesidenten
Venezuela Nr 3 Nr 2. Staatsmänner Venezuelas
Venezuela Nr 6. Die Wahrnehmung Niederländischer Interessen durch
Deutschland 1892-1910
Venezuela Nr 7. Kirche und Schule in Venezuela 1901-1911
Venezuela Nr 8. Militär und Marine 1914-1919
Venezuela Nr 9. Presse 1914-1915

Venezuela I.C.61 Schriftwechsel mit der Kaiserl. Minister-Residentur zu Caracas sowie mit anderen Missionen und fremden Kabinetten über die inneren Zustände und Verhältnisse Venezuelas 1869-1875

Ver. St. v. Amerika Nr 1. Allgemeine Angelegenheiten der Vereinigten Staaten von Nordamerika
Ver. St. v. Amerika Nr 5. Militär-Angelegenheiten der Vereinigten Staaten von Nordamerika
Ver. St. v. Amerika Nr 5a. Marine-Angelegenheiten der Vereinigten Staaten von Nordamerika
Ver. St. v. Amerika Nr 6. Amerikanische Staatsmänner
Ver. St. v. Amerika Nr 6 Nr 2. Personalien: Journalisten
Ver. St. v. Amerika Nr 11. Präsidenten der Vereinigten Staaten von Nordamerika
Ver. St. v. Amerika Nr 16. Beziehungen der Vereinigten Staaten von Nordamerika zu Deutschland
Ver. St. v. Amerika Nr 16secr. Beziehungen der Vereinigten Staaten von Nordamerika zu Deutschland
Ver. St. v. Amerika Nr 20a. Die Monroe-Doktrin
Ver. St. v. Amerika Nr 22. Beziehungen zu Venezuela

4. BAYERISCHES HAUPTSTAATSARCHIV, MUNICH. ABT. II: GEHEIMES STAATSARCHIV.

Bayerische Gesandschaft Berlin 1074. Politische Berichte und Instruktionen für das Jahr 1902
Bayerische Gesandschaft zu Berlin 1075. Politische Berichte und Instruktionen für das Jahr 1903
MA III 2680. Bayerische Gesandschaft in Berlin. Geschäftsberichte 1902
MA III 2681. Bayerische Gesandschaft in Berlin. Geschäftsberichte 1903
MA 76076. Äusserungen Seiner Majestät des Kaisers Wilhelm II 1900-1903
MA 80023. Die politischen Verhältnisse der Verein. Staaten von Venezuela 1874-1905
Abt. IV: Kriegsarchiv
Generalstab 320. Mittel- und Südamerikanische Staaten 1905-1914
MKr 43. Berichte des Militär-Bevollmächtigten in Berlin 1887-1907, 1914
MKr 45. Geheimschreiben des Militär-Bevollmächtigten in Berlin 1899-1908
MKr 1950-1951. Übertritt deutscher Offiziere in ausserdeutsche Armeen als Militärinstrukteure

MKr 3711. Fremde Orden. Venezuela

5. STAATSARCHIV, BREMEN.

3-A.3.V. Nr 99. Senats-Registratur. Reklamationen Deutschlands gegen die Vereinigten Staaten von Venezuela

6. STAATSARCHIV, HAMBURG.

CL. VII Lit. Kª No. 5, Vol. 21 Fasc. 1 Inv. 10. Handelskompagnien & Aktiengesellschaften. Gesuch der Venezuela-Plantagen-Gesellschaft m.b.H. um Erteilung der staatlichen Genehmigung zur Ausgabe von 6% Schuldverschreibungen auf den Inhaber im Betrage von M 1,000,000 . . . 1901

Dep. f. Handel, Schiffahrt und Gewerbe. Spezialakten XXXVII 60. Erkundigungen über den ehemaligen Präsidenten von Venezuela, Cipriano Castro 1911-1912

Hanseatische Gesandschaft in Berlin. Ältere Registratur, 0 1 f. Fasc. 18. Deutsche Diplomatische Vertretung in Maracaibo 1871-74

Hanseatische Gesandschaft in Berlin. Ältere Registratur, 0 1 f. Fasc. 26. Gesetzwidriges Verfahren des Juan M. Guzman bezw. seines Vertreters Kampraths 1878

Senat Cl.VI No 16°, Vol. 2 Fasc. 13. Beschwerden der hiesigen Handelskammer über den General Consul der Vereinigten Staaten von Venezuela, Herrn General Juan de Mato Guzman, welcher sodann enthoben ist. 1878

Senat Cl.VI No 16°, Vol. 1 Fasc. 17. Venezuela-Varia. Eingabe der Handelskammer an das Auswärtige Amt um Schutz der deutschen Interessen während der Wirren in Venezuela

Sen. Kom. f.d. Reichs- und auswärtigen Angel. Ältere Registratur, C I d 172. Wirtschaftliche Verhältnisse in Venezuela. Auskunft über dortige Firmen 1894-1914

Sen. Kom. f.d. Reichs- und auswärtigen Angel. Ältere Registratur, C I d 173. Forderungen Hamburger Firmen gegen die Regierung von Venezuela 1899-1913

Sen. Kom. f.d. Reichs- und auswärtigen Angel. P.II. Politik-7/94. Jahrgang 1894. Politische Lage der Vereinigten Staaten von Venezuela

Sen. Kom. f.d. Reichs- und auswärtigen Angel. I, S I k 19.1, Nebenakten zu Convolutum I

Senat. Auswanderungsamt II. A. No 13

7. HANDELSKAMMER, HAMBURG. COMMERZBIBLIOTHEK.

Jahresberichte der Handelskammer zu Hamburg 1900-1903
Protokoll der Handelskammer 1898-1908

8. EVANGELISCHES ZENTRALARCHIV, WEST BERLIN.

C VI 9. Kirchenbundesamt. Die deutschen Schulen und Lehrer im Aus-
lande
C VII Venezuela 8. Kirchenbundesamt. Das deutsche Kirchenwesen in
Venezuela, insbesondere die deutsche Gemeinde in Caracas
EO IV Generalia No 7a. Evangelischer Ober-Kirchenrat. Reichsschulfonds
EO IV Venezuela No 1. Evangelischer Ober-Kirchenrat. Die allgemeinen
kirchlichen Verhältnisse in Venezuela
EO IV Generalia No 7. Evangelischer Ober-Kirchenrat. Die Bewerbungen
von Lehrern um Schulstellen in der ausländischen Diaspora

9. FRIEDRICH KRUPP, HISTORISCHES ARCHIV, ESSEN-BREDENEY.

II B 27 Familien-Archiv Hügel. Briefe Alfred Krupps an Oscar von
Ernsthausen
IV 584 Briefe von Verschiedenen an Friedr. Krupp-Essen
IV 1060 Schienen Produktion und Schienen Aufträge 1882-1888
IV 1439 Briefwechsel zwischen Meyer und Goose
IV 1462 Briefe von C. Meyer an Goose
IV 1639 Briefe von Goose an C. Meyer
IV C 13 Familien-Archiv Hügel. Aufsichtsrat 1903-1905
IV C 15 Familien-Archiv Hügel. Aufsichtsrat 1909
IV C 16-19 Familien-Archiv Hügel. Briefwechsel Aufsichtsrat-Direk-
torium 1903/04-1907/09
IV C 116 Privatbureau Gustav Krupp v. B. u. H. 50 Millionen Anleihe

10. INSTITUT FÜR ZEITGESCHICHTE, MUNICH.

Bestand F 6, Akz. 306/52. Personalakte Canaris

II. German Democratic Republic

1. ZENTRALES STAATSARCHIV, POTSDAM.

Personal Papers: Friedrich von Holstein (90 Ho 5), vols. 1, 3-7, 10, 12
Wolff-Metternich zur Gracht (90 Wo 1), vol. 1

Alldeutscher Verband. Sitzungen des Geschäftsführenden Ausschusses. 1904 Gotha (43)

Auswärtiges Amt, Abt. Ib.

28363-381. Die Gesuche fremder Militärs um Erlaubnis den diesseitigen militärischen Übungen und Feldzügen beiwohnen zu dürfen

28567. Reisen Kaiserlicher Kriegsschiffe

Auswärtiges Amt, Abt. Ic.

52796. Das Kaiserliche Konsulat in La Guayra

Auswärtiges Amt, Abt. Ih.

51419. Abschluss von Konsular- resp. Nachlass-Verträgen mit Venezuela

Auswärtiges Amt, Abt. II.

12301-324. Handels- und Schiffahrtsverhältnisse mit Venezuela

12561. Marken- resp. Musterschutz in Venezuela und die darauf bezüglichen Verhandlungen

22681. Verfahren bei Benachrichtigungen der Kaiserlichen Missionen und Konsulämter von der Entsendung von Kriegsschiffen

33371-372. Nachrichten der Kaiserlichen Konsule im Staate Venezuela

50944/1. Mission der Republik Venezuela

50960-965. Kais. Mission in Venezuela

54108-109. Jahresberichte des Kaiserlichen Konsulats in Ciudad Bolívar 1887-1906

54110-111. Jahresberichte des Kaiserlichen Konsulats in La Guayra

54112-113. Jahresberichte des Kaiserl. Konsulats in Maracaibo 1887-1906

54114-116. Jahresberichte des Kaiserlichen Konsulats in Puerto Cabello 1888-1906

54117. Jahresberichte des Kaiserlichen Konsulats in Caracas 1894-1906

54118. Jahresberichte des Kaiserlichen Konsulats in Valencia

54119. Jahresberichte des Kaiserlichen Konsulats in San Cristóbal

Auswärtiges Amt, Abt. IIE.

15322-344. Eisenbahnen in Central- und Südamerika

15585-590. Nachrichten über das Eisenbahnwesen des Auslandes

Auswärtiges Amt, Abt. IIm.

4771. Marken resp. Musterschutz in Venezuela und die darauf bezüglichen Verhandlungen

Auswärtiges Amt, Abt. IIs.

13291. Meldungen über Fahrten der subventionierten Postdampfer

17661-664. Schiffahrtsgesellschaften. Hamburg-Amerika Linie

22351-356. Kaiserlich Deutsche Kriegsmarine

22416. Nachrichten über fremde Marinewesen

22427-487. Entsendung deutscher Kriegsschiffe

22533-539. Errichtung deutscher Kohlen- und Flottenstationen im Auslande und deutsche Kolonisationsprojekte

22544. Beziehungen der Kaiserlich Gesandten und Konsuln zur Kriegsmarine

22645. Bewegungen fremder Kriegsschiffe

22657-659. Seeunfälle S. M. Schiffe

3118. Besteuerungen von Schiffen und Schiffahrtsgesellschaften

8133-139. Lieferungen der Eisengiesserei und Maschinenfabrik von H. Gruson in Buckau-Magdeburg für fremde Regierungen

Auswärtiges Amt, Abt. IIu.

3134. Verzeichnis der Handelsverträge des deutschen Reiches mit dem Auslande

3520-25. Aufstellung von Adressenverzeichnissen ausländischer Importeure

2950-52. Waffenlieferungen deutscher Firmen an fremde Regierungen (Amerika)

2958-64. Trust und Kartellwesen im überseeischen Auslande

3168. Bedeutung der Deutschen Seeinteressen im Auslande

4713-18. Handels- und Schiffahrtsverhältnisse mit Venezuela

4778-79. Handelsvertragsverhandlungen Deutschlands mit Venezuela 1893-1909

4799. Wünsche des Interessenten bezüglich des Abschlusses von Handels-Verträgen mit Südamerika

4802. Die diesseitigen Beschwerden über Zollbehörden in Venezuela

4804-06. Deutsche Banken in Mittel- und Süd-Amerika 1895-1919

4819. Jahreshandelsberichte des Konsuls in Caracas

4820. Jahreshandelsberichte des Kaiserlichen Konsuls in Ciudad Bolívar

4834. Jahreshandelsberichte des Kaiserlichen Konsuls in Maracaibo

4846. Jahreshandelsberichte des Kaiserlichen Konsulats in Puerto Cabello

4871. Jahreshandelsberichte des Kaiserlichen Konsulats Valencia

4873. Jahreshandelsberichte des Kaiserlichen Konsulats in La Guayra

4878-79. Deutsche Techniker und Beamte im Diensten Süd- und Mittelamerikanischer Staaten

8598-610. Bedeutung der deutschen Seeinteressen im Auslande

12573. Handelsvertragsverhandlungen Deutschlands mit Venezuela

13298. Trusts und Kartellwesen im überseeischen Ausland

Auswärtiges Amt, Abt. IIw.
3128. Die leichtsinnige Kreditgewährung an Ausländer durch deutsche Kaufleute
8179-80. Waffenlieferungen deutscher Firmen an fremde Regierungen
8492. Lieferungen der Firma L. Löwe A.G. in Berlin
13293. F. Friedr. Krupp Act. Ges. Grusonwerk
Auswärtiges Amt, Abt. III.
28988-998. Gesuche fremder Regierungen für ihre Staatsangehörigen zum Eintritt in diesseitige Militär- Erziehungs- und Bildungsanstalten, desgleichen zur Dienstleistung bei diesseitigen Truppentheilen und der Kais. Marine
29357-364. Gesuche von Ausländern um Erlaubnis zum Eintritt in das Deutsche Militär oder in die Kriegsmarine, unter derselben Begünstigung wie den Inländern
33398. Gesuche um Befreiung aus den Militärdiensten Südamerikanischer Staaten
Auswärtiges Amt, Abt. IIIa.
34130. Beschwerden über Polizei Behörden in Venezuela
34162. Beschwerden über die Behandlung Deutscher im Auslande. Venezuela
Auswärtiges Amt, Abt. IIIb.
29044. Erlaubnis für Venezolaner zum Eintritt in diesseitige Militär- Erziehungs- und Lehranstalten, sowie zur Dienstleistung bzw. Information bei diesseitigen Truppenteilen und der Kaiserlichen Marine
29085. Deutsche Militärinstrukteure in Venezuela
31795. Fremdengesetzgebung in Venezuela
31935. Nachrichten über Heer und Marine in Venezuela
33367-369. Nachrichten aus und über Venezuela
33370. Austausch amtlicher Veröffentlichungen mit Venezuela
Deutsche Kolonial-Gesellschaft.
261-262. Südamerikanische Colonisations-Gesellschaft zu Leipzig
297. 61 Ko 2. Deutsch-Südamerikanische Gesellschaft
411. Caracaya-Plantagen-Gesellschaft
621. Deutsche Siedlungen in Südamerika
899. 61 KO 1. Ausschuss und Vorstandssitzungsprotokolle vom 6.12.1882—3.11.1885. Generalversammlung zu Eisenach vom 21.9.1884. Generalversammlung zu Berlin vom 22.2.1885
900, 901, 903-915. 61 KO 1. Ausschußsitzungsprotokolle 1885-1911
902. 61 KO 1. Sachregister. Protokolle und Ausschuss-Sitzungen. Berichte der Vorstandssitzungen und Hauptversammlungen 1888-1892

928-930. 61 KO 1. Vorstandssitzungsprotokolle 1886-1905
Kolonialwirtschaftliches Komitee.
   326. Südamerikanische Kolonisations-Gesellschaft Leipzig 1900
   345. Plantage Mariara (Ven.)
   346. Grosse Venezuela Eisenbahn-Gesellschaft Hamburg 1894-1914
Reichsamt des Innern.
   5441-42. Handelssachen Venezuela
   5443. Statistik über Venezuela
   5444-51. Zoll- und Steuersachen. Venezuela
   5453. Finanz-Sachen Venezuela
Reichs Justizamt.
   3346. Sammlung der Handels- und Schiffahrtsverträge Deutschlands mit
      dem Auslande
   3478. Freundschafts- Handels- und Schiffahrtsvertrag mit Venezuela
   3606. Die Militärkonvention

2. ZENTRALES STAATSARCHIV, DIENSTSTELLE MERSEBURG.

Auswärtiges Amt. Nr 949-953. Die Konsulate der Republik Venezuela in
   Preussen
Königliches Geheimes Civil-Cabinet.
   Nr 13361. Die Südamerikanischen Staaten Venezuela, Columbien,
      Ekuador, Peru, Bolivia, Argentinien, Chile, Paraguay u. Uruguay
      1873-1918
   Nr 21871. Die Kirchen- und Schulangelegenheiten der Süd-Amerika-
      nischen Staaten: Venezuela, Peru, Columbien, Ekuador, Bolivia, Ar-
      gentinien, Chile, Paraguay u. Uruguay 1873-1918
Königlich Preussische Gesandschaft in Hamburg.
   Nr 344. Mittel- und Südamerika 1911-1918
Ministerium für Handel und Gewerbe.
   CXIII-17. Nr 18, vol. I. Statistische und Handelsnachrichten über Ve-
      nezuela 1857-1926
   CXIII-17. Nr 22, vol. III. Handels- und Schiffahrtsverhältnisse mit der
      Republik Venezuela
   CXIII-17. Nr 22b. Handelsvertrag zwischen dem Deutschen Reich und
      Venezuela
Reichskanzlei.
   12. Vereinigte Staaten von Amerika
   810-12. Allerhöchste Kundgebungen
   813. Reden des Kaisers
   827. Prinz Heinrich von Preussen

832. Immediatvorträge, Audienzen
913. Kolonialpolitik
917. Schutz Deutscher Handelsbez. i. überseeischen Ländern
950. Flottengesetz
1385. Ordensverleihungen an Ausländer
1760. Einladungen, Audienzen
1979. Hamburger Schiffahrtsgesellschaften

3. STAATSARCHIV, DRESDEN.

Aussenministerium.
Nr 1635. Deutsche Kirchen und Schulen im Ausland 1880-1906
Nr 2039. Politische Verhältnisse in Venezuela 1902-34
Nr 2040. Politische Verhältnisse in Venezuela 1906-13. Supplement
Nr 3315. Korrespondenz des Minist. mit der Gesandschaft in Berlin 1902-09
Nr 4702. Waffen- und Munitionsverkauf ins Ausland 1895-1928
Nr 4732. Übertritt sächs. Offiziere im Militärdienste des Auslandes 1907-22
Nr 6805. Statistik des deutschen Warenverkehrs mit dem Auslande 1877-1912
Nr 7026. Abschliessung eines Handels- und Schiffahrts-Vertrags zwischen den Zollvereins-Staaten und der Republik Venezuela
Nr 9470. Fremde Fürsten u. Staatsoberhäupter
Gesandschaft Berlin.
Nr 257-59. Politische Angelegenheiten
Nr 1130. Waffen Ausfuhr
Nr 1131. Marinesachen
Nr 1748. Flottengesetz 1897/98
Nr 1749. Flottengesetz 1900
Nr 1750. Flottengesetz 1905/07
Wirtschaftsinstitut.
Nr 349. Der Handels- und Schiffahrtsvertrag mit Venezuela
Nr 359. Deutscher Wirtschaftsverband für Süd- und Mittel-Amerika

III. Great Britain

1. PUBLIC RECORD OFFICE, LONDON.

Admiralty I/7690. Foreign Office. 1902
        I/7696. Foreign Office. 1903

I/7697. Foreign Office. 1903
Foreign Office 80/357. Colonial Office to FO, 3 September 1894. Enclosure
German Minister von Bodman to Imperial Chancellory, Caracas, 25
July 1894

2. N. M. ROTHSCHILD ARCHIVES, LONDON.

RAL, VI/10. Ledgers Home
RAL, VI/11. Ledgers Foreign
RAL, XI/63. Letters received from Bleichröder, Berlin, 17-23
RAL, XI/64. Private Letters received from Bleichröder, Berlin, 1887-1893
RAL, XI/72. Letters received from Discount Co., Berlin, 1886-1913, 7-14
RAL, XI/73. Letters received from Discount Co., Frankfurt, 1901-1920,
0-1
RAL, XI/86. Letters received from M. A. Rothschild, Frankfurt, 36A-36B
RAL, XI/90. Letters received from M. M. Warburg, Hamburg, 18-21
RAL, XI/101. File 8: Von Hansemann, 26-31
RAL, XI/148. Letter Copy Books, General, 354-385
RAL, XI/176. Telegram Copy Books, 31-43

IV. United States of America

1. TENNESSEE STATE ARCHIVES, NASHVILLE, MANUSCRIPT DIVISION.

Eugene H. Plumacher Memoirs 1877-1890. Accession Number 442
Plumacher Papers, Accession Number 70-76

PRIMARY SOURCES: PUBLISHED DOCUMENTS, MEMOIRS

Berdrow, Wilhelm, ed. *Alfred Krupps Briefe 1826-1887*. Berlin, 1928.
Boelcke, Willi A., ed. *Krupp und die Hohenzollern in Dokumenten: Krupp-Korrespondenz mit Kaisern, Kabinettschefs und Ministern 1850-1918.* Frankfurt, 1970.
Bülow, Bernhard von. *Denkwürdigkeiten.* 4 vols. Berlin, 1930.
———. *Deutsche Politik.* Berlin, 1917.
———. *Reden.* 4 vols. Leipzig, 1910-1914.
Fürstenberg, Carl. *Die Lebensgeschichte eines deutschen Bankiers 1870-1914.* Berlin, 1931.
Halder, Franz. *Kriegstagebuch.* 3 vols. Stuttgart, 1962-1964.
Hohenlohe-Schillingsfürst, Chlodwig zu. *Denkwürdigkeiten.* 2 vols. Stuttgart/Leipzig, 1907.

————. *Denkwürdigkeiten der Reichskanzlerzeit.* Stuttgart/Berlin, 1931.

Lepsius, Johannes, et al., eds. *Die Grosse Politik der Europäischen Kabinette 1871-1914.* 40 vols. Berlin, 1922-1927.

McGill, Samuel. *Poliantea: Memorias del Coronel McGill.* Caracas, 1978.

Meisner, H. O., ed. *Denkwürdigkeiten des Generalfeldmarschalls Alfred Grafen von Waldersee.* 3 vols. Stuttgart, 1923-1925.

Morison, Elting E., ed. *Letters of Theodore Roosevelt.* 8 vols. Cambridge, Mass., 1951-1954.

Penzler, Johannes, ed. *Fürst Bülows Reden.* 3 vols. Berlin, 1907-1909.

————. *Die Reden Kaiser Wilhelms II.* 3 vols. Leipzig, 1913.

Rich, Norman, and M. H. Fisher, eds. *Die geheimen Papiere Friedrich von Holsteins.* 4 vols. Göttingen, 1956-1963.

————. *The Holstein Papers.* 4 vols. Cambridge, 1955-1963.

Schinckel, Max von. *Lebenserinnerungen.* Hamburg, 1929.

Schnee, Heinrich, ed. *Deutsches Kolonial-Lexikon.* 3 vols. Leipzig, 1920.

Selections from the Correspondence of Theodore Roosevelt and Henry Cabot Lodge 1884-1918. 2 vols. New York, 1925.

Tirpitz, Alfred von. *Erinnerungen.* Leipzig, 1920.

Vierhaus, Rudolf, ed. *Das Tagebuch der Baronin Spitzemberg: Aufzeichnungen aus der Hofgesellschaft des Hohenzollernreiches.* Göttingen, 1960.

Voigt, Wilhelm E. *Auf Vorposten: Ein Zeugnis deutscher evangelischer Arbeit im Auslande in Predigten und Reden.* Berlin, 1909.

PRIMARY SOURCES: GOVERNMENT PUBLICATIONS

Amtsblatt (Prussia)
Gaceta oficial (Venezuela)
Handbuch des Deutschtums im Auslande
Monthly Bulletin of the International Bureau of the American Republics
Nachrichten für Handel und Industrie
Nachrichten für Handel, Industrie und Landwirtschaft
Reichsanzeiger (Germany)
Statistik des Deutschen Reiches, Auswärtiger Handel des deutschen Zollgebiets

PRIMARY SOURCES: NEWSPAPERS

Alldeutsche Blätter
Berliner Börsen Courier

Berliner Neueste Nachrichten
Berliner Tageblatt
The Daily Chronicle
The Daily Telegraph
Deutsche Kolonialzeitung
Das Deutschtum im Auslande
Frankfurter Zeitung
Hamburger Correspondent
Hamburger Nachrichten
Hamburgische Börsen Halle
Hannoverscher Courier
Kölnische Volkszeitung
Kölnische Zeitung
Leipziger Neueste Nachrichten
Leipziger Tageblatt
Münchner Allgemeine Zeitung
National Zeitung
Neue Hamburger Börsenhalle
Neue Hamburger Zeitung
New York Herald
New York Sun
Norddeutsche Allgemeine-Zeitung
Die Post
Südamerikanische Rundschau
The Times
Der Tropenpflanzer
Vossische Zeitung
Washington Post
Die Zukunft

SECONDARY LITERATURE

A Student of History. "The Blockade of Venezuela." *History Today*, 15 (July 1965), 475-85.

Ahrensburg, Hermann. *Die deutsche Kolonie Tovar in Venezuela*. Jena, 1920.

Anderson, Pauline R. *The Background of Anti-English Feeling in Germany, 1890-1902*. Washington, D.C., 1939.

Baasch, Ernst. *Beiträge zur Geschichte der Handelsbeziehungen zwischen Hamburg und Amerika*. Hamburg, 1892.

Baasch, Ernst. *Geschichte Hamburgs 1814-1918.* Vol. II. Stuttgart/Gotha, 1925.

——. *Die Handelskammer zu Hamburg 1665-1915.* Vol. II. Hamburg, 1915.

Bairoch, Paul. "International Industrialization Levels from 1750 to 1980." *Journal of Economic History,* 11 (Spring 1982), 269-333.

Barkin, K. D. *The Controversy over German Industrialization 1890-1902.* Chicago, 1970.

Baumgart, Winfried. *Deutschland im Zeitalter des Imperialismus (1890-1914).* Frankfurt, 1972.

Beale, Howard K. *Theodore Roosevelt and the Rise of America to World Power.* New York, 1962.

Becker, Willy. *Fürst Bülow und England 1897-1909.* Greifswald, 1929.

Behrens, Hans Oscar. *Grundlagen und Entwicklung der regelmässigen deutschen Schiffahrt nach Südamerika.* Halle, 1905.

Berdrow, Wilhelm. *Alfred Krupp und sein Geschlecht: 150 Jahre Krupp-Geschichte 1787-1937.* Berlin, 1937.

Berghahn, Volker R. *Der Tirpitz-Plan: Genesis und Verfall einer innenpolitischen Krisenstrategie unter Wilhelm II.* Düsseldorf, 1971.

——. "Zu den Zielen des deutschen Flottenbaus." *Historische Zeitschrift,* 210 (1970), 34-100.

Berliner Handels-Gesellschaft. *Die Berliner Handels-Gesellschaft in einem Jahrhundert Deutscher Wirtschaft 1856-1956.* Berlin, n.d.

Boelcke, Willi A. *So kam das Meer zu uns: Die preussisch-deutsche Kriegsmarine in Übersee 1822 bis 1914.* Frankfurt, 1981.

Böhm, Ekkehard. *Überseehandel und Flottenbau: Hanseatische Kaufmannschaft und deutsche Seerüstung 1879-1902.* Düsseldorf, 1972.

Böhme, Helmut. *Deutschlands Weg zur Grossmacht.* Cologne, 1966.

Borcke, Kurt von. *Deutsche unter fremden Fahnen.* Berlin, 1938.

Borght, Richard van der. *Das Wirtschaftsleben Südamerikas insbesondere in seinen Beziehungen zu Deutschland.* Cöthen, 1919.

Brunn, Gerhard. "Deutscher Einfluss und Deutsche Interessen in der Professionalisierung einiger Lateinamerikanischer Armeen vor dem 1. Weltkrieg (1885-1914)." *Jahrbuch für Geschichte von Staat, Wirtschaft und Gesellschaft Lateinamerikas,* 6 (Cologne/Vienna 1969), 278-336.

——. *Deutschland und Brasilien (1889-1914).* Cologne/Vienna, 1971.

Bullen, R. J., et al., eds. *Ideas into Politics: Aspects of European History 1880-1950.* London/Sydney, 1984.

Bürger, Otto. *Venezuela.* Leipzig, 1922.

Carl, George E. "British Commercial Interests in Venezuela during the Nineteenth Century." Diss., Tulane University, 1968.

Carreras, Charles E. "United States Economic Penetration of Venezuela and its Effects on Diplomacy, 1895-1906." Diss., University of North Carolina, Chapel Hill, 1971.

Carroll, E. M. *Germany and the Great Powers 1866-1914*. New York, 1938.

Challener, Richard. *Admirals, Generals, and American Foreign Policy 1898-1914*. Princeton, 1973.

Cohen, Benjamin J. *The Question of Imperialism: The Political Economy of Dominance and Dependence*. New York, 1973.

Collingwood, R. G. *The Idea of History*. London, 1961.

Conway, J. S. *The Nazi Persecution of the Churches 1933-45*. New York, 1968.

Crist, Raymond. "Life on the Llanos of Venezuela." *Bulletin of the Geographical Society of Philadelphia*, 25 (April 1937), 13-25.

Däbritz, W. *David Hansemann und Adolph von Hansemann*. Krefeld, 1954.

Daennel, E. "Das Ringen der Weltmächte um Mittel- und Südamerika." *Meereskunde*, 146 (Berlin, 1919).

Deist, Wilhelm. *Flottenpolitik und Flottenpropaganda: Das Nachrichtenbureau des Reichsmarineamtes 1897-1914*. Stuttgart, 1976.

Deutsche Kultur in der Welt: Archiv für Politische, Geistige und Wirtschaftliche Interessen Deutschlands im Auslande, I (January 1915).

Engelbrecht, H. C., and F. C. Hanighen. *Merchants of Death: A Study of the International Armament Industry*. New York, 1934.

Epstein, Fritz T. "European Military Influences in Latin America." Ms., Library of Congress, Washington, D.C., 1941.

Erzberger, Matthias. *Die Rüstungsausgaben des Deutschen Reichs*. Stuttgart, 1914.

Farrar, L. L., Jr. *Arrogance and Anxiety: The Ambivalence of German Power, 1848-1914*. Iowa City, 1981.

Farrer, David. *The Warburgs*. London, 1974.

Feis, Herbert. *Europe: The World's Banker, 1870-1914*. New Haven, 1930.

Fieldhouse, David K. *The Colonial Empires from the Eighteenth Century*. New York, 1967.

————. *Economics and Empire, 1830-1914*. London, 1973.

————. *Economics of Imperialism*. Ithaca, N.Y., 1973.

————. " 'Imperialism': An Historiographical Revision." *Economic History Review*, 14 (December 1961), 187-209.

Fischer, Fritz. *War of Illusions: German Policies from 1911 to 1914*. New York, 1975.

Forbes, Ian L. D. "German Commercial Relations with South America, 1890-1914." Diss., University of Adelaide, 1975.

Frankel, Benjamin A. "Venezuela and the United States, 1810-1888." Diss., University of California, Berkeley, 1964.

Führer durch die Quellen zur Geschichte Lateinamerikas. Bremen, 1972.

Funke, Alfred. *Deutsche Siedlung über See: Ein Abriss ihrer Geschichte und ihr Gedeihen in Rio Grande do Sul.* Halle, 1902.

Die Geschichte der Ludw. Loewe Actiengesellschaft Berlin: 60 Jahre Edelarbeit 1869 bis 1929. Berlin, 1930.

Geschichte der Mauser-Werke. Berlin, 1938.

Gilmore, Robert L. *Caudillism and Militarism in Venezuela, 1810-1910.* Athens, Ohio, 1964.

Gollwitzer, Heinz. *Die Standesherren: Die politische und gesellschaftliche Stellung der Mediatisierten 1815-1918.* Stuttgart, 1957.

Grimm, Hans. *Volk ohne Raum.* Munich, 1926.

Gröner, Erich. *Die deutschen Kriegsschiffe 1815-1945.* 2 vols. Munich, 1966-1968.

Grothe, Hugo. *Die Deutschen in Übersee: Eine Skizze ihres Werdens, ihrer Verbreitung und kultureller Arbeit.* Berlin, 1932.

Gutsche, W. *Zur Imperialismus-Apologie in der BRD: "Neue" Imperialismusdeutungen in der BRD-Historiographie zur deutschen Geschichte 1898 bis 1917.* East Berlin, 1975.

Haebler, K. *Die überseeische Unternehmungen der Welser.* Leipzig, 1903.

Halle, Ernst von, ed. *Amerika: Seine Bedeutung für die Weltwirtschaft und seine wirtschaftlichen Beziehungen zu Deutschland insbesondere zu Hamburg.* Hamburg, 1905.

Hallgarten, G.W.F. *Imperialismus vor 1914: Die Soziologischen Grundlagen der Aussenpolitik Europäischer Grossmächte vor dem Ersten Weltkrieg.* 2 vols. Munich, 1963.

"Die Haltung der Alldeutschen zu Lateinamerika 1891-1918." Ms., Zentrales Staatsarchiv, Potsdam, 1964.

Hammond, Richard J. "Economic Imperialism: Sidelights of a Stereotype." *Journal of Economic History,* 22 (1961), 582-98.

Hampe, Peter. *Die "ökonomische Imperialismustheorie": Kritische Untersuchungen.* Munich, 1976.

Handbuch des Deutschtums im Auslande. Berlin, 1906.

Hell, Jürgen. "Die Politik des deutschen Reiches zur Umwandlung Südbrasiliens in ein überseeisches Neudeutschland (1890-1914)." Diss., East Berlin, 1966.

Henderson, W. O. *The Rise of German Industrial Power.* Berkeley/Los Angeles, 1975.

Hentschel, Volker. *Wirtschaft und Wirtschaftspolitik im wilhelminischen*

Deutschland: Organisierter Kapitalismus und Interventionsstaat? Stuttgart, 1978.

Herschel, Frank Bernard. *Entwicklung und Bedeutung der Hamburg-Amerika Linie.* Berlin, 1912.

Herwig, Holger H. *Alemania y el bloqueo internacional de Venezuela 1902/03.* Caracas, 1977.

―――. "German Imperialism and South America before the First World War: The Venezuelan Case 1902/03." In A. Fischer, G. Moltmann, and K. Schwabe, eds., *Russland-Deutschland-Amerika: Festschrift für Fritz T. Epstein zum 80. Geburtstag,* 117-130, Wiesbaden, 1978.

―――. *"Luxury" Fleet: The Imperial German Navy 1888-1918.* London, 1980.

―――. *Politics of Frustration: The United States in German Strategic Planning, 1888-1941.* Boston, 1976.

Herwig, Holger H., and David F. Trask. "Naval Operations Plans between Germany and the United States of America 1898-1913: A Study of Strategical Planning in the Age of Imperialism." *Militärgeschichtliche Mitteilungen,* 11 (1970), 5-32.

Hewitt, Clyde E. "Cipriano Castro, 'Man without a Country.' " *American Historical Review,* 55 (October 1949), 36-53.

―――. "Venezuela and the Great Powers, 1902-1909: A Study in International Investment and Diplomacy." Diss., University of Chicago, 1948.

Hilbert, L. "The Role of Military and Naval Attachés in the British and German Service with Particular Reference to those in Berlin and London and their Effect on Anglo-German Relations 1871-1914." Diss., Cambridge University, 1954.

Hildebrand, G. *Die Erschütterung der Industrieherrschaft und des Industriesozialismus.* Jena, 1910.

Hilferding, Rudolf. *Das Finanzkapital: Studie über die jüngste Entwicklung des Kapitalismus.* Vienna, 1910.

Hillgruber, Andreas. *Die gescheiterte Grossmacht: Eine Skizze des Deutschen Reiches 1871-1945.* Düsseldorf, 1980.

Himer, Kurt. *Die Hamburg-Amerika Linie: Im Sechsten Jahrzehnt ihrer Entwicklung 1897-1907.* Hamburg, 1907.

Historisches Archiv der Deutschen Bank, Frankfurt a. M. *Die Disconto-Gesellschaft 1851 bis 1901: Denkschrift zum 50jährigen Jubiläum.* Berlin, 1901.

Hobson, John A. *Imperialism: A Study.* London, 1902.

Hoffmann, W. G. *Das Wachstum der deutschen Wirtschaft seit der Mitte des 19. Jahrhunderts.* Berlin/Heidelberg/New York, 1965.

Hood, Miriam. *Gunboat Diplomacy 1895-1905: Great Power Pressure in Venezuela.* London, 1975.

Illi, Manfred. *Die deutsche Auswanderung nach Lateinamerika: Ein Literaturübersicht.* Munich, 1977.

Jaeger, Hans. *Unternehmer in der deutschen Politik (1890-1918).* Bonn, 1967.

Jerussalimski, A. S. *Die Aussenpolitik und die Diplomatie des deutschen Imperialismus Ende des 19. Jahrhunderts.* East Berlin, 1954.

Johnson, John J. *The Military and Society in Latin America.* Stanford, 1964.

——, ed. *The Role of the Military in Underdeveloped Countries.* Princeton, 1962.

Kannapin, Klaus. "Die deutsch-argentinischen Beziehungen von 1871 bis 1914 unter besonderer Berücksichtigung der Handels- und Wirtschaftsbeziehungen und der Auswanderungspolitik." Diss., East Berlin, 1968.

Kanya-Forstner, A. S. *The Conquest of the Western Sudan: A Study in French Military Imperialism.* Cambridge, 1969.

Kasdorf, Otto. *Der Wirtschaftskampf um Südamerika.* Berlin, 1916.

Katz, Friedrich. *Deutschland, Diaz und die Mexikanische Revolution.* East Berlin, 1964.

——. "Einige Grundzüge der Politik des deutschen Imperialismus in Lateinamerika von 1898 bis 1941." *Der deutsche Faschismus in Lateinamerika 1933-1943,* 9-69. East Berlin, 1966.

——. *The Secret War in Mexico: Europe, the United States and the Mexican Revolution.* Chicago, 1981.

Kennedy, Paul. "British and German Reactions to the Rise of American Power." In R. J. Bullen et al., eds., *Ideas into Politics: Aspects of European History 1880-1950,* 15-24. London/Sydney, 1984.

——. "The First World War and the International Power System." *International Security,* 9 (Summer 1984), 7-40.

——. "Imperial Cable Communication and Strategy, 1870-1914." *English Historical Review,* 86 (October 1971), 740-52.

——. *The Rise of the Anglo-German Antagonism 1860-1914.* London, 1980.

King, W.T.C. *History of the London Discount Market.* London, 1936.

Kjellén, Rudolf. *Der Staat als Lebensform.* Leipzig, 1917.

Klein, Fritz, ed. *Neue Studien zum Imperialismus vor 1914.* East Berlin, 1980.

Koch, Conrad. *La Colonia Tovar: Geschichte und Kultur einer aleman-nischen Siedlung in Venezuela.* Basel, 1969.

Körner, Emil. "Die Südamerikanischen Militärverhältnisse." *Deutsche Kultur in der Welt,* 1 (1915), 146-50, 219-25.

Kresse, Walter. *Die Fahrtgebiete der Hamburger Handelsflotte 1824-1888.* Hamburg, 1972.

Kubicek, R. V. *Economic Imperialism in Theory and Practice.* Durham, N.C., 1979.

Kuczynski, Jürgen. *Studien zur Geschichte des deutschen Imperialismus.* 2 vols. East Berlin, 1950-1952.

Lambi, Ivo N. *The Navy and German Power Politics, 1862-1914.* Boston, 1984.

Landes, David S. "Some Thoughts on the Nature of Economic Imperialism." *Journal of Economic History,* 21 (December 1961), 469-521.

―――. *The Unbound Prometheus.* Cambridge, 1969.

Langer, William L. *The Diplomacy of Imperialism, 1890-1902.* New York, 1932.

Lefferts, Walter. "The Cattle Industry of the Llanos." *Bulletin of the American Geographical Society,* 45 (1913), 180-87.

Leichner, Günther. "In Venezuela liegt ein Schwarzwalddorf: Hundertjährige Isolation." *Globus* (Munich, 1971), 4.

Lenin, V. I. *Imperialism, the Highest Stage of Capitalism.* New York, 1969.

―――. *Der Imperialismus als jüngste Etappe des Kapitalismus.* Hamburg, 1921.

Lichtheim, George. *Imperialism.* New York, 1971.

Lieuwen, Edwin. *Arms and Politics in Latin America.* New York, 1960.

―――. *Petroleum in Venezuela: A History.* Berkeley/Los Angeles, 1954.

Link, Arthur S., et al., eds. *The American People: A History.* Vol. II. Arlington Heights, Ill., 1981.

Livermore, Seward W. "Theodore Roosevelt, the American Navy, and the Venezuelan Crisis of 1902-1903." *Hispanic American Historical Review,* 51 (April 1946), 452-71.

Lombardi, John V. *Venezuela: The Search for Order, The Dream of Progress.* New York, 1982.

Lufft, Hermann A. L. *Die nordamerikanischen Interessen in Südamerika vor dem Weltkriege.* Jena, 1916.

Luxemburg, Rosa. *Die Akkumulation des Kapitals: Ein Beitrag zur ökonomischen Erklärung des Imperialismus.* Leipzig, 1921.

Mann, Golo, and August Nitschke, eds. *Propyläen Weltgeschichte: Eine Universalgeschichte.* Vol. VI. Berlin, 1964.

Marchtaler, Hildegard von. *Chronik der Firma Van Dissel, Rode & Co. Nachf. Hamburg gegründet 1893 und deren Vorgänger in Venezuela gegründet 1852*. Bremen, n.d.

Marder, Arthur J. *The Anatomy of British Sea Power: A History of British Naval Policy in the Pre-Dreadnought Era, 1880-1905*. New York, 1940.

Marschalck, Peter. *Deutsche Überseewanderung im 19. Jahrhundert: Ein Beitrag zur soziologischen Theorie der Bevölkerung*. Stuttgart, 1973.

Martin, Rudolf. *Jahrbuch des Vermögens und Einkommens der Millionäre in den drei Hansestädten (Hamburg, Bremen, Lübeck)*. Berlin, 1912.

Mathies, Otto. *Hamburgs Reederei 1814-1914*. Hamburg, 1924.

May, Ernest R., ed. *Knowing One's Enemies: Intelligence Assessment Before the Two World Wars*. Princeton, 1984.

Meissner, Walther. *Das wirtschaftliche Vordringen der Nordamerikaner in Südamerika*. Cöthen, 1919.

Menne, Bernhard. *Krupp: Deutschlands Kanonenkönige*. Zurich, 1937.

Mielke, Siegfried. *Der Hansa-Bund für Gewerbe, Handel und Industrie 1909-1914*. Göttingen, 1976.

Mombert, Paul. "Bevölkerungsproblem und Bevölkerungstheorie im Lichte des Weltkrieges." In *Die Wirtschaftswissenschaft nach dem Kriege, Festgabe für Lujo Brentano*. Vol. II. Munich/Leipzig, 1925.

Mommsen, Wolfgang J., ed. *Imperialismustheorien: Ein Überblick über die neueren Imperialismusinterpretationen*. Göttingen, 1977.

⸻. *Der Moderne Imperialismus*. Stuttgart, 1971.

Mönckmeier, Wilhelm. *Die deutsche überseeische Auswanderung*. Jena, 1912.

Moon, Parker T. *Imperialism and World Politics*. New York, 1937.

Mörner, Magnus. *Race Mixture in the History of Latin America*. Boston, 1967.

Morôn, Guillermo. *A History of Venezuela*. London, 1964.

Münch, Hermann. *Adolph von Hansemann*. Munich/Berlin, 1932.

Neuburger, Hugh. *German Banks and German Economic Growth from Unification to World War I*. New York, 1977.

Nunn, Frederick M. "Emil Körner and the Prussianization of the Chilean Army: Origins, Processes and Consequences, 1885-1920." *Hispanic American Historical Review*, 50 (May 1970), 300-22.

⸻. "Military Professionalism and Professional Militarism in Brazil 1870-1970: Historical Perspectives and Political Implications." *Journal of Latin American Studies*, 4 (May 1972), 29-54.

————. *Yesterday's Soldiers: European Military Professionalism in South America, 1890-1940.* Lincoln, Nebr., 1983.

Otto, Walter. *Anleiheübernahme-, Gründungs- und Beteiligungsgeschäfte der Deutschen Grossbanken in Übersee.* Berlin, 1910.

Owen, E.R.J., and R. B. Sutcliffe, eds. *Studies in the Theory of Imperialism.* London, 1972.

Parsons, Edward B. "The German-American Crisis of 1902-1903." *The Historian,* 33 (May 1971), 436-52.

Perkins, Dexter. *The Monroe Doctrine, 1867-1907.* Baltimore, 1937.

Petter, Wolfgang. "Die Stützpunktpolitik der preussisch-deutschen Kriegsmarine 1859-1883." Diss., Freiburg, 1975.

Pierard, R. V. "The German Colonial Society 1882-1914." Diss., Iowa State University, 1964.

Pierson, William W. "Foreign Influences on Venezuelan Political Thought, 1830-1930." *Hispanic American Historical Review,* 15 (1935), 3-42.

Platt, D.C.M. "The Allied Coercion of Venezuela, 1902-3—A Reassessment." *Inter-American Economic Affairs,* 15 (1962), 3-28.

————. *Finance, Trade and Politics in British Foreign Policy 1815-1914.* Oxford, 1968.

————. *Latin America and British Trade 1806-1914.* New York, 1972.

Poidevin, Raymond. *Les Relations économiques et financières entre la France et l'Allemagne de 1898 à 1914.* Paris, 1969.

Preiser, Erich. "Die Imperialismusdebatte: Rückschau und Bilanz." In *Wirtschaft und Wirtschaftsgeschichte: Festschrift zum 65. Geburtstag von Friedrich Lütge,* 355-70. Stuttgart, 1966.

Rachel, Hugo, et al., eds. *Berliner Grosskaufleute und Kapitalisten.* 3 vols. Berlin, 1967.

Radkau, Joachim, and Imanuel Geiss, eds. *Imperialismus im 20. Jahrhundert: Gedenkschrift für George W. F. Hallgarten.* Munich, 1976.

Rauschning, Hermann. *Gespräche mit Hitler.* New York, 1940.

Rayburn, John C. "Development of Venzuela's Iron Ore Deposits." *Inter-American Affairs,* 6 (1952), 52-70.

Riesser, Jakob. *Die deutschen Grossbanken und ihre Konzentration im Zusammenhange mit der Entwicklung der Gesamtwirtschaft in Deutschland.* Jena, 1910.

————. *Zur Entwicklungsgeschichte der deutschen Grossbanken mit besonderer Rücksicht auf die Konzentrationsbestrebungen.* Jena, 1906.

Rippy, J. Fred. *Latin America in World Politics: An Outline Survey.* New York, 1928.

Roehl, John C. G. *Germany without Bismarck: The Crisis of Government in the Second Reich, 1890-1900.* London, 1967.

Roehl, John C. G., and Nicolaus Sombart, eds. *Kaiser Wilhelm II: New Interpretations. The Corfu Papers.* Cambridge, 1982.

Rohrmann, Elsabea. *Max von Schinckel: Hanseatischer Bankmann im wilhelminischen Deutschland.* Hamburg, 1971.

Rosenbaum, Eduard, and A.-J. Sherman. *Das Bankhaus M . M . Warburg & Co. 1798-1938.* Hamburg, 1978.

Schaefer, Jürgen. *Deutsche Militärhilfe an Südamerika: Militär- und Rüstungsinteressen in Argentinien, Bolivien und Chile vor 1914.* Düsseldorf, 1974.

Schäfer, Hans-Bernd. *Imperialismusthesen und Handelsgewinne: Zur Theorie der Wirtschaftsbeziehungen zwischen Industrie- und Entwicklungsländern.* Düsseldorf, 1972.

Scharbius, Manfred. "Die ökonomischen Rivalitäten der imperialistischen Hauptmächte um Kuba und ihre Auswirkungen auf die wirtschaftliche Entwicklung der Insel (Vom Anfang der spanischen Kolonialherrschaft bis 1914)." Diss., East Berlin, 1970.

Schiff, Warren. "The Influence of the German Armed Forces and War Industry on Argentina, 1880-1914." *Hispanic American Historical Review*, 52 (August 1972), 436-55.

Schilling, K. "Beiträge zu einer Geschichte des radikalen Nationalismus in der Wilhelminischen Ära 1890-1909." Diss., Cologne, 1968.

Schottelius, Ursula. "Das Amerikabild der deutschen Regierung in der Ära Bülow, 1897-1909." Diss., Hamburg, 1956.

Schramm, Percy Ernst. "Die deutschen Überseekaufleute im Rahmen der Sozialgeschichte." *Bremisches Jahrbuch*, 49 (1964), 31-53.

———. *Deutschland und Übersee: Der Deutsche Handel mit den anderen Kontinenten, insbesondere Afrika, von Karl V. bis zu Bismarck.* Braunschweig/Berlin/Hamburg/Kiel, 1950.

———. *Hamburg, Deutschland und die Welt: Leistung and Grenzen Hanseatischen Bürgertums in der Zeit zwischen Napoleon I. und Bismarck. Ein Kapitel Deutscher Geschichte.* Hamburg, 1952.

———. *Kaufleute zu Haus und Über See: Hamburgische Zeugnisse des 17., 18. und 19. Jahrhunderts.* Hamburg, 1949.

Schüddekopf, Otto-Ernst. *Die Stützpunktpolitik des Deutschen Reiches 1890-1914.* Berlin, 1941.

Schuett, Alfred. *Die Finanzierung des Hamburger Aussenhandels.* Marburg, 1925.

Schumpeter, Joseph A. *Imperialism and Social Classes.* New York, 1951.

Scott, James Brown. *The International Conferences of American States 1889-1928.* New York, 1931.

Seidenzahl, Fritz. *100 Jahre Deutsche Bank 1870-1970.* Frankfurt, 1970.

Senelich, L. "Politics as Entertainment: Victorian Music-Hall Songs." *Victorian Studies,* 19 (December 1975), 149-80.

Sievers, Wilhelm. *Südamerika und die deutschen Interessen.* Stuttgart, 1903.

———. *Venezuela.* Hamburg, 1921.

———. *Zweite Reise in Venezuela in den Jahren 1892/93.* Hamburg, 1896.

Simon, Harry Arthur. *Die Banken und der Hamburger Überseehandel: Studien zur Frage der Zahlungsabwicklung und Kreditgewährung.* Stuttgart/Berlin, 1909.

Smith, Woodruff D. *The German Colonial Empire.* Chapel Hill, N.C., 1978.

———. "The Ideology of German Colonialism, 1840-1906." *Journal of Modern History,* 46 (1974), 641-62.

Stegmann, Dirk. *Die Erben Bismarcks: Parteien und Verbände in der Spätphase des wilhelminischen Deutschlands. Sammlungspolitik 1897-1918.* Cologne, 1970.

Steiner, Zara S. *The Foreign Office and Foreign Policy 1895-1914.* Cambridge, 1969.

Stenkewitz, Kurt. *Gegen Bajonette und Dividende: Die politische Krise in Deutschland am Vorabend des ersten Weltkrieges.* East Berlin, 1960.

Stoecker, Erika. *A.S. Jerussalimski: Geschichte im Leben eines sowj. Historikers und Kommunisten.* East Berlin, 1980.

Sullivan, William M. "The Rise of Despotism in Venezuela: Cipriano Castro, 1899-1908." Diss., University of New Mexico, 1974.

Tansill, Charles C. *The Purchase of the Danish West Indies.* Baltimore, 1932.

Tansill, R. H. "Los von England: Probleme des Nationalismus in der deutschen Wirtschaftsgeschichte." *Zeitschrift für die gesamte Staatswissenschaft,* 124 (1968).

Taylor, A.J.P. *Germany's First Bid for Colonies 1884-1885: A Move in Bismarck's European Policy.* London 1938.

Tirpitz, Alfred von. *Politische Dokumente I: Der Aufbau der deutschen Weltmacht.* Stuttgart/Berlin, 1924.

Townsend, Mary E. *The Rise and Fall of Germany's Colonial Empire 1884-1918.* New York, 1966.

Uhlich, Ingrid. "Die Politik des deutschen Kaiserreichs und der Grossmächte in Peru von 1871 bis zum Beginn des 1. Weltkrieges." Diss., East Berlin, 1971.

Vagts, Alfred. *Deutschland und die Vereinigten Staaten in der Weltpolitik.* 2 vols. New York, 1935.

Vale, A. "The Great Venezuelan Railway." *Railway Magazine,* 9 (July 1901), 38-43.

Veblen, Thorstein. *The Theory of the Leisure Class.* New York, 1967.

Volberg, Heinrich. *Deutsche Kolonialbestrebungen in Südamerika nach dem Dreissigjährigen Kriege, insbesondere die Bemühungen von Johann Joachim Becher.* Cologne/Vienna, 1977.

Wagemann, Ernst. "Die deutschen Kolonisten in Südamerika." *Schmollers Jahrbuch für Gesetzgebung, Verwaltung und Volkswirtschaft im Deutschen Reiche,* 39 (1915), 283-93.

Walker, Mack. *Germany and the Emigration 1816-1885.* Cambridge, Mass., 1964.

Wehler, Hans-Ulrich. *Der Aufstieg des amerikanischen Imperialismus: Studien zur Entwicklung des Imperium Americanum 1865-1900.* Göttingen, 1974.

—————. *Bismarck und der Imperialismus.* Cologne, 1969.

—————. *Krisenherde des Kaiserreichs 1871-1918: Studien zur deutschen Sozial- und Verfassungsgeschichte.* Göttingen, 1979.

—————. "Stützpunkte in der Karibischen See: Die Anfänge des amerikanischen Imperialismus auf Hispaniola." *Jahrbuch für Geschichte von Staat, Wirtschaft und Gesellschaft Lateinamerikas,* 2 (1965), 399-428.

Whale, P. B. *Joint Stock Banking in Germany.* London, 1930.

Wintzer, Wilhelm. *Der Kampf um das Deutschtum: Die Deutschen im tropischen Amerika.* Munich, 1900.

Winzen, Peter. *Bülows Weltmachtkonzept: Untersuchungen zur Frühphase seiner Aussenpolitik 1897-1901.* Boppard, 1977.

—————. "Die Englandpolitik Friedrich von Holsteins 1895-1901." Diss., Cologne, 1975.

Wulff, H. *Norddeutsche Bank in Hamburg 1856-1906.* Berlin, 1906.

Ybarra, T. R. *Young Man of Caracas.* New York, 1941.

Yoder, Lee Owen. "The Cattle Industry in Colombia and Venezuela." Diss., University of Chicago, 1926.

INDEX

Library of Congress Cataloging-in-Publication Data

Herwig, Holger H.
Germany's vision of empire in Venezuela 1871-1914.
Bibliography: p.
Includes index.
1. Germany—Foreign relations—Venezuela.
2. Venezuela—Foreign relations—Germany. 3. Germany—
Foreign relations—1871-1918. 4. Germany—Territorial
expansion—History. 5. Venezuela—History—Anglo-German
Blockade, 1902. I. Title.
DD120.V4H47 1986. 327.43087 86-9495
ISBN 0-691-05483-5 (alk. paper)

(continued from front flap)

Holger H. Herwig is Professor of History at Vanderbilt University. Among his works are *The German Naval Officer Corps: A Social and Political History, 1890-1918* (Oxford), *Politics of Frustration: The United States in German Strategic Planning, 1888-1941* (Little, Brown), and *"Luxury" Fleet: The Imperial German Navy, 1888-1918* (George Allen & Unwin).